Handbook of Fingerprint Recognition

Davide Maltoni
Dario Maio
Anil K. Jain
Salil Prabhakar

Handbook of
Fingerprint Recognition

INCLUDES
DVD-ROM

 Springer

Davide Maltoni
Biometric Systems Laboratory
University of Bologna
Cesena, 47023
Italy
maltoni@csr.unibo.it

Anil K. Jain
Department of Computer Science
    and Engineering
Michigan State University
East Lansing, MI 48824
USA
jain@cse.msu.edu

Dario Maio
DEIS-CSITE
University of Bologna
Bologna, 40136
Italy
dmaio@deis.unibo.it

Salil Prabhakar
DigitalPersona, Inc.
Redwood City, CA 94063
USA
salilp@digitalpersona.com

Library of Congress Cataloging-in-Publication Data
Handbook of fingerprint recognition / Davide Maltoni . . . [et al.]
    p. cm.
    Includes bibliographical references and index.
    ISBN 0-387-95431-7 (alk. paper)
    1. Fingerprints—Identification. 2. Fingerprints—Classification I. Maltoni, Davide
HV6074.H25 2003
363.25′8—dc21   2003042439

ISBN 0-387-95431-7   Printed on acid-free paper.

Printed in the United States of America.

9 8 7 6 5 4 3   Corrected second printing, 2005

springer.com

Contents

Preface

Overview

Biometric recognition refers to the use of distinctive physiological and behavioral characteristics (e.g., fingerprints, face, hang geometry, iris, gait, signature), called biometric identifiers or simply biometrics, for automatically recognizing a person. Questions such as "Is this person authorized to enter the facility?", "Is this individual entitled to access the privileged information?", and "Did this person previously apply for a job?" are routinely asked in a variety of organizations in both public and private sectors. Because biometric identifiers cannot be easily misplaced, forged, or shared, they are considered more reliable for person recognition than traditional token- (e.g., keys) or knowledge- (e.g., password) based methods. Biometric recognition can provide better security, higher efficiency, and increased user convenience. It is for these reasons that biometric systems are being either increasingly deployed or evaluated in a large number of government (e.g., welfare disbursement, national ID card, issuing of driver's license) and civilian (e.g., computer network logon, automatic teller machine, cellular phone, Web access, smartcard) applications.

A number of biometric technologies have been developed and several of them are being used in a variety of applications. Among these, fingerprints, face, iris, speech, and hand geometry are the ones that are most commonly used. Each biometric has its strengths and weaknesses and the choice of a particular biometric typically depends on the requirements of an application. Various biometric identifiers can also be compared on the following factors; universality, distinctiveness, permanence, collectability, performance, acceptability and circumvention. Because of the well-known distinctiveness (individuality) and persistence properties of fingerprints over time, fingerprints are the most widely used biometric characteristics. In fact, fingerprints and biometrics are often considered synonyms! Fingerprints have been routinely used in the forensics community for over one hundred years and automatic fingerprint identification systems were first installed almost fifty years back. While law enforcement agencies were the earliest adopters of the fingerprint recognition technology, more recently, increasing identity fraud has created a growing need for biometric technology for person recognition in a number of non-forensic applications.

Fingerprint recognition is a complex pattern recognition problem; designing algorithms capable of extracting salient features and matching them in a robust way is quite hard, especially in poor quality fingerprint images. There is a popular misconception that automatic fingerprint recognition is a fully solved problem since it was one of the first applications of machine pattern recognition almost fifty years ago. On the contrary, fingerprint recognition is still a challenging and important pattern recognition problem.

This book reflects the progress made in automatic techniques for fingerprint recognition over the past four decades. We attempted to organize, classify and present hundreds of existing approaches in a systematic way. We believe this would greatly facilitate both beginners and experts of different application domains who desire to explore not only the general concepts but also the intricate details of this fascinating technology.

Objectives

The aims and objectives of this book are to:
- introduce the readers to automatic techniques for fingerprint recognition. Introductory material is provided on all components/modules of a fingerprint recognition system;
- provide an in-depth survey of the state-of-the-art in fingerprint recognition;
- present in detail recent advances in fingerprint recognition, including sensing, feature extraction, matching and classification techniques, synthetic fingerprint generation, multimodal biometric systems, fingerprint individuality, and design of secure fingerprint systems;
- serve as the first complete reference book on fingerprint recognition, including an exhaustive bibliography.

Organization and Features

After an introductory chapter, the book chapters are organized logically into four parts: fingerprint sensing (Chapter 2); fingerprint representation, matching and classification (Chapters 3, 4, and 5); advanced topics, including synthetic fingerprints, multimodal biometric systems, and fingerprint individuality (Chapters 6, 7, and 8); and securing fingerprint systems (Chapter 9).

Chapter 1 introduces biometric systems and provides some historical remarks on fingerprints and their adoption in forensic and civilian recognition applications. All the topics that are covered in detail in the successive chapters are introduced here in brief. This will provide the reader an overview of the various book chapters and let her choose a personalized reading path. Other non-technical but important topics such as "applications" and "privacy issues" are also discussed. Some background in image processing and pattern recognition techniques is necessary to fully understand the majority of the book chapters. To facilitate readers who do not have this background, references to basic readings and introductory surveys on various topics are provided at the end of Chapter 1.

Chapter 2 surveys the existing fingerprint acquisition techniques: from the traditional "ink technique" to recent optical, capacitive, thermal, and ultrasonic on-line scanners, and discusses the factors that determine the quality of a fingerprint image. Chapter 2 also introduces the compression techniques that are used to store the fingerprint image data in a compact form.

Chapters 3, 4, and 5 provide an in-depth treatment of fingerprint feature extraction, representation, matching, classification, and retrieval algorithms. The existing techniques are divided into various categories to guide the reader through the large number of ideas proposed in more than 400 technical papers on the subject. The main approaches are explained in detail to help practitioners in the field understand the methodology used in commercial systems.

Chapters 6, 7, and 8 are specifically dedicated to the three cutting edge topics: synthetic fingerprint generation, multimodal biometric systems, and fingerprint individuality, respectively. Synthetic fingerprints have proven to be a valid substitute for real fingerprints for the design and benchmarking of fingerprint-based recognition systems. Multimodal biometric systems, that is, systems based on a combination of fingerprints with other biometrics (e.g., face) or a combination of different fingerprint feature extraction or matching algorithms, appear to be a promising research direction to overcome the intrinsic limitations of the existing solutions. Scientific evidence supporting fingerprint individuality is being increasingly demanded in forensic, civil and commercial applications, and this has generated interest in designing accurate fingerprint individuality models.

Finally, Chapter 9 discusses the design, implementation and administration of secure fingerprint-based biometric systems, whose building blocks (basic algorithms) have been presented in the previous chapters. Experience and care is necessary to design and develop secure systems. Techniques for securing biometric systems against attacks (to sensor, feature extraction and matching modules, template, and communication channels) are also discussed.

Contents of the DVD

The book includes a DVD that contains the four fingerprint databases used in the 2002 Fingerprint Verification Competition (FVC2002) and the four databases used in 2000 Fingerprint Verification Competition (FVC2000). The DVD also contains a demonstration version of the SFINGE software that can be used to generate synthetic fingerprint images. These real and synthetic fingerprint images will allow interested readers to evaluate various modules of their fingerprint recognition system and to compare their developments with the state-of-the-art algorithms.

Intended Audience

This book will be useful to researchers, practicing engineers, and students who wish to understand and/or develop fingerprint-based recognition systems. It would also be useful as a reference book for a graduate course on biometrics. For this reason, the book is written in an informal style and the concepts are explained in plain language. A number of examples are presented to visualize the concepts and methods before giving any mathematical definition. Although the core chapters on fingerprint feature extraction, matching and classification require some background in image processing and pattern recognition, the introduction, sensing and security chapters are accessible to a wider audience (e.g., developers of biometric applications, system integrators, security managers, designers of security systems).

Acknowledgments

A number of people helped in making this book a reality. Raffaele Cappelli of the University of Bologna wrote Chapter 6 on synthetic fingerprints, Sharath Pankanti of the IBM T. J. Watson Research Center and Arun Ross of Michigan State University provided portions of text and figures in Chapters 1, 7, and 8, and Alexander Ivanisov of Digital Persona Inc. provided invaluable suggestions throughout several revisions of Chapter 9. We also thank Wayne Wheeler and Wayne Yuhasz, editors at Springer, for their suggestions and keeping us on schedule for the production of the book.

This book explores automatic techniques for fingerprint recognition, from the first approaches introduced more than forty years ago to the current state-of-the-art algorithms. However, with the development of sensor technologies, the availability of faster processors at lower cost, and new emerging applications of biometrics, there continues to be vigorous activity in the design and development of faster, more accurate, and robust fingerprint recognition systems. As a result, new algorithms for fingerprint recognition will continue to appear in the literature even after this book goes to press. We hope that the fundamental concepts presented in this book will provide some constancy in this rapidly evolving and important field of automatic fingerprint recognition.

December 2002

Davide Maltoni
Dario Maio
Anil K. Jain
Salil Prabhakar

1
Introduction

1.1 Introduction

More than a century has passed since Alphonse Bertillon first conceived and then industriously practiced the idea of using body measurements for solving crimes (Rhodes, 1956). Just as his idea was gaining popularity, it faded into relative obscurity by a far more significant and practical discovery of the distinctiveness of the human fingerprints. In 1893, the Home Ministry Office, UK, accepted that no two individuals have the same fingerprints. Soon after this discovery, many major law enforcement departments embraced the idea of first "booking" the fingerprints of criminals, so that their records are readily available and later using leftover fingerprint smudges (latents), they could determine the identity of criminals. These agencies sponsored a rigorous study of fingerprints, developed scientific methods for visual matching of fingerprints and strong programs/cultures for training fingerprint experts, and applied the art of fingerprint recognition for nailing down the perpetrators (Scott (1951) and Lee and Gaensslen (2001)).

Despite the ingenious methods improvised to increase the efficiency of the manual approach to fingerprint indexing and search, the ever growing demands on manual fingerprint recognition quickly became overwhelming. The manual method of fingerprint indexing resulted in a highly skewed distribution of fingerprints into bins (types): most fingerprints fell into a few bins and this did not improve search efficiency. Fingerprint training procedures were time-intensive and slow. Furthermore, demands imposed by the painstaking attention needed to visually match the fingerprints of varied qualities, tedium of the monotonous nature of the work, and increasing workloads due to a higher demand on fingerprint recognition services, all prompted the law enforcement agencies to initiate research into acquiring fingerprints through electronic media and automate fingerprint recognition based on the digital representation of fingerprints. These efforts led to development of *Automatic Fingerprint Identification Systems* (AFIS) over the past few decades. Law enforcement agencies were the earliest adopters of the fingerprint recognition technology, more recently, however, increasing identity fraud has created a growing need for biometric technology for person recognition in a number of non-forensic applications.

Biometric recognition refers to the use of distinctive *physiological* (e.g., fingerprints, face, retina, iris) and *behavioral* (e.g., gait, signature) characteristics, called *biometric identifiers* (or simply biometrics) for automatically recognizing individuals. Perhaps all biometric identifiers are a combination of physiological and behavioral characteristics and they should not be exclusively classified into either physiological or behavioral characteristics. For example, fingerprints may be physiological in nature but the usage of the input device (e.g., how a user presents a finger to the fingerprint scanner) depends on the person's behavior. Thus, the input to the recognition engine is a combination of physiological and behavioral characteristics. Similarly, speech is partly determined by the biological structure that produces speech in an individual and partly by the way a person speaks. Often, a similarity can be noticed among parent, children, and siblings in their voice, gait, and even signature. The same argument applies to the face: faces of identical twins may be extremely similar at birth but during development, the faces change based on the person's behavior (e.g., lifestyle differences leading to a difference in bodyweight, etc.).

Is this person authorized to enter this facility? Is this individual entitled to access privileged information? Is the given service being administered exclusively to the enrolled users? Answers to questions such as these are valuable to business and government organizations. Because biometric identifiers cannot be easily misplaced, forged, or shared, they are considered more reliable for person recognition than traditional token- or knowledge-based methods. The objectives of biometric recognition are user convenience (e.g., money withdrawal without ATM card or PIN), better security (e.g., difficult to forge access), and higher efficiency (e.g., lower overhead for computer password maintenance). The tremendous success of fingerprint-based recognition technology in law enforcement applications, decreasing cost of fingerprint sensing devices, increasing availability of inexpensive computing power, and growing identity fraud/theft have all ushered in an era of fingerprint-based person recognition applications in commercial, civilian, and financial domains.

There is a popular misconception in the pattern recognition and image processing academic community that automatic fingerprint recognition is a fully solved problem inasmuch as it was one of the first applications of machine pattern recognition almost fifty years ago. On the contrary, fingerprint recognition is still a challenging and important pattern recognition problem.

With the increase in the number of commercial systems for fingerprint-based recognition, proper evaluation protocols are needed. The first fingerprint verification competition (FVC2000) was a good start in establishing such protocols (Maio et al., 2002a). As fingerprints (biometrics) get increasingly embedded into various systems (e.g., cellular phones), it becomes increasingly important to analyze the impact of biometrics on the overall integrity of the system and its social acceptability as well as the related security and privacy issues.

1.2 Biometric Systems

A *biometric system* is essentially a pattern recognition system that recognizes a person by determining the authenticity of a specific physiological and/or behavioral characteristic possessed by that person. An important issue in designing a practical biometric system is to determine how an individual is recognized. Depending on the application context, a biometric system may be called either a *verification* system or an *identification* system:

- a verification system authenticates a person's identity by comparing the captured biometric characteristic with her own biometric template(s) pre-stored in the system. It conducts one-to-one comparison to determine whether the identity claimed by the individual is true. A verification system either rejects or accepts the submitted claim of identity (*Am I whom I claim I am?*);
- an identification system recognizes an individual by searching the entire template database for a match. It conducts one-to-many comparisons to establish the identity of the individual. In an identification system, the system establishes a subject's identity (or fails if the subject is not enrolled in the system database) without the subject having to claim an identity (*Who am I?*).

The term *authentication* is also frequently used in the biometric field, sometimes as a synonym for verification; actually, in the information technology language, authenticating a user means to let the system know the user identity regardless of the mode (verification or identification). Throughout this book we use the generic term *recognition* where we are not interested in distinguishing between verification and identification.

The block diagrams of a verification system and an identification system are depicted in Figure 1.1; user enrollment, which is common to both tasks is also graphically illustrated. The enrollment module is responsible for registering individuals in the biometric system database (system DB). During the enrollment phase, the biometric characteristic of an individual is first scanned by a biometric reader to produce a raw digital representation of the characteristic. A quality check is generally performed to ensure that the acquired sample can be reliably processed by successive stages. In order to facilitate matching, the raw digital representation is usually further processed by a feature extractor to generate a compact but expressive representation, called a *template*. Depending on the application, the template may be stored in the central database of the biometric system or be recorded on a *magnetic card* or *smartcard* issued to the individual. The verification task is responsible for verifying individuals at the point of access. During the operation phase, the user's name or PIN (Personal Identification Number) is entered through a keyboard (or a keypad); the biometric reader captures the characteristic of the individual to be recognized and converts it to a digital format, which is further processed by the feature extractor to produce a compact digital representation. The resulting representation is fed to the feature matcher, which compares it against the template of a single user (retrieved from the system DB based on the user's PIN). In the identification task, no PIN is provided and the system compares the representation of the input biometric against the templates of all the users in the system database; the output is either the identity of an enrolled user or an alert message such as "user not identified." Because identification in large databases is computationally expensive, classification and indexing techniques are often deployed to limit the number of templates that have to be matched against the input.

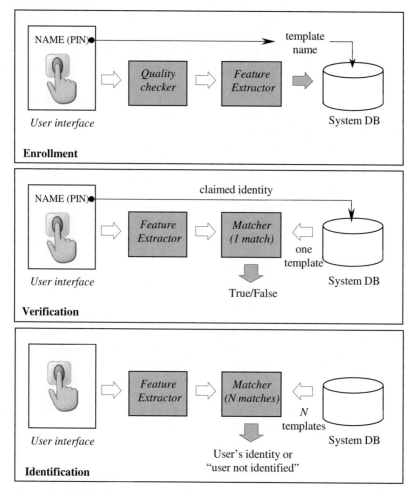

Figure 1.1. Block diagrams of enrollment, verification, and identification tasks.

Depending on the application domain, a biometric system could operate either as an *on-line* system or an *off-line* system. An on-line system requires the recognition to be performed quickly and an immediate response is imposed (e.g., a computer network logon application). On the other hand, an off-line system usually does not require the recognition to be performed immediately and a relatively long response delay is allowed (e.g., an employee background check application). Typically, on-line systems are *fully automatic* and require that the biometric characteristic be captured using a live-scan scanner, the enrollment process be unattended, there be no (manual) quality control, and the matching and decision be fully automatic. Off-line systems, however, are typically *semi-automatic*, where the biometric acquisition could be through an off-line scanner (e.g, scanning a fingerprint image from a latent or inked fingerprint card), the enrollment may be supervised (e.g., when a criminal is "booked," a forensic expert or a police officer may guide the fingerprint acquisition process), a manual quality check may be performed to ensure good quality acquisition, and the matcher may return a list of candidates which are then manually examined by a forensic expert to arrive at a final (human) decision.

An application could operate either in a *positive* or a *negative* recognition mode:

- in a positive recognition application, the system establishes whether the person is who he (implicitly or explicitly) claims to be. The purpose of a positive recognition is to prevent multiple people from using the same identity. For example, if only Alice is authorized to enter a certain secure area, then the system will grant access only to Alice. If the system fails to match the enrolled template of Alice with the input, a rejection results; otherwise, an acceptance results;
- in a negative recognition application, the system establishes whether the person is who he (implicitly or explicitly) denies being. The purpose of negative recognition is to prevent a single person from using multiple identities. For example, if Alice has already received welfare benefits and now she claims that she is Becky and would like to receive the welfare benefits of Becky (this is called "double dipping"), the system will establish that Becky is not who she claims to be. If the system fails to match the input biometric of Becky with a database of people who have already received benefits, an acceptance results; otherwise, a rejection results.

Note that although the traditional methods of user authentication such as passwords, PINs, keys, and tokens may work for positive recognition, negative recognition can only be established through biometrics. Furthermore, positive recognition application can operate both in verification or identification mode, but negative recognition applications cannot work in verification mode: in fact, the system has to search the entire archive to prove that the given input is not already present.

A biometric system can be classified according to a number of other application-dependent characteristics. Wayman (1999a) suggests that all the biometric applications may be classified into categories based on their characteristics:

1. cooperative versus non-cooperative,
2. overt versus covert,
3. habituated versus non-habituated,
4. attended versus non-attended,

> 5. standard versus non-standard operating environment,
> 6. public versus private, and
> 7. open versus closed.

Cooperative versus non-cooperative dichotomy refers to the behavior of the impostor in interacting with the system. For example, in a positive recognition system, it is in the best interest of an impostor to cooperate with the system to be accepted as a valid user. On the other hand, in a negative recognition system, it is in the best interest of the impostor not to cooperate with the system so that she does not get recognized. Electronic banking is an example of a cooperative application whereas an airport application to identify terrorists who will try to break the system is an example of a non-cooperative application.

If a user is aware that he is being subjected to a biometric recognition, the application is categorized as overt. If the user is unaware, the application is covert. Facial recognition can be used in a covert application while fingerprint recognition cannot be used in this mode (except for criminal identification based on latent fingerprints). Most commercial uses of biometrics are overt, whereas government, forensic, and surveillance applications are typically covert. Also, most verification applications are overt whereas identification applications generally fall in the covert category.

Habituated versus non-habituated use of a biometric system refers to how often the enrolled users are subjected to biometric recognition. For example, a computer network logon application typically has habituated users (after an initial "habituation" period) due to their use of the system on a regular basis. However, a driver's license application typically has non-habituated users since a driver's license is renewed only once in several years. This is an important consideration when designing a biometric system because the familiarity of users with the system affects recognition accuracy.

Attended versus non-attended classification refers to whether the process of biometric data acquisition in an application is observed, guided, or supervised by a human (e.g., a security officer). Furthermore, an application may have an attended enrollment but non-attended recognition. For example, a banking application may have a supervised enrollment when an ATM card is issued to a user but the subsequent uses of the biometric system for ATM transactions will be non-attended. Non-cooperative applications generally require attended operation.

Standard versus non-standard environments refer to whether the system is being operated in a controlled environment (such as temperature, pressure, moisture, lighting conditions, etc.). Typically, indoor applications such as computer network logon operate in a controlled environment whereas outdoor applications such as keyless car entry or parking lot surveillance operate in a non-standard environment. This classification is also important for the system designer as a more rugged biometric sensor is needed for a non-standard environment. Similarly, infrared face recognition may be preferred over visible-band face recognition for outdoor surveillance at night.

Public or private dichotomy refers to whether the users of the system are customers or employees of the organization deploying the biometric system. For example, a network logon application is used by the employees and managed by the information technology manager of the same company. Thus it is a private application. The use of biometric data in conjunction with electronic identity cards is an example of a public application.

Closed versus open systems refers to whether a person's biometric template is used for a single or multiple applications. For example, a user may use a fingerprint-based recognition system to enter secure facilities, for computer network logon, electronic banking, and ATM. Should all these applications use separate templates (databases) for each application, or should they all access the same template (database)? A closed system may be based on a proprietary template whereas an open system will need standard data formats and compression methods to exchange and compare information between different systems (most likely developed by different commercial vendors).

Note that the most popular commercial applications have the following attributes: cooperative, overt, habituated, attended enrollment and non-attended recognition, standard environment, closed, and private.

1.3 A Comparison of Various Biometrics

Any human physiological and/or behavioral characteristic can be used as a biometric identifier to recognize a person as long as it satisfies these requirements:

- *universality*, which means that each person should have the biometric;
- *distinctiveness*, which indicates that any two persons should be sufficiently different in terms of their biometric identifiers;
- *permanence*, which means that the biometric should be sufficiently invariant (with respect to the matching criterion) over a period of time;
- *collectability*, which indicates that the biometric can be measured quantitatively.

However, in a practical biometric system, there are a number of other issues that should be considered, including:

- *performance*, which refers to the achievable recognition accuracy, speed, robustness, the resource requirements to achieve the desired recognition accuracy and speed, as well as operational or environmental factors that affect the recognition accuracy and speed;
- *acceptability*, which indicates the extent to which people are willing to accept a particular biometric identifier in their daily lives;
- *circumvention*, which reflects how easy it is to fool the system by fraudulent methods.

A practical biometric system should have acceptable recognition accuracy and speed with reasonable resource requirements, harmless to the users, accepted by the intended population, and sufficiently robust to various fraudulent methods.

A number of biometric identifiers are in use in various applications (Figure 1.2). Each biometric has its strengths and weaknesses and the choice typically depends on the application. No single biometric is expected to effectively meet the requirements of all the applications. The match between a biometric and an application is determined depending upon the characteristics of the application and the properties of the biometric.

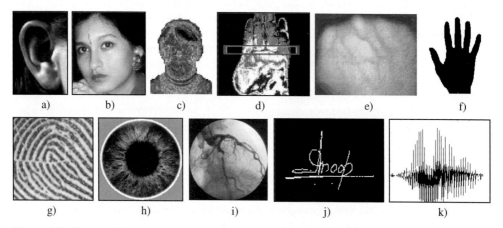

Figure 1.2. Some of the biometrics are shown: a) ear, b) face, c) facial thermogram, d) hand thermogram, e) hand vein, f) hand geometry, g) fingerprint, h) iris, i) retina, j) signature, and k) voice.

When choosing a biometric for an application the following issues have to be addressed:
- Does the application need verification or identification? If an application requires an identification of a subject from a large database, it needs a scalable and relatively more distinctive biometric (e.g., fingerprint, iris, or DNA).
- What are the operational modes of the application? For example, whether the application is attended (semi-automatic) or unattended (fully automatic), whether the users are habituated (or willing to be habituated) to the given biometrics, whether the application is covert or overt, whether subjects are cooperative or non-cooperative, and so on.
- What is the storage requirement of the application? For example, an application that performs the recognition at a remote server may require a small template size.
- How stringent are the performance requirements? For example, an application that demands very high accuracy needs a more distinctive biometric.
- What types of biometrics are acceptable to the users? Different biometrics are acceptable in applications deployed in different demographics depending on the cultural, ethical, social, religious, and hygienic standards of that society. The acceptability of a

biometric in an application is often a compromise between the sensitivity of a community to various perceptions/taboos and the value/convenience offered by biometrics-based recognition.

A brief introduction to the most common biometrics is provided below.

- *DNA*: DeoxyriboNucleic Acid (DNA) is the one-dimensional ultimate unique code for one's individuality, except for the fact that identical twins have identical DNA patterns. It is, however, currently used mostly in the context of forensic applications for person recognition. Several issues limit the utility of this biometric for other applications: i) contamination and sensitivity: it is easy to steal a piece of DNA from an unsuspecting subject that can be subsequently abused for an ulterior purpose; ii) automatic real-time recognition issues: the present technology for DNA matching requires cumbersome chemical methods (wet processes) involving an expert's skills and is not geared for on-line non-invasive recognition; iii) privacy issues: information about susceptibilities of a person to certain diseases could be gained from the DNA pattern and there is a concern that the unintended abuse of genetic code information may result in discrimination, for example, in hiring practices.

- *Ear*: It is known that the shape of the ear and the structure of the cartilaginous tissue of the pinna are distinctive. The features of an ear are not expected to be unique to an individual. The ear recognition approaches are based on matching the distance of salient points on the pinna from a landmark location on the ear.

- *Face*: The face is one of the most acceptable biometrics because it is one of the most common methods of recognition that humans use in their visual interactions. In addition, the method of acquiring face images is nonintrusive. Facial disguise is of concern in unattended recognition applications. It is very challenging to develop face recognition techniques that can tolerate the effects of aging, facial expressions, slight variations in the imaging environment, and variations in the pose of the face with respect to the camera (2D and 3D rotations).

- *Facial, hand, and hand vein infrared thermograms*: The pattern of heat radiated by the human body is a characteristic of each individual body and can be captured by an infrared camera in an unobtrusive way much like a regular (visible spectrum) photograph. The technology could be used for covert recognition and could distinguish between identical twins. A thermogram-based system is non-contact and non-invasive but sensing challenges in uncontrolled environments, where heat-emanating surfaces in the vicinity of the body, such as, room heaters and vehicle exhaust pipes, may drastically affect the image acquisition phase. A related technology using near-infrared imaging is used to scan the back of a clenched fist to determine hand vein structure. Infrared sensors are prohibitively expensive which is a factor inhibiting widespread use of the thermograms.

- *Gait*: Gait is the peculiar way one walks and is a complex spatio-temporal biometric. Gait is not supposed to be very distinctive, but is sufficiently characteristic to allow verification in some low-security applications. Gait is a behavioral biometric and may not stay invariant, especially over a large period of time, due to large fluctuations of body weight, major shift in the body weight, major injuries involving joints or brain, or due to inebriety. Acquisition of gait is similar to acquiring facial pictures and hence it may be an acceptable biometric. Because gait-based systems use a video-sequence footage of a walking person to measure several different movements of each articulate joint, it is computing and input intensive.

- *Hand and finger geometry*: Some features related to a human hand (e.g., length of fingers) are relatively invariant and peculiar (although not very distinctive) to an individual. The image acquisition system requires cooperation of the subject and captures frontal and side view images of the palm flatly placed on a panel with outstretched fingers. The representational requirements of the hand are very small (nine bytes in one of the commercially available products), which is an attractive feature for bandwidth- and memory-limited systems. Due to its limited distinctiveness, hand geometry-based systems are typically used for verification and do not scale well for identification applications. Finger geometry systems (which measure the geometry of only one or two fingers) may be preferred because of their compact size.

- *Iris*: Visual texture of the human iris is determined by the chaotic morphogenetic processes during embryonic development and is posited to be distinctive for each person and each eye (Daugman, 1999a). An iris image is typically captured using a non-contact imaging process. Capturing an iris image involves cooperation from the user, both to register the image of iris in the central imaging area and to ensure that the iris is at a predetermined distance from the focal plane of the camera. The iris recognition technology is believed to be extremely accurate and fast.

- *Keystroke dynamics*: It is hypothesized that each person types on a keyboard in a characteristic way. This behavioral biometric is not expected to be unique to each individual but it offers sufficient discriminatory information to permit identity verification. Keystroke dynamics is a behavioral biometric; for some individuals, one may expect to observe large variations from typical typing patterns. The keystrokes of a person using a system could be monitored unobtrusively as that person is keying in information.

- *Odor*: It is known that each object exudes an odor that is characteristic of its chemical composition and could be used for distinguishing various objects. A whiff of air surrounding an object is blown over an array of chemical sensors, each sensitive to a certain group of (aromatic) compounds. A component of the odor emitted by a human (or any animal) body is distinctive to a particular individual. It is not clear if the invariance in the body odor could be detected despite deodorant smells and varying chemical composition of the surrounding environment.

- *Retinal scan*: The retinal vasculature is rich in structure and is supposed to be a characteristic of each individual and each eye. It is claimed to be the most secure biometric since it is not easy to change or replicate the retinal vasculature. The image capture requires a person to peep into an eyepiece and focus on a specific spot in the visual field so that a predetermined part of the retinal vasculature may be imaged. The image acquisition involves cooperation of the subject, entails contact with the eyepiece, and requires a conscious effort on the part of the user. All these factors adversely affect public acceptability of retinal biometrics. Retinal vasculature can reveal some medical conditions (e.g., hypertension), which is another factor standing in the way of public acceptance of retinal scan-based biometrics.

- *Signature*: The way a person signs his name is known to be a characteristic of that individual. Although signatures require contact and effort with the writing instrument, they seem to be acceptable in many government, legal, and commercial transactions as a method of verification. Signatures are a behavioral biometric that change over a period of time and are influenced by physical and emotional conditions of the signatories. Signatures of some people vary a lot: even successive impressions of their signature are significantly different. Furthermore, professional forgers can reproduce signatures to fool the unskilled eye.

- *Voice*: Voice capture is unobtrusive and voice print is an acceptable biometric in almost all societies. Voice may be the only feasible biometric in applications requiring person recognition over a telephone. Voice is not expected to be sufficiently distinctive to permit identification of an individual from a large database of identities. Moreover, a voice signal available for recognition is typically degraded in quality by the microphone, communication channel, and digitizer characteristics. Voice is also affected by a person's health (e.g., cold), stress, emotions, and so on. Besides, some people seem to be extraordinarily skilled in mimicking others.

These various biometric identifiers described above are compared in Table 1.1. Note that fingerprint recognition has a very good balance of all the desirable properties. Every human being possesses fingerprints with the exception of any hand-related disabilities. Fingerprints are very distinctive (see Chapter 8); fingerprint details are permanent, even if they may temporarily change slightly due to cuts and bruises on the skin or weather conditions. Live-scan fingerprint sensors can easily capture high-quality images and they do not suffer from the problem of segmentation of the fingerprint from the background (e.g., unlike face recognition). However, they are not suitable for covert applications (e.g., surveillance) as live-scan fingerprint scanners cannot capture a fingerprint image from a distance without the knowledge of the person. The deployed fingerprint-based biometric systems offer good performance and fingerprint sensors have become quite small and affordable (see Chapter 2). Because fingerprints have a long history of use in forensic divisions worldwide for criminal investigations, they have a stigma of criminality associated with them. However, this is changing with the high demand of automatic recognition to fight identity fraud in our electronically interconnected society. With a marriage of fingerprint recognition, cryptographic techniques, and vitality detection, fingerprint systems are becoming quite difficult to circumvent (see Chapter 9). Fingerprint recognition is one of the most mature biometric technologies and is suitable for a large number of recognition applications. This is also reflected in revenues generated by various biometric technologies in the year 2002 (see Figure 1.3).

Biometric identifier	Universality	Distinctiveness	Permanence	Collectability	Performance	Acceptability	Circumvention
DNA	H	H	H	L	H	L	L
Ear	M	M	H	M	M	H	M
Face	H	L	M	H	L	H	H
Facial thermogram	H	H	L	H	M	H	L
Fingerprint	M	H	H	M	H	M	M
Gait	M	L	L	H	L	H	M
Hand geometry	M	M	M	H	M	M	M
Hand vein	M	M	M	M	M	M	L
Iris	H	H	H	M	H	L	L
Keystroke	L	L	L	M	L	M	M
Odor	H	H	H	L	L	M	L
Retina	H	H	M	L	H	L	L
Signature	L	L	L	H	L	H	H
Voice	M	L	L	M	L	H	H

Table 1.1. Comparison of biometric technologies. The data are based on the perception of the authors. High, Medium, and Low are denoted by H, M, and L, respectively.

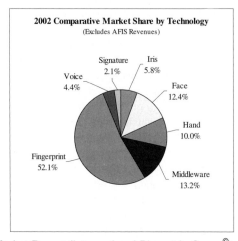

Figure 1.3. Biometric Market Report (International Biometric Group©) estimated the revenue of various biometrics in the year 2002 and showed that fingerprint-based biometric systems continue to be the leading biometric technology in terms of market share, commanding more than 50% of non-AFIS biometric revenue. Face recognition was second with 12.4%. Note that AFIS are used in forensic applications.

1.4 Biometric System Errors

For simplicity of exposition, the following discussion focuses on fingerprints, although it is valid for any other biometric identifier. The response of a matcher in a fingerprint recognition system is typically a *matching score s* (without loss of generality, ranging in the interval [0,1]) that quantifies the similarity between the input and the database template representations. The closer the score is to1, the more certain is the system that the two fingerprints come from the same finger; the closer the score is to 0, the smaller is the system confidence that the two fingerprints come from the same finger. The system decision is regulated by a *threshold t*: pairs of fingerprints generating scores higher than or equal to *t* are inferred as *matching pairs* (i.e., belonging to the same finger); pairs of fingerprints generating scores lower than *t* are inferred as *non-matching pairs* (i.e., belonging to different fingers).

A typical biometric verification system commits two types of errors: mistaking biometric measurements from two different fingers to be from the same finger (called *false match*) and mistaking two biometric measurements from the same finger to be from two different fingers (called *false non-match*). Note that these two types of errors are also often denoted as *false acceptance* and *false rejection*; a distinction has to be made between positive and negative recognition (see Section 1.2); in positive recognition systems (e.g., an access control system) a false match determines the false acceptance of an impostor, whereas a false non-match causes the false rejection of a genuine user. On the other hand, in a negative recognition application (e.g., preventing users from obtaining welfare benefits under false identities), a false match results in rejecting a genuine request, whereas a false non-match results in falsely accepting an impostor attempt. The notation "false match/false non-match" is not application dependent and therefore, in principle, is preferable to "false acceptance/false rejection." However, the use of false acceptance rate (FAR) and false rejection rate (FRR) is more popular and largely used in the commercial environment.

Verification system errors

From the design perspective, the biometric verification problem can be formulated as follows. Let the stored biometric template of a person be represented as T and the acquired input for recognition be represented by I. Then the null and alternate hypotheses are:

H_0: $I \neq T$, input does not come from the same person as the template;

H_1: $I = T$, input comes from the same person as the template.

The associated decisions are as follows.

D_0: person is not who she claims to be;

D_1: person is who she claims to be.

The verification involves matching T and I using a similarity measure $s(T,I)$. If the matching score is less than the system threshold t, then decide D_0, else decide D_1. The above terminology is borrowed from communication theory, where the goal is to detect a message in the presence of noise. H_0 is the hypothesis that the received signal is noise alone, and H_1 is the hypothesis that the received signal is message plus the noise. Such a hypothesis testing formulation inherently contains two types of errors:

Type I: false match (D_1 is decided when H_0 is true);

Type II: false non-match (D_0 is decided when H_1 is true).

False Match Rate (FMR) is the probability of type I error (also called significance level of the hypothesis test) and *False Non-Match Rate* (FNMR) is the probability of type II error:

FMR = $P(D_1 | H_0 = \text{true})$;

FNMR = $P(D_0 | H_1 = \text{true})$.

Note that (1 − FNMR) is also called the power of the hypothesis test.

To evaluate the accuracy of a biometric system one must collect scores generated from a number of fingerprint pairs from the same finger (the distribution $p(s|H_1 = \text{true})$ of such scores is traditionally called *genuine distribution*), and scores generated from a number of fingerprint pairs from different fingers (the distribution $p(s|H_0 = \text{true})$ of such scores is traditionally called *impostor distribution*). Figure 1.4 graphically illustrates the computation of FMR and FNMR over genuine and impostor distributions:

$$\text{FNMR} = \int_0^t p(s \,|\, H_1 = \text{true})\,ds \,,$$

$$\text{FMR} = \int_t^1 p(s \,|\, H_0 = \text{true})\,ds \,.$$

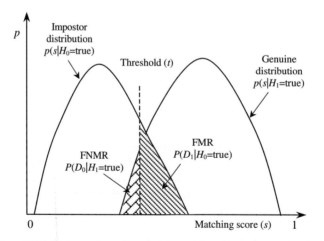

Figure 1.4. FMR and FNMR for a given threshold *t* are displayed over the genuine and impostor score distributions. From the drawing, it is evident that FMR is the percentage of impostor pairs whose matching score is greater than or equal to *t*, and FNMR is the percentage of genuine pairs whose matching score is less than *t*.

There is a strict tradeoff between FMR and FNMR in every biometric system (Golfarelli, Maio, and Maltoni, 1997). In fact, both FMR and FNMR are functions of the system threshold *t*, and we should, therefore, refer them as *FMR(t)* and *FNMR(t)*, respectively. If *t* is decreased to make the system more tolerant with respect to input variations and noise, then *FMR(t)* increases; vice versa, if *t* is raised to make the system more secure, then *FNMR(t)* increases accordingly. A system designer may not know in advance the particular application for which the system may be used (or a single system may be designed for a wide variety of applications). So it is advisable to report system performance at all operating points (threshold, *t*). This is done by plotting a *Receiver Operating Characteristic* (ROC) curve. A ROC curve is a plot of FMR against (1 − FNMR) for various decision thresholds (often FNMR is reported along the vertical axis instead of (1 − FNMR)). Figures 1.5.a through c show examples of score distributions, FMR(*t*) and FNMR(*t*) curves, and a ROC curve, respectively.

Besides the above distributions and curves, some "compact" indices are also used to summarize the accuracy of a verification system.

- *Equal-Error Rate* (EER) denotes the error rate at the threshold *t* for which false match rate and false non-match rate are identical: *FMR(t)* = *FNMR(t)* (see Figure 1.6). In practice, because the matching score distributions are not continuous (due to the finite number of matched pairs and the quantization of the output scores), an exact EER point might not exist. In this case, instead of a single value, an interval should be reported (Maio et al., 2000). Although EER is an important indicator, in practice, a fingerprint-based biometric system is rarely used at the operating point corresponding to EER, and often a more stringent threshold is set to reduce FMR in spite of a rise in FNMR.
- *ZeroFNMR* is the lowest FMR at which no false non-matches occur (see Figure 1.6).
- *ZeroFMR* is the lowest FNMR at which no false matches occur (see Figure 1.6).
- *Failure To Capture* (FTC) rate is associated with the automatic capture function of a biometric device and denotes the percentage of times the device fails to automatically capture the biometric when it is presented to a sensor. A high failure to capture rate makes the biometric device difficult to use.
- *Failure To Enroll* (FTE) rate denotes the percentage of times users are not able to enroll in the recognition system. There is a tradeoff between the FTE rate and the accuracy (FMR and FNMR) of a system. FTE errors typically occur when the recognition system performs a quality check to ensure that only good quality templates are stored in the database and rejects poor quality templates. As a result, the database contains only good quality templates and the system accuracy (FMR and FNMR) improves.
- *Failure To Match* (FTM) rate is the percentage of times the input cannot be processed or matched against a valid template because of insufficient quality. This is different from a false non-match error; in fact, in a failure to match error, the system is not able to make a decision, whereas in false non-match error, the system wrongly decides that the two inputs do not come from the same finger.

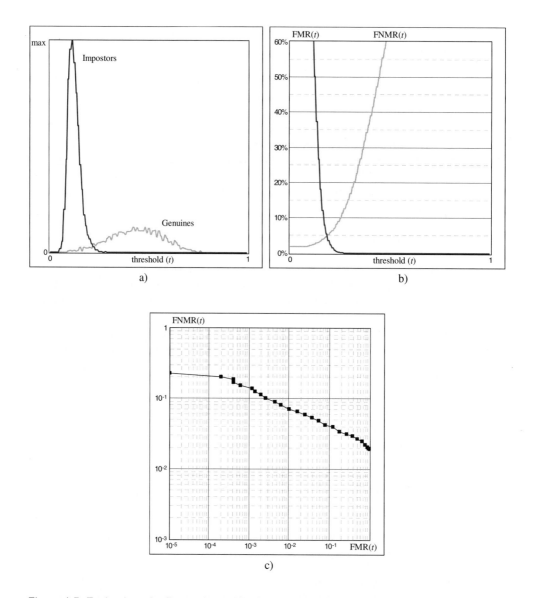

Figure 1.5. Evaluation of a fingerprint verification algorithm over FVC2002 (Maio et al., 2002b) database DB1: a) genuine and impostor distributions were computed from 2800 genuine pairs and 4950 impostor pairs, respectively; b) FMR(t) and FNMR(t) are derived from the score distributions in a); c) ROC curve is derived from the FMR(t) and FNMR(t) curves in b).

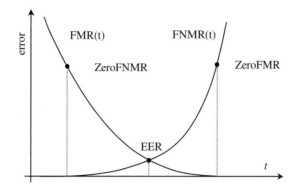
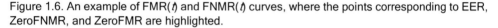

Figure 1.6. An example of FMR(*t*) and FNMR(*t*) curves, where the points corresponding to EER, ZeroFNMR, and ZeroFMR are highlighted.

For more formal definitions of errors in a fingerprint-based verification system, and practical suggestions on how to compute and report them for a given dataset, the reader should refer to the FVC2000 report (Maio et al. (2000); also included in the DVD accompanying this book) and Biometric Testing Best Practices, Version 2.01 (UKBWG, 2002).

The practical performance requirements of a biometric system are very much application related. From the viewpoint of system accuracy, an extremely low false non-match rate may be the primary objective. For example, in some forensic applications such as criminal identification, it is the false non-match rate that is a major concern and not the false match rate: that is, we do not want to miss a criminal even at the risk of manually examining a large number of potential matches identified by the biometric system. In forensic applications, it is the human expert that will make the final decision anyway. At the other extreme, a very low false match rate may be the most important factor in a highly secure access control application, where the primary objective is not to let in any impostors although we are concerned with the possible inconvenience to legitimate users due to a high false non-match rate. In between these two extremes are several civilian applications, where both false match rate and false non-match rate need to be considered. For example, in applications such as an ATM card verification a false match means a loss of several hundred dollars whereas a high false non-match rate may irritate the customers. Figure 1.7 graphically depicts the FMR and FNMR tradeoff preferred by different types of applications.

Identification system errors

How do the definitions of errors introduced above for fingerprint verification extend to fingerprint identification? Under some simplifying assumptions, an estimation of the performance in the identification mode can be inferred by the error estimates in the verification mode.

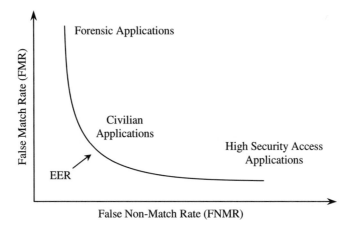

Figure 1.7. Typical operating points of different applications displayed on an ROC curve.

Let us assume that no indexing/retrieval mechanism is available (i.e., the entire database containing N templates has to be searched), and that a single template for each user is present in the database. Let $FNMR_N$ and FMR_N denote the identification false non-match rate and false match rate, respectively, then:

- $FNMR_N = FNMR$; in fact, the probability of falsely non-matching the input against the user template is the same as in verification mode (except that this expression does not take into account the probability that a false match may occur before the correct template is visited, see Cappelli, Maio, and Maltoni (2000c));
- $FMR_N = 1 - (1 - FMR)^N$; in fact, a false match occurs when the input falsely matches one or more templates in the database. FMR_N is then computed as one minus the probability that no false match is made with any of the database templates. In the above expression $(1 - FMR)$ is the probability that the input does not falsely match a single template, and $(1 - FMR)^N$ is the probability that it does not falsely match any of the database templates. If FMR is very small, then the above expression can be approximated by $FMR_N \cong N \cdot FMR$, and therefore we can state that the probability of false match increases linearly with the size of the database.

This result has serious implications for the design of large-scale identification systems. Usually, computation speed is perceived as the biggest problem in scaling an identification application. Actually, accuracy scales even worse than speed: in fact, consider an identification application with 10,000 users. We can certainly find a combination of a fast algorithm plus a fast architecture (eventually exploiting parallelism) capable of carrying out an identification in a few seconds. On the other hand, suppose that, for an acceptable FNMR, the FMR of the chosen algorithm is 10^{-5} (i.e., just one false match in 100,000 matches). Then the probability of falsely accepting an individual during identification is $FMR_N \cong 10\%$, and everyone has a good chance of gaining access to the system by trying to get in with all the ten fingers in their two hands. Multimodal biometric systems (see Chapter 7) seem to be the only obvious solution to accuracy scalability in large-scale automatic identification.

If the templates in the database have been classified/indexed (see Section 1.12 and Chapter 5), then only a portion of the database is searched during identification and this results in a different formulation of $FNMR_N$ and FMR_N:

- $FNMR_N = RER + (1-RER) \cdot FNMR$, where RER (Retrieval Error Rate) is the probability that the database template corresponding to the searched finger is wrongly discarded by the retrieval mechanism. The above expression is obtained using the following argument: in case the template is not correctly retrieved (this happens with probability RER), the system always generates a false non-match, whereas in the case where the retrieval returns the right template (this happens with probability $(1 - RER)$), the false non-match rate of the system is FNMR. Also, this expression is only an approximation as it does not consider the probability of falsely matching an incorrect template before the right one is retrieved (Cappelli, Maio, and Maltoni, 2000c);
- $FMR_N = 1 - (1 - FMR)^{N \cdot P}$, where P (also called *penetration rate*) is the average percentage of the database searched during the identification of an input fingerprint.

The exact formulation of errors in an identification system is derived in Cappelli, Maio, and Maltoni (2000c). The more complex case where the characteristics of the indexing/retrieval mechanism are known is also discussed there.

1.5 Evaluating Biometric Systems

Phillips et al. (2000) define three types of evaluation of biometric systems: *technology evaluation, scenario evaluation*, and *operational evaluation*.

- *Technology evaluation*: The goal of a technology evaluation is to compare competing algorithms from a single technology. Only algorithms compliant with a given input/output protocol are tested (sensing devices and application aspects are not taken into account). Testing of all the algorithms is carried out on one or more databases. Although sample data may be distributed for developmental or tuning purposes prior to the test, the actual testing must be done on data that have not previously been seen by algorithm developers. Because the database is fixed, the results of technology tests are repeatable. FVC2000 (Maio et al., 2002a) and FVC2002 (Maio et al., 2002b) are examples of technology evaluations of fingerprint verification algorithms. Section 4.7 discusses in more detail the comparison of fingerprint matching algorithms.
- *Scenario evaluation*: The goal of scenario evaluation is to determine the overall system performance in a prototype or simulated application. Testing is performed on a complete system in an environment that models a real-world target application. Each

tested system has its own acquisition device. Data collection across all tested systems has to be carried out in the same environment with the same population. Test results are repeatable only to the extent that the modeled scenario can be carefully controlled (UKBWG, 2002).

- *Operational evaluation*: The goal of operational testing is to determine the performance of a complete biometric system in a specific application environment with a specific target population. In general, operational test results are not repeatable because of unknown and undocumented differences between operational environments (UKBWG, 2002).

In scenario and operational evaluations, the accuracy of a biometric system depends heavily on several variables: the composition of the population (e.g., occupation, age, demographics, race), the environment, the system operational mode, and other application-specific constraints. In an ideal situation, one would like to characterize the application-independent performance of a recognition system and be able to predict the real operational performance of the system based on the application. Rigorous and realistic modeling techniques characterizing data acquisition and matching processes are the only way to grasp and extrapolate the performance evaluation results. In the case of fingerprint recognition, the results of fingerprint synthesis (see Chapter 6) exhibit many characteristics of finger appearance that can be exploited for simulations, but there do not exist any formal models for the data acquisition process under different conditions (e.g., different skin conditions, different distortions, different types of cuts and their states of healing, subtle user mischief, and adversarial testing conditions, etc.).

Until many aspects of biometric recognition algorithms and application requirements are clearly understood, the empirical, application-dependent evaluation techniques will be predominant and the evaluation results obtained using these techniques will be meaningful only for a specific database in a specific test environment and specific application. The disadvantage of the empirical evaluation is that it is not only expensive to collect the data for each evaluation, but it is also often difficult to objectively compare the evaluation results of two different systems. Depending upon the data collection protocol, the performance results can vary *significantly*. Biometric samples collected in a very controlled and non-realistic environment provide over-optimistic results that do not generalize well in practice.

For any performance metric to be able to generalize to the entire population of interest, the test data should i) be *representative* of the population and ii) contain enough samples from each category of the population (*large sample size*). Furthermore, the collection of two samples of the same biometric should be separated by a sufficient time period. Different applications, depending on whether the subjects are cooperative and habituated, or whether the target population is benevolent or subversive, may require a completely different sample set (Wayman, 2001). Size of the sample set is a very important factor in obtaining a reliable estimate of the error rates. The larger the size of the representative test samples, more reliable are the test results (smaller confidence interval). Data collection is expensive, therefore it is desirable to determine the smallest size of the database that will result in a given confidence interval. An estimation of the smallest database size is typically governed either by heuristics (Doddington et al., 1998) or by simplifying statistical assumptions (Wayman (2001) and UKBWG (2002)).

There are two methods of estimating confidence intervals: parametric and non-parametric. To simplify the estimation, both approaches typically assume independent and identically distributed (i.i.d.) test samples. Furthermore, parametric methods make strong assumptions about the form of the distribution. There is very little work on how to objectively test the validity of these assumptions (Kittler, Messer, and Sadeghi, 2001). A typical parametric approach models the test samples as independent Bernoulli trials and estimates the confidence intervals based on the resulting binomial distribution, inasmuch as a collection of correlated Bernoulli trials is also binomially distributed with a smaller variance (Viveros, Balasubramanian, and Mitas, 1984). Similarly, non-identically distributed test samples can be accommodated within the parametric approach by making some assumptions about the data. Wayman (2001) applied these methods to obtain estimates of accuracies as well as their confidence intervals. A nonparametric approach, such as bootstrap has been used by Bolle, Ratha, and Pankanti (1999) to estimate the error rates as well as their confidence intervals. The non-parametric approaches do not make any assumption about the form of the distributions. In addition, some nonparametric approaches such as bootstrapping techniques are known to be relatively immune to violations of i.i.d. assumptions. Bolle, Ratha, and Pankanti (2001) further explicitly modeled the weak dependence among typical fingerprint test sets by using a *subset bootstrap* technique. This technique obtains a better estimate of the error rate confidence intervals than the techniques that do not take the dependency among the test data into account.

In summary, the performance evaluation of a biometric system is empirical and the resulting measures cannot be completely understood/compared without carefully considering the methods that were used to acquire the underlying test data. Fortunately, the biometric community (e.g., United Kingdom Biometric Working Group) is making efforts towards establishing *best practices* guidelines (UKBWG, 2002) for performance evaluation so that egregious mistakes in data collection can be avoided and the test results presented in a consistent and descriptive manner.

1.6 History of Fingerprints

Human fingerprints have been discovered on a large number of archaeological artifacts and historical items (see Figure 1.8 for some examples). Although these findings provide evidence to show that ancient people were aware of the individuality of fingerprints, such awareness does not appear to have any scientific basis (Lee and Gaensslen (2001) and Moenssens (1971)). It was not until the late sixteenth century that the modern scientific fingerprint technique was first initiated (see Cummins and Midlo (1961), Galton (1892), and Lee and Gaensslen (2001)). In 1684, the English plant morphologist, Nehemiah Grew, published the first scientific paper reporting his systematic study on the ridge, furrow, and pore structure in fingerprints (Figure 9.a) (Lee and Gaensslen, 2001).

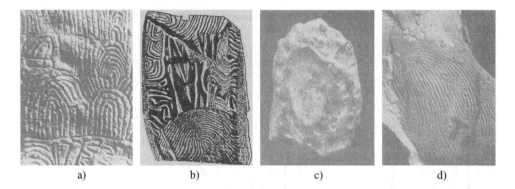

a)   b)   c)   d)

Figure 1.8. Examples of archaeological fingerprint carvings and historic fingerprint impressions: a) Neolithic carvings (Gavrinis Island) (Moenssens, 1971); b) standing stone (Goat Island, 2000 B.C.) (Lee and Gaensslen, 2001); c) a Chinese clay seal (300 B.C.) (Lee and Gaensslen, 2001); d) an impression on a Palestinian lamp (400 A.D.) (Moenssens, 1971). Although impressions on the Neolithic carvings and the Goat Island standing stones might not be used to indicate identity, there is sufficient evidence to suggest that the Chinese clay seal and impressions on the Palestinian lamp were used to indicate the identity of the providers. Figures courtesy of A. Moenssens, R. Gaensslen, and J. Berry.

Since then, a large number of researchers have invested huge amounts of effort on fingerprint studies. In 1788, a detailed description of the anatomical formations of fingerprints was made by Mayer (Moenssens, 1971) in which a number of fingerprint ridge characteristics were identified and characterized (Figure 1.9.b). Starting in 1809, Thomas Bewick began to use his fingerprint as his trademark (Figure 1.9.c), which is believed to be one of the most important milestones in the scientific study of fingerprint recognition (Moenssens, 1971). Purkinje, in 1823, proposed the first fingerprint classification scheme, which classified fingerprints into nine categories according to the ridge configurations (Figure 1.9.d) (Moenssens, 1971). Henry Fauld, in 1880, first scientifically suggested the individuality of fingerprints based on an empirical observation. At the same time, Herschel asserted that he had practiced fingerprint recognition for about 20 years (Lee and Gaensslen (2001) and Moenssens (1971)). These findings established the foundation of modern fingerprint recognition. In the late nineteenth century, Sir Francis Galton conducted an extensive study on fingerprints (Galton, 1892). He introduced the minutiae features for fingerprint matching in 1888.

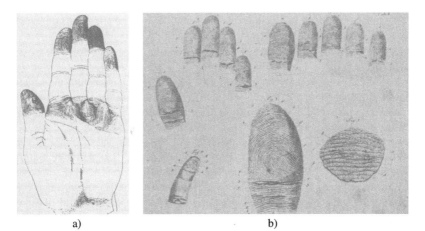

a)   b)

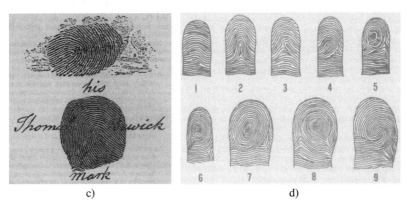

c)   d)

Figure 1.9. a) Dermatoglyphics drawn by Grew (Moenssens, 1971); b) Mayer's drawings of fingerprints (Cummins and Midlo, 1961); c) trademark of Thomas Bewick (Lee and Gaensslen, 2001); d) the nine patterns illustrated in Purkinje's thesis (Moenssens, 1971). Images courtesy of A. Moenssens, R. Gaensslen, and J. Berry.

An important advance in fingerprint recognition was made in 1899 by Edward Henry, who (actually his two assistants from India) established the well-known "Henry system" of fingerprint classification (Lee and Gaensslen, 2001). By the early twentieth century, the formations of fingerprints were well understood. The biological principles of fingerprints (Moenssens, 1971) are summarized below:

1. individual epidermal ridges and furrows have different characteristics for different fingerprints;

2. the configuration types are individually variable, but they vary within limits that allow for a systematic classification;
3. the configurations and minute details of individual ridges and furrows are permanent and unchanging.

The first principle constitutes the foundation of fingerprint recognition and the second principle constitutes the foundation of fingerprint classification.

In the early twentieth century, fingerprint recognition was formally accepted as a valid personal identification method and became a standard routine in forensics (Lee and Gaensslen, 2001). Fingerprint identification agencies were set up worldwide and criminal fingerprint databases were established (Lee and Gaensslen, 2001). Various fingerprint recognition techniques, including latent fingerprint acquisition, fingerprint classification, and fingerprint matching were developed. For example, the FBI fingerprint identification division was set up in 1924 with a database of 810,000 fingerprint cards (see Federal Bureau of Investigation (1984, 1991)).

With the rapid expansion of fingerprint recognition in forensics, operational fingerprint databases became so huge that manual fingerprint identification became infeasible. For example, the total number of fingerprint cards (each card contains one impression each of the 10 fingers of a person) in the FBI fingerprint database now stands well over 200 million from its original number of 810,000 and is growing continuously. With thousands of requests being received daily, even a team of more than 1300 fingerprint experts were not able to provide timely responses to these requests (Lee and Gaensslen, 2001). Starting in the early 1960s, the FBI, Home Office in the UK, and Paris Police Department began to invest a large amount of effort in developing automatic fingerprint identification systems (Lee and Gaensslen, 2001). Based on the observations of how human fingerprint experts perform fingerprint recognition, three major problems in designing AFISs were identified and investigated: digital fingerprint acquisition, local ridge characteristic extraction, and ridge characteristic pattern matching. Their efforts were so successful that today almost every law enforcement agency worldwide uses an AFIS. These systems have greatly improved the operational productivity of law enforcement agencies and reduced the cost of hiring and training human fingerprint experts.

Automatic fingerprint recognition technology has now rapidly grown beyond forensic applications into civilian applications. In fact, fingerprint-based biometric systems are so popular that they have almost become the synonym for biometric systems.

1.7 Formation of Fingerprints

Fingerprints are fully formed at about seven months of fetus development and finger ridge configurations do not change throughout the life of an individual except due to accidents such as bruises and cuts on the fingertips (Babler, 1991). This property makes fingerprints a very attractive biometric identifier. Biological organisms, in general, are the consequence of the interaction of genes and environment. It is assumed that the phenotype is uniquely determined by the interaction of a specific genotype and a specific environment. Physical appearance and fingerprints are, in general, a part of an individual's phenotype. Fingerprint formation is similar to the growth of capillaries and blood vessels in angiogenesis. The general characteristics of the fingerprint emerge as the skin on the fingertip begins to differentiate. The differentiation process is triggered by the growth in size of the volar pads on the palms, fingers, soles, and toes. However, the flow of amniotic fluids around the fetus and its position in the uterus change during the differentiation process. Thus the cells on the fingertip grow in a microenvironment that is slightly different from hand to hand and finger to finger. The finer details of the fingerprints are determined by this changing microenvironment. A small difference in microenvironment is amplified by the differentiation process of the cells. There are so many variations during the formation of fingerprints that it would be virtually impossible for two fingerprints to be exactly alike. But, because the fingerprints are differentiated from the same genes, they are not totally random patterns either.

The extent of variation in a physical trait due to a random development process differs from trait to trait. By definition, identical twins can not be distinguished based on DNA. Typically, most of the physical characteristics such as body type, voice, and face are very similar for identical twins and automatic recognition based on face and hand geometry will most likely fail to distinguish them. Although the minute details in the fingerprints of identical twins are different (Jain, Prabhakar, and Pankanti, 2002), a number of studies have shown significant correlation in the fingerprint class (i.e., whorl, right loop, left loop, arch, tented arch) of identical (monozygotic) twin fingers; correlation based on other generic attributes of the fingerprint such as ridge count, ridge width, ridge separation, and ridge depth has also been found to be significant in identical twins (Lin et al., 1982). In dermatoglyphics studies, the maximum generic difference between fingerprints has been found among individuals of different races. Unrelated persons of the same race have very little generic similarity in their fingerprints, parent and child have some generic similarity as they share half the genes, siblings have more similarity, and the maximum generic similarity is observed in monozygotic (identical) twins, which is the closest genetic relationship (Cummins and Midlo, 1943).

1.8 Individuality of Fingerprints

Although the word "fingerprint" is popularly perceived as synonymous with individuality, uniqueness of fingerprints is not an established fact but an empirical observation. With the stipulation of widespread use of fingerprints, however, there is a rightfully growing public concern about the scientific *basis* underlying individuality of fingerprints. Lending erroneous legitimacy to these observations will have disastrous consequences, especially if fingerprints will be ubiquitously used to establish positive person recognition for reasons of efficiency, convenience, and reliability in fighting growing identity fraud in society. Furthermore, automated fingerprint matching systems do not use the entire discriminatory information in the fingerprints, but only a parsimonious representation extracted by a machine unsupervised by human fingerprint experts.

The amount of distinctive information available in a fingerprint is also being questioned. A leading popular article by Simon Cole, "The Myth of Fingerprints," in The New York Times, May 13, 2001, stated that "the fingerprints may be unique in the sense that, as Gottfried Wilhelm Leibniz argued, all natural objects can be differentiated if examined in enough detail." Cole (2001a) further argues that uniqueness may be valid when *entire* prints are compared but not for prints depicting small portions of a finger; the print size is even more significant in the view of the newer chip-based fingerprint sensors that cover only a small portion of the finger (unlike the nail-to-nail rolled inked fingerprints used in many criminal fingerprint investigations). A Wall Street Journal article by D. Costello, "Families: The Perfect Deception: Identical Twins," on February 12, 1999 speculated that identical twin fingerprints are 95% similar. The same article also quoted a security expert stating, "identical twins would probably pass most of biometric (which includes fingerprint) security technology." Finally, the US Supreme Court Daubert vs. Merrell Dow Pharmaceuticals, Inc. (113 S. Ct. 2786, 1993) hearing started a closer scrutiny of the UK Home Office observation in 1893 that fingerprints are unique. Although the Supreme Court conceded that fingerprints are unique, it subsequently sought (through the United States Department of Justice) to sponsor a systematic study to examine a sound and indisputable scientific basis of fingerprint individuality information.

Thus uniqueness of fingerprints is neither a bygone conclusion nor has it been systematically studied. Obviously, there is enormous public interest in this crucial and contemporary topic. Chapter 8 explores answers to some of these fingerprint individuality questions. More specifically, it presents the examination of fingerprint individuality information in the context of an automated fingerprint matching system in detail and lays out the implications of a fingerprint individuality model in terms of verification and identification systems. An estimate of the information content (cryptographic strength) in fingerprints directly corresponds to the probability of success of a brute force attack on a fingerprint template, that is, the likelihood of generating a synthetic fingerprint input template that matches the registered fingerprint template of an enrolled user.

1.9 Fingerprint Sensing and Storage

Based on the mode of acquisition, a fingerprint image may be classified as off-line or live-scan. An off-line image is typically obtained by smearing ink on the fingertip and creating an inked impression of the fingertip on paper. The inked impression is then digitized by scanning the paper using an optical scanner or a high-quality video camera. A live-scan image, on the other hand, is acquired by sensing the tip of the finger directly, using a sensor that is capable of digitizing the fingerprint on contact. A special kind of off-line images, extremely important in forensic applications, are the so-called *latent* fingerprints found at crime scenes. The oily nature of the skin results in the impression of a fingerprint being deposited on a surface that is touched by a finger. These latent prints can be "lifted" from the surface by employing certain chemical techniques.

The main parameters characterizing a digital fingerprint image are: resolution, area, number of pixels, geometric accuracy, contrast, and geometric distortion. To maximize compatibility between digital fingerprint images and to ensure good quality of the acquired fingerprint impressions, the US Criminal Justice Information Services (the largest division within the FBI) released a set of specifications that regulate the quality and the format of both fingerprint images and FBI-compliant off-line/live-scan scanners (Appendix F and Appendix G of CJIS (1999)). Most of the commercial live-scan devices, designed for the non-AFIS market, do not meet FBI specifications but, on the other hand, are usually more user friendly, compact, and significantly cheaper.

There are a number of live-scan sensing mechanisms (e.g., optical FTIR, capacitive, thermal, pressure-based, ultrasound, etc.) that can be used to detect the ridges and valleys present in the fingertip. Figure 1.10 shows an off-line fingerprint image acquired with the ink technique, a latent fingerprint image, and some live-scan images acquired with different types of commercial live-scan devices.

Although optical scanners have the longest history, the new solid-state sensors are gaining great popularity because of their compact size and the ease of embedding them into laptop computers, cellular phones, smart pens, and the like. Figure 1.11 shows some examples of fingerprint sensors embedded in a variety of computer peripherals and other devices.

Chapter 2 of this book discusses fingerprint sensing technologies, provides some indications about the characteristics of commercially available scanners and shows images acquired with a number of devices in different operating conditions (good quality fingers, poor quality fingers, dry and wet fingers). One of the main causes of accuracy drop in fingerprint-based systems is the small sensing area. To overcome (or at least to reduce) this problem, mosaicking techniques attempt to build a complete fingerprint representation from a set of smaller partially overlapping images.

Storing raw fingerprint images may be problematic for large AFISs. In 1995, the size of the FBI fingerprint card archive contained over 200 million items, and archive size was increasing at the rate of 30,000 to 50,000 new cards per day. Although the digitization of fingerprint cards seemed to be the most obvious choice, the resulting digital archive could become extremely large. In fact, each fingerprint card, when digitized at 500 dpi requires about 10 Mbytes of storage. A simple multiplication by 200 million yields the massive storage requirement of 2000 terabytes for the entire archive. The need for an effective compression technique was then very urgent. Unfortunately, neither the well-known lossless methods nor the JPEG methods were found to be satisfactory. A new compression technique (with small acceptable loss), called Wavelet Scalar Quantization (WSQ), became the FBI standard for the compression of 500 dpi fingerprint images. Besides WSQ, a number of other compression techniques, as surveyed in Chapter 2, have been proposed.

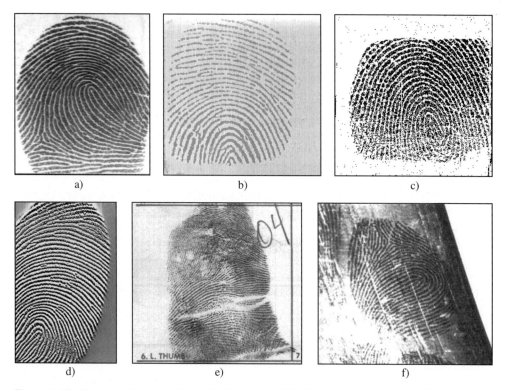

Figure 1.10. Fingerprint images from: a) a live-scan FTIR-based optical scanner; b) a live-scan capacitive scanner; c) a live-scan piezoelectic scanner; d) a live-scan thermal scanner; e) an off-line inked impression; f) a latent fingerprint.

1.10 Fingerprint Representation and Feature Extraction

The representation issue constitutes the essence of fingerprint recognition system design and has far-reaching implications for the design of the rest of the system. The pixel intensity values in the fingerprint image are typically not invariant over the time of capture and there is a need to determine salient features of the input fingerprint image that can discriminate between identities as well as remain invariant for a given individual. Thus the problem of representation is to determine a measurement (feature) space in which the fingerprint images belonging to the same finger form a compact cluster and those belonging to different fingers occupy different portions of the space (low *intra-class* variation and high *inter-class* variations).

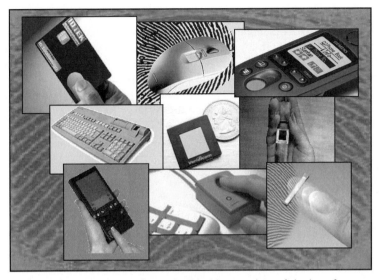

Figure 1.11. Fingerprint sensors can be embedded in a variety of devices for user recognition purposes.

A good fingerprint representation should have the following two properties: *saliency* and *suitability*. Saliency means that a representation should contain distinctive information about the fingerprint. Suitability means that the representation can be easily extracted, stored in a compact fashion, and be useful for matching. Saliency and suitability properties are not generally correlated. A salient representation is not necessarily a suitable representation. In addition, in some biometrics applications, storage space is at a premium. For example, in a smartcard application, typically about 2 Kbytes of storage are available. In such situations, the representation also needs to be parsimonious.

Image-based representations, constituted by raw pixel intensity information, are prevalent among the recognition systems using optical matching and correlation-based matching. However, the utility of the systems using such representation schemes may be limited due to factors such as brightness variations, image quality variations, scars, and large global distortions present in the fingerprint image. Furthermore, an image-based representation requires a considerable amount of storage. On the other hand, an image-based representation preserves the maximum amount of information, makes fewer assumptions about the application domain, and therefore has the potential to be robust to wider varieties of fingerprint images. For instance, it is extremely difficult to extract robust features from a (degenerate) finger devoid of any ridge structure.

The fingerprint pattern, when analyzed at different scales, exhibits different types of features.

- At the global level, the ridge line flow delineates a pattern similar to one of those shown in Figure 1.12. *Singular points*, called loop and delta (denoted as squares and triangles, respectively in Figure 1.12), are a sort of control points around which the ridge lines are "wrapped" (Levi and Sirovich, 1972). Singular points and coarse ridge line shape are very important for fingerprint classification and indexing (see Chapter 5), but their distinctiveness is not sufficient for accurate matching. External fingerprint shape, orientation image, and frequency image also belong to the set of features that can be detected at the global level.

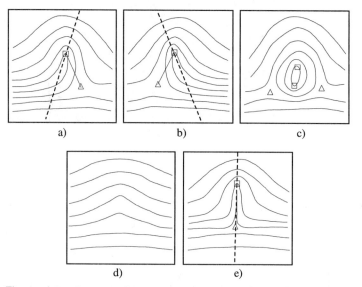

Figure 1.12. Fingerprint patterns as they appear at a coarse level: a) left loop; b) right loop; c) whorl; d) arch; and e) tented arch; squares denote loop-type singular points, and triangles delta-type singular points.

- At the local level, a total of 150 different local ridge characteristics, called *minute details*, have been identified (Moenssens, 1971). These local ridge characteristics are not evenly distributed. Most of them depend heavily on the impression conditions and quality of fingerprints and are rarely observed in fingerprints. The two most prominent ridge characteristics, called *minutiae* (see Figure 1.13), are: *ridge termination* and *ridge bifurcation*. A ridge ending is defined as the ridge point where a ridge ends abruptly. A ridge bifurcation is defined as the ridge point where a ridge forks or diverges into branch ridges. Minutiae in fingerprints are generally stable and robust to fingerprint impression conditions. Although a minutiae-based representation is characterized by a high saliency, a reliable automatic minutiae extraction can be problematic in low-quality fingerprints (hence the suitability of this kind of representation is not optimal).

- At the very-fine level, intra-ridge details can be detected. These are essentially the finger *sweat pores* (see Figure 1.13) whose position and shape are considered highly distinctive. However, extracting pores is feasible only in high-resolution fingerprint images (e.g., 1000 dpi) of good quality and therefore this kind of representation is not practical for most applications.

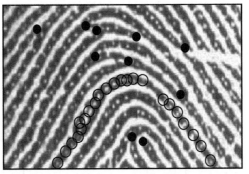

Figure 1.13. Minutiae (black-filled circles) in a portion of fingerprint image; sweat pores (empty circles) on a single ridge line.

Chapter 3 describes fingerprint anatomy and introduces the techniques available for processing fingerprint images and extracting salient features. Specific sections are dedicated to the definition and description of approaches for computing local ridge orientation, local ridge frequency, singular points, and minutiae. Particular emphasis is placed on fingerprint segmentation (i.e., isolation of fingerprint area from the background), fingerprint image enhancement, and binarization, which are very important intermediate steps in the extraction of salient features.

1.11 Fingerprint Matching

Reliably matching fingerprint images is an extremely difficult problem, mainly due to the large variability in different impressions of the same finger (i.e., large intra-class variations). The main factors responsible for the intra-class variations are: displacement, rotation, partial overlap, non-linear distortion, variable pressure, changing skin condition, noise, and feature extraction errors. Therefore, fingerprints from the same finger may sometimes look quite different whereas fingerprints from different fingers may appear quite similar (see Figure 1.14).

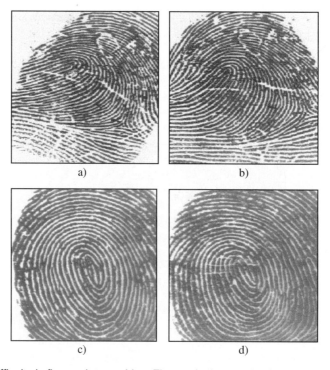

a)   b)

c)   d)

Figure 1.14. Difficulty in fingerprint matching. Fingerprint images in a) and b) look different to an untrained eye but they are impressions of the same finger. Fingerprint images in c) and d) look similar to an untrained eye but they are from different fingers.

Human fingerprint examiners, in order to claim that two fingerprints are from the same finger, evaluate several factors: i) global pattern configuration agreement, which means that two fingerprints must be of the same type, ii) qualitative concordance, which requires that the corresponding minute details must be identical, iii) quantitative factor, which specifies that at least a certain number (a minimum of 12 according to the forensic guidelines in the United States) of corresponding minute details must be found, and iv) corresponding minute details, which must be identically inter-related. In practice, complex protocols have been defined for fingerprint matching and a detailed flowchart is available to guide fingerprint examiners in manually performing fingerprint matching.

Automatic fingerprint matching does not necessarily follow the same guidelines. In fact, although automatic minutiae-based fingerprint matching is inspired by the manual procedure, a large number of approaches have been designed over the last 40 years, and many of them have been explicitly designed to be implemented on a computer. A (three-class) categorization of fingerprint matching approaches is:

- *correlation-based matching*: two fingerprint images are superimposed and the correlation (at the intensity level) between corresponding pixels is computed for different alignments (e.g., various displacements and rotations);
- *minutiae-based matching*: minutiae are extracted from the two fingerprints and stored as sets of points in the two-dimensional plane. Minutiae matching essentially consists of finding the alignment between the template and the input minutiae sets that results in the maximum number of minutiae pairings;
- *ridge feature-based matching*: minutiae extraction is difficult in very low-quality fingerprint images, whereas other features of the fingerprint ridge pattern (e.g., local orientation and frequency, ridge shape, texture information) may be extracted more reliably than minutiae, even though their distinctiveness is generally lower. The approaches belonging to this family compare fingerprints in term of features extracted from the ridge pattern.

Given a complex operating environment, it is critical to identify a set of valid assumptions upon which the fingerprint matcher design could be based. Often there is a choice between whether it is more effective to exert more constraints by incorporating better engineering design or to build a more sophisticated similarity function for the given representation. For instance, in a fingerprint matcher, one could constrain the elastic distortion altogether and design the matcher based on a rigid transformation assumption or allow arbitrary distortions and accommodate the variations in the input images using a clever matcher. In light of the operational environments mentioned above, the design of the matching algorithm needs to establish and characterize a realistic model of the variations among the representations of mated pairs.

Chapter 4 of this book is entirely dedicated to the fingerprint matching problem. After the analysis of the main critical points, the matching problem is formally presented, the above three classes of matching techniques are discussed, and the related literature is surveyed in detail. Particular emphasis is given to minutiae matching and both global and local minutiae matching algorithms are introduced. A separate section is dedicated to the non-linear distortion affecting fingerprint impressions and to the design of distortion-tolerant matchers. Chapter 4 is concluded with some practical suggestions for the estimation and comparison of the performance of fingerprint matching algorithms.

1.12 Fingerprint Classification and Indexing

Large volumes of fingerprints are collected and stored every day in a wide range of applications, including forensics, access control, and driver's license registration. Automatic identification based on fingerprints requires the input fingerprint to be matched with a large number of fingerprints stored in a database (e.g., the FBI database contains more than 200 million fingerprint cards). To reduce the search time and computational complexity, it is desirable to classify these fingerprints in an accurate and consistent manner such that the input fingerprint needs to be matched only with a subset of the fingerprints in the database. Fingerprint classification is a technique used to assign a fingerprint to one of the several pre-specified types already established in the literature (see Figure 1.12). Fingerprint classification can be viewed as a coarse-level matching of the fingerprints. An input fingerprint is first matched to one of the pre-specified types and then it is compared to a subset of the database corresponding to that fingerprint type. For example, if the fingerprint database is binned into five classes, and a fingerprint classifier outputs two classes (primary and secondary) with extremely high accuracy, then the identification system will only need to search two of the five bins, thus decreasing (in principle) the search space 2.5-fold. Unfortunately, only a limited number of major fingerprint categories have been identified (e.g., five), the distribution of fingerprints into these categories is not uniform, and there are many "ambiguous" fingerprints (see Figure 1.15), whose exclusive membership cannot be reliably stated even by human experts. In fact, the definition of each fingerprint category is both complex and vague. A human inspector needs a long period of experience to reach a satisfactory level of performance in fingerprint classification. About 17% of the 4000 images in the NIST Special Database 4 (Watson and Wilson, 1992a) have two different ground truth labels. This means that even human experts could not agree on the true class of the fingerprint for about 17% of the fingerprint images in this database. Therefore, in practice, fingerprint classification is not immune to errors and does not offer much selectivity for fingerprint searching in large databases.

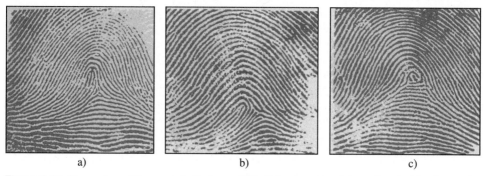

a)   b)   c)

Figure 1.15. Examples of fingerprints that are difficult to classify; a) tented arch; b) a loop; c) a whorl; it seems that all the fingerprints shown here should be in the loop category.

To overcome this problem, some authors have proposed methods based on "continuous classification" or on other indexing techniques. In continuous classification, fingerprints are not partitioned into non-overlapping classes, but each fingerprint is characterized with a numerical vector summarizing its main features. The continuous features obtained are used for indexing fingerprints through spatial data structures and for retrieving fingerprints by means of spatial queries.

Chapter 5 of this book covers fingerprint classification and indexing techniques. The fingerprint classification literature is surveyed in detail and the proposed methods are categorized into one or more of the following families: rule-based approaches, syntactic approaches, structural approaches, statistical approaches, neural networks, and multiple classifiers. A separate section introduces the "standard" notation used to compute classification performance and compares existing methods on NIST Special Database 4 (Watson and Wilson, 1992a) and NIST Special Database 14 (Watson, 1993a) which are the most commonly used benchmarks for fingerprint classification studies. Fingerprint sub-classification (i.e., a multilevel partitioning strategy) and continuous classification are then discussed and the associated retrieval strategies are introduced and compared.

1.13 Synthetic Fingerprints

Performance evaluation of fingerprint recognition systems is very data dependent. Therefore the acquisition conditions, database size, and confidence intervals must be specified when reporting the results. Typically, to obtain tight confidence intervals at very low error rates, large databases of representative fingerprint images are required. Moreover, once a fingerprint database has been used for testing and optimizing a system, successive testing cycles require new databases previously unseen by the system.

Unfortunately, collection of large fingerprint databases is not only expensive in terms of time and money, it is also problematic because of the repetitive monotony of the work (which often leads to collection errors) and of privacy legislation protecting the use of personal data. In several contexts, a synthetic generation of realistic fingerprint images will solve these problems. The most desirable property of such a synthetic fingerprint generator is that it correctly models the various inter-class and intra-class variations in fingerprint images observed in nature. In particular, it should be able to generate realistic "impressions" of the same "virtual finger," by simulating:
- different touching areas;
- non-linear distortions produced by non-orthogonal pressure of the finger against the sensor;
- variations in the ridge line thickness given by pressure intensity or by skin dampness;
- small cuts on the fingertip and other kinds of noise.

Chapter 6 describes a synthetic fingerprint generator (Cappelli, Maio, and Maltoni, 2002b) that meets the above requirements and is able to produce very realistic examples of fingerprint images (see Figure 1.16).

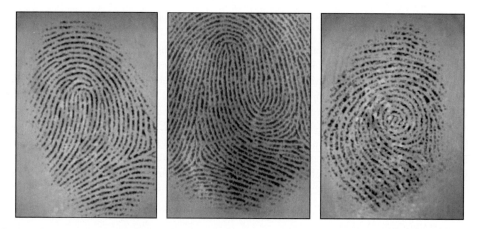

Figure 1.16. Synthetic fingerprint images generated with the software tool SFINGE, whose demo version accompanies this book.

The mathematical models on which the generator is based are introduced, together with visual examples of the intermediate steps. Part of the chapter is dedicated to the validation of the synthetic generator, that is, to the definition of measures and criteria that help to understand how realistic the generated synthetic fingerprints are, not simply on the basis of their appearance, but also from the point of view of fingerprint matching algorithms. Finally, the concluding section briefly describes a software tool that is provided with the DVD that accompanies this book. This tool implements synthetic generation and can be used to create a synthetic fingerprint step by step, observing the effects of various parameter values on the resulting fingerprint image.

1.14 Multimodal Biometric Systems

How can the performance of a fingerprint-based recognition system be improved? There comes a stage in the development of any biometric recognition system where it becomes increasingly difficult to achieve significantly better performance from a given biometric identifier and the need to explore other sources for improvement becomes a practical necessity. The *integration* approach to improve performance can take any number of different forms. One could combine a biometrics scheme with non-biometrics- (possession- or knowledge-) based schemes. For instance, combining a possession-based (e.g., smartcard) authentication with biometric recognition will relieve the burden of higher performance from the biometrics component without increasing the risk of an impostor acceptance. However, these solutions reintroduce some of the problems inherent in the possession- and knowledge-based techniques for personal recognition which is not desirable. This implies that for the desired performance improvement, we may need to rely on integrating multiple biometrics.

Multiple biometrics can also alleviate several practical problems in biometrics-based personal recognition. For instance, although a biometric identifier is supposed to be *universal* (each person in the target population should possess it), in practice, no biometric identifier is truly universal. Similarly, the biometric identifiers are not always sensed (failure to capture rate) or measured (failure to enroll rate, failure to match rate) by a practical biometric system. That is, some small fraction of the target population may possess biometric identifiers that are not easily quantifiable by the given biometric system. Consequently, the recognition system cannot handle this fraction of the population based on that particular biometric identifier. Furthermore, different biometrics may not be acceptable to different sections of the target population. In highly secure systems, reinforcement of evidence from multiple independent biometric identifiers offers increasingly irrefutable proof of the identity of the authorized person. It is also extremely difficult for an intruder to fake all the biometric traits of a genuine user in order to circumvent the system. The assumptions of universality, collectability, acceptability, and integrity are more realistically accommodated when person recognition is based on information from several biometric identifiers.

The output from multiple biometric sensors could be used to create a more reliable and/or extensive (spatially, temporally, or both) input acquisition (Brooks and Iyengar, 1997). Multiple modalities of biometrics can be combined at the feature, matcher score, or matcher decision levels. The representations extracted from many biometric sensors could be collated and the decisions could be made based on the augmented feature vector. The integration at sensor or representation level assumes a strong interaction among the input measurements and such integration schemes are referred to as *tightly coupled integrations* (Clark and Yuille, 1990). The *loosely coupled systems*, on the other hand, assume very little or no interaction among the inputs (e.g., face and finger) and integration occurs at the output of relatively autonomous agents, each agent independently assessing the input from its own perspective.

Focus of most multimodal biometrics research has been on loosely coupled systems. The loosely coupled systems are not only simpler to implement, they are more feasible in commonly confronted integration scenarios. A typical scenario for integration is two biometric systems (often proprietary) independently acquiring inputs and making an autonomous assessment of the "match" based on their respective identifiers; although the decisions or scores of individual biometric systems are available for integration, the features used by one biometric system are not accessible to the other biometric system. Decision-level and matcher score-level integration can provably deliver at least as good or better performance than any single constituent biometric (Hong, Jain, and Pankanti, 1999). With the advent of the API standards (e.g., BioAPI; www.bioapi.org), we expect to see score- or decision-level integration of fingerprints with other biometric identifiers.

Tightly coupled multimodal biometric integration is much harder. The National Institute of Standards and Technology (NIST) and the American Association of Motor Vehicle Administrators (AAMVA) introduced initiatives on interoperability that have led to common formats of fingerprint representations for easy exchange of data among vendors (Ratha et al., 1999). A limitation of these approaches is that these schemes force vendors to use the least common denomination of the representation as a basis of data sharing (e.g., minutiae) and consequently, there may be degradation in performance when one vendor is using the features extracted by another vendor. It remains to be seen whether there will be any development of *feature language*specification that will facilitate describing blackbox features for which blackbox matchers can be developed.

Chapter 7 introduces the reader to the various advantages of designing a multimodal biometric system and presents arguments from the multiclassifier literature that a (carefully designed) integrated system is expected to result in a significant improvement in recognition accuracy. Various combination schemes are categorized on the basis of architecture (e.g., cascade, hierarchical, and parallel), level of fusion (e.g., feature, confidence, rank, and abstract), fusion strategy (e.g., sum and product), and selection/training (e.g., stacking, bagging, and boosting) approaches for individual modalities. Five most common fusion scenarios in a fingerprint recognition system are briefly discussed. The chapter concludes by reviewing the most successful multimodal biometric systems designed to date.

1.15 Designing Fingerprint Recognition Systems

The major issues in designing a fingerprint recognition system include: defining the system working mode (verification or identification), choosing hardware and software components and making them work together, dealing with exceptions and poor quality fingerprint images, and defining effective administration and optimization policy.

As mentioned in Section 1.2, a fingerprint-based system may operate either in verification or identification mode. As a rule of thumb, when the number of users is large (e.g., >1000) it is recommended that the system designer choose the verification mode unless identification is strictly necessary.[1] In fact, it is significantly more difficult to design an identification system than a verification system. For an identification system, both speed and accuracy are critical (see the computation of identification error in Section 1.2). In case neither binning nor clever retrieval mechanisms are available, an identification system needs to explore the entire template database to establish an identity. Even if a classification/indexing is used, it is doubtful that a one-finger-indexing mechanism can reach the desirable efficiency and accuracy on a large database.

---

1 Negative recognition applications cannot work in verification mode: in fact, the system has to search the entire archive to prove that the input is not already present. Sometimes, also in positive applications, the system must necessarily work in identification mode, due to the practical impossibility of using an input device to enter a PIN.

If the system designer/integrator is also the developer of the feature extraction and matching (and eventually classification/retrieval) algorithms, then she certainly has the necessary knowledge to combine all the pieces and to select the optimal fingerprint scanner and computing platform. In the biometric field, developers/integrators of systems and applications are not always the producers of hardware devices and core software, and therefore, care must be taken when choosing basic hardware and software components. The system designer should take into account several factors:

- proven technology: have the hardware and software components been tested by third parties? Are the test results available? Is the vendor available to prove in some way that the claimed performance is true?
- system interoperability and standards: is the system compliant with emerging standards? Is the software compliant with all the platforms and operating systems of interest?
- cost/performance tradeoff: the optimal point in the cost/performance tradeoff strongly depends on the application requirements. The cheapest solution is not necessarily the best choice; biometrics is not infallible, and the success/failure of an application often depends on how much of the customer expectation is met;
- available documentation, examples, and support.

Vendors may supply an SDK (Software Development Kit) in the form of libraries for one or more operating systems. These libraries typically include a series of primitives that allow different tasks to be performed (e.g., acquisition, feature extraction, matching, template storage, etc.). The system/application designer is usually in charge of developing specific routines for:

- implementing ad hoc enrollment stages;
- storing and retrieving template and user information in/from a centralized/distributed database;
- defining the user search order in an identification application. For example, the template of the users most frequently accessing the system may be matched before those of infrequent users;
- defining policies and administration modules to let the system administration define and control system behavior. This includes setting the system security options (system threshold, number of trials, alarms, etc.) and logging information about access attempts.

An important point, when designing a fingerprint-based biometric system/application is to decide from the beginning how to deal with users whose fingerprint quality is very poor. Although the percentage of users with "unusable" fingerprints (they are often called "goats" by some authors (Doddington et al., 1998) is very small, they cannot be ignored, especially in large-scale applications. There are several options to deal with goats:

- in the enrollment stage, choose the best quality finger and eventually enroll more fingers or more instances of the same finger;

- define user-dependent system thresholds. In particular, the system threshold should be relaxed by the system administrator for goats (to reduce false non-match rate) and maintained at the default level for other users. This is in general preferable than decreasing the system threshold for all the users, because an impostor who intends to "imitate" an enrolled user usually is not aware of who is a goat, and in any case should posses a finger similar to that of a goat. In Doddington et al. (1998) jargon (see also Campbell (1997) and Pankanti, Ratha, and Bolle (2002)), users whose biometrics can be easily imitated are referred to as "lambs" whereas users who are the most dangerous imitators are referred to as "wolves";
- use an additional biometric (multimodal biometric system);
- use an additional non-biometric. For example, using a computer-generated difficult password (frequently changed) could be an acceptable authentication alternative for a limited number of users.

System administration and optimization are also very important issues. An administrator should briefly instruct users the first time they use the system and, in particular, make them familiar with the live-scan device. An attended enrollment is often preferable to check the quality of input, select the best finger, and eventually relax the user-dependent threshold (if this option is available). The administration is also in charge of setting the global security threshold, controlling the state of the acquisition devices (the live-scan scanners tend to become dirty with use and therefore, the quality of the input images tends to deteriorate), and to monitor access attempts. In particular, in case some users find difficult accessing the system, the administration should understand the underlying reasons: a new enrollment could solve the problem in the case of some physical variations in the finger (e.g., a recent injury or scratch); retraining users on how to properly interact with the scanner could be sufficient in several other cases. Monitoring the system log could also be very useful to discover if the system is being subjected to attacks by fraudulent users.

In the next section (and in more detail in Chapter 9) we discuss the techniques that can be used to design secure fingerprint-based systems capable of resisting various types of attacks.

1.16 Securing Fingerprint Recognition Systems

Maintaining the integrity of a fingerprint recognition system is critical and requires resolving the frauds involving *repudiation* (e.g., users denying having accessed the system), *coercion* (e.g., users claiming to have been forced into the system), *contamination* (e.g., an erroneous acquisition of fingerprint not associated with the intended user), and *circumvention* (e.g., unauthorized user illegitimately gaining access to the system). The security issues ensure that the intruders will neither be able to access the individual information/measurements (e.g., obtain user fingerprint information from the database, insert spurious new fingerprints into the database) nor be able to pose as other individuals by electronically interjecting ("replay attack") stale and fraudulently obtained biometrics measurements (e.g., surreptitiously lifted fingerprints from surfaces touched by the individuals, fingerprint information tapped from a communication channel) into the system. The access protection may sometimes involve physical protection of the data or detection of the fraudulent physical access to the data (e.g., tamper-proof enclosures). When the system and/or its communication channels are vulnerable to open physical access, cryptographic methods should be employed to protect the biometric information.

A typical approach to protecting biometric information closely follows the path of mainstream security research: encrypting fingerprint data using various standard cryptographic mechanisms. Although many standard encryption technologies could be applied independent of the biometrics, some fingerprint-specific techniques exist. For instance, Soutar and Tomko (1996) envisage a practical system of private DES-like encryption based on Fourier transform of fingerprints. In another approach, Ratha, Connell, and Bolle (1999) propose i) a system of using secret transformation of the biometric measurements and ii) using secret manipulation of frequency domain descriptors of the biometric measurements to render them useless to intruders.

Invisible watermarking of fingerprint images may assure the database administrators that all the images in the database are authentic and are not tampered with by an intruder (Yeung and Pankanti, 2000) in situations where the biometrics are needed for visual inspection without having to decrypt the coded message for such operations. A further requirement is that such watermarked images do not interfere with feature extraction/matching. Such mechanisms of protection reduce the risk of unauthorized "insertion" of spurious records into the database.

Typical approaches to resist "replay" attacks also follow mainstream cryptographic strategies, which rely on introducing (encrypted) time/session sensitive challenge response mechanisms to authenticate the source/destination of the encrypted transmission. Ratha, Connell, and Bolle (1999) have proposed to exploit stochastic noise in the biometric measurements to make sure the stale measurements are rejected by the system. Some biometric systems update their template representations to adapt to the temporally varying nature of the biometric identifier (e.g., finger scratch or cut). Emerging standards like X.9.84 ensure that incremental changes in template are not substantial so as to prevent inadvertent or intentional (insider) attacks to gradually change one identity into the other.

How well one can guess a given fingerprint by brute force depends on the invariant information (see Chapters 8 and 9) in the fingerprints and the number of attempts typically offered to the user. Inherently, fingerprints have significantly high information content which is substantially larger than weak passwords (e.g., date of birth, mother's maiden name) chosen by a typical naive user. A leading biometric API, BioAPI, has explicit controls in its framework to stymie guessing of biometric information (e.g., fingerprint minutiae) by hackers using the feedback offered by the matcher based on optimization strategies such as *hill climbing*. On the other hand, fingerprint data standardization (e.g., Common Biometric Exchange File Format (CBEFF)) when used in isolation offers to somewhat weaken the security of the system by publishing the basic format of the data and thus offering information to the culprits to enable them to use the stolen data in multiple systems (e.g., Hill (2001)). Similarly, by making the functionality public, common API systems may become more prone to hacker attacks than the systems designed with unknown software architecture. Security standards such as ANSI Standard X.9.84 ensure that the known software API structure is minimally exposed to adverse hacking attacks (e.g., through encryption).

Denial-of-service attacks can be particularly problematic in any (biometric or non-biometric) system. Biometric systems often face additional vulnerabilities in this aspect because of the nature of the sensors and because of high bandwidth requirements in the case of centralized recognition services. Biometric sensors are often sensitive and fragile. Many live-scan fingerprint scanners involve optical imaging and are prone to breakage on intentional show of force. Solid-state fingerprint sensors can often be damaged using malicious electric discharge. All sensors requiring optical contact can be rendered practically useless by scratching the glass platens. Developments in contact-less and ultrasonic sensors promise design of more robust fingerprint sensors. On the other hand, forgetting a password or misplacing a token is a known problem in denying access to otherwise legitimate users.

Of particular interest among the various biometric circumvention measures is that of checking whether the source of the input signal is a live genuine biometric (finger) and distinguishing it from a signal originating from a fraud (e.g., tight-fitting latex glove having impression of the genuine finger). The premise of a liveness test is that if the finger (surface) is live, the impression made by it represents the person to whom the finger belongs. One of the approaches of detecting vitality is to use one or more vital signs (e.g., pulse, temperature) that are not particular to the individual but are common to the entire target population. The live-scan optical scanners use a frustrated total internal reflection mechanism for differentially imaging the fingerprint ridges and the fingerprint valleys. Such mechanisms are somewhat inherently resistant to attacks from two-dimensional replay of the fingerprint image. High-resolution fingerprint scanning can reveal characteristic sweat pore structure of skin (Roddy and Stosz, 1997) that is difficult to replicate in an artificial finger. The skin tone of a live finger turns white/yellow when pressed against a glass platen. This effect can be exploited for detecting a live finger. The blood flow in a live finger and its pulsation can be detected by careful measurement of light reflected/transmitted through the finger. Difference in action potentials across two specific points on a live fingerprint muscle can also be used to distinguish it from a dead finger. The electrical properties of a live finger can be ascertained rather effortlessly in some solid-state fingerprint scanners. Measuring complex impedance of the finger can be a useful attribute to distinguish a live finger from its lifeless counterpart. Finally, a live finger typically generates sweat; in a solid-state sensor, the characteristic temporal evolution of the signal can determine liveness of a finger (Derakhshani et al., 2002). Any combination of pulse rate, electrocardiographic signals, spectral characteristics of human tissue, percentage of oxygenation of blood, bloodflow, hematocrit, biochemical assays of tissue, electrical plethysmography, transpiration of gases, electrical property of skin, blood pressure, and differential blood volumes can be used to detect a live finger.

The most important objection to biometrics from a security analysis point of view is that of *key replacement* (Schneier, 1999): what happens when a biometric (e.g., finger) measurement is compromised? Although, in the fingerprint scenario, 10 unique fingerprints offer multiple chances to replace the *key*, the finite number of choices is often not acceptable in many situations. It is hoped that, in a well-designed system with sufficient checks, the compromised keys are rendered useless for biometric recognition.

Chapter 9 discusses in brief various threats such as denial of service, circumvention, repudiation, contamination, covert acquisition, collusion, and coercion that are typical to a recognition application. A number of potential attack points in a fingerprint-based recognition system are also enumerated that include attacks on the sensor, on the feature extraction, matching, and database modules, and on the communication channels. For each type of attack, a dedicated section discusses the existing and potential methods of safeguarding the fingerprint recognition system against that attack. For example, Section 9.6 discusses the attack on the communication channels, presents a brief overview of cryptographic techniques, and discusses the advantages and disadvantages of using competing algorithms.

1.17 Applications of Fingerprint Recognition Systems

Fingerprint recognition is a rapidly evolving technology that has been widely used in forensics such as criminal recognition and prison security, and has a very strong potential to be widely adopted in a broad range of civilian applications (see Table 1.2 and Figure 1.17).

Forensic	Government	Commercial
Corpse Identification, Criminal Investigation, Terrorist Identification, Parenthood Determination, Missing Children, etc.	National ID card, Correctional Facility, Driver's License, Social Security, Welfare Disbursement, Border Control, Passport Control, etc.	Computer Network Logon, Electronic Data Security, E-Commerce, Internet Access, ATM, Credit Card, Physical Access Control, Cellular Phones, Personal Digital Assistant, Medical Records Management Distance Learning, etc.

Table 1.2. Most of the fingerprint recognition applications are divided here into three categories. Traditionally, forensic applications have used manual biometrics, government applications have used token-based systems, and commercial applications have used knowledge-based systems. Fingerprint recognition systems are now being increasingly used for all these sectors. Note that over one billion dollars in welfare benefits are annually claimed by "double dipping" welfare recipients in the United States alone.

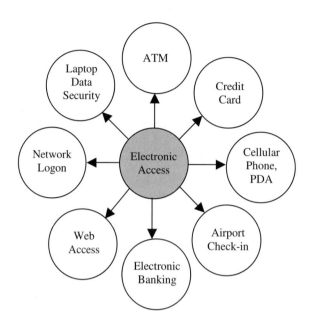

Figure 1.17. Various electronic access applications in widespread use that require automatic recognition.

These applications may be divided into the following groups: i) applications such as banking, electronic commerce, and access control, in which biometrics will replace or enforce the current token- or knowledge-based techniques and ii) applications such as welfare and immigration in which neither the token-based nor the knowledge-based techniques are currently being used.

Information system/computer network security, such as user authentication and access to databases via remote login, is one of the most important application areas for fingerprint recognition. It is expected that more and more information systems/computer networks will be secured with fingerprints with the rapid expansion of the Internet. Applications such as medical information systems, distance learning, and e-publishing are already benefiting from deployment of such systems. *Electronic commerce and electronic banking* are also important and emerging application areas of biometrics due to the rapid progress in electronic transactions. These applications include electronic fund transfers, ATM security, check cashing, credit card security, smartcard security, on-line transactions, and so on. Currently, there are several large fingerprint security projects under development in these areas, including credit card security (MasterCard) and smartcard security (IBM and American Express).

The *physical access control* market is currently dominated by token-based technology. However, it is increasingly shifting to fingerprint-based biometric techniques. The introduction of fingerprint-based biometrics in *government benefits distribution programs* such as welfare disbursement has already resulted in substantial savings in deterring multiple claimants. In addition, *customs and immigration initiatives* such as the *INS* Passenger Accelerated Service System (INSPASS) which permits faster immigration procedures based on hand geometry will greatly increase operational efficiency. Fingerprint-based *national ID systems* provide a unique ID to the citizens and integrate different government services. Fingerprint-based *voter and driver registration* provides registration facilities for voters and drivers. Fingerprint-based *time/attendance monitoring systems* can be used to prevent any abuses of the current token-based/manual systems. Fingerprint-based recognition systems will replace passwords and tokens in a large number of applications. Their use will increasingly reduce identity theft and fraud and protect privacy.

As fingerprint technology matures, there will be increasing interaction among market, technology, and applications. The emerging interaction is expected to be influenced by the added value of the technology, the sensitivities of the user population, and the credibility of the service provider. It is too early to predict where and how fingerprint technology would evolve and be mated with which applications, but it is certain that fingerprint-based recognition will have a profound influence on the way we will conduct our daily business.

1.18 Privacy Issues

Privacy is the ability to lead one's own life free from intrusions, to remain anonymous, and to control access to one's own personal information. Since privacy deals with personal information, there needs to be an enforceable, objective definition of a person's identity. As the magnitude of (identity) fraud increases and as we are increasingly being asked to prove our identity to strangers in remote communities, we believe there will be a tendency to lower the standards of suspecting validity of claimed identity (by the government and industry) for authorizing an important transaction. Strong biometrics such as fingerprints will increasingly come into play for positively recognizing people because the other conventional technologies (e.g., knowledge-based or token-based) cannot deliver such function. For instance, US legislation requires the use of strong recognition schemes such as biometric identifier for controlling access to sensitive medical records to authorized personnel. Some applications have envisaged using biometrics for anonymous access. For instance, these applications will index sensitive individual information without explicitly specifying a name and the access mechanisms will entail specific biometric-based recognition (e.g., allow access to these records if the person's left index fingerprint matches the fingerprint associated with this record). Furthermore, by requiring automated access mechanisms through a secure biometric system, it is hoped that all the accesses to the privileged information can be tracked, thereby increasing the accountability of transactions within the information systems. Thus it is clear that biometric identifiers, especially the strong biometric identifiers such as fingerprints, will be useful for enhancing the integrity of systems holding personal information.

The person recognition value provided by a biometric identifier has almost no objectionable aspect to it from the perspective of the mainstream population and it is almost universally agreed that it provides positive person recognition better than existing conventional technologies. The objections to biometric recognition are based on the following arguments. Some of the privacy concerns surrounding biometrics may be related to personal sensitivities and connotations. Human recognition is traditionally conceived as a mutually reciprocal action between two individuals. Methods of automatic recognition of individuals, especially those based on biometrics, may be perceived as undignifying to humans. Religious objections to the use of biometrics interpret biometric recognition as "the mark of beast" by citing somewhat dubious biblical references.[2] Some people have raised concerns about hygiene of biometric scanners requiring contact. Given that we routinely touch many objects (e.g., money) touched by strangers, this objection may be considered as a frivolous excuse. There may be negative connotations associated with some biometrics (fingerprints, faces, and DNA) due to their prevalent use in criminal investigation. Despite the *criminal* stigma associated with fingerprints, a CNN poll on September 27, 2001 found that fingerprints rate high in social acceptability.

Although person recognition functionality of biometrics appears to be relatively nonintrusive, stronger criticisms are being leveled against the other capabilities of biometric identifiers.

- *Unintended Functional Scope*: Because biometric identifiers are biological in origin, some additional (possibly statistical) personal information may be gleaned from the scanned biometric measurements. For instance, it has been long known that certain malformed fingers may be statistically correlated with certain genetic disorders (Babler (1991), Penrose (1965), and Mulvhill (1969)). With rapid advancement in human genome research, the fear of inferring further information from biological measurements may be imminent. Such derived medical information may become a basis for systematic discrimination against the perceived "risky" sections of population.

- *Unintended Application Scope*: Strong biometric identifiers such as fingerprints allow the possibility of person recognition. For instance, persons legally maintaining multinyms (say, for safety reasons) can be found out based on their fingerprints. The ability to link bits and pieces of behavioral information about individuals enrolled in widely different applications based on biometric identifiers is often construed as accumulation of power over individuals and leaving them with even fewer choices. One of the specific concerns about biometrics is that they are not typically secret. By acquiring strong biometrics identifiers (either covertly or overtly without permission), one has the capacity to track an identified individual. It has been argued that auto-

---

2 "He also forced everyone, small and great, rich and poor, free and slave, to receive a mark on his right hand or on his forehead, so that no one could buy or sell unless he had the mark, which is the name of the beast or the number of his name." (Revelation 13:16-17)

matically gathering individual information based on biometric identifiers accrues unfair advantage to people in power and reduces the sovereignty of private citizens. In the case of fingerprints, presently there is no technology to automatically/routinely capture fingerprints covertly to facilitate effortless tracking.[3]

- *Covert recognition*: Biometrics are not secrets. It is often possible to obtain biometric samples (e.g., face) without the knowledge of the person. This permits covert recognition of previously enrolled people; consequently, the persons who desire to remain anonymous in any particular situation may be denied their privacy due to biometric recognition. Although currently there is no technology for snooping fingerprints of sufficient quality to positively identify persons, we cannot exclude that in the future such technology might become commonplace.

The possible abuse of biometric information (or their derivatives) and related accountability procedures can be addressed through legislation by government/public (e.g., EU legislation against sharing of biometric identifiers and personal information (Woodward, 1999)), assurance of self-regulation (e.g., self-regulation policies of the International Biometrics Industry Association (IBIA)) by the biometric industry, and autonomous enforcement by regulatory independent organizations (e.g., a Central Biometric Authority). Until such consensus is reached, there may be a reluctance to provide (either raw or processed) biometrics measurements to centralized applications and to untrustworthy applications with a potential to share biometric data with other applications. As a result, applications delivering recognition capability in a highly decentralized fashion will be favored.

In biometric verification applications, one way to decentralize a biometric system is by storing the biometric information in a decentralized (encrypted) database over which the individual has complete control. For instance, one could store the fingerprint template of a user in a smartcard that is issued to the user. In addition, if the smartcard is integrated with a small fingerprint sensor, the input fingerprint retrieved from the sensor can be directly compared with the template on the smartcard and the decision delivered (possibly in encrypted form) to the outside world. Such a smartcard-sensor integrated decentralized system permits all the advantages of biometric-based recognition without many of the stipulated privacy problems associated with biometrics. The available smartcard-based fingerprint recognition commercial products offer fingerprint sensing and matching on the smartcard, but usually the feature extraction component is performed on the host PC. However, since the technology for delivering compact feature extraction and matching exists today, we believe it is a matter of time before completely decentralized fingerprint-based recognition is delivered from smartcard-sensor integrated systems for pervasive person recognition.

---

3 Although there is touchless (direct) fingerprint scanning technology available, it is expected to work in close cooperation of the subject at a very close distance. There is presently no technology capable of video snooping of fingerprints.

1.19 Summary

Fingerprint recognition has come a long way since its inception more than 100 years ago. The first primitive live-scan scanners designed by Cornell Aeronautical Lab/North American Aviation, Inc. were unwieldy beasts with many problems as compared to the sleek, inexpensive, and relatively miniscule sensors available today. Over the past few decades, research and active use of fingerprint matching and indexing have also advanced our understanding of individuality information in fingerprints and efficient ways of processing this information. Increasingly inexpensive computing power, cheap fingerprint sensors, and demand for security/efficiency/convenience have lead to the viability of fingerprint matching for every-day positive person recognition in the last few years.

There is a popular misconception that automatic fingerprint matching is a fully solved problem since it was one of the first applications of automatic pattern recognition. Despite notions to the contrary, there are a number of challenges that remain to be overcome in designing a completely automatic and reliable fingerprint matcher, especially when fingerprint images are of poor quality. Although automatic systems are successful, the level of sophistication of automatic systems in matching fingerprints today cannot rival that of a dedicated, well-trained, fingerprint expert. Still, automatic fingerprint matching systems offer a reliable, rapid, consistent, and cost-effective solution in a number of traditional and newly emerging applications. Performance of various stages of a recognition system, including feature extraction, classification, and minutiae matching, do not degrade gracefully with deterioration in the quality of the fingerprints. As mentioned earlier, significant research appears to be necessary to enable us to develop feature extraction systems that can reliably and consistently extract a diverse set of features that provide rich information comparable to those commonly used by the fingerprint experts.

In most pattern recognition applications (e.g., optical character recognition), the best-performing commercial systems use a combination of matchers, matching strategies, and representations. There is limited work in combining multiple fingerprint matchers (Chapter 7); more research/evaluation of such techniques is needed. The proprietary set of features used by the system vendors and lack of a meaningful information exchange standard makes it difficult, if not impossible, for the system designers to leverage the complementary strengths of different commercial systems.

It is not an exaggeration to state that research in automatic fingerprint recognition has been mostly an exercise in imitating the performance of a human fingerprint expert without access to the many underlying information-rich features an expert is able to glean by visual examination. The lack of such a rich set of informative features in automatic systems is mostly due to the unavailability of complex modeling and image processing techniques that can reliably and consistently extract detailed features in the presence of noise. Perhaps, using the human intuition-based manual fingerprint recognition approach may not be the most appropriate basis for the design of automatic fingerprint recognition systems; there may be a need for exploring radically different features (see Chapter 4) rich in discriminatory information, robust methods of fingerprint matching, and more ingenious methods for combining fingerprint matching and classification that are amenable to automation.

Only a few years back, it seemed as though interest in fingerprint matching research was waning. As mentioned earlier, due to a continuing increase in identity fraud, there is a growing need for positive person recognition. Lower fingerprint sensor prices, inexpensive computing power, and our (relatively better) understanding of individuality information in fingerprints (compared to other biometrics) have attracted a lot of commercial interest in fingerprint-based person recognition. Consequently, dozens of fingerprint recognition vendors have mush-roomed in the last few years, and the market revenue is expected to constantly grow over the next five years (see Figure 1.18.a). Reliable pervasive embedded applications of fingerprint-based recognition (e.g., in a smartcard or in a cell phone) may not be far behind. Scientific research on fingerprint recognition is also receiving more attention; proof of this is the exponentially increasing number of scientific publications per year on this topic (see Figure 1.18.b). We strongly believe that higher visibility of (and liability from) performance limitations of commercial fingerprint recognition applications would fuel much stronger research interest in some of the most difficult research problems in fingerprint-based recognition. Some of these difficult problems will entail solving not only the core pattern recognition challenges but also confronting very challenging system engineering issues related to security and privacy.

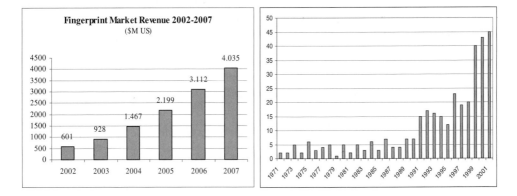

Figure 1.18. a) Biometric Market Report (International Biometric Group©) predicts that total fingerprint revenues, including law enforcement and large-scale public sector usage, will grow rapidly. The maximum growth is expected in the PC/Network Access and e-Commerce market. b) The number of scientific papers published on fingerprint research in last 30 years shows gaining interest in fingerprint recognition research.

On a more speculative note, we wonder whether the protection of personal privacy the way we formulate it today, is a fundamentally flawed concept (Brin, 1998); we need to refine our concept of privacy to accommodate the new "values" created by the automated information society (Nissenbaum, 2001). With the advent of rapidly developing technologies, if rich and resourceful people will be able to covertly (either using biometrics or otherwise) access information about all individuals in society, will we all agree to suffer the indignity of universal transparency (through perhaps silicon chip transponders implanted into the bodies of human beings (McGinity, 2000)) to achieve universal accountability in society? Certainly, these chip technologies are more attractive in terms of their recognition performance and mutability of their signature. It then remains to be seen in the years to come, whether we would prefer to engineer biometric systems that will recognize us in a natural way, to engineer our bodies so that they are more easily identifiable by the machines, or to engineer a system in between the two extremes. An answer to this question will be based on how biometric-based recognition will be perceived by our society faced with the problem of effectively combating increasing identity fraud.

Further introductory readings (books, special issues, and survey papers) on the different aspects of fingerprint recognition (including forensic practices and AFIS) can be found in: Scott (1951), Chapel (1971), Moenssens (1971), Eleccion (1973), Swonger (1973), Banner and Stock (1975a, 1975b), Riganati (1977), Cowger (1983), Wilson and Woodard (1987), Mehtre and Chatterjee (1991), Federal Bureau of Investigation (1984, 1991), Overton and Richardson (1991), Hollingum (1992), Miller (1994), Shen and Khanna (1997), Ashbaugh (1999), Jain et al. (1999, 2001), Maio and Maltoni (1999b), Jain and Pankanti (2000, 2001, 2001b), Jain, Hong, and Pankanti (2000), Pankanti, Bolle, and Jain (2000) and Lee and Gaensslen (2001).

1.20 Image-processing and Pattern Recognition Background

Some background in image processing and pattern recognition techniques is necessary to fully understand the majority of the book chapters (especially Chapters 3 to 7). To facilitate readers who do not have this background, references to basic readings and introductory surveys on various topics are listed below.

Image processing

- A.K. Jain, *Fundamentals of Digital Image Processing*, Prentice-Hall, Englewood Cliffs, NJ, 1988.
- R.C. Gonzalez and R.E. Woods, *Digital Image Processing* (2nd edition), Prentice-Hall, Englewood Cliffs, NJ, 2002.

- D.A. Forsyth and J. Ponce, *Computer Vision: A Modern Approach*, Prentice-Hall, Englewood Cliffs, NJ, 2002.
- J. Parker, *Algorithms for Image Processing and Computer Vision*, John Wiley, New York, 1996.
- L.G. Shapiro and G. Stockman, *Computer Vision*, Prentice-Hall, Englewood Cliffs, NJ, 2001.
- J.C. Russ, *The Image Processing Handbook* (3rd edition), CRC Press, Boca Raton, FL, 1999.
- R. Bracewell, *The Fourier Transform and Its Applications* (3rd edition), McGraw-Hill, New York, 1999.
- S. Mallat, *A Wavelet Tour of Signal Processing*, Academic, New York, 1997.

Pattern recognition

- R.O. Duda, P.E. Hart, and D.G. Stork, *Pattern Classification* (2nd edition), Wiley-Interscience, New York, 2000.
- P.A. Devijver and J. Kittler, *Pattern Recognition: A Statistical Approach*, Prentice-Hall, Englewood Cliffs, NJ, 1982.
- T. Pavlidis, *Structural Pattern Recognition*, Springer-Verlag, New York, 1977.
- A.K. Jain and R.C. Dubes, *Algorithms for Clustering Data*, Prentice-Hall, Englewood Cliffs, NJ, 1988.
- A.K. Jain, R. Duin, and J. Mao, "Statistical Pattern Recognition: A Review," *IEEE Transactions on Pattern Analysis and Machine Intelligence*, vol. 22, pp. 4–37, January 2000.
- A.K. Jain, M.N. Murty, and P.J. Flynn, "Data Clustering: A Review," *ACM Computing Surveys*, vol. 31, no. 3, pp. 264–323, September 1999.
- C.M. Bishop, *Neural Networks for Pattern Recognition*, Oxford University Press, Oxford, 1995.
- A.K. Jain, J. Mao, and M. Mohiuddin "Neural Networks: A Tutorial," *IEEE Computer*, vol. 29, no. 3, pp. 31–44, March 1996.
- J. Kittler and F. Roli (eds.), *Multiple Classifier Systems, First, Second and Third International Workshops* (MCS 2000, 2001, and 2002), *Proceedings, Lecture Notes in Computer Science* 1857, 2096, and 2364, Springer, New York, 2000, 2001, and 2002.

Major journals in image processing and pattern recognition

- *IEEE Transactions on Pattern Analysis and Machine Intelligence*
- *Pattern Recognition*
- *Pattern Recognition Letters*

- *IEEE Transactions on Neural Networks*
- *Computer Vision and Image Understanding*
- *IEEE Transactions on Image Processing*

2
Fingerprint Sensing

2.1 Introduction

Historically, in law enforcement applications, the acquisition of fingerprint images was performed by using the so-called "ink-technique": the subject's finger was spread with black ink and pressed against a paper card; the card was then scanned by using a common paper-scanner, producing the final digital image. This kind of process is referred to as *off-line* fingerprint acquisition or off-line sensing. A particular case of off-line sensing is the acquisition of a latent fingerprint from a crime scene (Colins, 1992). Nowadays, most civil and criminal AFIS accept *live-scan* digital images acquired by directly sensing the finger surface with an electronic fingerprint scanner. No ink is required in this method, and all that a subject has to do is press his finger against the flat surface of a live-scan scanner. To maximize compatibility between digital fingerprint images and ensure good quality of the acquired fingerprint impressions, the US Criminal Justice Information Services released a set of specifications that regulate the quality and format of both fingerprint images and FBI-compliant off-line/live-scan scanners (ref. to Appendix F and Appendix G of CJIS (1999)).

Although AFIS has greatly benefited from the use of live-scan acquisition techniques, this innovation is undoubtedly more important for a broad range of civil and commercial applications where user-friendliness, low-cost, and reliability are being increasingly demanded. Certainly, an employee cannot be expected to ink his fingertip every time he has to logon to his personal computer or to carry out an electronic transaction; neither could we imagine a large diffusion of fingerprint-based biometric techniques if the cost of the acquisition devices was that of the expensive FBI-compliant scanners. Therefore, in the last decade several companies have developed live-scan acquisition scanners designed for the non-AFIS market, with the aim of providing effective solutions to the challenging problem of person recognition (Jain, Bolle, and Pankanti, 1999). Certainly, these sensors do not have the characteristics of the AFIS ones, but are more user friendly, smaller, and significantly cheaper. This chapter, after an introduction on the characteristics of fingerprint images, surveys the main sensor technologies, and discusses the sensing-area versus accuracy tradeoff. Designing low-cost and small-size scanners is the main aim of most scanner producers; on the other hand, it is important for reliable fingerprint recognition that the fingerprint images possess certain characteristics. Relaxing such constraints may lead to a significant (and sometimes unacceptable) decrease in fingerprint recognition accuracy.

The general structure of a fingerprint scanner is shown in Figure 2.1: a *sensor* reads the finger surface and converts the analogue reading in the digital form through an A/D (Analog to Digital) converter; an interface module is responsible for communicating (sending images, receiving commands, etc.) with external devices (e.g., a personal computer). Throughout this chapter we use the terms "scanner" and "sensor" with different meanings: with sensor we denote the internal component of a fingerprint scanner that reads the finger surface. The different technologies the sensors are based on (e.g., optical, solid-state, ultrasound, etc.) are surveyed in Section 2.4.

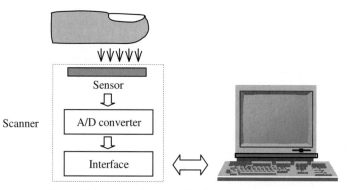

Figure 2.1. Block diagram of a fingerprint scanner.

In practice, there exist several variants of the schema in Figure 2.1: some fingerprint scanners do not have an integrated A/D converter and an external frame grabber is needed to transform their analogue output signal. Furthermore, some embedded system-on-chips have been proposed (Anderson et al. (1991), Shigematsu et al. (1999), and Jung et al. (1999)) where, besides the sensor, a processing board is embedded into the chip in order to locally process and/or match the fingerprint data. The design of secure fingerprint-based biometric systems requires protection/encryption mechanisms to be implemented in the biometric scanners. Chapter 9 discusses the techniques used to protect fingerprint scanners against various attacks and to discard fake fingers presented to the sensors.

Most of the personal recognition systems do not store fingerprint images but store only numerical features extracted from them (see Chapter 3). However, in certain applications (e.g., driver's license), it may be necessary to store the acquired fingerprint images in a database. Storing millions of fingerprint images (as in a large AFIS), or transmitting raw fingerprint data through low-bandwidth networks, is particularly demanding in terms of space/time. Hence, ad hoc compression techniques have been proposed and one of them, Wavelet Scalar Quantization (WSQ), has been adopted as a standard by the FBI; Section 2.7 briefly discusses fingerprint image compression.

2.2 Fingerprint Images

The main parameters characterizing a digital fingerprint image are as follows.

- *Resolution*: This indicates the number of dots or pixels per inch (*dpi*). 500 dpi is the minimum resolution for FBI-compliant scanners and is met by many commercial devices; 250 to 300 dpi is probably the minimum resolution that allows the extraction algorithms to locate the minutiae in fingerprint patterns (see Sections 3.1 and 3.8). Minutiae play a primary role in fingerprint matching, since most of the algorithms rely on the coincidence of minutiae to declare whether the two fingerprint impressions are of the same finger (see Section 4.3). Figure 2.2 shows the same fingerprint portion sub-sampled at different resolutions; decreasing the resolution results in a greater difficulty in resolving ridges from valleys and isolating minutiae points. Images acquired at 200 to 300 dpi are often matched through correlation techniques (see Section 4.2) which seem to tolerate lower resolutions better (Wilson, Watson, and Paek, 2000).

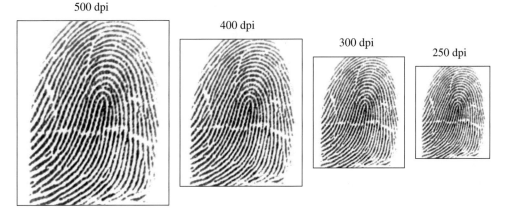

Figure 2.2. The fingerprint on the left, acquired at 500 dpi, is progressively sub-sampled at lower resolutions: 400, 300, and 250 dpi, respectively.

- *Area*: The size of the rectangular area sensed by a fingerprint scanner is a fundamental parameter. The larger the area, the more ridges and valleys are captured and the more distinctive the fingerprint becomes. An area greater than or equal to 1×1 square inches (as required by FBI specifications) permits a full plain fingerprint impression to be acquired. In most of the recent fingerprint scanners aimed at non-AFIS market, area is sacrificed to reduce cost and to have a smaller device size. Small-area scanners do not allow a whole fingerprint to be captured, and the users encounter difficulties in re-presenting the same portion of the finger. This may result in a small overlap between different acquisitions of the same finger, leading to false non-match errors. The tradeoff between sensing area and accuracy is discussed in Section 2.6.

- *Number of pixels*: The number of pixels in a fingerprint image can be simply derived by the resolution and the fingerprint area: a scanner working at r dpi over an area of $height(h) \times width(w)$ $inch^2$ has $rh \times rw$ pixels. If the area is expressed in mm^2, the formula must include the mm–inch conversion and therefore the number of pixels is: $r \cdot (h/25.4) \times r \cdot (w/25.4)$. For example, a scanner working at 500 dpi over an area of 20.32×15.24 mm^2 produces images of $500 \cdot (20.32/25.4) \times 500 \cdot (15.24/25.4) = 400 \times 300$ pixels. Obviously, the equation is invertible and each value {resolution, area, number of pixels} may be uniquely determined given the other two.

- *Dynamic range (or depth)*: This denotes the number of bits used to encode the intensity value of each pixel. Color information is not considered useful for fingerprint recognition and therefore almost all the available fingerprint scanners acquire grayscale images. The FBI standard for pixel bit depth is 8 bits, which yields 256 levels of gray. Actually, some sensors capture only 2 or 3 bits of real fingerprint information and successively stretch the dynamic range to 8 bits in software (Xia and O'Gorman, 2003). No definitive study has been conducted to show how recognition performance decreases when bit depth is decreased. However, it is understood that some degree of bit depth above 1 bit is necessary for good performance of many feature extraction algorithms.

- *Geometric accuracy*: This is usually specified by the maximum geometric distortion introduced by the acquisition device, and expressed as a percentage with respect to x and y directions. Most of the optical fingerprint scanners introduce geometric distortion which, if not compensated, alters the fingerprint pattern depending on the relative position of the finger on the sensor surface.

- *Image quality*: It is not easy to precisely define the quality of a fingerprint image, and it is even more difficult to decouple the fingerprint image quality from the intrinsic finger quality or status. In fact, when the ridge prominence is very low (especially for manual workers and elderly people), when the fingers are too moist or too dry, or when they are incorrectly presented, most of the scanners produce poor quality images (Figure 2.3). The FBI specifications cover only some numerical aspects such as

MTF (Modulation Transfer Function) and SNR (Signal-to-Noise Ratio) concerning the fidelity of reproduction with respect to the original pattern. In practice, other scanner characteristics, such as the ability of dealing with dry and wet fingers should also be taken into account.

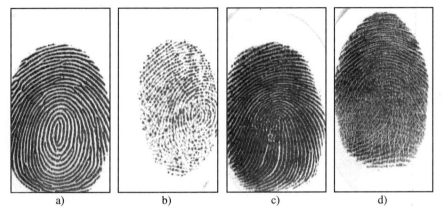

a)   b)   c)   d)

Figure 2.3. Examples of fingerprint images acquired with an optical scanner: a) a good quality fingerprint; b) a fingerprint left by a dry finger; c) a fingerprint left by a wet finger, d) an intrinsically bad fingerprint.

All the above characteristics have a bearing on the accuracy of the recognition system and they do not independently affect the performance. For example, let us suppose there is a 1% decrease in accuracy when resolution is dropped from 500 to 400 dpi, and there is 1% decrease in accuracy when the dynamic range is changed from 8 bits to 4 bits; simultaneously reducing to 400 dpi and 4 bits may decrease the accuracy by more than 2%.

2.3 Off-line Fingerprint Acquisition

Although the first fingerprint scanners were introduced more than 30 years ago, nowadays, the ink-technique (Reed and Meier (1990) and Lee and Gaensslen (2001)) is still used in law enforcement applications. Live-scan acquisition techniques are now being employed in AFIS. As a result, the databases built by law enforcement agencies over a period of time contain both the fingerprint images acquired by off-line scanners and live-scan scanners and the AFIS matching algorithms are expected to interoperate on these different types of images. In the ink-technique the finger skin is first spread with black ink and then pressed against a paper card; the card is then converted into digital form by means of a paper-scanner or by using a high-quality CCD camera. The default resolution is 500 dpi. If not executed with care, the ink-

technique produces images including regions with missing information, due to excessive inki-
ness or due to ink deficiency. On the other hand, an advantage of this technique is the possibility of producing *rolled* impressions (by rolling "nail-to-nail" a finger against the card, thus
producing an unwrapped representation of the whole pattern) which carries more information
with respect to the flat (or *dab*) impressions obtained by simply pressing the finger against the
flat surface of a scanner. Actually, hardware and software techniques have been introduced
(Bolle, Ratha, and Connell, 1998) to enable live-scan fingerprint scanners to produce rolled
impressions. Figure 2.4 reports some examples of digitization from cards taken from NIST
Special Database 14 (Watson, 1993a).

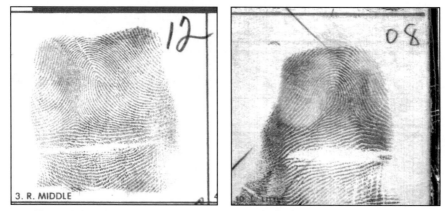

Figure 2.4. Rolled fingerprint images acquired off-line with the ink technique.

In forensics, a special kind of fingerprints, called *latent fingerprints*, is of great interest.
Constant perspiration exudation of sweat pores on fingerprint ridges and intermittent contact
of fingers with other parts of the human body and various objects leave a film of moisture
and/or grease on the surface of the fingers. In touching an object (e.g., a glass), the film of
moisture and/or grease is transferred to the object and leaves an impression of the ridges
thereon. This type of fingerprint is called a latent fingerprint. In this case, a real three-
dimensional finger is not available and a copy of the latent print has to be lifted from the surface or the object where it was left. Latent fingerprints are usually poorly visible and their detection often requires some means of development and enhancement (Figure 2.5). In the past,
powder dusting, ninhydrin spraying, iodine fuming, and silver nitrate soaking were the four
most commonly used techniques of latent print development (Lee and Gaensslen, 2001).
These techniques are quite effective under normal circumstances but are not appropriate in
special cases when fingerprints are deposited on particular objects or surfaces (e.g., wet surfaces, untreated wood, human skin). New procedures have been developed based on new

chemical reagents, instruments, and systematic approaches involving a combination of methods (Lee and Gaensslen, 2001).

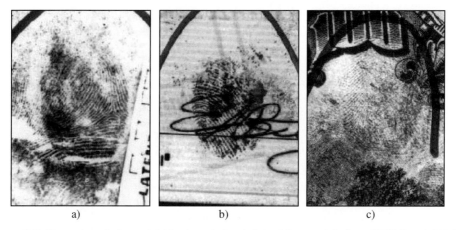

Figure 2.5. Examples of a) good, b) bad, and c) ugly latent fingerprints from NIST Special Database 27 (Garris and McCabe, 2000).

2.4 Live-scan Fingerprint Sensing

The most important part of a fingerprint scanner is the sensor (or sensing element), which is the component where the fingerprint image is formed. Almost all the existing sensors belong to one of the three families: optical, solid-state, and ultrasound.

Optical sensors

- *Frustrated Total Internal Reflection (FTIR)*: This is the oldest and most used live-scan acquisition technique today (Hase and Shimisu (1984) and Bahuguna and Corboline (1996)). The finger touches the top side of a glass prism, but while the ridges enter in contact with the prism surface, the valleys remain at a certain distance (see Figure 2.6); the left side of the prism is illuminated through a diffused light (a bank of light-emitting diodes (LED) or a film planar light). The light entering the prism is reflected at the valleys, and randomly scattered (absorbed) at the ridges. The lack of reflection allows the ridges (which appear dark in the image) to be discriminated from the valleys (appearing bright). The light rays exit from the right side of the prism and are focused through a lens onto a CCD or CMOS image sensor. Because FTIR devices sense a three-dimensional surface, they cannot be easily deceived by presentation of a photograph or printed image of a fingerprint.

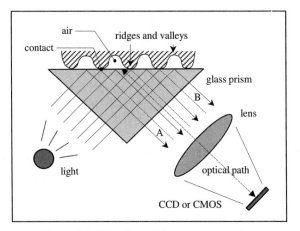

Figure 2.6. FTIR-based fingerprint sensing.

A simple optical device like that shown in Figure 2.6 introduces geometrical distortions. The most evident one is known as trapezoidal distortion; an example is shown in Figure 2.6. Since the fingerprint plane is not parallel to the CCD plane, rays A and B have different lengths, and this results in a stretching or compression of the image regions which is a function of their distance from the optical axis. Compensation for this distortion may be optics-based (by using ad hoc pre-molded plastic lenses or holograms as proposed by Seigo, Shin, and Takashi (1989) and Igaki et al. (1992)) or software-based (calibration techniques).

When a finger is very dry, it does not make uniform contact with the sensor surface. To improve the formation of fingerprints from dry fingers, whose ridges do not contain sweat particles, some scanner producers use silicone coating, which favors the contact of the skin with the prism. With the aim of reducing the cost of the optical devices, plastic is nowadays often used instead of glass for prisms and lenses, and CMOS cameras are mounted instead of more expensive CCDs.

In spite of a generally better image quality and the possibility of larger sensing areas, FTIR-based devices cannot be miniaturized unlike other optical techniques (e.g., optical fibers) or solid-state devices. In fact, the length of the optical path (i.e., the distance between the prism external surface and the image sensor) cannot be significantly reduced without introducing severe optical distortion at the image edges; using one or more intermediate mirrors may help in assembling working solutions in reasonably small packages, but even if these are suitable for embedding into a mouse or a keyboard, they are still too large to be integrated into a PDA or a mobile phone.

- *FTIR with a sheet prism*: Using a sheet prism made of a number of "prismlets" adjacent to each other (see Figure 2.7), instead of a single large prism, allows the size of the mechanical assembly to be reduced to some extent (Chen and Kuo (1995), Zhou, Qiao, and Mok (1998) and Xia and O'Gorman (2003)): in fact, even if the optical path remains the same, the sheet prism is nearly flat. However, the quality of the acquired images is generally lower than traditional FTIR techniques using glass prisms.

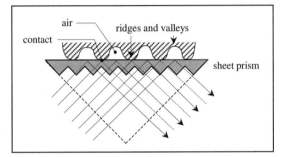

Figure 2.7. The use of a sheet prism in FTIR fingerprint acquisition.

- *Optical fibers*: A significant reduction of the packaging size can be achieved by substituting prism and lens with a fiber-optic platen (Fujieda, Ono, and Sugama (1995) and Dowling and Knowlton (1988)). The finger is in direct contact with the upper side of the platen; on the opposite side, a CCD or CMOS, tightly coupled with the platen, receives the finger residual light conveyed through the glass fibers (see Figure 2.8). Unlike the FTIR devices, here the CCD/CMOS is in direct contact with the platen (without any intermediate lens), and therefore its size has to cover the whole sensing area. This may result in a high cost for producing large area sensors.

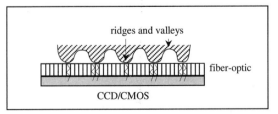

Figure 2.8. A sensor based on optical fibers. Residual light emitted by the finger is conveyed through micro-optical guides to the array of pixels that constitute the CCD/CMOS.

- *Electro-optical*: These devices are constituted of two main layers; the first layer contains a polymer that, when polarized with the proper voltage, emits light that depends on the potential applied on one side (see Figure 2.9). As ridges touch the polymer and the valleys do not, the potential is not the same across the surface when a finger is placed on it and the amount of light emitted varies, thus allowing a luminous representation of the fingerprint pattern to be generated. The second layer, strictly coupled with the first one, consists of a photodiode array (embedded in the glass) which is responsible for receiving the light emitted by the polymer and converting it into a digital image (Young et al., 1997). Some commercial sensors use just the first light-emitting layer for the image formation and a standard lens and CMOS for the image acquisition and digitization. In spite of great miniaturization, images produced by commercial scanners based on this technology are not yet comparable in quality with the FTIR images.

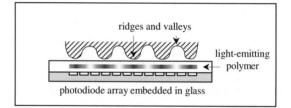

Figure 2.9. Electro-optical fingerprint sensor.

- *Direct reading*: A direct reading device uses a high-quality camera to directly focus the fingertip. The finger is not in contact with any surface, but the scanner is equipped with a mechanical support that facilitates the user in presenting the finger at a uniform distance. Such a device may overcome some problems such as periodically cleaning the sensor surface and may be perceived to be more hygienic, but obtaining well-focused and high-contrast images is very difficult.

Solid-state sensors

Although solid-state sensors (also known as silicon sensors) have been proposed in patent literature since the 1980s, it was not until the middle 1990s that these became commercially available (Xia and O'Gorman, 2003). Solid-state sensors were designed to overcome the size and cost problems which, at the time seemed to be a barrier against the deployment of fingerprint recognition systems in various applications. Actually, as discussed in the following, the cost of silicon sensors is not any lower than optical ones, especially when a very small sensing area is not acceptable. All silicon-based sensors consist of an array of pixels, each pixel being a tiny sensor itself. The user directly touches the surface of the silicon: neither optical components nor external CCD/CMOS image sensors are needed. Four main effects have been proposed to convert the physical information into electrical signals: capacitive, thermal, electric field, and piezoelectric.

- *Capacitive*: This is the most common method used today within the silicon-based sensor arena (Tsikos (1982), Edwards (1984), Knapp (1994), Inglis et al. (1998), Setlak (1999), Lee et al. (1999), and Dickinson et al. (2000)). A capacitive sensor is a two-dimensional array of micro-capacitor plates embedded in a chip (see Figure 2.10). The other plate of each micro-capacitor is the finger skin itself. Small electrical charges are created between the surface of the finger and each of the silicon plates when a finger is placed on the chip. The magnitude of these electrical charges depends on the distance between the fingerprint surface and the capacitance plates (Tartagni and Guerieri, 1998). Thus fingerprint ridges and valleys result in different capacitance patterns across the plates.

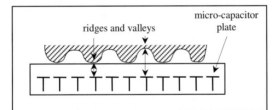

Figure 2.10. Capacitive sensing.

An accurate capacitance measurement is quite difficult to make and adjust, and each sensor has its own method to get enough sensitivity to make a difference between the ridges and the valleys. The capacitive sensors, like the optical ones, cannot be easily deceived by presentation of a flat photograph or printed image of a fingerprint since they measure the distances and therefore only a three-dimensional surface can be sensed.

A critical component of capacitive sensors is the surface coating: the silicon chip needs to be protected from chemical substances (e.g., sodium) that are present in finger perspiration. But a coating that is too thick increases the distance between the pixels and the finger too much, and the distinction between a ridge and a valley decreases, especially with poor quality fingers, where the depth of a valley is in the range of a micron. As a result, the coating must be as thin as possible (a few microns), but not too thin, as it will not be resistant to mechanical abrasion. Also, capacitive sensors sense the electrical field: electrostatic discharges (ESD) from the fingertip can cause large electrical fields that could severely damage the device itself. Therefore, proper protection and grounding is necessary to avoid ESD, chemical corrosion, and physical scratches to the sensor surface (Thomas and Bryant (2000) and Setlak et al. (2000)).

An interesting property of capacitive sensors is the possibility of adjusting some electrical parameters to deal with non-ideal skin conditions (wet and dry fingers); a drawback is the need for frequently cleaning the surface to prevent the grease and dirt from compromising image quality.

- *Thermal*: These sensors are made of pyro-electric material that generates current based on temperature differentials (Edwards (1984) and Mainguet, Pegulu, and Harris (1999)). The fingerprint ridges, being in contact with the sensor surface, produce a different temperature differential than the valleys, which are away from the sensor surface. The sensors are typically maintained at a high temperature by electrically heating them up, to increase the temperature difference between the sensor surface and the finger ridges. The temperature differential produces an image when contact occurs, but this image soon disappears because the thermal equilibrium is quickly reached and the pixel temperature is stabilized. Hence a sweeping method (as explained in Section 2.5) may be necessary to acquire a stable fingerprint image. On the other hand, thermal sensing has some advantages: it is not sensitive to ESD and it can accept a thick protective coating (10 to 20 microns) because the thermal information (heat flow) can easily propagate through the coating.

- *Electric field*: In this arrangement, the sensor consists of a drive ring that generates a sinusoidal signal and a matrix of active antennas that receives a very small amplitude signal transmitted by the drive ring and modulated by the derma structure (subsurface of the finger skin). The finger must be simultaneously in contact with both the sensor and the drive ring. To image a fingerprint, the analogue response of each (row, column) element in the sensor matrix is amplified, integrated, and digitized.

- *Piezoelectric*: Pressure-sensitive sensors have been designed that produce an electrical signal when mechanical stress is applied to them. The sensor surface is made of a non-conducting dielectric material which, on encountering pressure from the finger, generates a small amount of current (this effect is called the piezoelectric effect). The strength of the generated current depends on the pressure applied by the finger on the sensor surface. Since ridges and valleys are present at different distances from the sensor surface, they result in different amounts of current. Unfortunately, these materials are typically not sensitive enough to detect the difference and, moreover, the protective coating blurs the resulting image. An alternative solution is to use micro-mechanical switches (a cantilever made of silicon). Coating is still a problem and, in addition, this device delivers a binary image, leading to minimal information.

2.5 Touch versus Sweep   65

Ultrasound sensors

Ultrasound sensing may be viewed as a kind of *echography*. It is based on sending acoustic signals toward the fingertip and capturing the echo signal (see Figure 2.11). The echo signal is used to compute the range image of the fingerprint and, subsequently, the ridge structure itself. The sensor has two main components: the transmitter, which generates short acoustic pulses, and the receiver, which detects the responses obtained when these pulses bounce off the fingerprint surface (Schneider and Wobschall (1991) and Bicz et al. (1999)). This method images the subsurface of the finger skin (even through thin gloves); therefore, it is resilient to dirt and oil accumulations that may visually mar the fingerprint. Good quality images may be obtained by this technology. However, the scanner is large with mechanical parts and quite expensive. Moreover, it takes a few seconds to acquire an image. Hence, this technology is not yet mature enough for large-scale production.

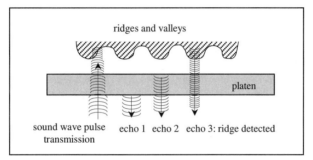

Figure 2.11. The basic principle of the ultrasound technique. Characteristic of sound waves is the ability to penetrate materials, giving a partial echo at each impedance change.

2.5 Touch versus Sweep

Most of the sensors available today use the *touch* method: the finger is simply put on the scanner, without moving it. The main advantage of this method is its simplicity: very little user training is required. On the other hand, this method has some drawbacks.

- Depending on the sensor technology and the operating conditions, the sensor can soon become dirty and must be cleaned periodically. Some people are reluctant to put their finger in the same place after someone else for hygiene reasons, especially if it looks dirty.

- A more-or-less-visible latent fingerprint remains on the sensor once the finger has been removed. In some cases, the sensor may be triggered to read this latent image as an input, and some countermeasures have to be adopted to prevent this.
- Rotation of the finger may be a problem for recognition: some matching algorithms do not accept large rotation (e.g., more than ±20°) of the finger. Generally, a guiding mechanism helps the finger to be always placed in the same way to avoid this.
- There is a strict tradeoff between the cost and the size of the sensing area. This is especially true for solid-state sensors, where the cost mainly depends on the area of the chip die. A larger die costs more due to fewer dies per wafer and lower yield; furthermore, large dies are more likely to include defects, resulting in a higher number of discarded chips. A typical capacitive touch sensor has a size of 15 mm by 15 mm, which is large for a chip.

With the main aim of reducing the cost, especially in silicon sensors, another sensing method has been proposed: to *sweep* the finger over the sensor. Since the sweeping consists of a vertical movement only, the chip must be as wide as a finger; on the other hand, in principle, the height of the sensor could be as low as one pixel: actually, since the finger movement speed is unknown and it can vary during the sweeping, the only way to reliably combine the different fingerprint readings (slices) is by requiring a certain degree of overlap between them. As a result, heights greater than one pixel are typically used. At the end of the sweep, a single fingerprint image has to be reconstructed from the slices. This could be done "on-the-fly" by combining the slices as they are delivered by the sensor (see Figure 2.12). In practice, using the sweeping technique, the size of the silicon sensor can be reduced by a factor of ten and the cost reduced commensurately (Xia and O'Gorman, 2003).

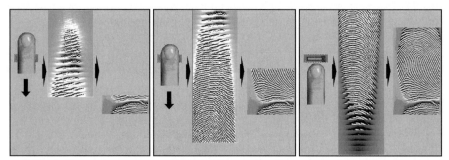

Figure 2.12. As the user sweeps her finger on the sensor, the sensor delivers new image slices, which are combined into a two-dimensional image.

The sweeping method was initially introduced in conjunction with thermal sensors, because sweeping was necessary to have a working "thermal" device. In fact, as discussed in

Section 2.4, the image vanishes very quickly because of the thermal equilibrium between the finger and the sensor. However, the equilibrium is continuously broken when sweeping, as ridges and valleys touch the pixels alternately, introducing a continuous temperature change. Nowadays, both the touch and sweep methods are being used with different sensor technologies. Optical scanners that use the sweeping method have also been proposed.

Unlike the touch devices, the sweep sensors always look clean since the finger itself cleans the sensor during usage, no latent fingerprint remains, and there is practically no rotation as the finger is always swept in the same direction (with the help of some mechanical guidance built in the scanner packaging). However, there are some drawbacks as well.

- The first times a novice user interacts with a sweep-based sensor, he may encounter some difficulties in performing the sweeping properly (i.e., without sharp speed changes, or discontinuity), and in general, it is less natural than using a touch-based device. In short, sweep sensors have a higher "habituation" period than touch sensors.
- The interface must be able to capture a sufficient number of fingerprint slices to follow the finger sweep speed. This may be difficult with interfaces with slow throughput, but does not constitute a problem with the available microprocessors and I/O interfaces.
- The full fingerprint image must be reconstructed from the slices; this process is time consuming and usually produces errors, especially in the case of poor quality fingerprints and non-uniform sweep speed.

Image reconstruction from slices

The sweep method allows the cost of a sensor to be significantly reduced, but requires reliable reconstruction to be performed. Figure 2.13 shows the block diagram of an algorithmic approach designed for a thermal sensor that delivers slices of 280×30 pixels. The main stages are as follows.

- *Slice quality computation*: For each slice, a single global quality measure and several local measures are computed by using an image contrast estimator; all successive stages are driven by these measures.
- *Slice pair registration*: For each pair of consecutive slices, the only possible transformation is assumed to be a global translation $[\Delta x, \Delta y]$, where the Δy component is dominant, but a limited Δx is also allowed to cope with lateral movements of the finger during sweeping. Finding the translation vector, or in other words, registering the two slices involves a search over the space of all possible translation vectors.
- *Relaxation*: When the quality of slices is low, the registration may fail and give incorrect translation vectors. Assuming a certain continuity of the finger speed during sweeping allows analogous hypotheses to be generated on the continuity of the translation vectors. The translation vectors' continuity may be obtained through a method

called relaxation (Rosenfeld and Kak, 1976) which has the nice property of smoothing the samples without affecting the correct measurements too much.

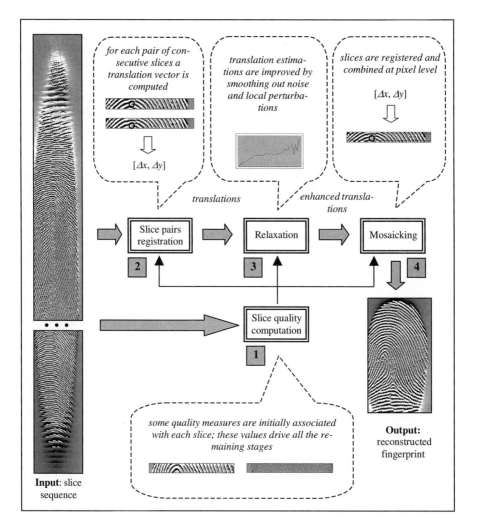

Figure 2.13. An algorithm for fingerprint reconstruction from slices. All the steps are performed sequentially on the whole set of slices. The output of the slice pair registration is a set of translation estimates that are globally enhanced by the relaxation step. These improved estimates drive the mosaicking phase in order to reconstruct the whole fingerprint image.

- *Mosaicking*: The enhanced translation vectors produced by the relaxation stage are used to register and superimpose the slices. Finally, each pixel of the reconstructed output image is generated by performing a weighted sum of the intensities of the corresponding pixels in the slices.

2.6 Fingerprint Scanners and their Features

Several fingerprint scanners, based on the sensing technologies surveyed in Section 2.4, are commercially available. Certainly, the main characteristics of a fingerprint scanner depend on the specific sensor mounted which in turn determines the image features (dpi, area, and dynamic range), size, cost, and durability. Other features should be taken into account when a fingerprint scanner has to be chosen for a specific application.

- *Interface*: FBI-compliant scanners often have analogue output (e.g., RS-170) and a frame grabber is necessary to digitize the images. This introduces an extra cost and usually requires an internal board to be mounted in the host. On the other hand, in non-AFIS devices, the analogue-to-digital conversion is performed by the scanner itself and the interface to the host is usually through a simple Parallel Port or USB connection.
- *Frames per second*: This indicates the number of images the scanner is able to acquire and send to the host in a second. A high frame rate (e.g., larger than 5 frames/sec) better tolerates movements of the finger on the sensors and allows a more friendly interaction with the scanner. It can also provide a natural visual feedback during the acquisition.
- *Automatic finger detection*: Some scanners automatically detect the presence of a finger on the acquisition surface, without requiring the host to continually grab and process frames; this allows the acquisition process to be automatically initiated as soon as the user's finger touches the sensor.
- *Encryption*: As discussed in Chapter 9, securing the communication channel between the scanner and the host is an effective way of securing a system against attacks. For this purpose, some commercial scanners implement state-of-the-art symmetric and public-key encryption capability.
- *Supported operating systems*: Depending on the application and the infrastructure where the fingerprint scanners have to be employed, compatibility with more operating systems, and in particular the support of open-source operating systems such as Linux, could be an important feature.

Table 2.1 lists some commercial scanners designed for the non-AFIS markets, whose cost is less than $200 US. Except for ultrasound scanners, which are not ready for mass-market applications yet, Table 2.1 includes at least one scanner for each technology.

	Technology	Company	Model	Dpi	Area (h×w)	Pixels
Optical	FTIR	Biometrika www.biometrika.it/eng/	FX2000	569	0.98"×0.52"	560×296 (165,760)
	FTIR	Digital Persona www.digitalpersona.com	UareU2000	440	0.67"×0.47"	316×228 (72,048)
	FTIR (sweep)	Kinetic Sciences www.kinetic.bc.ca	K-1000	up to 1000	0.002"×0.6"	2×900 (H×900)
	FTIR	Secugen www.secugen.com	Hamster	500	0.64"×0.54"	320×268 (85,760)
	Sheet prism	Identix www.identix.com	DFR 200	380	0.67"×0.67"	256×256 (65,535)
	Fiber optic	Delsy www.delsy.com	CMOS module	508	0.71"×0.47"	360×240 (86,400)
	Electro-optical	Ethentica www.ethentica.com	TactilSense T-FPM	403	0.76"×0.56"	306×226 (69,156)
Solid-state	Capacitive (sweep)	Fujitsu www.fme.fujitsu.com	MBF300	500	0.06"×0.51"	32×256 (H×256)
	Capacitive	Infineon www.infineon.com	FingerTip	513	0.56"×0.44"	288×224 (64,512)
	Capacitive	ST-Microelectronics us.st.com	TouchChip TCS1AD	508	0.71"×0.50"	360×256 (92,160)
	Capacitive	Veridicom www.veridicom.com	FPS110	500	0.60"×0.60"	300×300 (90,000)
	Thermal (sweep)	Atmel www.atmel.com	FingerChip AT77C101B	500	0.02"×0.55"	8×280 (H×280)
	Electric field	Authentec www.authentec.com	AES4000	250	0.38"×0.38"	96×96 (9,216)
	Piezoelectric	BMF www.bm-f.com	BLP-100	406	0.92"×"0.63	384×256 (98,304)

Table 2.1. Some commercial scanners, grouped by technology. Technologies are presented in the order of Section 2.4, and within each technology, companies are listed in alphabetical order. The table reports for each scanner, the resolution, the sensing area, and the number of pixels. For sweep sensors, the vertical number of pixels varies depending on the length of the sweep, and therefore, cannot be determined a priori.

Figures 2.14 through 2.17 compare the same finger (a good-quality finger, a dry finger, a wet finger, and a poor quality finger, respectively) as acquired by using some of the scanners listed in Table 2.1.

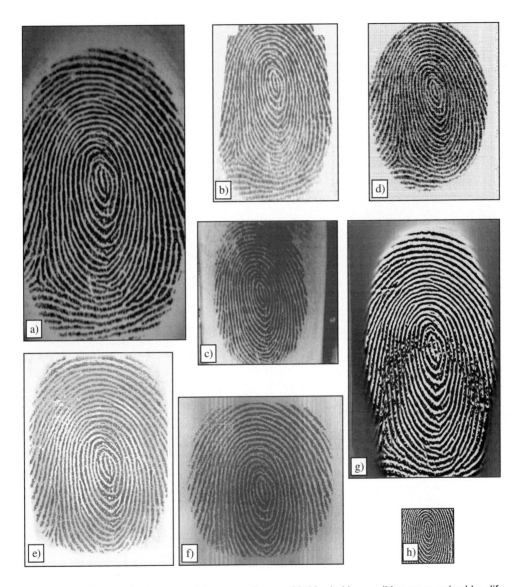

Figure 2.14. Fingerprint images of the same finger with ideal skin condition as acquired by different commercial scanners. Images are reported with right proportions: a) Biometrika FX2000, b) Digital Persona UareU2000, c) Identix DFR200, d) Ethentica TactilSense T-FPM, e) ST-Microelectronics TouchChip TCS1AD, f) Veridicom FPS110, g) Atmel FingerChip AT77C101B, h) Authentec AES4000.

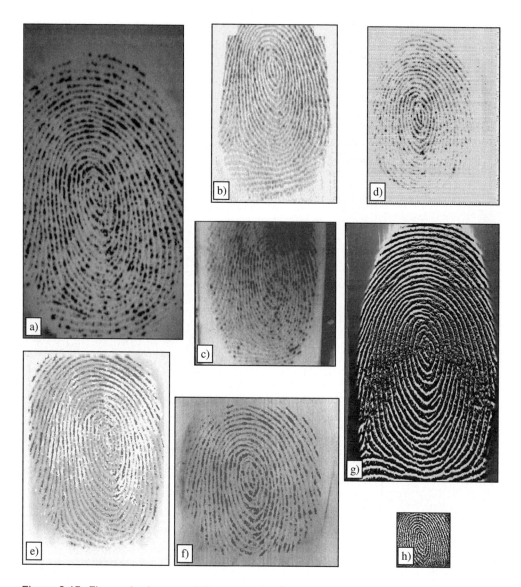

Figure 2.15. Fingerprint images of the same dry finger as acquired by different commercial scanners. Images are reported with right proportions: a) Biometrika FX2000, b) Digital Persona UareU2000, c) Identix DFR200, d) Ethentica TactilSense T-FPM, e) ST-Microelectronics TouchChip TCS1AD, f) Veridicom FPS110, g) Atmel FingerChip AT77C101B, h) Authentec AES4000.

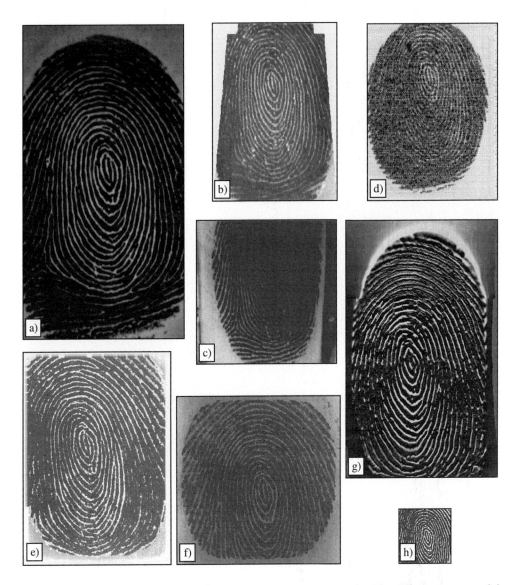

Figure 2.16. Fingerprint images of the same wet finger as acquired by different commercial scanners. Images are reported with right proportions: a) Biometrika FX2000, b) Digital Persona UareU2000, c) Identix DFR200, d) Ethentica TactilSense T-FPM, e) ST-Microelectronics TouchChip TCS1AD, f) Veridicom FPS110, g) Atmel FingerChip AT77C101B, h) Authentec AES4000.

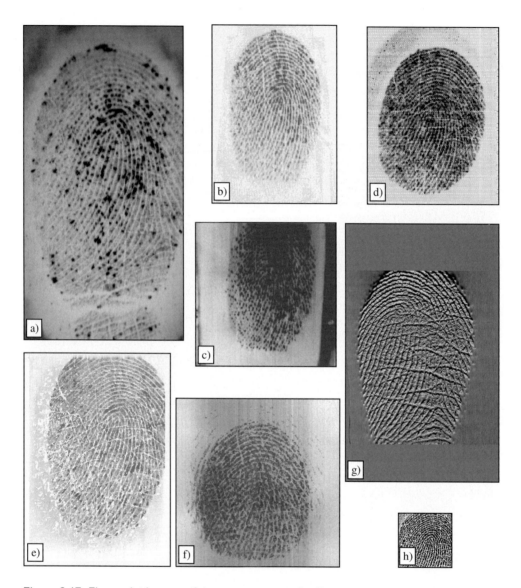

Figure 2.17. Fingerprint images of the same poor quality finger as acquired by different commercial scanners. Images are reported with right proportions: a) Biometrika FX2000, b) Digital Persona UareU2000, c) Identix DFR200, d) Ethentica TactilSense T-FPM, e) ST-Microelectronics TouchChip TCS1AD, f) Veridicom FPS110, g) Atmel FingerChip AT77C101B, h) Authentec AES4000.

2.7 Sensing Area versus Accuracy Tradeoff

In the previous sections, the main sensing technologies and their peculiarities have been discussed. Certainly, each technology has its pros and cons, and can be better or worse than another depending on the weight given to different factors: resolution, area, image quality, size, cost, robustness, and so on. In particular, an important tradeoff between accuracy and cost involves the sensing area. Sensor manufacturers tend to reduce the sensing area in order to lower the cost of their devices. In fact, in general, independently of the sensor technology, the larger the area sensed by a device, the greater is the device cost. This is especially true for silicon-based sensors where, since the finger directly touches the sensor's active elements, there is no possibility of magnification/reduction and the cost increases linearly with the area (in square millimeters) of silicon. The above principle also holds for optical and ultrasound sensors where, given a desired resolution, requiring a bigger area involves adopting larger optical and mechanical parts, more expensive electronic components, and larger packaging.

Recognizing fingerprints acquired through small-area sensors is difficult due to the possibility of having too little overlap between different acquisitions of the same finger. If a minutiae-based matching algorithm (see Section 4.3) is used, in the case of small overlap between the fingerprints, the number of minutiae correspondences might significantly decrease (see Section 8.4) and the matching algorithm would not be able to make a decision with high certainty (Yau et al. (2000), Pankanti, Prabhakar, and Jain (2002) and Jain and Ross (2002b)). This effect is even more marked on intrinsically poor quality fingers, where only a subset of the minutiae can be extracted and used with sufficient reliability. A small overlap also affects the reliability of both correlation-based and ridge feature-based matching techniques, since the amount of information available for the matching is reduced.

Jain, Prabhakar, and Ross (1999) compared the performance of a given matching algorithm on two fingerprint databases containing the same subjects and acquired with the same protocol: the first database was collected with a large sensing area FTIR optical scanner (640×480 pixels, 500 dpi) and the second database was gathered with a capacitive solid-state sensor (300×300 pixels, 500 dpi). In their experiments, Jain, Prabhakar, and Ross (1999) observed substantial differences in the resulting verification accuracy (see Figure 2.18).

Other experimental evidence can be extrapolated from the FVC2000 and FVC2002 results (Maio et al. (2000) and Maio et al. (2002b)). Although these competitions were not aimed at comparing sensors but only matching algorithms, it is evident that, if the same algorithm performs differently on databases collected under the same conditions but using different scanners, and if this happens for the majority of algorithms, then the scanner itself is primarily responsible for the difference in performance. In FVC2000 (Maio et al., 2000), databases DB1 and DB2 were collected under the same conditions (typology of volunteers, number of sessions, training, and constraints): DB1 was collected with an FTIR optical scanner and DB2 was collected with a capacitive solid-state sensor. Both scanners have approximately the same resolution and the same area. Most of the algorithms performed similarly, even though the images in the two databases appear to be visually quite different. This suggests that the sensor technology (optical or capacitive) did not play a primary role in the resulting performance. Database DB3 was collected with a large-area optical sensor, but the acquisition conditions were not comparable with those of DB1 and DB2. Database DB3 is more "difficult" than the others because the users were explicitly requested to exaggerate distortions and include fingerprints of children (that typically have lower area, more improper placements, and higher ridge frequency).

In FVC2002 (Maio et al., 2002b), DB1, DB2, and DB3 were acquired under the same conditions: DB1 and DB2 with two large area FTIR optical scanners (388×374 pixels, 500 dpi and 560×296 pixels, 569 dpi, respectively) and DB3 with a smaller area capacitive sensor (300×300 pixel, 500 dpi). A significant difference was observed in the average performance of the matching algorithms on {DB1, DB2} and DB3. Although the average EER (Equal Error Rate) was approximately the same for DB1 and DB2, it was about 250% higher on DB3.

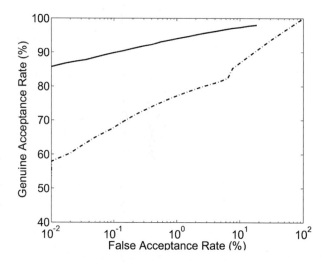

Figure 2.18. The results of the experiments performed by Jain, Prabhakar, and Ross (1999). The solid line denotes the performance of a fingerprint verification algorithm over a database collected through a large-area FTIR optical scanner, whereas the dashed line denotes the performance of the same algorithm over a database acquired through a smaller area capacitive solid-state sensor. The false match rate is here referred to as False Acceptance Rate (FAR). The false non-match rate (here referred to as False Rejection Rate, FRR) is the complement (to 100%) of the Genuine Acceptance Rate (GAR) shown along the ordinate of the graph: FRR = (100% − GAR). For example, for FAR = 0.1%, FRR ≈ 10% for the FTIR scanner and FRR ≈ 32% for the capacitive one.

To deal with small sensing areas, some vendors equip their scanners with mechanical guides with the aim of constraining the finger position so that roughly the same fingerprint portion is captured in different acquisition sessions. In any event, due to the different sizes of fingers of different users and the difficulty of integrating the guides in certain applications, this solution is not satisfactory.

An interesting alternative is designing an algorithm capable of dealing with a small sensor area. A feasible approach is sketched in Figure 2.19, where multiple acquisitions of a finger are performed during the user enrollment, and a "mosaic" is automatically built and stored as a reference fingerprint. This technique is known as fingerprint *mosaicking*. At recognition time, the user touches the sensor once, and the small fingerprint area captured is matched against the whole reference fingerprint. Different approaches could be adopted to combine multiple (partially overlapping) fingerprint images into a full fingerprint image (Brown, 1992). A simple idea is to exploit the same algorithm used for matching: in fact, a side effect of matching two fingerprints is the derivation of the transformation (e.g., displacement and rotation) between the two fingerprints; given this information, pasting more images into a single large image can be accomplished by superimposing the aligned images and by appropriately weighting the intensity of the corresponding pixels. The main difficulty in creating a mosaicked image is that, often, the alignment between the various impressions/pieces cannot be completely recovered.

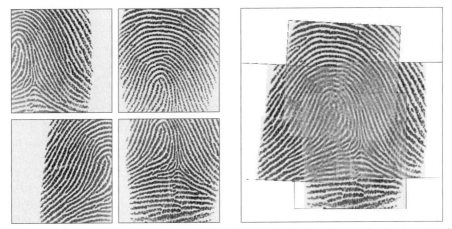

Figure 2.19. A fingerprint mosaic image obtained by combining four fingerprint images acquired with a 0.51 × 0.51 square inch optical sensor working at 500 dpi.

In practice, for minutiae-based matching algorithms, instead of recreating the whole fingerprint image, it may be more convenient to build the mosaic at minutiae level, that is, rearranging the minutiae from each fingerprint impression into a single map. Practical implementations of this approach, known in the literature as *template consolidation* or *template improvement*, are discussed in Yau et al. (2000), Toh et al. (2001), Jain and Ross (2002b), and Ramoser, Wachmann, and Bischof (2002).

The Jain and Ross (2002b) mosaicking algorithm combines two impressions of a finger by first aligning the fingerprint images by using the Iterative Closest Point (ICP) algorithm (Besl and McKay, 1992). A low-pass filter is initially applied to the images and the pixel intensities are sub-sampled to a narrow gray-scale range of [10,20] to ensure a fairly smooth change in the surface corresponding to the range image of the fingerprints (see Figure 3.7 for an example of surface representation of a fingerprint image). The images are then segmented into foreground and background; an alignment between the two foreground images is estimated using the ICP algorithm, and a composite image is created by taking an average of the corresponding pixel intensities (see Figure 2.20). Jain and Ross (2002b) compared the mosaicking of fingerprints at the gray-scale image representation level with a mosaicking at the minutiae representation level and found the former to outperform the latter. Their results on 320 query images showed an improvement of ~4% in the accuracy of a fingerprint verification system when two impressions of each finger were combined to form a composite template at the gray-scale intensity level.

Figure 2.20. Combination of two impressions of a finger (on the left) into one composite fingerprint image (on the right) using the Jain and Ross (2002b) method. ©IEEE.

Other mosaicking techniques were proposed by Bolle, Ratha, and Connell (1998) and Zhou et al. (2001) with the aim of obtaining a rolled fingerprint impression from a sequence of dab fingerprint images acquired through a live-scan scanner. In particular, the Bolle, Ratha, and Connell (1998) mosaicking algorithm consists of the following steps: i) segment fingerprint foreground and background areas in each fingerprint image, ii) use the foreground mask to weight each image's contribution, iii) stack the weighted gray-scale frames to compute the mosaicked gray-scale image, and iv) stack the foreground masks to compute a confidence index at each pixel. Because all the fingerprint images to be combined are acquired in a single rolling of a fingerprint, the authors assume that the images are already aligned. Furthermore, the foreground masks are shrunk so that only the central portion of each image with the best contrast and least distortion is used.

2.8 Storing and Compressing Fingerprint Images

Storing fingerprint images is not a serious problem for non-AFIS applications, because generally, only numerical features extracted from fingerprint images are archived to be successively used for the user recognition. Also, in a few non-AFIS applications, where the images are required to be stored, the number of users enrolled in the database is generally quite low.

Things are very different in AFIS: in 1995, the size of the FBI fingerprint card archive (each card is a paper form where, besides textual information, all 10 fingerprints from two hands of an individual are impressed through the ink technique) was over 200 million, occupying an acre of filing cabinets in the J. Edgar Hoover building in Washington, DC. (Hopper, Brislawn, and Bradley, 1993). Furthermore, the archive size was increasing at the rate of 30,000 to 50,000 new cards per day. The digitization of fingerprint cards was an obvious choice, although the size of the resulting digital archive was problematic. Each fingerprint impression, when digitized at 500 dpi, produces an image of 768×768 pixels at 256 gray-levels. An uncompressed representation of such an image requires 589,824 bytes and about 10 Mbytes are necessary to encode a single card (both a dab and rolled impression of each finger are present on the card). A simple multiplication by 200 million yields the massive storage capacity of 2000 terabytes for the entire archive. Another problem was the long delay involved in transmitting a fingerprint image over a band-limited communication channel: about three hours for transmitting a single image over a 9600 baud channel. The need for an effective compression technique was very urgent. Unfortunately, neither the well-known lossless methods nor the JPEG compression method was satisfactory. The former typically provide a compression ratio of 2 when applied to gray-scale fingerprint images and the latter, at the FBI target compression ratio (0.75 bit per pixel, i.e., about 1:10.7), produces block artifacts and loses many small details (e.g., ridge pores) (see Figure 2.21.c). A new compression technique (with small acceptable loss), called Wavelet Scalar Quantization (WSQ), was then developed on the basis of the work by Hopper and Preston (1991), Bradley, Brislawn, and Hopper (1992), Hopper, Brislawn, and Bradley (1993) and Brislawn et al. (1996). Due to its superiority with respect to other general-purpose compression techniques, WSQ became the FBI standard for the compression of 500 dpi fingerprint images. WSQ is based on adaptive scalar quantization of a discrete wavelet transform (Hopper, Brislawn, and Bradley, 1993). The WSQ encoder performs sequential steps:

1. the fingerprint image is decomposed into a number of spatial frequency sub-bands (typically 64) using a Discrete Wavelet Transform (DWT);

    2.   the resulting DWT coefficients are quantized into discrete values; this is the step that leads to the loss of information and makes it very difficult to invert the process to obtain the exact starting image;

    3.   the quantized sub-bands are concatenated into several blocks (typically three to eight) and compressed using an adaptive Huffman run-length encoding.

A compressed image can be decoded into the original image (with certain loss) by applying the equivalents of the above steps in reverse order (i.e., Huffman decoding, quantization decoding, and Inverse Discrete Wavelet Transform (IDWT)).

WSQ can compress a fingerprint image by a factor of 10 to 25 (see Figure 2.21). A typical compression ratio of 10 to 15 seems to be most appropriate, as higher compression ratios result in an unacceptable degradation of the fingerprint image.

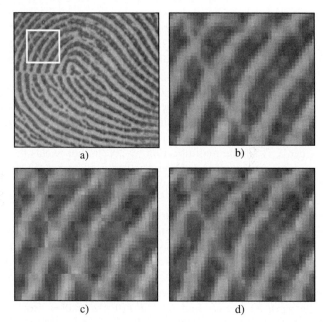

Figure 2.21. Fingerprint compression: a) the central section of a fingerprint image scanned at 500 dpi resolution; b) the marked portion of the image in a); c) the marked portion of the image in a) after the image was compressed using a generic JPEG (www.jpeg.org) image compression algorithm; and d) the marked portion of the image in a) is shown after the image was compressed using the WSQ compression algorithm. Both JPEG and WSQ examples used a compression ratio of 1:12.9; JPEG typically introduces blocky artifacts and obliterates detailed information. Images courtesy of Chris Brislawn, Los Alamos National Laboratory.

Fingerprint compression is still an active area of research. Improvements and efficient implementations of the basic WSQ approaches have been proposed (Kasaei, Deriche, and Boashash (1997) and Deriche, Kasaei, and Bouzerdoum (1999)), however, alternative approaches have been investigated where the compression relies on explicitly extracting features from fingerprints instead of encoding raw pictorial information (Abdelmalek et al. (1984) and Chong et al. (1992)). For example, in Chong et al. (1992), after binarization and thinning of the fingerprint image (see Section 3.8), the one-pixel-wide ridges are encoded by B-spline curves. This allows a compression ratio of 1:20 to 1:25 to be achieved, but only a feature-based representation of the image is used and the gray-scale fingerprint image cannot be reconstructed.

Another compression method based on feature extraction, but which allows the gray-scale image to be reconstructed, was proposed by Gokmen, Ersoy, and Jain (1996) and Ersoy, Ercal, and Gokmen (1999). The binarized and thinned (one-pixel wide) ridges and valleys are encoded through differential chain codes. Gray-scale values along ridges and valleys are also encoded. This allows a sparse representation (e.g., with holes) of the fingerprint image to be obtained. To reconstruct a full gray-scale image, the authors used the Hybrid Image Model (Gokmen and Jain, 1997), which starts from a sparse image (i.e., where not all the pixel values are known) and generates a dense image by imposing the smoothness constraint by means of regularization theory.

2.9 Summary

Recent developments in fingerprint scanners have focused on reducing both their cost and size. Although lower cost and size are essential to enable a wide deployment of the technology in civilian applications, some of these developments have been made at the expense of fingerprint image quality (e.g., dpi resolution, etc.). Some manufacturers have reduced the sensor size to such an extent that recognition accuracy has been significantly compromised. Mosaicking and template consolidation techniques have been introduced to compensate for a small sensing area. Although these approaches are useful in practice, they require a more complicated enrollment and it is not always possible to perform a reliable fingerprint image reconstruction from the partially overlapping fingerprint portions. Sweep sensors seem to be a valid alternative, because in spite of low cost, they do not sacrifice area. On the other hand, they involve a higher failure to acquire rate due to incorrect finger sweeping, and they require the image to be reconstructed from the slices, which remains a challenging task and involves extra computation.

We expect that while the market will continue to drive down scanner prices, it will also require higher-quality products at the same time. Manufacturers will continue to innovate low-cost small-size scanner designs, but they will also take care that their products deliver high quality-images of large areas of the finger. Until now, sensor manufacturers have provided a scanner with the same characteristics for all applications. With the deployment of fingerprint recognition systems in a number of different applications, we believe that application-specific fingerprint scanners will emerge. In general, the following properties are desirable in fingerprint scanners, and an application may choose among them based on the price: i) automatic finger detection (i.e., scanner automatically determines if a finger has approached it and alerts the system), ii) automatic fingerprint capture (i.e., scanner automatically determines which frame in the fingerprint video has the best quality), iii) temporary storage for the captured fingerprint image (to be transferred or processed even after the finger has left the scanner), iv) vitality detection (i.e., the scanner can determine if the finger belongs to a living human being), v) compression (compressed image will require less storage and bandwidth when transferred to the system), vi) image processing (certain applications will benefit from feature extraction carried out on the sensor itself; the transfer of the template will also require less bandwidth than the image), vii) matching (certain applications would like the matching to be performed on the sensor for security reasons), viii) inclusion of a smartcard reader or template database storage, and ix) cryptographic security protocol(s) implemented in the scanner to carry out secure communication. We also expect to see "wireless" fingerprint scanners that will be embedded into multifunction devices (Driscoll (1994) and Uchida (2000)).

3
Fingerprint Analysis and Representation

3.1 Introduction

A fingerprint is the reproduction of a fingertip epidermis, produced when a finger is pressed against a smooth surface. The most evident structural characteristic of a fingerprint is a pattern of interleaved *ridges* and *valleys*; in a fingerprint image, ridges (also called ridge lines) are dark whereas valleys are bright (see Figure 3.1). Ridges vary in width from 100 μm, for very thin ridges, to 300 μm for thick ridges. Generally, the period of a ridge/valley cycle is about 500 μm (Stosz and Alyea, 1994). Injuries such as superficial burns, abrasions, or cuts do not affect the underlying ridge structure, and the original pattern is duplicated in any new skin that grows.

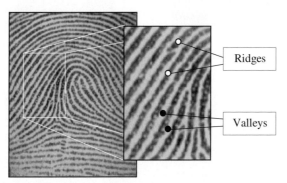

Figure 3.1. Ridges and valleys on a fingerprint image.

Ridges and valleys often run in parallel; sometimes they bifurcate and sometimes they terminate. When analyzed at the global level, the fingerprint pattern exhibits one or more regions where the ridge lines assume distinctive shapes (characterized by high curvature, frequent termination, etc.). These regions (called *singularities* or *singular regions*) may be classified into three typologies: *loop*, *delta*, and *whorl* (see Figure 3.2). Singular regions belonging to loop, delta, and whorl types are typically characterized by ∩, Δ, and O shapes, respectively. Sometimes whorl singularities are not explicitly introduced because a whorl type can be described in terms of two facing loop singularities.

Several fingerprint matching algorithms pre-align fingerprint images according to a landmark or a center point, called the *core*. Henry (1900) defines the core point as "the north most point of the innermost ridge line." In practice, the core point corresponds to the center of the north most loop type singularity. For fingerprints that do not contain loop or whorl singularities (e.g., those belonging to the Arch class in Figure 3.3), it is difficult to define the core. In these cases, the core is usually associated with the point of maximum ridge line curvature. Unfortunately, due to the high variability of fingerprint patterns, it is difficult to reliably locate a registration (core) point in all the fingerprint images. Singular regions are commonly used for fingerprint classification (see Figure 3.3), that is, assigning a fingerprint to a class among a set of distinct classes, with the aim of simplifying search and retrieval (ref. Chapter 5).

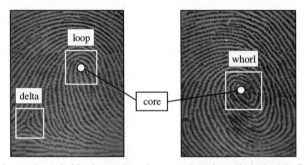

Figure 3.2. Singular regions (white boxes) and core points (small circles) in fingerprint images.

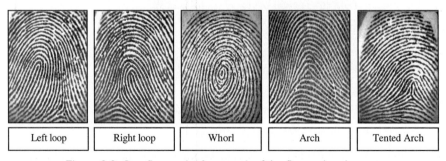

| Left loop | Right loop | Whorl | Arch | Tented Arch |

Figure 3.3. One fingerprint from each of the five major classes.

At the local level, other important features, called *minutiae* can be found in the fingerprint patterns. Minutia means small detail; in the context of fingerprints, it refers to various ways that the ridges can be discontinuous. For example, a ridge can suddenly come to an end (termination), or can divide into two ridges (bifurcation). Sir Francis Galton (1822–1911) was the first person to categorize minutiae and to observe that they remain unchanged over an individual's lifetime (Galton, 1892). Minutiae are sometimes called "Galton details" in his honor. Although several types of minutiae can be considered (the most common types are shown in Figure 3.4.a), usually only a coarse classification is adopted to deal with the practical difficulty in automatically discerning the different types with high accuracy. The American National Standards Institute (ANSI, 1986) proposed a minutiae taxonomy based on four classes: *terminations*, *bifurcations*, *trifurcations* (or crossovers), and *undetermined*. The FBI minutiae-coordinate model (Wegstein, 1982) considers only terminations and bifurcations: each minutia is denoted by its class, the x- and y-coordinates and the angle between the tangent to the ridge line at the minutia position and the horizontal axis (Figures 3.4.b and 3.4.c). In practice, an ambiguity exists between termination and bifurcation minutiae; depending on the finger pressure against the surface where the fingerprint is left, terminations may appear as bifurcations and vice versa.

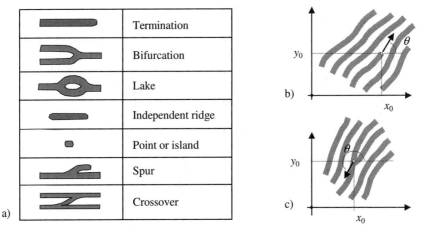

Figure 3.4. a) The most common minutiae types; b) a termination minutia: $[x_0, y_0]$ are the minutia coordinates; θ is the angle that the minutia tangent forms with the horizontal axis; c) a bifurcation minutia: θ is now defined by means of the termination minutia corresponding to the original bifurcation that exists in the negative image.

Figure 3.5.a shows a portion of the fingerprint image where the ridge lines appear as dark traces on a light background; two terminations (1,2) and one bifurcation (3) are shown. Note that on the negative image (Figure 3.5.b) the corresponding minutiae take the same positions, but their type is exchanged: terminations appear as bifurcations and vice versa (this property is known as termination/bifurcation *duality*).

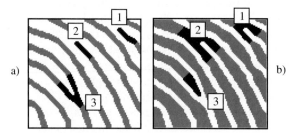

Figure 3.5. The termination/bifurcation duality on a) a binary image and b) its negative image.

If a fingerprint image is acquired at a high resolution (e.g., 1000 dpi), it is possible to clearly identify the *sweat pores* (Stosz and Alyea, 1994) which may range in size from 60 to 250 μm (see Figure 3.6). In fact, each ridge of the epidermis (outer skin) is dotted with sweat pores along its entire length and anchored to the dermis (inner skin) by a double row of peglike protuberances, or papillae. Although pore information (number, position, shape, etc.) is highly distinctive, very few automatic matching techniques use pores since their reliable detection requires very high resolution and good quality fingerprint images.

Figure 3.6. A fingerprint portion where skin sweat pores are well evident.

3.2 Fingerprint Image Processing and Feature Extraction

Although some fingerprint matching techniques directly compare images through correlation-based methods (see Section 4.2), the gray-scale image intensities are known to be an unstable representation. Most of the fingerprint recognition and classification algorithms require a feature extraction stage for identifying salient features.

The features extracted from fingerprint images often have a direct physical counterpart (e.g., singularities or minutiae), but sometimes they are not directly related to any physical traits (e.g., local orientation image or filter responses). Features may be used either for matching or their computation may serve as an intermediate step for the derivation of other features. For example, some preprocessing and enhancement steps are often performed to simplify the task of minutiae extraction.

Throughout this book, a fingerprint image is often represented as a two-dimensional surface. Let $\mathbf{I}$ be a gray-scale fingerprint image with g gray-levels, and $\mathbf{I}[x,y]$ be the gray-level of pixel $[x,y]$ in $\mathbf{I}$. Let $z = S(x,y)$ be the discrete surface corresponding to the image $\mathbf{I}$: $S(x,y) = \mathbf{I}[x,y]$. By associating bright pixels with gray-levels close to 0 and dark pixels with gray-levels close to $g-1$, the fingerprint ridge lines (appearing dark in $\mathbf{I}$) correspond to surface ridges, and the spaces between the ridge lines (appearing bright in $\mathbf{I}$) correspond to surface valleys (Figure 3.7).

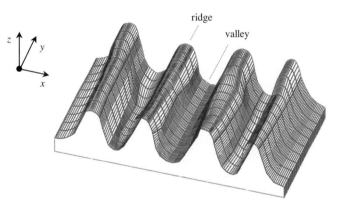

Figure 3.7. A surface S corresponding to a small area of a fingerprint. Reprinted with permission from Maio and Maltoni (1997). ©IEEE.

3.3 Estimation of Local Ridge Orientation

Let $[x,y]$ be a generic pixel in a fingerprint image. The local ridge orientation at $[x,y]$ is the angle θ_{xy} that the fingerprint ridges, crossing through an arbitrary small neighborhood centered at $[x,y]$, form with the horizontal axis. Because fingerprint ridges are not directed, θ_{xy} is an unoriented direction lying in $[0..180°[$. In the rest of the book we use the term *orientation* to denote an unoriented direction in [0..180°[, and the term *direction* to indicate an oriented direction in [0..360°[.

Instead of computing local ridge orientation at each pixel, most of the fingerprint processing and feature extraction methods estimate the local ridge orientation at discrete positions (this reduces computational efforts and allows further estimates to be obtained through interpolation). The fingerprint *orientation image* (also called *directional image*), first introduced by Grasselli (1969), is a matrix **D** whose elements encode the local orientation of the fingerprint ridges. Each element θ_{ij}, corresponding to the node $[i,j]$ of a square-meshed grid located over the pixel $[x_i,y_j]$, denotes the average orientation of the fingerprint ridges in a neighborhood of $[x_i,y_i]$ (see Figure 3.8). An additional value r_{ij} is often associated with each element θ_{ij} to denote the reliability (or consistency) of the orientation. The value r_{ij} is low for noisy and seriously corrupted regions and high for good quality regions in the fingerprint image.

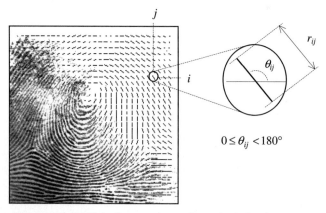

Figure 3.8. A fingerprint image faded into the corresponding orientation image computed over a square-meshed grid of size 16×16. Each element denotes the local orientation of the fingerprint ridges; the element length is proportional to its reliability.

The simplest and most natural approach for extracting local ridge orientation is based on computation of gradients in the fingerprint image. The gradient $\nabla(x_i,y_j)$ at point $[x_i,y_j]$ of **I**, is a two-dimensional vector $[\nabla_x(x_i,y_j), \nabla_y(x_i,y_j)]$, where ∇_x and ∇_y components are the derivatives of **I** in $[x_i,y_j]$ with respect to the x and y directions, respectively. It is well known that the gradient phase angle denotes the direction of the maximum pixel-intensity change. Therefore, the direction θ_{ij} of a hypothetical edge that crosses the region centered at $[x_i,y_j]$ is orthogonal to the gradient phase angle at $[x_i,y_j]$. This method, although simple and efficient, has some drawbacks. First, using the classical Prewitt or Sobel convolution masks (Gonzales and Woods, 1992) to determine ∇_x and ∇_y components of the gradient, and computing θ_{ij} as the arctangent of the

∇_y / ∇_x ratio, presents problems due to the non-linearity and discontinuity around 90°. Second, a single orientation estimate reflects the ridge–valley orientation at too fine a scale and is generally very sensitive to the noise in the fingerprint image; on the other hand, simply averaging gradient estimates is not possible due to the circularity of angles: the average orientation between 5° and 175° is not 90° (as an arithmetic average would suggest) but 0°. Furthermore, the concept of average orientation is not always well defined; consider the two orthogonal orientations 0° and 90°; is the correct average orientation 45° or 135°?

Kass and Witkin (1987) proposed a simple but elegant solution to the above problem, which allows local gradient estimates to be averaged. Their basic idea is to double the angles, so that each element of **D** is encoded by the vector:

$$\mathbf{d}_{ij} = \left[r_{ij} \cdot \cos 2\theta_{ij}, r_{ij} \cdot \sin 2\theta_{ij} \right], \tag{1}$$

where $2\theta_{ij}$ is used in place of θ_{ij} to discount the circularity of angles. Averaging the angles in a local $n \times n$ window, to obtain a more robust estimate $\overline{\mathbf{d}}$, is simply performed by separately averaging the two (x and y) components:

$$\overline{\mathbf{d}} = \left[\frac{1}{n^2} \sum_{i,j} r_{ij} \cdot \cos 2\theta_{ij}, \frac{1}{n^2} \sum_{i,j} r_{ij} \cdot \sin 2\theta_{ij} \right]. \tag{2}$$

Computing the average between two orthogonal orientations with Equation (2) involves summing two vectors facing each other, and therefore the length of the resulting vector is zero. This indicates that the vector is meaningless, independent of its orientation.

Based on the above idea, an effective method may be derived for computing the fingerprint orientation image (Rao (1990), Ratha, Chen, and Jain (1995), and Bazen and Gerez (2002b)). For example, Ratha, Chen, and Jain (1995) computed the dominant ridge orientation θ_{ij} by combining multiple gradient estimates within a 17×17 window centered at $[x_i, y_j]$:

$$\theta_{ij} = 90° + \frac{1}{2} \arctan\left(\frac{2G_{xy}}{G_{xx} - G_{yy}} \right),$$

$$G_{xy} = \sum_{h=-8}^{8} \sum_{k=-8}^{8} \nabla_x(x_i + h, y_j + k) \cdot \nabla_y(x_i + h, y_j + k),$$

$$G_{xx} = \sum_{h=-8}^{8} \sum_{k=-8}^{8} \nabla_x(x_i + h, y_j + k)^2,$$

$$G_{yy} = \sum_{h=-8}^{8} \sum_{k=-8}^{8} \nabla_y(x_i + h, y_j + k)^2,$$

where ∇_x and ∇_y are the x- and y-gradient components computed through 3×3 Sobel masks. Bazen and Gerez (2002b) have shown that this method is mathematically equivalent to the principal component analysis of the autocorrelation matrix of the gradient vectors. Another gradient-based method, independently proposed by Donahue and Rokhlin (1993), relies on least-squares minimization to perform the averaging of orientation estimates, and leads to the same expressions.

Different approaches to the computation of the orientation image, not directly based on the gradient computation, have been proposed by Stock and Swonger (1969), Mehtre et al. (1987), and Kawagoe and Tojo (1984). Stock and Swonger (1969) evaluated the local ridge orientation on the basis of pixel alignments relative to a fixed number of reference orientations. The total fluctuation of the gray-scale is expected to be smallest along the orientation of the ridges and largest in the orthogonal direction. Kawagoe and Tojo (1984) made a straight comparison against four edge templates to extract a rough directional estimate in each 2×2 pixel neighborhood. These estimates were then arithmetically averaged over a larger region to obtain a more accurate measure. These approaches do not provide very accurate estimates mainly because of the small number of fixed possible orientations.

Finally, other techniques have been proposed by Rao and Balck (1980), O'Gorman and Nickerson (1989), Srinivasan and Murthy (1992), Beyer, Lake, and Lougheed (1993), Hung (1993), Shumurun et al. (1994), Mardia et al. (1997), and Almansa and Lindeberg (2000).

The reliability r_{ij} of the estimates θ_{ij} can be derived by the concordance (or coherence) of different orientation estimates in a neighborhood of $[x_i,y_j]$ (Kass and Witkin (1987) and Bazen and Gerez (2002b)). In fact, due to the continuity and smoothness of fingerprint ridges, sharp orientation changes often denote unreliable estimation. Jain et al. (1997) computed the concordance of the orientations according to their variance in small 5×5 neighborhoods whereas Donahue and Rokhlin (1993) computed this according to the residual of the least-square minimization.

The orientation image **D**, computed from poor quality fingerprints may contain several unreliable elements due to local scratches or cluttered noise (Figure 3.9.a). In this situation, a regularization or smoothing step is very useful in enhancing **D**: a local average, performed by using Equation (2), is a valid technique (Candela et al., 1995). Figure 3.9.c shows an example of orientation image smoothing.

Other interesting regularization approaches have been proposed by Kawagoe and Tojo (1984), O'Gorman and Nickerson (1989), Pradenas (1997), and Perona (1998). Sherlock and Monro (1993) proposed an effective mathematical model to synthesize a fingerprint orientation image from the position of loops and deltas alone. Their work is quite different from those discussed until now: instead of starting from a fingerprint image, the authors take as input only the position of the singularities. Obviously, some simplifying assumptions have been made and the model does not cover all the variabilities of fingerprint patterns (in nature, different ridge pattern fingerprints may present the same singularities at the same locations); on the other hand, this model can be very useful for several purposes such as orientation image restoration, fingerprint data compression, synthetic fingerprint generation (see Chapter 6), and so on. Improvements of this method have been proposed by Vizcaya and Gerhardt (1996) and Araque et al. (2002). These new models introduce more degrees of freedom to better cope with fingerprint pattern variability.

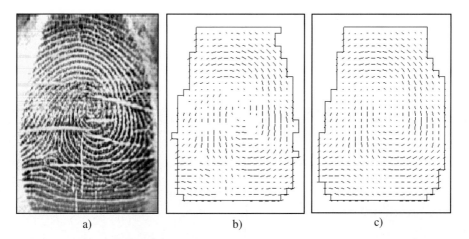

Figure 3.9. a) A poor quality fingerprint image; b) the orientation image of the fingerprint in a) is computed through the Donahue and Rokhlin (1993) method; the orientation of several elements is clearly inconsistent and a regularization step appears necessary; c) the orientation image is the result of the local averaging of each element in b) in its 3×3 window according to Equation (2).

3.4 Estimation of Local Ridge Frequency

The local ridge frequency (or density) f_{xy} at point $[x,y]$ is the inverse of the number of ridges per unit length along a hypothetical segment centered at $[x,y]$ and orthogonal to the local ridge orientation θ_{xy}. A frequency image $\mathbf{F}$, analogous to the orientation image $\mathbf{D}$, can be defined if the frequency is estimated at discrete positions and arranged into a matrix.

The local ridge frequency varies across different fingers, and may also noticeably vary across different regions in the same fingerprint (see Figure 3.10). Hong, Wan, and Jain (1998) estimate local ridge frequency by counting the average number of pixels between two consecutive peaks of gray-levels along the direction normal to the local ridge orientation (see Figure 3.11). For this purpose, the surface S corresponding to the fingerprint is sectioned with a plane parallel to the z-axis (see Figure 3.7) and orthogonal to local ridge orientation. The frequency f_{ij} at $[x_i,y_j]$ is computed as follows.

1. A 32×16 *oriented window* centered at $[x_i,y_j]$ is defined in the ridge coordinate system (i.e., rotated to align the y-axis with the local ridge orientation).
2. The *x-signature* of the gray-levels is obtained by accumulating, for each column x, the gray-levels of the corresponding pixels in the oriented window. This is a sort of

averaging that makes the gray-level profile smoother and prevents ridge peaks from being obscured due to small ridge breaks or pores.

3. f_{ij} is determined as the inverse of the average distance between two consecutive peaks of the *x*-signature.

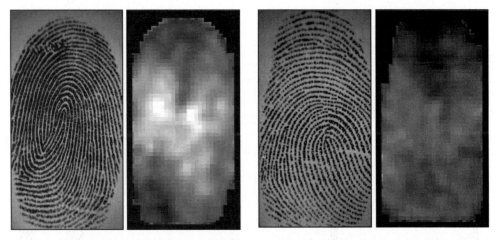

Figure 3.10. Two fingerprint images and the corresponding frequency image computed with the method proposed by Maio and Maltoni (1998a). A local 3×3 averaging is performed after frequency estimation to reduce noise. Light blocks denote higher frequencies. It is quite evident that significant changes may characterize different fingerprint regions and different average frequencies may result from different fingers.

The method is simple and fast. However, it is difficult to reliably detect consecutive peaks of gray-levels in the spatial domain in noisy fingerprint images. In this case, the authors suggest using interpolation and low-pass filtering.

Jiang (2000) also computes the local ridge frequency starting from the *x*-signatures (see Figure 3.11). However, instead of measuring the distances in the spatial domain, he makes use of a high-order spectrum technique called *mix-spectrum*. The ridge patterns in a fingerprint image are noisy periodic signals; when they deviate from a pure sinusoid shape, their energy is distributed to their fundamental frequency and harmonics. The mix-spectrum technique enhances the fundamental frequency of the signal by exploiting the information contained in the second and third harmonic.

In the method proposed by Maio and Maltoni (1998a), the ridge pattern is locally modeled as a sinusoidal-shaped surface, and the variation theorem is exploited to estimate the unknown frequency. The variation V of a function h in the interval $[x_1, x_2]$ is the amount of "vertical" change in h:

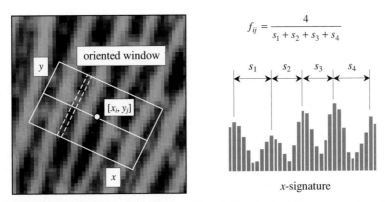

$$f_{ij} = \frac{4}{s_1 + s_2 + s_3 + s_4}$$

Figure 3.11. An oriented window centered at $[x_i, y_j]$; the dashed lines show the pixels whose gray-levels are accumulated for a given column of the x-signature (Hong, Wan, and Jain, 1998). The x-signature on the right clearly exhibits five peaks; the four distances between consecutive peaks are averaged to determine the local ridge frequency.

$$V(h) = \int_{x_1}^{x_2} \left| \frac{dh(x)}{dx} \right| \cdot dx \quad .$$

If the function h is periodic at $[x_1, x_2]$ or the amplitude changes within the interval $[x_1, x_2]$ are small, the variation may be expressed as a function of the average amplitude α_m and the average frequency f (see Figure 3.12).

$$V(h) = (x_2 - x_1) \cdot 2\alpha_m \cdot f \quad .$$

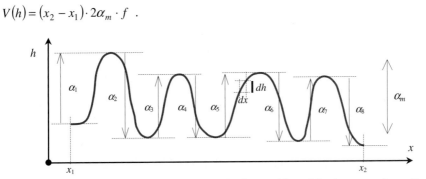

Figure 3.12. The variation of the function h in the interval $[x_1, x_2]$ is the sum of amplitudes α_1, $\alpha_2, ..., \alpha_8$ (Maio and Maltoni, 1998a). If the function is periodic or the function amplitude does not change significantly within the interval of interest, the average amplitude α_m can be used to approximate the individual α. Then the variation may be expressed as $2\alpha_m$ multiplied by the number of periods of the function over the interval.

Therefore, the unknown frequency can be estimated as

$$f = \frac{V(h)}{2 \cdot (x_2 - x_1) \cdot \alpha_m}.$$

(3)

Maio and Maltoni (1998a) proposed a practical method based on the above theory. The variation and the average amplitude of a two-dimensional ridge pattern are estimated from the first- and second-order partial derivatives and the local ridge frequency is computed from Equation (3). Two examples of frequency images computed using this method are shown in Figure 3.10.

Kovacs-Vajna, Rovatti, and Frazzoni (2000) proposed a two-step procedure: first, the average ridge distance is estimated for each 64×64 sub-block of the image that is of sufficient quality and then this information is propagated, according to a diffusion equation, to the remaining regions. Two methods are considered in the first step: geometric and spectral. In the geometric approach, the central points of the ridges are computed on a regular grid and the ridge distances are measured on straight lines passing through these points. Unlike the x-signature approach, distances are directly measured in the two-dimensional image; several estimates on the same image block are performed to compensate for the noise. The second method is based on a search of the maxima in the Fourier power spectrum of each sub-block. Here too, the method works on two-dimensional signals. The invariance with respect to the local ridge orientations is obtained by performing the maxima search radially: in fact, all the components (harmonics) having the same distance from the origin denote the same frequency.

Almansa and Lindeberg (1997, 2000) use scale space theory to locally estimate ridge width; their approach relies upon combinations of normalized derivatives computed pointwise.

3.5 Segmentation

The term *segmentation* is generally used to denote the separation of fingerprint area (foreground) from the image background; examples of segmentation are shown in Figures 3.9 and 3.10 where the background is removed from the processed images. Separating the fingerprint area is useful to avoid extraction of features in noisy areas of the fingerprint and background. Some authors use the term segmentation to indicate the transformation of the fingerprint image from gray-scale to black and white; throughout this book the latter processing is referred to as *fingerprint binarization*.

Because fingerprint images are striated patterns, using a global or local thresholding technique (Gonzales and Woods, 1992) does not allow the fingerprint area to be effectively isolated. In fact, what really discriminates foreground and background is not the average image intensities but the presence of a striped and oriented pattern in the foreground and of an isotropic pattern (i.e., which does not have a dominant orientation) in the background. If the image background were always uniform and lighter than the fingerprint area, a simple approach based on local intensity could be effective for discriminating foreground and background; in practice, the presence of noise (such as that produced by dust and grease on the surface of live-scan fingerprint scanners) requires more robust segmentation techniques.

Mehtre et al. (1987) isolated the fingerprint area according to local histograms of ridge orientations. Ridge orientation is estimated at each pixel and a histogram is computed for each 16×16 block. The presence of a significant peak in a histogram denotes an oriented pattern, whereas a flat or near-flat histogram is characteristic of an isotropic signal. The above method fails when a perfectly uniform block is encountered (e.g., a white block in the background) because no local ridge orientation may be found. To deal with this case, Mehtre and Chatterjee (1989) proposed a composite method that, besides histograms of orientations, computes the gray-scale variance of each block and, in the absence of reliable information from the histograms, assigns the low-variance blocks to the background.

Ratha, Chen, and Jain (1995) assigned each 16×16 block to the foreground or the background according to the variance of gray-levels in the orthogonal direction to the ridge orientation. They also derive a quality index from the block variance (see Figure 3.13). The underlying assumption is that the noisy regions have no directional dependence, whereas regions of interest exhibit a very high variance in a direction orthogonal to the orientation of ridges and very low variance along ridges.

Maio and Maltoni (1997) discriminated foreground and background by using the average magnitude of the gradient in each image block; in fact, because the fingerprint area is rich in edges due to the ridge/valley alternation, the gradient response is high in the fingerprint area and small in the background.

In the method proposed by Shen, Kot, and Koo (2001), eight Gabor filters (refer to Section 3.7) are convolved with each image block, and the variance of the filter responses is used both for fingerprint segmentation and for the classification of the blocks, according to their quality, as "good," "poor," "smudged," or "dry."

Bazen and Gerez (2001b) proposed a pixel-wise segmentation technique, where three features (gradient coherence, intensity mean, and intensity variance) are computed for each pixel, and a linear classifier associates the pixel with the background or the foreground. A supervised technique is used to learn the optimal parameters for the linear classifier for each specific acquisition sensor. A final morphological post-processing step (Gonzales and Woods, 1992) is performed to eliminate holes in both the foreground and background and to regularize the external silhouette of the fingerprint area. Their experimental results showed that this method provides accurate results; however, its computational complexity is markedly higher than most of the previously described block-wise approaches.

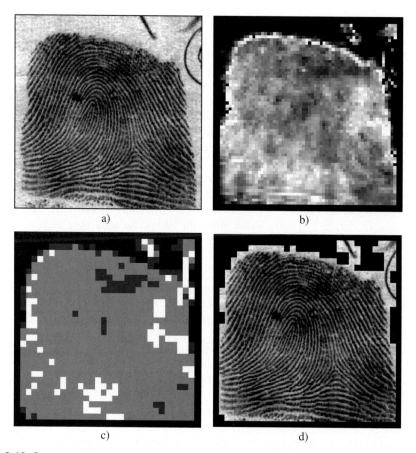

Figure 3.13. Segmentation of a fingerprint image as proposed by Ratha, Chen, and Jain (1995): a) original image; b) variance field; c) quality image derived from the variance field: a quality value "good," "medium," "poor" or "background" is assigned to each block according to its variance; d) segmented image. ©Elsevier.

3.6 Singularity and Core Detection

Most of the approaches proposed in the literature for singularity detection operate on the fingerprint orientation image. In the rest of this section, the main approaches are coarsely classified and a subsection is dedicated to each family of algorithms.

Poincaré method index

An elegant and practical method based on the Poincaré index was proposed by Kawagoe and Tojo (1984). Let $\mathbf{G}$ be a vector field and C be a curve immersed in $\mathbf{G}$; then the Poincaré index $P_{\mathbf{G},C}$ is defined as the total rotation of the vectors of $\mathbf{G}$ along C (see Figure 3.14).

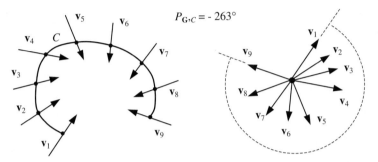

Figure 3.14. The Poincaré index computed over a curve C immersed in a vector field $\mathbf{G}$.

Let $\mathbf{G}$ be the field associated with a fingerprint orientation image[1] $\mathbf{D}$ and let $[i,j]$ be the position of the element θ_{ij} in the orientation image; then the Poincaré index $P_{\mathbf{G},C}(i,j)$ at $[i,j]$ is computed as follows.

- The curve C is a closed path defined as an ordered sequence of some elements of $\mathbf{D}$, such that $[i,j]$ is an internal point;
- $P_{\mathbf{G},C}(i,j)$ is computed by algebraically summing the orientation differences between adjacent elements of C. Summing orientation differences requires a direction (among the two possible) to be associated at each orientation. A solution to this problem is to randomly select the direction of the first element and assign the direction closest to that of the previous element to each successive element. It is well known and can be easily shown that, on closed curves, the Poincaré index assumes only one of the discrete values: $0°$, $\pm180°$, and $\pm360°$. In the case of fingerprint singularities:

$$P_{\mathbf{G},C}(i,j) = \begin{cases} 0° & \text{if } [i,j] \text{ does not belong to any singular region} \\ 360° & \text{if } [i,j] \text{ belongs to a whorl type singular region} \\ 180° & \text{if } [i,j] \text{ belongs to a loop type singular region} \\ -180° & \text{if } [i,j] \text{ belongs to a delta type singular region.} \end{cases}$$

---

1 Note that a fingerprint orientation image is not a true vector field inasmuch as its elements are unoriented directions.

Figure 3.15 shows three portions of orientation images. The path defining C is the ordered sequence of the eight elements $\mathbf{d}_k$ ($k = 0..7$) surrounding $[i,j]$. The direction of the elements $\mathbf{d}_k$ is chosen as follows: $\mathbf{d}_0$ is directed upward; $\mathbf{d}_k$ ($k = 1..7$) is directed so that the absolute value of the angle between $\mathbf{d}_k$ and $\mathbf{d}_{k-1}$ is less than or equal to 90°. The Poincaré index is then computed as

$$P_{\mathbf{G},C}(i,j) = \sum_{k=0..7} angle\left(\mathbf{d}_k, \mathbf{d}_{(k+1) \bmod 8}\right).$$

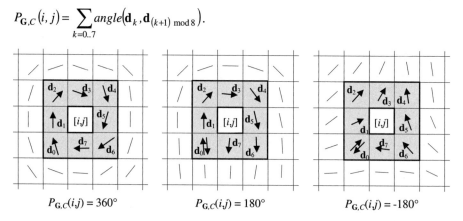

$P_{\mathbf{G},C}(i,j) = 360°$ $P_{\mathbf{G},C}(i,j) = 180°$ $P_{\mathbf{G},C}(i,j) = -180°$

Figure 3.15. Example of computation of the Poincaré index in the 8-neighborhood of points belonging (from the left to the right) to a whorl, loop, and delta singularity, respectively. Note that for the loop and delta examples (center and right), the direction of $\mathbf{d}_0$ is first chosen upward (to compute the angle between $\mathbf{d}_0$ and $\mathbf{d}_1$) and then successively downward (when computing the angle between $\mathbf{d}_7$ and $\mathbf{d}_0$).

An example of singularities detected by the above method is shown in Figure 3.16.a.

An interesting implementation of the Poincaré method for locating singular points was proposed by Bazen and Gerez (2002b): according to Green's theorem, a closed line integral over a vector field can be calculated as a surface integral over the rotation of this vector field; in practice, instead of summing angle differences along a closed path, the authors compute the "rotation" of the orientation image (through a further differentiation) and then perform a local integration (sum) in a small neighborhood of each element. Bazen and Gerez (2002b) also provided a method for associating an orientation with each singularity; this is done by comparing the orientation image around each detected singular point with the orientation image of an ideal singularity of the same type.

Singularity detection in noisy or low-quality fingerprints is difficult and the Poincaré method may lead to the detection of false singularities (Figure 3.17). Regularizing the orientation image through a local averaging, as discussed in Section 3.3, is often quite effective in preventing the detection of false singularities.

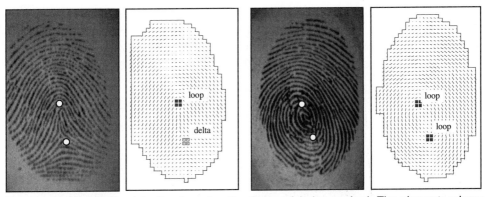

Figure 3.16. Singularity detection by using the Poincaré index method. The elements whose Poincaré index is 180° (loop) or -180° (delta) are enclosed by small boxes. Usually, more than one point (four points in these examples) is found for each singular region: hence, the center of each singular region can be defined as the barycenter of the corresponding points.

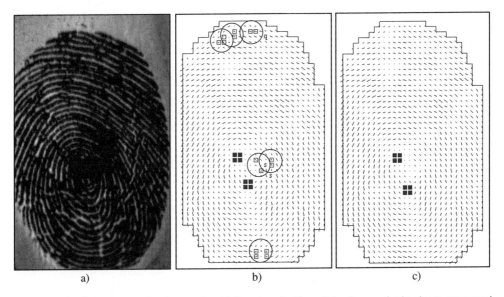

a)   b)   c)

Figure 3.17. a) A poor quality fingerprint; b) the singularities of the fingerprint in a) are extracted through the Poincaré method (circles highlight the false singularities); c) the orientation image has been regularized and the Poincaré method no longer provides false alarms.

Based on the observation that only a limited number of singularities can be present in a fingerprint, Karu and Jain (1996) proposed to iteratively smooth the orientation image (through averaging) until a valid number of singularities is detected by the Poincaré index. In fact, a simple analysis of the different fingerprint classes (refer to Chapter 5 for a more detailed discussion) shows that:

- arch fingerprints do not contain singularities;
- left loop, right loop, and tented arch fingerprints contain one loop and one delta;
- whorl fingerprints contain two loops (or one whorl) and two deltas.

Methods based on local characteristics of the orientation image

Some authors have proposed singularity detection approaches where the fundamental idea is to explore the orientation image regions characterized by high irregularity, curvature, or symmetry. In fact, the singularities are the only foreground regions where a dominant orientation does not exist and ridges assume high curvature. Srinivasan and Murthy (1992) extract singularities according to the local histogram of the orientation image; in fact, the points where the local histogram does not exhibit a well-pronounced peak are likely to belong to singular regions. By analyzing the predominant orientation in some predefined sectors around the candidate points, the Srinivasan and Murthy method is able to discriminate between loop and delta singularities.

The irregularity operator, introduced by Cappelli et al. (1999) can be exploited to coarsely locate singular regions: the irregularity of $\mathbf{d}_{ij}$ is computed over a 3×3 neighborhood of $[i,j]$:

$$irregularity(i, j) = 1 - \frac{\left\| \sum\limits_{h=-1..1} \sum\limits_{k=-1..1} \mathbf{d}_{i+h\,j+k} \right\|}{\sum\limits_{h=-1..1} \sum\limits_{k=-1..1} \left\| \mathbf{d}_{i+h\,j+k} \right\|}, \tag{4}$$

where $\|\mathbf{d}\|$ is the norm of vector $\mathbf{d}$. It is easy to prove that the irregularity operator returns 0 if all the elements are parallel to each other (minimum irregularity), and its value smoothly approaches 1 when discordance increases (maximum irregularity). Note that the $\mathbf{d}_{ij}$ are characterized by unoriented directions; therefore, for a practical application of Equation (4), the elements $\mathbf{d}_{ij}$ have to be encoded as in Equation (1). Figure 3.18 shows an example of the irregularity map.

Koo and Kot (2001) used a multi-resolution approach to determine the singularities with single pixel accuracy. At each resolution, they derive from the orientation image a curvature image whose blocks indicate the local degree of ridge curvature. High-curvature blocks, which denote singularities, are retained and analyzed at finer resolutions. The block-resolution pyramid consists of four levels: 11×11, 7×7, 3×3 and 1×1. At the finest resolution, the neighborhood of each detected singular point is further analyzed to discriminate between loop and delta singularities. Nilsson and Bigun (2002a, b) also proposed a multi-resolution analysis to extract the singularities from the orientation field by using two complex filters tuned to detect points of symmetry. The two filters (one for loop type singularity and one for delta-type singularity) are correlated at each position in the orientation image and the points where the response of any one filter is high are retained.

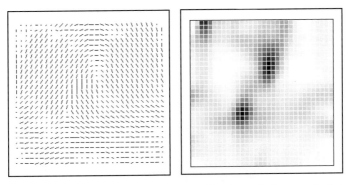

Figure 3.18. An orientation image and the corresponding irregularity map that clearly identifies the regions (dark cells) containing the singularities.

Partitioning-based methods

Some authors noted that partitioning the orientation image in regions characterized by homogeneous orientation implicitly reveals the position of singularities. Hung and Huang (1996) coarsely discretize the orientation image by using a very small number of orientation values. Each orientation value determines a region. The borderline between two adjacent regions is called a fault-line. By noting that fault lines converge towards loop singularities and diverge from deltas, the authors define a geometrical method for determining the convergence and divergence points. In Maio and Maltoni (1996) and Cappelli et al. (1999), the orientation image is partitioned by using an iterative clustering algorithm and a set of dynamic masks, respectively (Figure 3.19). Rämö et al. (2001) implicitly partition the orientation image in correspondence with the points where the x- and y-orientation components (refer to Equation (1)) cross the zero. An efficient method is then introduced to extract singularities based on the contemporary zero crossings of both orientation components.

Core detection and fingerprint registration

Once the singularities have been extracted, the core position may be simply defined as the location of the north most loop. Some problems arise with the arch type fingerprints that do not have singularities, and sometimes present a quite flat flow field where no discriminant positions can be located. When the core point is detected with the aim of registering fingerprint images (thus obtaining invariance with respect to x,y displacement), its location may be quite critical and an error at this stage often leads to a failure of subsequent processing (e.g., matching). On the other hand, if the core has to be used only for fingerprint registration, it is not important to find the north most loop exactly and any stable point in the fingerprint pattern is suitable.

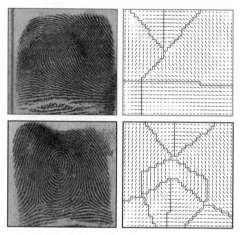

Figure 3.19. Orientation image partitioning with the MASK approach (Cappelli et al., 1999). The intersections between region border lines denote fingerprint singularities. ©IEEE.

One of the first automatic methods for fingerprint registration was proposed by Wegstein (1982). This method, known as R92, searches the core point independently of the other singularities. The core is searched by scanning (row by row) the orientation image to find *well-formed arches*; a well-formed arch is denoted by a sextet (set of six) of adjacent elements whose orientations comply with several rules controlled by many parameters. One sextet is chosen among the valid sextets by evaluating the orientation of the elements in adjacent rows. The exact core position is then located through interpolation (Figure 3.20). Although quite complicated and heuristic, R92 usually gives good results and is able to localize the core point with sub-block accuracy. This algorithm was a fundamental component of the fingerprint identification systems used by the FBI and is still extensively used by other authors (e.g., Candela et al. (1995)).

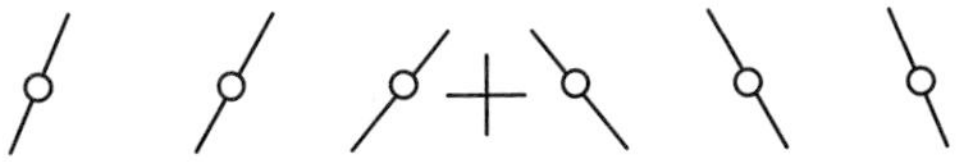

Figure 3.20. The core point "+" located on the chosen sextet.

Several other ideas for the location of stable registration points have been proposed. Novikov and Kot (1998) define the core as the crossing point of the lines normal to the ridges (Figure 3.21) and use the Hough transform (Ballard, 1981) to determine its coordinates. Similarly, Rerkrai and Areekul (2000) define the *focal point* as the point where pairs of straight lines normal to the ridges intersect. Because the ridges do not draw perfect concentric circumferences around the core, the normal lines (dashed lines in Figure 3.21) do not exactly cross at a single point and a sort of average point has to be defined as the center of curvature. Novikov and Kot (1998) compute this average point in a least squares sense, whereas Rerkrai and Areekul (2000) compute the barycenter of the crossing between pairs of normals. Although the focal point (or the center of curvature) does not necessarily correspond to the core point, it has been experimentally demonstrated to be quite stable with respect to fingerprint variation (displacement, rotation, distortion, etc.). Therefore, it can be reliably used for fingerprint registration. The main problem of these methods is in isolating a fingerprint region characterized by a single center of curvature. In fact, if the selected fingerprint region contains more than one singularity, the result may be unpredictable.

Figure 3.21. The straight lines normal to the ridges identify a valid registration point that corresponds to the center of curvature.

Finally, Jain et al. (2000) proposed a multi-resolution approach for locating the north most loop type singularities (core) based on integration of sine components in two adjacent regions R_I and R_{II} (Figure 3.22). The geometry of the two regions is designed to capture the maximum curvature in concave ridges. At each scale and for each candidate position [x,y], the sine components of the orientation image are integrated over the two regions resulting in the values SR_I and SR_{II}. The points $[x,y]$ that maximize the quantity $(SR_I - SR_{II})$ are retained as candidate positions and analyzed at a finer resolution.

Miscellanea

Other approaches for singularity or core detection, besides those already described, have been proposed by Tou and Hankley (1968), Aushermann et al. (1973), Rao, Prasad, and Sharma (1974), Rao and Balck (1978, 1980), Chang (1980), Drets and Liljenstrom (1998), Tico and Kuosmanen (1999b), and Cho et al. (2000).

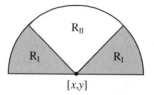

Figure 3.22. Regions of integration of the sine components in the method proposed by Jain et al. (2000).

3.7 Enhancement

The performance of minutiae extraction algorithms and other fingerprint recognition techniques relies heavily on the quality of the input fingerprint images. In an ideal fingerprint image, ridges and valleys alternate and flow in a locally constant direction. In such situations, the ridges can be easily detected and minutiae can be precisely located in the image. Figure 3.23.a shows an example of a good quality fingerprint image. However, in practice, due to skin conditions (e.g., wet or dry, cuts, and bruises), sensor noise, incorrect finger pressure, and inherently low-quality fingers (e.g., elderly people, manual workers), a significant percentage of fingerprint images (approximately 10%, according to our experience) is of poor quality like those in Figures 3.23.b and c. In many cases, a single fingerprint image contains regions of good, medium, and poor quality where the ridge pattern is very noisy and corrupted (Figure 3.24). In general, there are several types of degradation associated with fingerprint images:
1.   the ridges are not strictly continuous; that is, the ridges have small breaks (gaps);
2.   parallel ridges are not well separated. This is due to the presence of noise which links parallel ridges, resulting in their poor separation;
3.   cuts, creases, and bruises.

These three types of degradation make ridge extraction extremely difficult in the highly corrupted regions. This leads to the following problems in minutiae extraction: i) a significant number of spurious minutiae are extracted, ii) a large number of genuine minutiae are missed, and iii) large errors in the location (position and orientation) of minutiae are introduced. In order to ensure good performance of the ridge and minutiae extraction algorithms in poor quality fingerprint images, an enhancement algorithm to improve the clarity of the ridge structure is necessary.

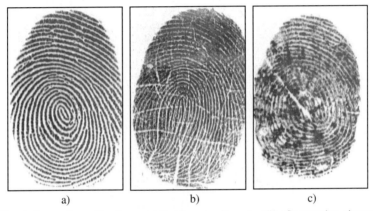

a)   b)   c)

Figure 3.23. a) A good quality fingerprint; b) a medium quality fingerprint characterized by scratches and ridge breaks; c) a poor quality fingerprint containing a lot of noise.

A fingerprint expert is often able to correctly identify the minutiae by using various visual clues such as local ridge orientation, ridge continuity, ridge tendency, and so on. In theory, it is possible to develop an enhancement algorithm that exploits these visual clues to improve image quality. Generally, for a given fingerprint image, the fingerprint areas resulting from the segmentation step may be divided into three categories (Figure 3.24):

- *well-defined region*, where ridges are clearly differentiated from each another;
- *recoverable region*, where ridges are corrupted by a small amount of gaps, creases, smudges, links, and the like, but they are still visible and the neighboring regions provide sufficient information about their true structure;
- *unrecoverable region*, where ridges are corrupted by such a severe amount of noise and distortion that no ridges are visible and the neighboring regions do not allow them to be reconstructed.

Good quality regions, recoverable, and unrecoverable regions may be identified according to several criteria; in general, image contrast, orientation consistency, ridge frequency, and other local features may be combined to define a quality index. The goal of an enhancement algorithm is to improve the clarity of the ridge structures in the recoverable regions and mark the unrecoverable regions as too noisy for further processing.

Usually, the input of the enhancement algorithm is a gray-scale image. The output may either be a gray-scale or a binary image, depending on the algorithm. General-purpose image enhancement techniques do not produce satisfying and definitive results for fingerprint image enhancement. However, contrast stretching, histogram manipulation, normalization (Hong, Wan, and Jain, 1998), and Wiener filtering (Greenberg et al., 2000) have been shown to be effective as initial processing steps in a more sophisticated fingerprint enhancement algorithm.

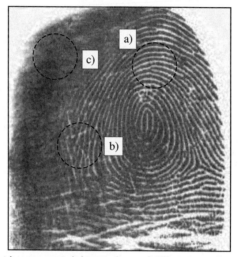

Figure 3.24. A fingerprint image containing regions of different quality: a) a well-defined region; b) a recoverable region; c) an unrecoverable region.

The normalization approach used by Hong, Wan, and Jain (1998) determines the new intensity value of each pixel in an image as

$$\mathbf{I}'[x, y] = \begin{cases} m_0 + \sqrt{(\mathbf{I}[x, y] - m)^2 \cdot v_0 / v} & \text{if } \mathbf{I}[x, y] > m \\ m_0 - \sqrt{(\mathbf{I}[x, y] - m)^2 \cdot v_0 / v} & \text{otherwise,} \end{cases}$$

where m and v are the image mean and variance and m_0 and v_0 are the desired mean and variance after the normalization. The above normalization process is a pixel-wise operation (the value of each pixel only depends on its previous value and some global parameters) and does not change the ridge and valley structures. In particular, it is not able to fill small ridge breaks, fill intra-ridge holes, or separate parallel touching ridges. Figure 3.25 shows an example.

The most widely used technique for fingerprint image enhancement is based on *contextual filters*. In conventional image filtering, only a single filter is used for convolution throughout the image. In contextual filtering, the filter characteristics change according to the local context. Usually, a set of filters is pre-computed and one of them is selected for each image region. In fingerprint enhancement, the context is often defined by the local ridge orientation and local ridge frequency. In fact, the sinusoidal-shaped wave of ridges and valleys is mainly defined by a local orientation and frequency that varies slowly across the fingerprint area. An appropriate filter that is tuned to the local ridge frequency and orientation can efficiently remove the undesired noise and preserve the true ridge and valley structure.

Figure 3.25. An example of normalization with the method described in Hong, Wan and Jain (1998) using ($m_0 = 100$, $v_0 = 100$). ©IEEE.

Several types of contextual filters have been proposed in the literature for fingerprint enhancement. Although they have different definitions, the intended behavior is almost the same: 1) provide a low-pass (averaging) effect along the ridge direction with the aim of linking small gaps and filling impurities due to pores or noise; 2) perform a bandpass (differentiating) effect in the direction orthogonal to the ridges to increase the discrimination between ridges and valleys and to separate parallel linked ridges.

The method proposed by O'Gorman and Nickerson (1988, 1989) was one of the first to use contextual filtering for fingerprint enhancement; the authors defined a mother filter based on four main parameters of fingerprint images at a given resolution: minimum and maximum ridge width, and minimum and maximum valley width. The filter is bell-shaped (see Figure 3.26), elongated along the ridge direction, and cosine tapered in the direction normal to the ridges. The local ridge frequency is assumed constant and therefore, the context is defined only by the local ridge orientation. Once the mother filter has been generated, a set of 16 rotated versions (in steps of 22.5°) is derived. The image enhancement is performed by convolving each point of the image with the filter in the set whose orientation best matches the local ridge orientation. Depending on some input parameters, the output image may be gray-scale or binary. Examples of image binarizations using this technique are shown in Figures 3.31.b and 3.34.a.

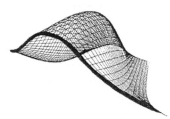

Figure 3.26. The shape of the filter proposed by O'Gorman and Nickerson (1989). ©Elsevier.

Sherlock, Monro, and Millard (1992, 1994) performed contextual filtering in the Fourier domain; in fact, it is well-known that a convolution in the spatial domain corresponds to a point-by-point multiplication in the Fourier domain (Gonzales and Woods, 1992). The filter is defined in the frequency domain by the function:

$$H(\rho,\theta) = H_{radial}(\rho) \cdot H_{angle}(\theta),$$

where H_{radial} depends only on the local ridge spacing $\rho = 1/f$ and H_{angle} depends only on the local ridge orientation θ. Both H_{radial} and H_{angle} are defined as bandpass filters and are characterized by a mean value and a bandwidth. A set of n discrete filters is derived by their analytical definition. Actually, in the experiments, to reduce the number of filters, only a single value is used for the local ridge frequency and, therefore, the context is determined only by the orientation. The Fourier transform $\mathbf{P}_i$, $i = 1..n$ of the filters is pre-computed and stored. Filtering an input fingerprint image $\mathbf{I}$ is performed as follows (see Figure 3.27).

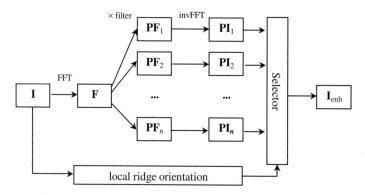

Figure 3.27. Enhancement of the fingerprint image I according to the Sherlock, Monro, and Millard (1994) method.

- The FFT (Fast Fourier Transform) **F** of **I** is computed;
- each filter $\mathbf{P}_i$ is point-by-point multiplied by **F,** thus obtaining n filtered image transforms $\mathbf{PF}_i$, $i = 1..n$ (in the frequency domain);
- inverse FFT is computed for each $\mathbf{PF}_i$ resulting in n filtered images $\mathbf{PI}_i$, $i = 1..n$ (in the spatial domain).

The enhanced image $\mathbf{I}_{enh}$ is obtained by setting, for each pixel $[x,y]$, $\mathbf{I}_{enh}[x,y] = \mathbf{PI}_k[x,y]$, where k is the index of the filter whose orientation is the closest to θ_{xy}.

Hong, Wan, and Jain (1998) proposed an effective method based on Gabor filters. Gabor filters have both frequency-selective and orientation-selective properties and have optimal joint resolution in both spatial and frequency domains (Daugman (1985) and Jain and Farrokhnia (1991)). As shown in Figure 3.28, a Gabor filter is defined by a sinusoidal plane wave (the second term of Equation (5)) tapered by a Gaussian (the first term in Equation (5)). The even symmetric two-dimensional Gabor filter has the following form.

$$g(x, y : \theta, f) = \exp\left\{-\frac{1}{2}\left[\frac{x_\theta^2}{\sigma_x^2} + \frac{y_\theta^2}{\sigma_y^2}\right]\right\} \cdot \cos(2\pi f \cdot x_\theta), \tag{5}$$

where θ is the orientation of the filter, and $[x_\theta, y_\theta]$ are the coordinates of $[x,y]$ after a clockwise rotation of the Cartesian axes by an angle of $(90°-\theta)$.

$$\begin{bmatrix} x_\theta \\ y_\theta \end{bmatrix} = \begin{bmatrix} \cos(90° - \theta) & \sin(90° - \theta) \\ -\sin(90° - \theta) & \cos(90° - \theta) \end{bmatrix} \begin{bmatrix} x \\ y \end{bmatrix} = \begin{bmatrix} \sin\theta & \cos\theta \\ -\cos\theta & \sin\theta \end{bmatrix} \begin{bmatrix} x \\ y \end{bmatrix}.$$

In the above expressions, f is the frequency of a sinusoidal plane wave, and σ_x and σ_y are the standard deviations of the Gaussian envelope along the x- and y-axes, respectively.

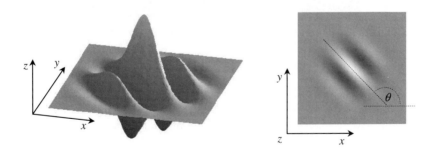

Figure 3.28. Graphical representation (lateral view and top view) of the Gabor filter defined by the parameters $\theta = 135°$, $f = 1/5$, and $\sigma_x = \sigma_y = 3$.

To apply Gabor filters to an image, the four parameters ($\theta, f, \sigma_x, \sigma_y$) must be specified. Obviously, the frequency of the filter is completely determined by the local ridge frequency and the orientation is determined by the local ridge orientation. The selection of the values σ_x and σ_y involves a tradeoff. The larger the values, the more robust the filters are to the noise in the fingerprint image, but also the more likely to create spurious ridges and valleys. On the other hand, the smaller the values, the less likely the filters are to introduce spurious ridges and valleys but then they will be less effective in removing the noise. In fact, from the Modulation Transfer Function (MTF) of the Gabor filter, it can be shown that increasing σ_x, σ_y decreases the bandwidth of the filter and vice versa. Based on empirical data, Hong, Wan and Jain (1998) set $\sigma_x = \sigma_y = 4$. To make the enhancement faster, instead of computing the best-suited contextual filter for each pixel "on the fly," a set $\{g_{ij}(x,y) | i = 1..n_o, j = 1..n_f\}$ of filters are a priori created and stored, where n_o is the number of discrete orientations $\{\theta_i | i = 1..n_o\}$ and n_f the number of discrete frequencies $\{f_j | j = 1..n_f\}$. Then each pixel [x,y] of the image is con-volved, in the spatial domain, with the filter $g_{ij}(x,y)$ such that θ_i is the discretized orientation closest to θ_{xy} and f_j is the discretized frequency closest to f_{xy}. Figure 3.29 shows an example of the filter set for $n_o = 8$ and $n_f = 3$. Figure 3.30 shows the application of Gabor-based contextual filtering on medium and poor quality images.

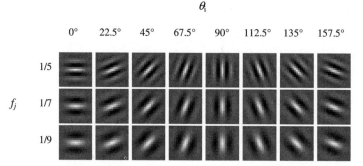

Figure 3.29. A graphical representation of a bank of 24 ($n_o = 8$ and $n_f = 3$) Gabor filters where $\sigma_x = \sigma_y = 4$.

Greenberg et al. (2000) noted that by reducing the value of σ_x with respect to σ_y, the filtering creates fewer spurious ridges and is more robust to noise. In practice, reducing σ_x results in increasing the frequency bandwidth, independently of the angular bandwidth which remains unchanged; this allows the filter to better tolerate errors in local frequency estimates. Analogously, one could decrease σ_y in order to increase the angular bandwidth as pointed out by Sherlock, Monro, and Millard (1994). Their method increases the angular bandwidth near the singularities where the ridges are characterized by higher curvatures and the orientation changes rapidly.

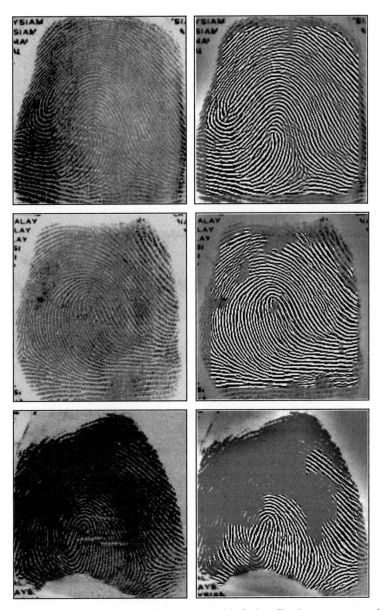

Figure 3.30. Examples of fingerprint enhancement with Gabor filtering as proposed by Hong, Wan, and Jain (1998). On the right, the enhanced recoverable regions are superimposed on the corresponding input images. ©IEEE.

Finally, the method by Erol, Halici, and Ongun (1999) relates the filter bandwidth to the local orientation reliability encoded by r_{ij}, whereas the Bernard et al. (2002) approach reduces the filter bandwidth if none of the responses to an initial set of filters exceeds a certain threshold.

The output of a contextual fingerprint enhancement can be a gray-scale, near-binary, or binary image, usually depending on the filter parameters chosen. When selecting the appropriate set of filters and tuning their parameters, one should keep in mind that the goal is not to produce a good visual appearance of the image but facilitate robustness of the successive feature extraction steps. If the filters are tuned to strongly increase the contrast and suppress the noise, the estimation of the local context (orientation and frequency) may be erroneous in poor quality areas and the filtering is likely to produce spurious structures (Jiang, 2001). For example, an iterative application of Gabor filters has been used by Cappelli, Maio, and Maltoni (2000b) (refer to Chapter 6) to generate a synthetic fingerprint pattern; in this case the filters generate completely nonexistent ridge patterns.

The need of an effective enhancement is particularly important in poor quality fingerprints where only the recoverable regions carry information necessary for the matching. On the other hand, computing local information (context) with sufficient reliability in poor quality fingerprint images is very challenging and the risk is to make things worse. To overcome this problem, Kamei and Mizoguchi (1995), Hong et al. (1996), and Bernard et al. (2002) proposed to apply all the filters of a given set at each point in the image (as in Figure 3.27). A "selector" then chooses the best response from all the filter responses. In the method by Kamei and Mizoguchi (1995), the selection is performed by minimizing an energy function that includes terms that require orientation and frequency to be locally smooth. In the approach by Bernard et al. (2002), the selection is performed according to the maximum response. However, unlike most of the Gabor-based methods, phase information coming from the real and the imaginary part of Gabor filters is also used for the final image enhancement. Unfortunately, the approaches that require convolution of an image with a large number of filters are computationally expensive, so they do not find application in practical on-line systems.

Another interesting technique that is able to perform a sort of contextual filtering without requiring explicitly computing local ridge orientation and frequency was proposed by Watson, Candela, and Grother (1994) and Willis and Myers (2001). Each 32×32 block in the image is enhanced separately; the Fourier transform of the block is multiplied by its power spectrum raised to a power k:

$$\mathrm{I}_{enh}[x, y] = F^{-1}\left\{ F\left(\mathrm{I}[x, y] \right) \times \left| F\left(\mathrm{I}[x, y] \right) \right|^{k} \right\}.$$

The power spectrum contains information about the underlying dominant ridge orientation and frequency and the multiplication has the effect of enhancing the block accordingly. Watson, Candela, and Grother (1994) set $k = 0.6$ whereas Willis and Myers (2001) proposed a more aggressive $k = 1.4$. Unfortunately, to avoid discontinuities at the edges between adjacent blocks, a large amount of overlap between the neighboring blocks (e.g., 24 pixels) is necessary and this significantly increases the enhancement time.

Other fingerprint enhancement approaches can be found in Asai et al. (1975), Berdan and Chiralo (1978), Nakamura, Nagaoka, and Minami (1986), Danielsson and Ye (1988), Sasakawa, Isogai, and Ikebata (1990), Kaymaz and Mitra (1993), Mehtre (1993), Bergengruen (1994), Sherstinsky and Picard (1994, 1996), Szu et al. (1995), Almansa and Lindeberg (1997, 2000), Pradenas (1997), Park and Smith (2000), Greenberg et al. (2000), Ghosal et al. (2000a, b), Simon-Zorita et al. (2001a, b), Cheng, Tian, and Zhang (2002) and Kim, Kim, and Park (2002).

3.8 Minutiae Detection

Most automatic systems for fingerprint comparison are based on minutiae matching (see Chapter 4); hence, reliable minutiae extraction is an extremely important task and a lot of research has been devoted to this topic. Although rather different from one another, most of the proposed methods require the fingerprint gray-scale image to be converted into a binary image. Some binarization processes greatly benefit from an a priori enhancement (see Section 3.7); on the other hand, some enhancement algorithms directly produce a binary output, and therefore the distinction between enhancement and binarization is sometimes faded. The binary images obtained by the binarization process are usually submitted to a thinning stage which allows for the ridge line thickness to be reduced to one pixel (Figure 3.31). Finally, a simple image scan allows the detection of pixels that correspond to minutiae.

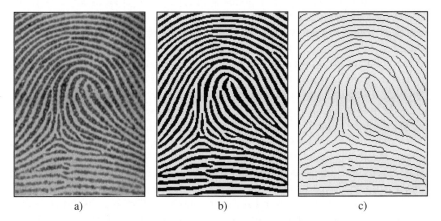

a)   b)   c)

Figure 3.31. a) A fingerprint gray-scale image; b) the image obtained after a binarization of the image in a); c) the image obtained after a thinning of the image in b). Reprinted with permission from Maio and Maltoni (1997). ©IEEE.

Some authors have proposed minutiae extraction approaches that work directly on the gray-scale images without binarization and thinning. This choice is motivated by these considerations:

- a significant amount of information may be lost during the binarization process;
- binarization and thinning are time consuming; thinning may introduce a large number of spurious minutiae;
- in the absence of an a priori enhancement step, most of the binarization techniques do not provide satisfactory results when applied to low-quality images.

Binarization-based methods

The general problem of image binarization has been widely studied in the fields of image processing and pattern recognition (Trier and Jain, 1995). The easiest approach uses a *global threshold* t and works by setting the pixels whose gray-level is lower than t to 0 and the remaining pixels to 1. In general, different portions of an image may be characterized by different contrast and intensity and, consequently, a single threshold is not sufficient for a correct binarization. For this reason, the *local threshold* technique changes t locally, by adapting its value to the average local intensity. In the specific case of fingerprint images, which are sometimes of very poor quality, a local threshold method cannot always guarantee acceptable results and more effective fingerprint-specific solutions are necessary. In the rest of this section, the main binarization methods used for fingerprints are briefly summarized.

The FBI "minutiae reader" designed by Stock and Swonger (1969) (see also Stock (1977)) binarizes the image through a composite approach based on a local threshold and a "slit comparison" formula that compares pixel alignment along eight discrete directions. In fact, it is observed that for each pixel that belongs to a ridge line, there exists an orientation (the ridge line orientation) whose average local intensity is higher than those of the remaining orientations (which cross different ridges and valleys).

Moayer and Fu (1986) proposed a binarization technique based on an iterative application of a Laplacian operator and a pair of dynamic thresholds. At each iteration, the image is convolved through a Laplacian operator and the pixels whose intensity lies outside the range bounded by the two thresholds are set to 0 and 1, respectively. The thresholds are progressively moved towards a unique value so that a guaranteed convergence is obtained. A similar method was proposed by Xiao and Raafat (1991a, b) who, after the convolution step, employed a local threshold to deal with regions with different contrast.

A fuzzy approach to image enhancement proposed by Verma, Majumdar, and Chatterjee (1987) that uses an adaptive threshold to preserve the same number of 1 and 0 pixels for each neighborhood forms the basis of their binarization technique. The image is initially partitioned in small regions and each region is processed separately. Each region is submitted to the following steps: smoothing, fuzzy coding of the pixel intensities, contrast enhancement, binarization, 1s and 0s counting, fuzzy decoding, and parameter adjusting. This sequence is repeated until the number of 1s approximately equals the number of 0s.

Coetzee and Botha (1993) presented a binarization technique based on the use of edges in conjunction with the gray-scale image. Edge extraction is performed by using the standard Marr and Hildreth (1980) algorithm. Then, the ridges are tracked by two local windows: one in the gray-scale image and the other in the edge image; in the gray-scale domain, the binarization is performed with a local threshold, whereas in the edge-image, a blob-coloring routine is used to fill the area delimited by the two ridge edges. The resulting binary image is the logical OR of the two individual binary images.

Ratha, Chen, and Jain (1995) introduced a binarization approach based on peak detection in the gray-level profiles along sections orthogonal to the ridge orientation (see Figure 3.32). A 16 × 16 oriented window is centered around each pixel [x,y]. The gray-level profile is obtained by projection of the pixel intensities onto the central section. The profile is smoothed through local averaging; the peaks and the two neighboring pixels on either side of each peak constitute the foreground of the resulting binary image (see Figure 3.33).

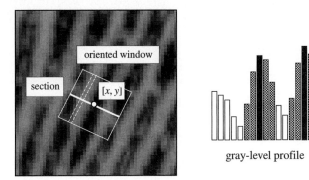

gray-level profile

Figure 3.32. An example of a gray-level profile obtained through projection of pixel intensities on the segment centered at [x,y] and normal to the local ridge orientation θ_{xy}.

Sherstinsky and Picard (1996) designed a complex method for fingerprint binarization that employs a dynamic non-linear system called "M–lattice." This method is based on the reaction-diffusion model first proposed by Turing in 1952 to explain the formation of animal patterns such as zebra stripes.

Domeniconi, Tari, and Liang (1998) modeled fingerprint ridges and valleys as sequences of local maxima and saddle points. Maxima and saddle points are detected by evaluating the gradient ∇ and the Hessian matrix **H** at each point. The Hessian of a two-dimensional surface $S(x,y)$ is a 2×2 symmetric matrix whose elements are the second-order derivatives of S with respect to x^2, xy, and y^2. The eigenvectors of **H** are the directions along which the curvature of S is extremized. Let **p** be a stationary point (i.e., a point such that ∇ in **p** is **0**) and let λ_1 and λ_2

be the eigenvalues of $\mathbf{H}$ in $\mathbf{p}$. Then $\mathbf{p}$ is a local maximum if $\lambda_1 \leq \lambda_2 < 0$ and is a saddle point if $\lambda_1 \cdot \lambda_2 < 0$. Since ridges may gradually change their intensity values along the ridge direction, causing the surface to have either positive or negative slope, the algorithm also considers non-stationary points $\mathbf{p}$ such that the gradient directions φ_1 and φ_2 at two neighboring points $\mathbf{p}_1$ and $\mathbf{p}_2$ (located along the normal to the ridge) face each other: $angle(\varphi_1,\ \varphi_2) \cong 180°$. The authors also proposed an edge-linking algorithm to connect the ridge pixels detected in the first stage.

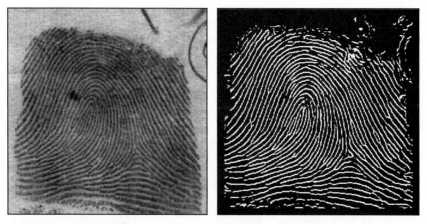

Figure 3.33. An example of fingerprint binarization using the Ratha, Chen, and Jain (1995) method. ©Elsevier.

A slightly different topological approach was proposed by Tico and Kuosmanen (1999) who treated a fingerprint image as a noisy sampling of the underlying continuous surface (Figure 3.7) and approximated it by orthogonal Chebyshev polynomials. Ridge and valley regions are discriminated by the sign of the maximal normal curvature of this continuous surface (Wang and Pavlidis, 1993). The maximal normal curvature along a given direction $\mathbf{d}$ may be computed as $\mathbf{d}^T \mathbf{H} \mathbf{d}$, where $\mathbf{H}$ is the Hessian matrix, and therefore the second-order derivatives have to be estimated at each point.

Abutaleb and Kamel (1999) used a genetic algorithm (Goldberg, 1989) to discriminate ridges and valleys along the gray-level profile of scanned lines. The proposed optimization criterion is aimed at increasing the correlation between adjacent gray-levels along fingerprint sections.

Most of the enhancement algorithms based on contextual filtering (discussed in Section 3.7) may produce a clear binary image for appropriately chosen parameters. In any case, even when the output of the contextual filtering is a gray-scale image, a simple local thresholding technique often results in satisfactory binarization. Examples of binary images obtained through the O'Gorman and Nickerson (1989) approach are shown in Figures 3.31.b and

3.34.a. Analogous results may be obtained through the contextual filtering techniques proposed by Donahue and Rokhlin (1993), Mehtre (1993), Sherlock, Monro, and Millard (1992, 1994), Watson, Candela, and Grother (1994), and Hong, Wan, and Jain (1998). Figure 3.34 shows the results obtained by binarizing a portion of a good quality fingerprint image through some of the methods described in this section; contextual filtering-based methods a) and d) produced the most regular binary ridge patterns.

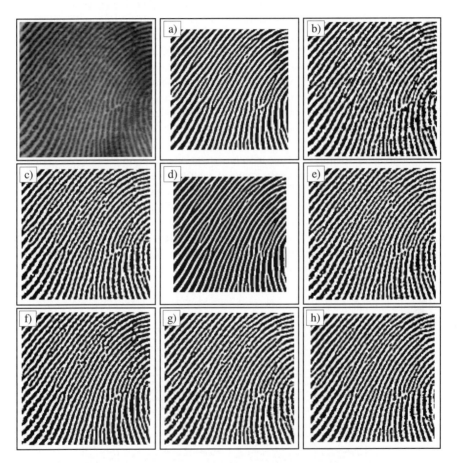

Figure 3.34. A portion of a good quality fingerprint image and its binarization through some of the methods discussed in this section: a) O'Gorman and Nickerson (1989); b) Verma, Majumdar, and Chatterjee (1987); c) local threshold approach; d) Sherlock, Monro, and Millard (1994); e) Xiao and Raafat (1991b); f) Moayer and Fu (1986); g) Stock and Swonger (1969); h) Watson, Candela, and Grother (1994).

Minutiae detection from binary images is usually performed after an intermediate thinning step that reduces the width of the ridges to one pixel. Unfortunately, thinning algorithms are rather critical and the aberrations and irregularity of the binary-ridge boundaries have an adverse effect on the *skeletons* (i.e., the one-pixel-width ridge structure), resulting in "hairy" growths (spikes) that lead to the detection of spurious minutiae.

With the aim of improving the quality of the binary images, some researchers have introduced regularization techniques which usually work by filling holes (see Figure 3.35), removing small breaks, eliminating bridges between ridges, and other artifacts. For this purpose, Coetzee and Botha (1993) identify holes and gaps by tracking the ridge line edges through adaptive windows and remove them using a simple blob-coloring algorithm. Hung (1993) uses an adaptive filtering technique to equalize the width of the ridges: narrow ridges in under-saturated regions are expanded and thick ridges in over-saturated regions are shrunk. To remove the spikes that often characterize the thinned binary images, Ratha, Chen, and Jain (1995) implement a morphological "open" operator (Gonzales and Woods, 1992) whose structuring element is a small box oriented according to the local ridge orientation. Fitz and Green's (1996) approach removes small lines and dots both in the ridges and valleys of binary images through an application of four morphological operators on a hexagonal grid. Wahab, Chin, and Tan (1998) correct the binary image at locations where orientation estimates deviate from their neighboring estimates. This correction is performed by substituting the noisy pixels according to some oriented templates. Luo and Tian (2000) implement a two-step method, where the skeleton extracted at the end of the first step is used to improve the quality of the binary image based on a set of structural rules; a new skeleton is then extracted from the improved binary image. Finally, Ikeda et al. (2002) use morphological operators to enhance ridges and valleys in the fingerprint binary image; their implementation is suitable to be efficiently mapped on a compact pixel-parallel architecture.

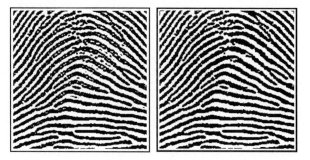

Figure 3.35. The result of eliminating small holes from both the ridges and valleys of the binary image; input image is shown on the left and the output is shown on the right. The filtering is performed by computing the connected components of the image and by removing the components whose area (number of pixels) is smaller than a given threshold.

As far as thinning techniques are concerned (Lam, Lee, and Suen, 1992), a large number of approaches are available in the literature due to the central role of this processing step in many pattern recognition applications: character recognition, document analysis, map and drawing vectorization, and so on. Hung (1993) used the algorithm by Arcelli and Baja (1984); Ratha, Chen, and Jain (1995) adopted a technique included in the HIPS library (Landy, Cohen, and Sperling, 1984), Mehtre (1993) employed the parallel algorithm described in Tamura (1978) and Coetzee and Botha (1993) used the method by Baruch (1988).

Once a binary skeleton has been obtained, a simple image scan allows the pixel corresponding to minutiae to be detected: in fact the pixels corresponding to minutiae are characterized by a *crossing number* different from 2. The crossing number $cn(\mathbf{p})$ of a pixel $\mathbf{p}$ in a binary image is defined (Arcelli and Baja, 1984) as half the sum of the differences between pairs of adjacent pixels in the 8-neighborhood of $\mathbf{p}$:

$$cn(\mathbf{p}) = \frac{1}{2} \sum_{i=1..8} \left| val(\mathbf{p}_{i \bmod 8}) - val(\mathbf{p}_{i-1}) \right|,$$

where $\mathbf{p}_0$, $\mathbf{p}_1$, ..., $\mathbf{p}_7$ are the pixels belonging to an ordered sequence of pixels defining the 8-neighborhood of $\mathbf{p}$ and $val(\mathbf{p}) \in \{0,1\}$ is the pixel value. It is simple to note (Figure 3.36) that a pixel $\mathbf{p}$ with $val(\mathbf{p}) = 1$:

- is an intermediate ridge point if $cn(\mathbf{p}) = 2$;
- corresponds to a termination minutia if $cn(\mathbf{p}) = 1$;
- defines a more complex minutia (bifurcation, crossover, etc.) if $cn(\mathbf{p}) \geq 3$.

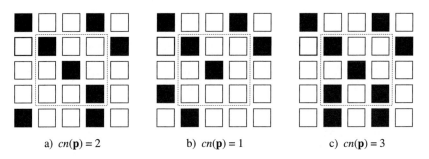

a) $cn(\mathbf{p}) = 2$ b) $cn(\mathbf{p}) = 1$ c) $cn(\mathbf{p}) = 3$

Figure 3.36. a) intra-ridge pixel; b) termination minutia; c) bifurcation minutia.

Figure 3.37 shows two examples of minutiae extraction from binary thinned images. Leung et al.'s (1991) method extracts the minutiae from thinned binary images but, instead of using the crossing number, the authors use a three-layer perceptron neural network. In some approaches, minutiae are detected from binary images without any intermediate thinning: Weber (1992) first performed an image enhancement by bandpass filtering in the frequency domain and then did binarization via a local threshold. Finally, the minutiae are detected from the thick binary ridges through a ridge tracking algorithm. Székely and Székely (1993) developed a minutiae detection technique based on the computation of the orientation image divergence. The foundation of this method lies in the use of a divergence operator in order to discern fingerprint pattern discontinuities that correspond to minutiae.

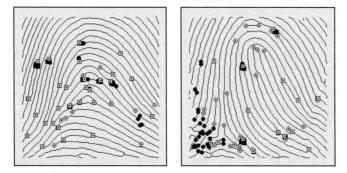

Figure 3.37. Examples of minutiae detection on binary skeletons. White circles and white boxes denote terminations and bifurcations, respectively; black circles and black boxes denote filtered minutiae (see Section 3.9).

Direct gray-scale extraction

With the aim of overcoming some of the problems related to fingerprint image binarization and thinning (e.g., the presence of spurious minutiae in the case of irregular ridge edges), some authors have proposed direct gray-scale extraction methods.

Leung, Engeler, and Frank (1990) introduced a neural network-based approach where a multi-layer perceptron analyzes the output of a rank of Gabor filters applied to the gray-scale image. The image is first transformed into the frequency domain where the filtering takes place; the resultant magnitude and phase signals constitute the input to a neural network composed of six sub-networks, each of which is responsible for detecting minutiae at a specific orientation; a final classifier is employed to combine the intermediate responses.

Maio and Maltoni (1997) proposed a direct gray-scale minutiae extraction technique, whose basic idea is to track the ridge lines in the gray-scale image, by "sailing" according to the local orientation of the ridge pattern. From a mathematical point of view, a ridge line is defined as a set of points that are local maxima along one direction. The ridge line extraction algorithm attempts to locate, at each step, a local maximum relative to a section orthogonal to the ridge direction. By connecting the consecutive maxima, a polygonal approximation of the ridge line can be obtained.

Given a starting point $[x_c,y_c]$ and a starting direction θ_c, the *ridge line following* algorithm (see Figure 3.38) computes a new point $[x_t,y_t]$ at each step by moving μ pixels from the current point $[x_c,y_c]$ along direction θ_c. Then it computes the *section set* Ω as the set of points belonging to the section segment lying on the *xy*-plane and having median point $[x_t,y_t]$, direction orthogonal to θ_c and length $2\sigma+1$. A new point $[x_n,y_n]$, belonging to the ridge line, is chosen among the local maxima of an enhanced version of the set Ω. The point $[x_n,y_n]$ becomes the current point $[x_c,y_c]$ and a new direction θ_c is computed (Figure 3.38).

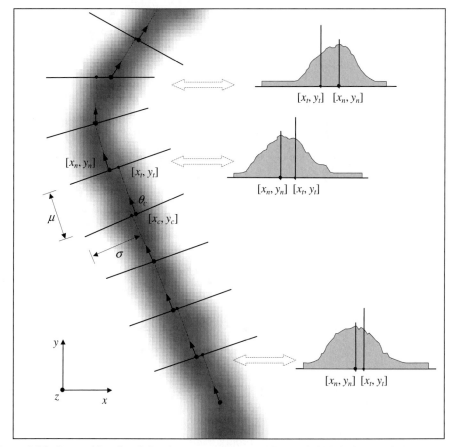

Figure 3.38. Some ridge line following steps (Maio and Maltoni, 1997). On the right, some sections are shown. ©IEEE.

The optimal value of the parameters μ and σ can be determined according to the average thickness of the image ridge lines. The algorithm runs until one among four stop criteria becomes true. In particular, when a ridge line terminates or intersects another ridge line (location of a minutia), the algorithm stops and returns the characteristics (type, coordinates and direction) of the detected minutia. The ridge line following algorithm extracts a ridge line given a starting point and a direction. By exploiting such an algorithm, it is possible to define a schema for extracting all the ridge lines in an image and, consequently, detect all the minutiae. The main problems arise from the difficulty of examining each ridge line only once and locating the intersections with the ridge lines already extracted. For this purpose, an auxiliary image **T** of the same dimension as **I** is used. **T** is initialized by setting its pixel values to 0; each time a new ridge line is extracted from **I**, the pixels of **T** corresponding to the ridge line are labeled. The pixels of **T** corresponding to a ridge line are the pixels belonging to the ε-pixel thick polygonal, which links the consecutive maximum points $[x_n,y_n]$ located by the ridge line following algorithm (Figure 3.39).

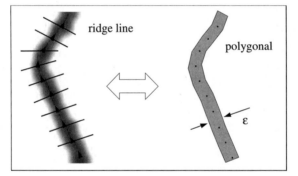

Figure 3.39. A ridge line and the corresponding ε-pixel thick polygonal (Maio and Maltoni, 1997). ©IEEE.

Let **G** be a regular square-meshed grid superimposed on the image **I**. For each node of G, the minutiae detection algorithm searches the nearest ridge line and tracks it by means of the ridge line following routine. Because the initial point can be anywhere in the middle of a ridge line, the tracking is executed alternately in both directions. The auxiliary image **T,** which is updated after each ridge line following, provides a simple and effective way to discover ridge line intersections and to avoid multiple trackings. Figure 3.40 shows the results obtained by applying the minutiae detection algorithm to a sample fingerprint. Maio and Maltoni (1997) compared their method with four binarization thinning-based approaches and concluded that direct gray-scale extraction can significantly reduce processing time as well as the number of spurious minutiae resulting from thinning algorithms.

Jiang, Yau, and Ser (1999, 2001) proposed a variant of the Maio and Maltoni (1997) method, where the ridge following step μ is dynamically adapted to the change of ridge contrast and bending level. Referring to Figure 3.38, a long step is executed if there is little variation in the gray-level intensity along the segment $[x_c,y_c]$ $[x_t,y_t]$, and the ridge bending is low. On the other hand, high bending level of the ridge (possibly facing a ridge bifurcation) or large intensity variations (possibly facing a termination) will result in a short step. Using a dynamic step speeds up the tracing while maintaining good precision.

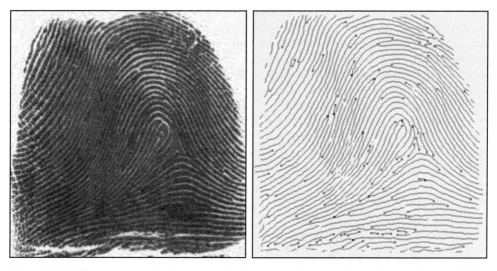

Figure 3.40. Minutiae detection on a sample fingerprint by using the Maio and Maltoni (1997) method. Contextual filtering is performed on "touched" pixels during ridge line following. The ridge lines are represented through the corresponding polylines of **T**. Termination minutiae are denoted by gray boxes and bifurcation minutiae are denoted by black boxes.

Liu, Huang, and Chan (2000) introduced another modification of the Maio and Maltoni (1997) method. Instead of tracking a single ridge, the algorithm simultaneously tracks a central ridge and the two surrounding valleys. For this purpose, they search a central maximum and two adjacent minima in each section Ω. Minutiae are detected where the relation < minimum, maximum, minimum > is altered. Here too, the ridge following step μ is dynamically adjusted according to the distances between lateral minima from the central maximum. This approach does not need an a priori setting of some parameters such as the maximum bending angle (which determines a stopping criterion in the original algorithm) and the step μ.

The Chang and Fan (2001) approach is aimed at discriminating the true ridge maxima in the sections Ω obtained during ridge line following. Two thresholds are initially determined based on the gray-level histogram decomposition. The histogram is modeled as a sum of three Gaussian contributions associated with the background, valleys, and ridges, respectively. The mean, variance, and probability of each Gaussian is estimated and two thresholds are derived for successive characterization of maxima and minima of the sections Ω. A set of rules is employed to discriminate real ridge points from background noise and intra-ridge variations.

Nilsson and Bigun (2001) proposed using Linear Symmetry (LS) properties computed by spatial filtering (Bigun and Granlund, 1987) via separable Gaussian filters and Gaussian derivative filters. Minutiae are identified in the gray-scale image as points characterized by the lack of symmetry. In fact, whereas a non-minutia point is characterized by a direction (i.e., the minutiae angle) along which an infinitesimal translation leaves the pattern least variant, minutiae are local discontinuities of the LS vector field.

Finally, Bolle et al. (2002) addressed the problem of precisely and consistently locating the minutiae points in the gray-scale fingerprint pattern. In fact, different feature extraction algorithms tend to locate the minutiae at slightly different positions (depending on their operational definition of minutia and the intermediate processing steps) and this may lead to interoperability problems. Bolle et al. (2002) provided a formal definition of minutia based on the gray-scale image that allows the location and orientation of an existing minutia to be more precisely determined.

3.9 Minutiae Filtering

A post-processing stage is often useful in removing the spurious minutiae detected in highly corrupted regions or introduced by previous processing steps (e.g., thinning). Two main post-processing types have been proposed:
  • structural post-processing, and
  • minutiae filtering in the gray-scale domain.

Structural post-processing

Simple structural rules may be used to detect many of the false minutiae that usually affect thinned binary fingerprint images. Xiao and Raafat (1991b) identified the most common false minutiae structures and introduced an ad hoc approach to remove them (Figure 3.41). The underlying algorithm is rule-based and requires some numerical characteristics associated with the minutiae as input: the length of the associated ridge(s), the minutia angle, and the number of facing minutiae in a neighborhood. As shown in Figure 3.41, the algorithm connects facing endpoints (a, b), removes bifurcations facing with endpoints (c) or with other bifurcations (d), and removes spurs (e), bridges (f), triangles (g), and ladder structures (h).

Hung (1993) exploited the minutiae duality (Figure 3.5) to purify false minutiae extracted from binary thinned images. In particular, both ridge and valley skeletons are extracted and only ridge minutiae having a counterpart (of complementary type) in the valley skeleton are retained. A graph is defined for both ridge and valley skeletons by assigning a vertex to each termination and bifurcation and by assigning an edge to each ridge. Each edge is characterized by the length of the corresponding ridge, and the degree of a vertex is given by the number of converging edges. Spurs (i.e., very short edges) and holes (i.e., loops with a very small diameter) are first removed by considering some property of the ridge graph. Bridges between adjacent ridges are then removed by exploiting their relation with breaks in the dual space.

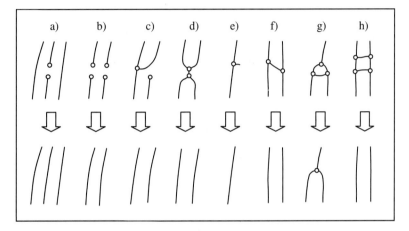

Figure 3.41. The most common false-minutiae structures (on the first row) and the structural changes resulting from their removal (second row).

Farina, Kovacs-Vajna, and Leone (1999) introduced some optimized variants of the previously proposed rules and algorithms. Spurs and bridges are removed based on the observation that in a "spurious" bifurcation, only two branches are generally aligned whereas the third one is almost orthogonal to the other two. Short ridges are removed on the basis of the relationship between the ridge length and the average distance between ridges. Terminations and bifurcations are then topologically validated: they are removed if topological requirements are not satisfied; they are classified as less reliable if the requirements are not fully satisfied; they are considered as highly reliable minutiae otherwise. An example is shown in Figure 3.42.

A slightly different implementation of spurious minutiae removal has been proposed by Kim, Lee, and Kim (2001). In their work, local orientation and flow of ridges are key factors for post-processing to avoid eliminating true minutiae.

The Bhanu, Boshra, and Tan (2000) filtering method verifies each minutia, detected from the thinned binary image, through correlation with logical templates (i.e., template matching) adapted to the local ridge orientation. In Bhanu and Tan (2001b), an evolution of the above method is proposed where templates are not static, but are learned in a supervised manner from examples.

Minutiae filtering in the gray-scale domain

A direct gray-scale minutiae filtering technique reexamines the gray-scale image in the spatial neighborhood of a detected minutia with the aim of verifying the presence of a real minutia.

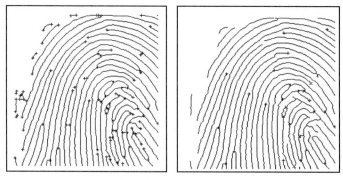

Figure 3.42. Minutiae post-processing according to Farina, Kovacs-Vajna, and Leone (1999). On the right, most of the false minutiae present in the thinned binary image (on the left) have been removed. ©Elsevier.

Maio and Maltoni (1998b) used a shared-weights neural network to verify the minutiae detected by their gray-scale algorithm (Maio and Maltoni, 1997). The minutiae neighborhoods in the original gray-scale image are normalized, with respect to their angle and the local ridge frequency, before passing them to a neural network classifier, which classifies them as termination, bifurcation, and non-minutia. Figure 3.43.b shows the same minutiae neighborhoods of Figure 3.43.a after the normalization. To take advantage of the termination/bifurcation duality, both the original neighborhood and its negative version constitute the input to the neural network classifier. Additionally, to avoid the problems related to training large networks, the dimensionality of the normalized neighborhoods is reduced through the Karhunen–Loeve transform (Jolliffe, 1986). A typical three-layer neural network architecture has been adopted, where a partial weight sharing allows the termination/bifurcation duality to be exploited (Figure 3.44). In fact, the weight sharing requires the same type of processing to be performed by the first layer of neurons both on the positive and the negative neighborhoods. This network has more degrees of freedom with respect to a three-layer (26–10–2) perceptron trained both on the positive and the negative versions of the same neighborhood, and used twice for each classification.

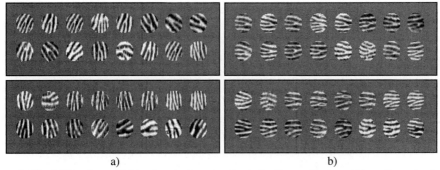

Figure 3.43. a) Minutiae neighborhoods (termination minutiae at the top, bifurcation minutiae at the bottom) as they appear in the original gray-scale images; b) the same neighborhoods have been normalized with respect to minutiae angle and local ridge frequency (Maio and Maltoni, 1998b). ©IEEE.

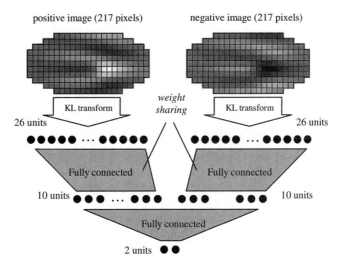

Figure 3.44. The neural network architecture to classify gray-scale minutiae neighborhoods into termination, bifurcation, and non-minutiae (Maio and Maltoni, 1998b). ©IEEE.

In this case, both the positive and negative images convey contemporary information to the third layer, which acts as the final decision maker. Experimental results proved that this filtering method, in spite of a certain increase in missed minutiae, provides significant reduction in false minutiae and exchanged minutiae (i.e., a termination detected as bifurcation and vice versa) errors.

The Prabhakar et al. (2000) minutiae verifier operates on the gray-scale neighborhoods extracted from the original image after enhancement through Gabor filtering (Hong, Wan, and Jain, 1998). Minutiae neighborhoods are normalized with respect to minutiae angle and local ridge frequency. The resulting patterns are classified through a Learning Vector Quantizer (Kohonen et al., 1992) trained in a supervised fashion to discriminate between minutiae and non-minutiae. The authors obtained a classification accuracy of 87% and a reduction of about 4% fingerprint matching error when their minutiae verification algorithm was embedded into the minutiae-based fingerprint verification system described in Jain et al. (1997).

3.10 Estimation of Ridge Count

Absolute position, direction, and type of minutiae (e.g., termination or bifurcation) are not the only features that may be used for fingerprint recognition. In fact, forensic experts and latent fingerprint examiners have often used *ridge count* to increase the reliability of their analysis (Henry, 1900). Ridge count is an abstract measurement of the distances between any two points in a fingerprint image (Lin and Dubes, 1983). Let **a** and **b** be two points in a fingerprint; then the ridge count between **a** and **b** is the number of ridges intersected by segment **ab** (Figure 3.45).

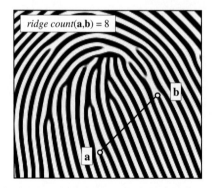

Figure 3.45. In this example the number of ridges intersected by segment **ab** (ridge count between **a** and **b**) is 8.

Ridge count has been typically used in forensic matching because of the difficulty of human experts to work in the Euclidean space. However, because the early automatic systems were developed from an intuitive design geared towards duplicating the performance of human experts in matching fingerprints, ridge counts were used in the early AFIS systems but they soon disappeared into oblivion. Recently, with an increased interest in improving the performance of fingerprint recognition systems in commercial applications, several authors (e.g., Germain, Califano, and Colville (1997), Jiang and Yau (2000), and Ratha et al. (2000)) have used ridge counts as features.

Although the general definition of ridge count includes measuring the number of ridges between any two points in the fingerprint images, typically, **a** and **b** (refer to Figure 3.45) coincide with stationary points in the fingerprint pattern (e.g., position of the singularities or position of the minutiae). For example, in forensic AFIS it is common to count the ridges between core and delta.

There exist two main approaches for counting the number of ridges between two points **a** and **b** in a fingerprint image:

- determine the number of (0 to 1) transitions along the segment **ab** in a binarized image;
- determine the number of local maxima in the section **ab** of a gray-scale image. Refer to the x-signature method (Figure 3.11) for an example of a possible implementation.

In both cases, the estimation of ridge count may be problematic in noisy areas, near singularities, near minutiae, and when the segment orientation is close to the underlying ridge orientation. Kovacs-Vajna (2000) matched the ridge profiles between pairs of minutiae using the dynamic time warping technique. This method is conceptually similar to ridge counting, even if it cannot be directly used to estimate the ridge count but only to verify that the ridge–valley profiles between two pairs of corresponding points are similar.

3.11 Summary

Most of the early work in fingerprint analysis was based on general-purpose image processing techniques. Recent developments in fingerprint analysis have taken two important directions. Novel fingerprint features that particularly focus on optimizing the salient discriminatory information in fingerprints have emerged. For example, Kaymaz and Mitra (1992) proposed ridge line-based features, Stosz and Alyea (1994) proposed sweat pores as features and Jain et al. (2000) proposed texture-based features. Also, algorithms designed specifically for processing fingerprint images have been proposed. For example, O'Gorman and Nickerson (1988) proposed contextual filtering for fingerprint enhancement. Similarly, Hong, Wan, and Jain (1998) developed an enhancement algorithm based on Gabor filters whose parameters were derived based on fingerprint properties and Pankanti et al. (2002) proposed an algorithm to quantify the quality of fingerprint images based on the properties of the fingerprints. Robust feature extraction remains a challenging problem, especially in poor quality fingerprints. Development of fingerprint-specific image processing techniques is necessary in order to solve some of the outstanding problems. For example, explicitly measuring (and restoring or masking) noise such as creases, cuts, dryness, smudginess, and the like will be helpful in reducing feature extraction errors. Algorithms that can extract discriminative non-minutiae-based features in fingerprint images and integrate them with the available features and matching strategies will improve fingerprint matching accuracy. New (perhaps, model-based) methods for computation (or restoration) of the orientation image in very low-quality images is also desirable to reduce feature extraction errors.

4
Fingerprint Matching

4.1 Introduction

A fingerprint matching algorithm compares two given fingerprints and returns either a degree of similarity (without loss of generality, a score between 0 and 1) or a binary decision (mated/non-mated). Only a few matching algorithms operate directly on grayscale fingerprint images; most of them require that an intermediate fingerprint representation be derived through a feature extraction stage (refer to Chapter 3). Without loss of generality, hereafter we denote the representation of the fingerprint acquired during enrollment as the *template* ($\mathbf{T}$) and the representation of the fingerprint to be matched as the *input* ($\mathbf{I}$). In case no feature extraction is performed, the fingerprint representation coincides with the grayscale fingerprint image itself; hence, throughout this chapter, we denote both raw fingerprint images and fingerprint feature vectors (e.g., minutiae) with $\mathbf{T}$ and $\mathbf{I}$.

The fingerprint feature extraction and matching algorithms are usually quite similar for both fingerprint verification and identification problems. This is because the fingerprint identification problem (i.e., searching for an input fingerprint in a database of N fingerprints) can be implemented as a sequential execution of N one-to-one matches (verifications) between pairs of fingerprints. The fingerprint classification and indexing techniques are usually exploited to speed up the search (refer to Chapter 6) in fingerprint identification problems.

Matching fingerprint images is an extremely difficult problem, mainly due to the large variability in different impressions of the same finger (i.e., large *intra-class* variations). The main factors responsible for intra-class variations are summarized below.

- *Displacement*: The same finger may be placed at different locations on the sensor during different acquisitions resulting in a (global) translation of the fingerprint area. A finger displacement of just 2 mm (imperceptible to the user) results in a translation of about 40 pixels in a fingerprint image scanned at a resolution of 500 dpi.
- *Rotation*: The same finger may be rotated at different angles with respect to the sensor surface during different acquisitions. In spite of the finger "guide" mounted in

certain commercial scanners, involuntary finger rotations of up to ±20 degrees with respect to vertical orientation can be observed in practice.

- *Partial overlap*: Finger displacement and rotation often cause part of the fingerprint area to fall outside the sensor's "field of view," resulting in a smaller overlap between the foreground areas of the template and the input fingerprints. This problem is particularly serious for small-area sensors (see Section 2.7).

- *Non-linear distortion*: The act of sensing maps the three-dimensional shape of a finger onto the two-dimensional surface of the sensor. This mapping results in a non-linear distortion in successive acquisitions of the same finger due to skin plasticity. Often, fingerprint matching algorithms disregard the characteristic of such a mapping, and consider a fingerprint image as non-distorted by assuming that it was produced by a correct finger placement; a finger placement is correct when the user:
  1. approaches the finger to the sensor through a movement that is orthogonal to the sensor surface;
  2. once the finger touches the sensor surface, the user does not apply traction or torsion.

  However, due to skin plasticity, the components of the force that are non-orthogonal to the sensor surface produce non-linear distortions (compression or stretching) in the acquired fingerprints. Distortion results in the inability to match fingerprints as rigid patterns.

- *Pressure and skin condition*: The ridge structure of a finger would be accurately captured if ridges of the part of the finger being imaged were in uniform contact with the sensor surface. However, finger pressure, dryness of the skin, skin disease, sweat, dirt, grease, and humidity in the air all confound the situation, resulting in a non-uniform contact. As a consequence, the acquired fingerprint images are very noisy and the noise strongly varies in successive acquisitions of the same finger depending on the magnitude of the above cited causes.

- *Noise*: It is mainly introduced by the fingerprint sensing system; for example, residues are left over on the glass platen from the previous fingerprint capture.

- *Feature extraction errors*: The feature extraction algorithms are imperfect and often introduce measurement errors. Errors may be made during any of the feature extraction stages (e.g., estimation of orientation and frequency images, detection of the number, type, and position of the singularities, segmentation of the fingerprint area from the background, etc.). Aggressive enhancement algorithms may introduce inconsistent biases that perturb the location and orientation of the reported minutiae from their gray-scale counterparts. In low-quality fingerprint images, the minutiae extraction process may introduce a large number of spurious minutiae and may not be able to detect all the true minutiae.

The pairs of images in Figure 4.1 visually show the high variability (large *intra-class* variations) that can characterize two different impressions of the same finger.

Figure 4.1. Each row shows a pair of impressions of the same finger, taken from the FVC2002 DB1 (Maio et al., 2002b), which were falsely non-matched by most of the algorithms submitted to FVC2002. The main cause of difficulty is a very small overlap in the first row, high non-linear distortion in the second row, and very different skin conditions in the third row.

On the other hand, as evident from Figure 4.2, fingerprint images from different fingers may sometimes appear quite similar (small *inter-class* variations), especially in terms of global structure (position of the singularity, local ridge orientation, etc.). Although the probability that a large number of minutiae from impressions of two different fingers will match is extremely small (refer to Chapter 8), fingerprint matchers aim to find the "best" alignment. They often tend to declare that a pair of the minutiae "match" even when they are not perfectly coincident.

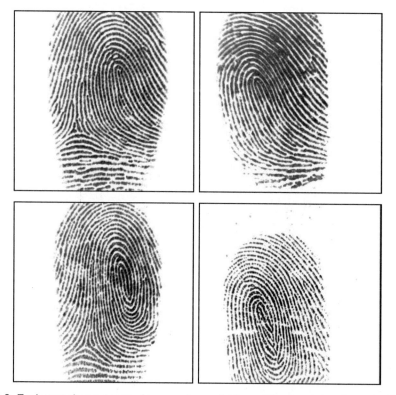

Figure 4.2. Each row shows a pair of impressions of different fingers, taken from the FVC2002 databases (Maio et al., 2002b) which were falsely matched by some of the algorithms submitted to FVC2002.

A large number of automatic fingerprint matching algorithms have been proposed in the pattern recognition literature. Most of these algorithms have no difficulty in matching good quality fingerprint images. However, fingerprint matching remains a challenging pattern recognition problem to date due to the difficulty in matching low-quality and partial fingerprints. In the case of human-assisted AFIS, a quality-checking algorithm can be used to acquire and insert only good quality fingerprints into the database. Furthermore, the processing of "difficult" latent fingerprints can be supervised. However, human intervention is not feasible in unattended on-line fingerprint recognition systems, which have increasingly been demanded in commercial applications.

A coarse analysis of the false non-match errors produced by the various fingerprint matching algorithms that participated in FVC2000 showed that most errors were made on about 15 to 20% poor quality fingerprints. In other words, typically, 20% of the database is responsible for about 80% of the false non-match errors (Maio et al., 2002b). Some advances in the state of the art of fingerprint recognition technology was demonstrated two years later at FVC2002 (Maio et al., 2002b) (see Table 4.1), where some of the submitted algorithms correctly matched many poor quality fingerprints. However, there is still a need to continually develop more robust systems capable of dealing with very poor quality fingerprint images.

The large number of approaches to fingerprint matching can be coarsely classified into three families.

- *Correlation-based matching*: Two fingerprint images are superimposed and the correlation between corresponding pixels is computed for different alignments (e.g., various displacements and rotations). Correlation-based techniques are described in Section 4.2.
- *Minutiae-based matching*: This is the most popular and widely used technique, being the basis of the fingerprint comparison made by fingerprint examiners. Minutiae are extracted from the two fingerprints and stored as sets of points in the two-dimensional plane. Minutiae-based matching essentially consists of finding the alignment between the template and the input minutiae sets that results in the maximum number of minutiae pairings. Sections 4.3 and 4.4 are dedicated to minutiae matching techniques.
- *Ridge feature-based matching*: Minutiae extraction is difficult in very low-quality fingerprint images. However, whereas other features of the fingerprint ridge pattern (e.g., local orientation and frequency, ridge shape, texture information) may be extracted more reliably than minutiae, their distinctiveness is generally lower. The approaches belonging to this family compare fingerprints in term of features extracted from the ridge pattern. In principle, correlation- and minutiae-based matching could be conceived of as subfamilies of ridge feature-based matching, inasmuch as the pixel intensity and the minutiae positions are themselves features of the finger ridge pattern; throughout this book we address them separately, and in Section 4.6 we discuss only those matching techniques that use neither minutiae nor pixel intensity as a fingerprint representation.

Algorithm	EER (%)	FMR 100 (%)	FMR 1000 (%)	Zero FMR (%)	REJ_{enr} (%)	REJ_{match} (%)	Enroll time (sec)	Match time (sec)
PA15 (c)	0.19	0.15	0.28	0.38	0.00	0.00	0.11	1.97
PA27 (c)	0.33	0.28	0.56	1.44	0.00	0.00	2.12	1.98
PB27 (c)	0.41	0.34	0.59	1.29	0.00	0.00	1.23	1.13
PB15 (c)	0.77	0.77	1.04	1.29	0.00	0.00	0.07	0.22
PB05 (c)	0.92	1.46	1.87	2.29	0.00	0.00	0.48	0.52
PA08 (c)	0.99	1.12	2.07	3.11	0.00	0.00	0.56	0.56
PA35 (c)	1.18	1.32	2.71	4.21	0.00	0.00	4.05	1.65
PA02 (o)	1.31	1.34	1.80	2.22	0.32	0.20	0.81	1.23
PB35 (c)	1.42	1.51	2.71	4.60	0.00	0.00	0.77	0.66
PA13 (o)	2.18	2.49	3.48	10.29	0.00	0.14	0.17	0.48
PA45 (c)	2.22	3.05	4.96	6.27	0.00	0.00	0.52	0.62
PA26 (c)	2.50	3.08	4.30	6.14	0.00	0.00	0.54	0.63
PA34 (c)	3.31	4.71	7.55	10.89	0.00	0.00	0.53	0.65
PA24 (a)	3.76	5.17	8.48	12.04	0.07	0.05	0.57	0.59
PA19 (c)	4.19	6.47	9.60	13.19	0.00	0.00	0.18	0.18
PA29 (o)	4.24	7.01	11.20	15.14	0.00	0.00	0.65	0.66
PA14 (c)	5.21	7.27	9.73	11.69	0.00	0.00	0.68	1.76
PA07 (c)	5.46	11.88	20.55	25.47	0.00	0.00	0.20	0.54
PA31 (c)	5.72	31.95	75.12	79.91	0.00	0.00	0.01	3.15
PA28 (c)	6.05	15.58	31.83	48.50	0.00	0.00	0.48	0.77
PA21 (a)	6.07	10.77	18.62	33.69	0.43	0.63	0.80	0.84
PA10 (c)	6.16	7.66	8.88	9.74	0.00	0.00	1.81	1.81
PA42 (c)	6.40	11.29	16.01	19.87	1.04	1.63	0.49	0.50
PA32 (c)	6.72	10.46	15.03	18.26	0.39	0.93	0.33	0.56
PA12 (c)	7.12	11.98	16.36	20.12	0.07	0.05	0.24	0.28
PA20 (a)	9.04	13.66	18.17	22.82	0.00	0.00	0.13	0.15
PA18 (c)	12.09	27.79	29.17	36.59	0.86	0.40	0.68	0.70
PA22 (a)	14.66	38.09	53.57	65.32	0.00	0.25	0.57	0.65
PA16 (a)	16.79	26.29	32.96	43.87	0.00	0.53	1.16	1.19
PA25 (o)	39.10	90.33	96.59	99.34	2.50	1.81	0.52	0.63
PA03 (a)	50.00	100.00	100.00	100.00	0.00	100.00	7.05	5.01

Table 4.1. Results extracted from the FVC2002 report (Maio et al., 2002b). ERR denotes the average Equal Error Rate over the four databases used in FVC2002. FMR100, FMR1000, and ZeroFMR are the false non-match rates when the false match rate is 1/100, 1/1000, and zero, respectively. REJ_{enr} and REJ_{match} are the rejection at enrollment and rejection at matching, that is, the percentage of fingerprints that the algorithms are not able to process. The last two columns are the average time for the enrollment of a fingerprint and the average time for matching a fingerprint against a template, respectively. In the first column, a character is used to indicate if the algorithm owner is a company (c), an academic organization (a), or other (o).

Many other techniques have also been proposed in the literature that, in principle, could be associated with one of the above families according to the features used, but we prefer to categorize them separately on the basis of the matching technique. These include the neural network-based approaches (Sjogaard, (1992), Baldi and Chauvin (1993), Quek, Tan, and Sagar (2001), and Coetzee and Botha (1990)) and the attempts made to carry out fingerprint matching using parallel processors or with other dedicated architectures (Gowrishankar (1989), Ratha, Rover, and Jain (1996) and Prabhakar and Rao (1989)).

Finally, to provide a more complete panorama of the techniques proposed in the past, we cite some early works presented in AFIS, academic, and commercial environments: Banner and Stock (1974, 1975a, b), Millard (1975), Singh, Gyergyek, and Pavesic (1977), Hoshino et al. (1980), Liu et al. (1982), Millard (1983), Li and Zhang (1984), and Sparrow and Sparrow (1985a, b).

4.2 Correlation-based Techniques

Let $\mathbf{T}$ and $\mathbf{I}$ be the two fingerprint images corresponding to the template and the input fingerprint, respectively. Then an intuitive measure of their diversity is the sum of squared differences (*SSD*) between the intensities of the corresponding pixels:

$$SSD(\mathbf{T},\mathbf{I}) = \|\mathbf{T}-\mathbf{I}\|^2 = (\mathbf{T}-\mathbf{I})^{\mathrm{T}}(\mathbf{T}-\mathbf{I}) = \|\mathbf{T}\|^2 + \|\mathbf{I}\|^2 - 2\mathbf{T}^{\mathrm{T}}\mathbf{I}, \tag{1}$$

where the superscript "T" denotes the transpose of a vector. If the terms $\|\mathbf{T}\|^2$ and $\|\mathbf{I}\|^2$ are constant, the diversity between the two images is minimized when the cross-correlation (*CC*) between $\mathbf{T}$ and $\mathbf{I}$ is maximized:

$$CC(\mathbf{T},\mathbf{I}) = \mathbf{T}^{\mathrm{T}}\mathbf{I}. \tag{2}$$

Note that the quantity $-2 \cdot CC(\mathbf{T},\mathbf{I})$ appears as the third term in Equation (1). The cross-correlation (or simply correlation) is then a measure of image similarity. Due to the displacement and rotation that unavoidably characterize two impressions of a given finger, their similarity cannot be simply computed by superimposing $\mathbf{T}$ and $\mathbf{I}$ and applying Equation (2).

Let $\mathbf{I}^{(\Delta x, \Delta y, \theta)}$ represent a rotation of the input image $\mathbf{I}$ by an angle θ around the origin (usually the image center) and shifted by Δx, Δy pixels in directions x and y, respectively; then the similarity between the two fingerprint images $\mathbf{T}$ and $\mathbf{I}$ can be measured as

$$S(\mathbf{T},\mathbf{I}) = \max_{\Delta x, \Delta y, \theta} CC\!\left(\mathbf{T}, \mathbf{I}^{(\Delta x, \Delta y, \theta)}\right). \tag{3}$$

The direct application of Equation (3) rarely leads to acceptable results (see Figure 4.3.a) mainly due to the following problems.

1. Non-linear distortion makes impressions of the same finger significantly different in terms of global structure; in particular, the elastic distortion does not significantly alter the fingerprint pattern locally, but since the effects of distortion get integrated in image space, two global fingerprint patterns cannot be reliably correlated (see Figure 4.3.b).

2. Skin condition and finger pressure cause image brightness, contrast, and ridge thickness to vary significantly across different impressions (see Figure 4.3.c). The use of more sophisticated correlation measures such as the *normalized cross-correlation* or the *zero-mean normalized cross-correlation* (Crouzil, Massip-Pailhes, and Castan, 1996) may compensate for contrast and brightness variations and applying a proper combination of enhancement, binarization, and thinning steps (performed on both **T** and **I**) may limit the ridge thickness problem. Hatano et al. (2002) proposed using the *differential correlation*, which is computed as the maximum correlation minus the minimum correlation, in a neighborhood of the point where the correlation is maximum. In fact, due to the cyclic nature of fingerprint patterns, if two corresponding portions of the same fingerprint are slightly misaligned with respect to their optimum matching position, the correlation value falls sharply whereas two non-corresponding portions exhibit a flatter correlation value in the neighborhood of the optimum matching position. Hatano et al. (2002) reported a significant accuracy improvement with respect to the conventional correlation method.

3. A direct application of Equation (3) is computationally very expensive. For example, consider two 400×400 pixel images; then the computation of the cross-correlation (Equation (2)) for a single value of the $(\Delta x, \Delta y, \theta)$ triplet would require 16,000 multiplications and 16,000 summations (neglecting border effects). If $\Delta x, \Delta y$ were both sampled with a one-pixel step in the range $[-200,200]$, and θ with step $1°$ in the range $[-30°,30°]$ we would have to compute $401 \times 401 \times 61$ cross-correlations, resulting in about 1569 billion multiplications and summations (i.e., more than one hour on a 500 MIPS computer).

The fingerprint distortion problem (point 1 in the above list) is usually addressed by computing the correlation locally instead of globally: a set of local regions (whose typical size may be 24×24 or 32×32) is extracted from the template image **T** and each of them is independently correlated with the whole input image **I** (Bazen et al., 2000). The local regions may be defined in several ways:

- their union completely covers **T** and their intersection is null (full coverage without any overlap);
- their union completely covers **T** and they locally overlap (full coverage with overlap);
- only certain "interesting" regions are selected from **T**. For example, Yahagi, Igaki and Yamagishi (1990), Kovacs-Vajna (2000), and Beleznai et al. (2001) select small windows around the minutiae, whereas Bazen et al. (2000) consider selective regions

that are distinctively localized in the input image (i.e., which fit well at the right location, but do not fit at other locations). Three different criteria are given by Bazen et al. (2000) to identify such selective regions in the template image: regions around minutiae, regions where ridges have a high curvature, and regions that exhibit a low (auto)correlation at other locations in the template image itself.

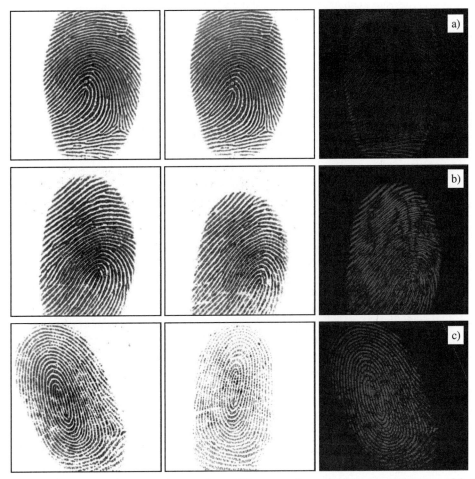

Figure 4.3. Each row shows two impressions of the same finger and the absolute value of their difference for the best alignment (i.e., that maximize correlation). In the first row, a) the two impressions are very similar and their images correlate well (the residual is very small). In the second row, b), and third row, c), due to high distortion and skin condition, respectively, the residuals are high and the global correlation methods fail.

When fingerprint correlation is carried out locally, the correlation estimates at different regions may be simply combined to obtain a similarity measure (e.g., the number of estimates exceeding a certain threshold divided by the total number of estimates). In addition to the values of the correlation, the coordinates of the points where each region has maximum correlation can be exploited to strengthen the matching (*consolidation* step): in fact, the spatial relationship (distances, angles, etc.) between the regions in the template and their mates in the input image is required to be preserved (Bazen et al., 2000). In any case, there is no guarantee that using such a consolidation step is really advantageous.

As to the computational complexity of the correlation technique, smart approaches may be exploited to achieve efficient implementations.

- The correlation theorem (Gonzales and Woods, 1992) states that computing the correlation in the spatial domain (operator $\otimes$) is equivalent to performing a point-wise multiplication in the Fourier domain; in particular,

$$\mathbf{T} \otimes \mathbf{I} = F^{-1}\left(F^*(\mathbf{T}) \times F(\mathbf{I})\right), \tag{4}$$

  where $F(.)$ is the Fourier transform of an image, $F^{-1}(.)$ is the inverse Fourier transform, "*" denotes the complex conjugate, and "$\times$" denotes the point-by-point multiplication of two vectors. The result of Equation (4) is a correlation image whose value at the pixel $[x,y]$ denotes the correlation between $\mathbf{T}$ and $\mathbf{I}$ when the displacement is $\Delta x = x$ and $\Delta y = y$. Equation (4) does not take into account rotation, which has to be dealt with separately; in any case, the computational saving is very high when correlation is performed globally (Coetzee and Botha, 1993) and considerable when it is performed locally by using medium-size regions.

- Computing the maximum correlation need not necessarily be done in a sequential, exhaustive manner; multi-resolution approaches, space-searching techniques (gradient descent), and other heuristics can be adopted to reduce the number of evaluations.

- The Fourier–Mellin transform (Sujan and Mulqueen, 2002) may be used instead of the Fourier transform to achieve rotation invariance in addition to translation invariance; on the other hand, some additional steps (such as the log–polar coordinate transformation) have to be performed, but that can reduce the accuracy of this solution.

- The approach proposed by Wilson, Watson, and Paek (1997) partitions both $\mathbf{T}$ and $\mathbf{I}$ into local regions and computes the maximum correlation (in the Fourier domain) between any pair of regions. This method suffers from "border effects" because of the partial overlapping between the different blocks, but can considerably speed up the whole matching process.

- It is well known that correlation between two signals can be computed by an optical system that uses lenses to derive the Fourier transform of the images and a joint transform correlator for their matching. Several systems have been proposed in the literature for optical fingerprint matching: McMahon et al. (1975), Fielding, Homer, and

Makekau (1991), Grycewicz (1995, 1996), Rodolfo, Rajbenbach, and Huignard (1995), Grycewicz and Javidi (1996), Petillot, Guibert, and de Bougrenet (1996), Soifer et al. (1996), Gamble, Frye, and Grieser (1992), Wilson, Watson, and Paek (1997), Kobayashi and Toyoda (1999), and Watson, Grother, and Casasent (2000). However, these optical systems usually suffer from rotation and distortion variations and the hardware/optical components are complex and expensive; therefore, optical fingerprint matching technology has not reached satisfactory maturity yet.

4.3 Minutiae-based Methods

Minutiae matching is certainly the most well-known and widely used method for fingerprint matching, thanks to its strict analogy with the way forensic experts compare fingerprints and its acceptance as a proof of identity in the courts of law in almost all countries.

Problem formulation

Let $\mathbf{T}$ and $\mathbf{I}$ be the representation of the template and input fingerprint, respectively. Unlike in correlation-based techniques, where the fingerprint representation coincides with the fingerprint image, here the representation is a feature vector (of variable length) whose elements are the fingerprint minutiae. Each minutia may be described by a number of attributes, including its location in the fingerprint image, orientation, type (e.g., ridge termination or ridge bifurcation), a weight based on the quality of the fingerprint image in the neighborhood of the minutia, and so on. Most common minutiae matching algorithms consider each minutia as a triplet $\mathbf{m} = \{x, y, \theta\}$ that indicates the x, y minutia location coordinates and the minutia angle θ:

$$\mathbf{T} = \{\mathbf{m}_1, \mathbf{m}_2, ..., \mathbf{m}_m\}, \quad \mathbf{m}_i = \{x_i, y_i, \theta_i\}, \quad i = 1..m$$
$$\mathbf{I} = \{\mathbf{m}_1', \mathbf{m}_2', ..., \mathbf{m}_n'\}, \quad \mathbf{m}_j' = \{x_j', y_j', \theta_j'\}, \quad j = 1..n,$$

where m and n denote the number of minutiae in $\mathbf{T}$ and $\mathbf{I}$, respectively.

A minutia $\mathbf{m}_j'$ in $\mathbf{I}$ and a minutia $\mathbf{m}_i$ in $\mathbf{T}$ are considered "matching," if the *spatial distance* (sd) between them is smaller than a given tolerance r_0 and the *direction difference* (dd) between them is smaller than an angular tolerance θ_0:

$$sd(\mathbf{m}_j', \mathbf{m}_i) = \sqrt{(x_j' - x_i)^2 + (y_j' - y_i)^2} \leq r_0, \qquad \text{and} \tag{5}$$

$$dd(\mathbf{m}_j', \mathbf{m}_i) = \min\left(|\theta_j' - \theta_i|, 360° - |\theta_j' - \theta_i|\right) \leq \theta_0. \tag{6}$$

Equation (6) takes the minimum of $|\theta_j' - \theta_i|$ and $360° - |\theta_j' - \theta_i|$ because of the circularity of angles (the difference between angles of 2° and 358° is only 4°). The *tolerance boxes* (or hyper-spheres) defined by r_0 and θ_0 are necessary to compensate for the unavoidable errors made by feature extraction algorithms and to account for the small plastic distortions that cause the minutiae positions to change.

Aligning the two fingerprints is a mandatory step in order to maximize the number of matching minutiae. Correctly aligning two fingerprints certainly requires *displacement* (in x and y) and *rotation* (θ) to be recovered, and likely involves other geometrical transformations:

- *scale* has to be considered when the resolution of the two fingerprints may vary (e.g., the two fingerprint images have been taken by scanners operating at different resolutions);
- other *distortion-tolerant* geometrical transformations could be useful to match minutiae in case one or both of the fingerprints is affected by severe distortions.

In any case, tolerating a higher number of transformations results in additional degrees of freedom to the minutiae matcher: when a matcher is designed, this issue needs to be carefully evaluated, as each degree of freedom results in a huge number of new possible alignments which significantly increases the chance of incorrectly matching two fingerprints from different fingers.

Let *map*(.) be the function that maps a minutia $\mathbf{m}'_j$ (from **I**) into $\mathbf{m}''_j$ according to a given geometrical transformation; for example, by considering a displacement of $[\Delta x, \Delta y]$ and a counterclockwise rotation θ around the origin[1]:

$$map_{\Delta x,\Delta y,\theta}\left(\mathbf{m}'_j = \{x'_j, y'_j, \theta'_j\}\right) = \mathbf{m}''_j = \{x''_j, y''_j, \theta'_j + \theta\}, \quad \text{where}$$

$$\begin{bmatrix} x''_j \\ y''_j \end{bmatrix} = \begin{bmatrix} \cos\theta & -\sin\theta \\ \sin\theta & \cos\theta \end{bmatrix} \begin{bmatrix} x'_j \\ y'_j \end{bmatrix} + \begin{bmatrix} \Delta x \\ \Delta y \end{bmatrix}.$$

Let *mm*(.) be an indicator function that returns 1 in the case where the minutiae $\mathbf{m}''_j$ and $\mathbf{m}_i$ match according to Equations (5) and (6):

$$mm\left(\mathbf{m}''_j, \mathbf{m}_i\right) = \begin{cases} 1 & sd\left(\mathbf{m}''_j, \mathbf{m}_i\right) \le r_0 \quad \text{and} \quad dd\left(\mathbf{m}''_j, \mathbf{m}_i\right) \le \theta_0 \\ 0 & \text{otherwise.} \end{cases}$$

Then, the matching problem can be formulated as

$$\underset{\Delta x,\Delta y,\theta,P}{\text{maximize}} \sum_{i=1}^{m} mm\left(map_{\Delta x,\Delta y,\theta}\left(\mathbf{m}'_{P(i)}\right), \mathbf{m}_i\right), \tag{7}$$

where $P(i)$ is an unknown function that determines the *pairing* between **I** and **T** minutiae; in particular, each minutia has either exactly one mate in the other fingerprint or has no mate at all:

---

1 The origin is usually selected as the minutiae centroid (i.e., the average point); before the matching step, minutiae coordinates are adjusted by subtracting the centroid coordinates.

1. $P(i) = j$ indicates that the mate of the $\mathbf{m}_i$ in $\mathbf{T}$ is the minutia $\mathbf{m}'_j$ in $\mathbf{I}$;
2. $P(i) = $ null indicates that minutia $\mathbf{m}_i$ in $\mathbf{T}$ has no mate in $\mathbf{I}$;
3. a minutia $\mathbf{m}'_j$ in $\mathbf{I}$, such that $\forall\ i = 1..m$, $P(i) \neq j$ has no mate in $\mathbf{T}$;
4. $\forall\ i = 1..m,\ k = 1..m,\ i \neq k \Rightarrow P(i) \neq P(k)$ or $P(i) = P(k) = $ null (this requires that each minutia in $\mathbf{I}$ is associated with a maximum of one minutia in $\mathbf{T}$).

Note that, in general, $P(i) = j$ does not necessarily mean that minutiae $\mathbf{m}'_j$ and $\mathbf{m}_i$ match in the sense of Equations (5) and (6) but only that they are the most likely pair under the current transformation.

Expression (7) requires that the number of minutiae mates be maximized, independently of how strict these mates are; in other words, if two minutiae comply with Equations (5) and (6), then their contribution to expression (7) is made independently of their spatial distance and of their direction difference. Alternatives to expression (7) may be introduced where the residual (i.e., the spatial distance and the direction difference between minutiae) for the optimal alignment is also taken into account.

Solving the minutiae matching problem (expression (7)) is trivial when the correct alignment ($\Delta x, \Delta y, \theta$) is known; in fact, the pairing (i.e., the function P) can be determined by setting for each $i = 1..m$:

- $P(i) = j$ if $\mathbf{m}''_j = map_{\Delta x, \Delta y, \theta}\left(\mathbf{m}'_j\right)$ is closest to $\mathbf{m}_i$ among the minutiae $\left\{ \mathbf{m}''_k = map_{\Delta x, \Delta y, \theta}(\mathbf{m}'_k) \mid k = 1..n,\ mm(\mathbf{m}''_k, \mathbf{m}_i) = 1 \right\}$;
- $P(i) = $ null if $\forall\ k = 1..n,\ mm\left(map_{\Delta x, \Delta y, \theta}(\mathbf{m}'_k), \mathbf{m}_i\right) = 0$.

To comply with constraint 4 above, each minutia $\mathbf{m}''_j$ already mated has to be marked, to avoid mating it twice or more. Figure 4.4 shows an example of minutiae pairing given a fingerprint alignment.

To achieve the optimum pairing (according to Equation (7)), a slightly more complicated scheme should be adopted: in fact, in the case when a minutia of $\mathbf{I}$ falls within the tolerance hyper-sphere of more than one minutia of $\mathbf{T}$, the optimum assignment is that which maximizes the number of mates (refer to Figure 4.5 for a simple example).

The maximization in (7) can be easily solved if the function P (minutiae correspondence) is known; in this case, the unknown alignment ($\Delta x, \Delta y, \theta$) can be determined in the least square sense (Umeyana (1991) and Chang et al. (1997)). Unfortunately, in practice, neither the alignment parameters nor the correspondence function P are known and, therefore, solving the matching problem is very hard. A brute force approach, that is, evaluating all the possible solutions (correspondences and alignments) is prohibitive as the number of possible solutions is exponential in the number of minutiae (the function P is more than a permutation due to the possible null values). A few brute force approaches have also been proposed in the literature;

for example, Huvanandana, Kim, and Hwang (2000) proposed coarsely quantizing the minutiae locations and performing an exhaustive search to find the optimum alignment.

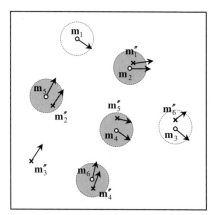

Figure 4.4. Minutiae of I mapped into T coordinates for a given alignment. Minutiae of T are denoted by **o**s, whereas I minutiae are denoted by ×s. Note that I minutiae are referred to as **m″**, because what is shown in the figure is their mapping into T coordinates. Pairing is performed according to the minimum distance. The dashed circles indicate the maximum spatial distance. The gray circles denote successfully mated minutiae; minutia $\mathbf{m}_1$ of T and minutia $\mathbf{m}''_3$ of I have no mates, minutiae $\mathbf{m}_3$ and $\mathbf{m}''_6$ cannot be mated due to their large direction difference.

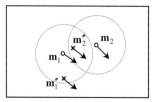

Figure 4.5. In this example, if $\mathbf{m}_1$ were mated with $\mathbf{m}''_2$ (the closest minutia), $\mathbf{m}_2$ would remain unmated; however, pairing $\mathbf{m}_1$ with $\mathbf{m}''_1$, allows $\mathbf{m}_2$ to be mated with $\mathbf{m}''_2$, thus maximizing Equation (7).

In the pattern recognition literature the minutiae matching problem has been generally addressed as a *point pattern matching* problem. Even though a small difference exists due to the presence of a direction associated with each minutia point, the two problems may be approached analogously. Because of its central role in many pattern recognition and computer vision tasks (e.g., object matching, remote sensing, camera calibration, motion estimation), point pattern matching has been extensively studied yielding families of approaches known as *relaxation methods, algebraic and operational research solutions, tree-pruning approaches, energy-minimization methods, Hough transform,* and so on.

Approaches to point pattern matching

- *Relaxation.* The relaxation approach (e.g., Rosenfeld and Kak (1976) and Ranade and Rosenfeld (1993)) iteratively adjusts the confidence level of each corresponding pair of points based on its consistency with other pairs until a certain criterion is satisfied. At each iteration r, the method computes $m \cdot n$ probabilities p_{ij} (probability that point i corresponds to point j):

$$p_{ij}^{(r+1)} = \frac{1}{m} \sum_{h=1}^{m} \left[\max_{k=1...n} \left\{ c(i,j;h,k) \cdot p_{ij}^{(r)} \right\} \right], \quad i = 1..m, \quad j = 1..n, \quad (8)$$

  where $c(i,j;h,k)$ is a compatibility measure between the pairing (i,j) and (h,k), which can be defined according to the consistency of the alignments necessary to map point j into i and point k into h. Equation (8) increases the probability of those pairs that receive substantial support by other pairs, and decreases the probability of the remaining ones. At convergence, each point i may be associated with the point j such that $p_{ij} = \max_s \{p_{is}\}$, where s is any other point in the set. Although a number of modified versions of this algorithm have been proposed to reduce the matching complexity (Ton and Jain, 1989), these algorithms are inherently slow due to their iterative nature.

- *Algebraic and operational research solutions.* Hong and Tan (1988), and Sprinzak and Werman (1994) proposed algebraic methods for point pattern matching under the restrictive hypotheses that $n = m$ and that an exact alignment may be recovered under an affine transformation. Solutions to point pattern matching may also be derived from some problems which are known in the field of operational research as assignment problems or bipartite graph matching (Murty (1992) and Gold and Rangarajan (1996)).

- *Tree pruning.* Tree-pruning approaches attempt to find the correspondence between the two point sets by searching over a tree of possible matches while employing different tree-pruning methods (e.g., branch and bound) to reduce the search space (Baird, 1984). To prune the tree of possible matches efficiently, this approach tends to impose a number of requirements on the input point sets, such as an equal number of points ($n = m$) and no outliers (points without correspondence). These requirements are difficult to satisfy in practice, especially in fingerprint minutiae matching.

- *Energy minimization.* These methods define a function that associates an *energy* with each solution of the problem. Optimal solutions are then derived by minimizing the energy function by using a stochastic algorithm such as the genetic algorithm (Ansari, Chen, and Hou, 1992) or simulated annealing (Starink and Backer, 1995). These methods tend to be very slow and are unsuitable for real-time minutiae matching.

- *Hough transform.* The Hough transform-based approach (Ballard (1981) and Stockman, Kopstein, and Benett (1982)) converts point pattern matching to the problem of detecting peaks in the Hough space of transformation parameters. It discretizes the parameter space and accumulates evidence in the discretized space by deriving transformation parameters that relate two sets of points using a substructure of the feature matching technique. A hierarchical Hough transform-based algorithm may be used to reduce the size of the accumulator array by using a multi-resolution approach. Hough transform-based approaches are quite popular for minutiae matching; a more in-depth analysis of this method is provided below.

Hough transform-based approaches for minutiae matching

Ratha et al. (1996) proposed a Hough transform-based minutiae matching approach, whose underlying alignment transformation, besides displacement and rotation, also includes scale. The space of transformations consists of quadruples (Δx, Δy, θ, s), where each parameter is discretized (denoted by the symbol $^+$) into a finite set of values:

$$\Delta x^+ \in \left\{ \Delta x_1^+, \Delta x_2^+, ..., \Delta x_a^+ \right\} \quad \Delta y^+ \in \left\{ \Delta y_1^+, \Delta y_2^+, ..., \Delta y_b^+ \right\},$$
$$\theta^+ \in \left\{ \theta_1^+, \theta_2^+, ..., \theta_c^+ \right\} \quad s^+ \in \left\{ s_1^+, s_2^+, ..., s_d^+ \right\}.$$

A four-dimensional array **A**, with one entry for each of the parameter discretizations, is initially reset and the following algorithm is used to accumulate evidence:

for each $\mathbf{m}_i$, $i = 1..m$

for each $\mathbf{m}'_j$, $j = 1..n$

for each $\theta^+ \in \left\{ \theta_1^+, \theta_2^+, ..., \theta_c^+ \right\}$

  if $dd\left(\theta'_j + \theta^+, \theta_i\right) < \theta_0$ // the minutiae directions after the rotation are sufficiently close as per equation (6)

    for each $s^+ \in \left\{ s_1^+, s_2^+, ..., s_d^+ \right\}$

$$\left\{ \begin{bmatrix} \Delta x \\ \Delta y \end{bmatrix} = \begin{bmatrix} x_i \\ y_i \end{bmatrix} - s^+ \cdot \begin{bmatrix} \cos\theta^+ & -\sin\theta^+ \\ \sin\theta^+ & \cos\theta^+ \end{bmatrix} \begin{bmatrix} x'_j \\ y'_j \end{bmatrix} \right.$$ // the *map* function including scale

$\Delta x^+, \Delta y^+$ = quantization of Δx, Δy to the nearest bin

$\mathbf{A}[\Delta x^+, \Delta y^+, \theta^+, s^+] = \mathbf{A}[\Delta x^+, \Delta y^+, \theta^+, s^+] + 1$

    }

At the end of the accumulation process, the best alignment transformation $(\Delta x^*, \Delta y^*, \theta^*, s^*)$ is then obtained as

$$\left(\Delta x^*, \Delta y^*, \theta^*, s^*\right) = arg \max_{\Delta x^+, \Delta y^+, \theta^+, s^+} \mathbf{A}\left[\Delta x^+, \Delta y^+, \theta^+, s^+\right]$$

and the minutiae pairing is performed as previously explained (in "Problem Formulation" subsection). To increase robustness of the Hough transform, it is common to cast a vote not only in the discretized bin, but also in its nearest neighbors; hence, in the above pseudo-code, the accumulator update can be substituted by a simple procedure that updates all the entries in the neighborhood of the selected bin.

An efficient parallel implementation of the above algorithm, whose complexity is $O(m \times n \times c \times d)$, was introduced by Ratha, Rover, and Jain (1995), where dedicated hardware consisting of a Field Programmable Gate Array (FPGA)-based point pattern matching processor was designed.

An alternative approach to point pattern matching, as proposed by Chang et al. (1997) consists of the main steps:

1. detect the minutiae pair (called the *principal pair*) that receives the maximum *Matching Pair Support* (MPS) and the alignment parameters (θ, s) that can match most minutiae between $\mathbf{T}$ and $\mathbf{I}$. The principal pair that has maximum MPS is determined through a Hough transform-based voting process;

2. the remaining minutiae mates (i.e., the function P) are then determined once the two fingerprints have been registered to superimpose the minutiae constituting the principal pair;

3. the exact alignment is computed in the least square sense once the correspondence function is known.

To accomplish Step 1, which is at the core of this approach, the algorithm considers segments defined by pairs of minutiae $\overline{\mathbf{m}_{i2}\mathbf{m}_{i1}}$ in $\mathbf{T}$ and $\overline{\mathbf{m}'_{j2}\mathbf{m}'_{j1}}$ in $\mathbf{I}$ and derives, from each pair of segments, the parameters θ and s simply as

$$\theta = angle\left(\overline{\mathbf{m}_{i2}\mathbf{m}_{i1}}\right) - angle\left(\overline{\mathbf{m}'_{j2}\mathbf{m}'_{j1}}\right), \tag{9}$$

$$s = \frac{length\left(\overline{\mathbf{m}_{i2}\mathbf{m}_{i1}}\right)}{length\left(\overline{\mathbf{m}'_{j2}\mathbf{m}'_{j1}}\right)}. \tag{10}$$

A transformation $(\Delta x, \Delta y, \theta, s)$, which aligns the two segments, must necessarily involve a scale change by an amount given by the ratio of the two segment lengths, and a rotation by an angle equal to the difference between the two segment angles (see Figure 4.6).

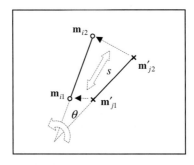

Figure 4.6. The transformation that aligns the two segments involves a rotation and a scale change as defined by Equations (9) and (10).

The principal pair and the parameters (θ^*, s^*) are determined as

$maxMPS = 0$ // maximum Matching Pair Support
for each $\mathbf{m}_{i1}$, $i1 = 1..m$
for each $\mathbf{m}'_{j1}$, $j1 = 1..n$ // $\mathbf{m}_{i1}, \mathbf{m}'_{j1}$ is the current pair for which MPS has be to estimated
   { Reset $\mathbf{A}$ // the accumulator array
     for each $\mathbf{m}_{i2}$, $i2 = 1..m$, $i2 \neq i1$
     for each $\mathbf{m}'_{j2}$, $j2 = 1..n$, $j2 \neq j1$

        { θ, s are computed from $\overline{\mathbf{m}_{i2}\mathbf{m}_{i1}}$, $\overline{\mathbf{m}'_{j2}\mathbf{m}'_{j1}}$ according to Equations (9) and (10)
          θ^+, s^+ = quantization of θ, s to the nearest bins
          $\mathbf{A}[\theta^+, s^+] = \mathbf{A}[\theta^+, s^+] + 1$
        }
     $MPS = \max_{\theta^+, s^+} \mathbf{A}\left[\theta^+, s^+\right]$
     if $MPS \geq maxMPS$
       { $maxMPS = MPS$
       $\left(\theta^*, s^*\right) = arg \max_{\theta^+, s^+} \mathbf{A}\left[\theta^+, s^+\right]$
       Principal pair $= (\mathbf{m}_{i1}, \mathbf{m}'_{j1})$

       }
   }

Some heuristics were introduced by Chang et al. (1997) to reduce the number of segments considered and therefore, to limit the computational complexity. An example of minutiae matching by the above method is shown in Figure 4.7.

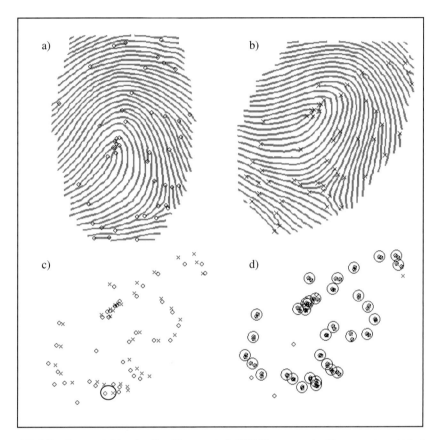

Figure 4.7. Minutiae matching by the Chang et al. (1997) approach. Figures a) and b) show the minutiae extracted from the template and the input fingerprint, respectively; c) the minutiae are coarsely superimposed and the principal pair is marked with an ellipse; d) each circle denotes a pair of minutiae as mated by the algorithm at the end of Step 3.

Another approach was introduced by Udupa, Garg, and Sharma (2001) who significantly improved an idea earlier published by Weber (1992). In this case, no scale change is allowed (rigid transformation) and the algorithm is simpler than the previous ones:

1. the segments identified by pairs of minutiae $\overline{\mathbf{m}_{i2}\mathbf{m}_{i1}}$ in $\mathbf{T}$ and $\overline{\mathbf{m}'_{j2}\mathbf{m}'_{j1}}$ in $\mathbf{I}$ are considered, and from each pair of segments that have approximately the same length (remember that the transformation is rigid), the alignment parameters (Δx, Δy, θ) are derived;

2. for each alignment (Δx, Δy, θ) obtained in Step 1), **T** and **I** are superimposed and the pairing between the remaining minutiae is determined, resulting in a number of mated pairs;

3. the top ten alignments (i.e., those giving the larger number of mates) are checked for consistency; in case of matching fingerprints, a majority of these alignments are mutually consistent, whereas for non-matching fingerprints they are not. A score is computed based on the fraction of mutually consistent transformations.

The final score is determined by combining the maximum number of mated pairs, the fraction of mutually consistent alignments, and the topological correspondence (i.e., minutiae direction and ridge counts) for the top ten alignments. The Hough transform is not explicitly used here, but the consistency check made in Step 3) is, in principle, very similar to the accumulation of evidence which characterizes the Hough transform. To reduce the computational complexity of their methods, Udupa, Garg, and Sharma (2001) suggest to filter out most of the candidate alignments in Step 1) early on according to the consistency of minutiae directions and of the ridge counts along the two segments.

Other algorithms based on minutiae matching are described in Pernus, Kovacic, and Gyergyek (1980), Mehtre and Murthy (1986), Gunawardena and Sagar (1991), Costello, Gunawardena, and Nadiadi (1994), and Johannesen et al. (1996).

Minutiae matching with pre-alignment

Embedding fingerprint alignment into the minutiae matching stage (as the methods presented in the previous section do), certainly leads to the design of robust algorithms, which are often able to operate with noisy and incomplete data. On the other hand, the computational complexity of such methods does not provide a high matching throughput (e.g., 10,000 matches per second), as required by AFIS or civil systems.

Storing pre-aligned templates in the database and pre-aligning the input fingerprint before the minutiae matching can be a valid solution to speed up the 1:N identification. In theory, if a perfect pre-alignment could be achieved, the minutiae matching could be reduced to a simple pairing. Two main approaches for pre-alignment have been investigated.

*   *Absolute pre-alignment*: Each fingerprint template is pre-aligned, independently of the others, before storing it in the database. Matching an input fingerprint **I** with a set of templates requires **I** to be independently registered just once, and the resulting aligned representation to be matched with all the templates. The most common absolute pre-alignment technique translates the fingerprint according to the position of the core point (see Section 3.6). Unfortunately, reliable detection of the core is very difficult in noisy images and in arch type patterns, and a registration error at this level is likely to result in a matching error. Absolute pre-alignment with respect to rotation is even more critical; some authors proposed using the shape of the external fingerprint silhouette (if available), the orientation of the core delta segment (if a delta exists),

the average orientation in some regions around the core (Wegstein, 1982), or the orientations of the singularities (Bazen and Gerez, 2002b). In any case, no definite solution has been proposed for a reliable pre-alignment to date and, therefore, the design of a robust system requires the minutiae matcher to tolerate pre-alignment errors to some extent.

- *Relative pre-alignment*: The input fingerprint **I** has to be pre-aligned with respect to each template **T** in the database; 1:*N* identification requires *N* independent pre-alignments. Relative pre-alignment may determine a significant speed up with respect to the algorithms that do not perform any pre-alignment, but cannot compete in terms of efficiency with absolute pre-alignment. However, relative pre-alignment is in general more effective (in terms of accuracy) than absolute pre-alignment, because the features of the template **T** may be used to drive the registration process.

The M82 method, developed for minutiae-based fingerprint matching in the FBI's Integrated AFIS (IAFIS) (Wegstein (1972), Wegstein and Rafferty (1978) and Wegstein (1982)), performs a coarse absolute pre-alignment according to the core position (detected through the R92 method; ref. Section 3.6) and the average orientation of two regions located at the two sides of the core (see Figure 4.8).

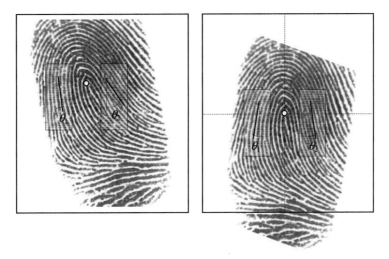

Figure 4.8. The fingerprint on the right has been translated to move the core point to the image center and rotated to minimize the difference between the angles θ_1 and θ_2.

After the coarse absolute pre-alignment of both **T** and **I** minutiae, M82 determines a list of candidate minutiae pairs by considering the minutiae that are closer than a given distance (this heavily relies on the assumption of a correct coarse pre-alignment); the matching degree of each candidate pair is consolidated according to the compatibility with other pairs. The list is sorted with respect to the degree of matching; the top pair is selected as the principal pair and all the remaining minutiae are translated accordingly. In a second stage, a deformation tensor, which allows the matching to tolerate small linear distortion and rotations, is determined (see Figure 4.9).

Relative pre-alignment may be performed in several ways; for example:

- by superimposing the singularities,
- by correlating the orientation images (template matching), or
- by correlating ridge features (e.g., length and orientation of the ridges).

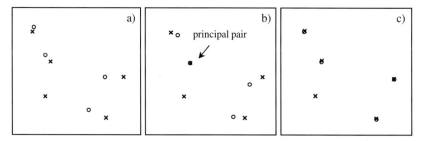

Figure 4.9. a) An example of minutiae matching as performed by M82, starting from a coarse absolute pre-alignment; b) the two minutiae sets after alignment with respect to the principal pair; c) the final result obtained after applying the correction given by the deformation/rotation tensor.

An interesting minutiae matching approach that exploits ridge features for relative pre-alignment was proposed by Jain, Hong, and Bolle (1997); see also Hong and Jain (1996) and Jain et al. (1997). The relative pre-alignment is based on the observation that minutiae registration can be performed by registering the corresponding ridges. In fact, each minutia in a fingerprint is associated with a ridge; during the minutiae extraction stage, when a minutia is detected and recorded, the ridge on which it resides is also recorded. The ridge is represented as a planar curve, with its origin coincident with the minutia and its x-coordinate being in the same direction as the minutia direction. Also, this planar curve is normalized (in scale) with respect to the average ridge frequency. By matching these ridges (see Figure 4.10) the parameters (Δx, Δy, θ) may be recovered. The ridge matching task proceeds by iteratively matching pairs of ridges until a pair is found whose matching degree exceeds a certain threshold. The pair found is then used for relative pre-alignment.

To tolerate local distortion and minutiae extraction errors (false and missing minutiae, location errors) Jain, Hong, and Bolle (1997), instead of using the classical pairing based on tolerance boxes, propose an adaptive elastic matching algorithm:

1. each minutia in **T** and **I** is converted to a polar coordinate system with respect to the reference minutia in its set (the reference minutia is that associated with the ridge selected during pre-alignment);
2. both **T** and **I** are transformed into symbolic strings by concatenating each minutia in the increasing order of radial angle.

The two strings are matched with a dynamic programming technique (Cormen, Leiserson, and Rivest, 1990) to find their *edit distance*. The edit distance between two strings is the minimum cost of transformations (symbol insertion, symbol deletion, symbol exchange) necessary to make the two strings coincident (Bunke, 1993). Matching minutiae representations by their edit distance tolerates missing and spurious minutiae as these are dealt with as symbol insertion and deletion. Radial and angular minutiae errors are handled by defining the cost of symbol exchange proportional to the position difference. However, some problems are due to "order flips" possibly inserted in Step 2, which could be solved by exhaustive reordering and matching within a local angular window. Figure 4.11 shows an example of minutiae matching by the Jain, Hong, and Bolle (1997) approach.

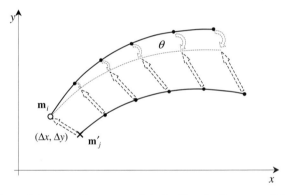

Figure 4.10. Matching of the two ridges associated with minutiae **m**$_i$ of T and **m**$'_j$ of I. Both ridges are sampled with step size equal to the average inter-ridge distance (sampling points are denoted by small black dots in the figure) and the matching is carried out by correlating the *y*-coordinates of the sampling points.

A variant of the above method was proposed by Luo, Tian, and Wu (2000), where ridge matching was performed in a slightly different manner: instead of correlating the *y*-coordinates of the sampled points along the two ridges, the authors matched distances and relative angles of the sampled points. The minutiae matching stage also deviated at some points: ridge information was fused into the computation of the edit distance and variable bounding boxes were introduced to deal with distortion.

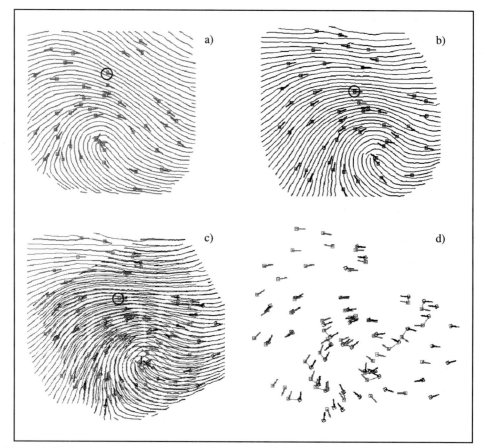

Figure 4.11. Result of applying the Jain, Hong, and Bolle (1997) matching algorithm to an input fingerprint b) and a template fingerprint a). c) Pre-alignment result based on the minutiae marked with circles and the associated ridges; ridges and minutiae of I and T are gray and black, respectively. d) Matching results where paired minutiae are connected by gray lines. ©IEEE.

Avoiding alignment

Fingerprint alignment is certainly a critical and time-consuming step. To overcome problems involved in alignment, and to better cope with local distortions, some authors perform minutiae matching locally (as discussed in Section 4.4). A few other attempts have been proposed that try to globally match minutiae without requiring explicit recovery of the parameters of the transformation. Bazen and Gerez (2001a) introduced an *intrinsic coordinate system* (ICS) whose axes run along hypothetical lines defined by the local orientation of the fingerprint pattern. First, the fingerprint is partitioned in regular regions (i.e., regions that do not contain singular points). In each regular region, the ICS is defined by the orientation field. When using intrinsic coordinates instead of pixel coordinates, minutiae are defined with respect to their position in the orientation field (Figure 4.12). Translation, displacement, and distortion move minutiae with the orientation field they are immersed in and therefore do not change their intrinsic coordinates. On the other hand, some practical problems such as reliably partitioning the fingerprint in regular regions and unambiguously defining intrinsic coordinate axes in low-quality fingerprints still remain to be solved.

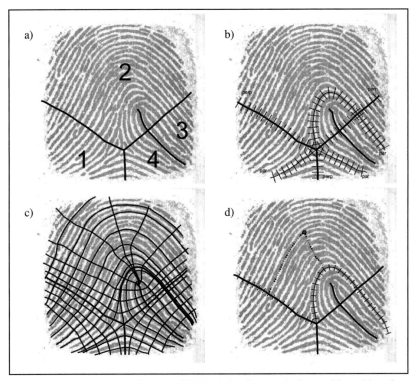

Figure 4.12. Intrinsic Coordinate System (ICS): a) the fingerprint is partitioned into four regular regions; b) each region is spanned by two axes, one parallel to the ridge orientation, and one perpendicular to the ridges; c) iso-coordinates in the ICS spaces; d) intrinsic coordinates of a given minutia. Reprinted with permission from Bazen and Gerez (2001a). ©Springer-Verlag.

4.4 Global versus Local Minutiae Matching

Local minutiae matching consists of comparing two fingerprints according to local minutiae structures; local structures are characterized by attributes that are invariant with respect to global transformation (e.g., translation, rotation, etc.) and therefore are suitable for matching without any a priori global alignment. Matching fingerprints based only on local minutiae arrangements relaxes global spatial relationships which are highly distinctive and therefore reduce the amount of information available for discriminating fingerprints. Global versus local matching is a tradeoff among simplicity, low computational complexity, and high distortion-tolerance (local matching), and high distinctiveness on the other hand (global matching). Interesting approaches have been proposed where the advantages of both methods are exploited (Jiang and Yau (2000) and Ratha et al. (2000)): a fast local matching is initially carried out for recovering alignment or an early rejection of very different fingerprints; a *consolidation* step is then performed to check whether the postulated coincidence hypotheses hold at global level.

Hrechak and McHugh (1990) associate an eight-dimensional feature vector $\mathbf{v}_i = [v_{i1}, v_{i2}, ..., v_{i8}]$ to each minutia $\mathbf{m}_i$, where v_{ij} is the number of occurrences of minutiae of type j in a neighborhood of the minutia $\mathbf{m}_i$. The minutiae types considered are dots, ridge endings, bifurcations, island, spurs, crossovers, bridges, and short ridges (ref. Section 3.1). These vectors are invariant with respect to fingerprint alignment and can be easily matched; however, the difficulty of automatically discriminating various minutiae types with sufficient reliability diminishes the practical applicability of this method.

Chen and Kuo (1991) and Wahab, Chin, and Tan (1998) enriched the local structures initially proposed by Hrechak and McHugh (1990) by including in the feature vectors: i) the distance and ii) the ridge count between the central minutia and each surrounding minutia, iii) the relative orientation of each surrounding minutia with respect to the central one, and iv) the angle between the orientation of the central minutia and the direction of the segment connecting the surrounding minutia to the central one. Local structures are then compared by correlation or tree-matching.

Fan, Liu, and Wang (2000) perform a geometric clustering of minutiae points. Each cluster is represented by the rectangular bounding box enclosing all the minutiae associated with it. During the matching stage, search for an optimal assignment between clusters of $\mathbf{T}$ and $\mathbf{I}$ is made by using a fuzzy bipartite weighted graph matching, where the clusters of $\mathbf{T}$ are the right nodes of a fuzzy bipartite weighted graph and the $\mathbf{I}$ clusters are the left nodes of the graph. Willis and Myers (2001) also group minutiae, by counting the number of minutiae falling inside the cells of a "dart board" pattern of wedges and rings; fixed-length feature vectors are obtained from the groupings which are partially invariant with respect to rotation and translation.

Jiang and Yau (2000) and Ratha et al. (2000) propose interesting two-stage minutiae matchers where a consolidation step is used to enforce the result of local matching. In Jiang and Yau (2000) local structures are formed by a central minutia and its two nearest-neighbor minutiae; the feature vector $\mathbf{v}_i$ associated with the minutia $\mathbf{m}_i$, whose nearest neighbors are minutiae $\mathbf{m}_j$ (the closest to $\mathbf{m}_i$) and $\mathbf{m}_k$ (the second closest) is:

$$\mathbf{v}_i = [d_{ij}, d_{ik}, \theta_{ij}, \theta_{ik}, \varphi_{ij}, \varphi_{ik}, n_{ij}, n_{ik}, t_i, t_j, t_k],$$

where d_{ab} is the distance between minutiae $\mathbf{m}_a$ and $\mathbf{m}_b$, θ_{ab} is the direction difference between the angles θ_a and θ_b of $\mathbf{m}_a$ and $\mathbf{m}_b$, φ_{ab} is the direction difference between the angle θ_a of $\mathbf{m}_a$ and the direction of the edge connecting $\mathbf{m}_a$ to $\mathbf{m}_b$, n_{ab} is the ridge count between $\mathbf{m}_a$ and $\mathbf{m}_b$, and t_a is the minutia type of $\mathbf{m}_a$ (Figure 4.13).

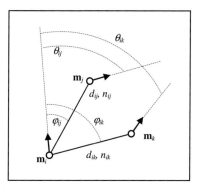

Figure 4.13. Features of the local structures used by Jiang and Yau (2000).

Local minutiae matching is performed by computing, for each pair of minutiae $\mathbf{m}_i$ and $\mathbf{m}'_j$, $i = 1..m$, $j = 1..n$, a weighted distance between their vectors $\mathbf{v}_i$ and $\mathbf{v}'_j$. The best matching pair is then selected and used for registering the two fingerprints. In the second stage (consolidation), the feature vectors of the remaining aligned pairs are matched and a final score is computed by taking into account the different contributions (first stage and second stage).

Ratha et al. (2000) more formally defined the concept of local structure by using graph notation. The *star* associated with the minutia $\mathbf{m}_i$ for a given distance $d_{\max}$ is the graph $S_i = (V_i, E_i)$ consisting of:

- the set of vertices V_i containing all the minutiae $\mathbf{m}_j$ whose distance $d(.,.)$ from $\mathbf{m}_i$ is less than or equal to $d_{\max}$: $V_i = \{ \mathbf{m}_j \mid sd(\mathbf{m}_i, \mathbf{m}_j) \leq d_{\max} \}$;
- the set of edges $E_i = \{\mathbf{e}_{ij}\}$, where $\mathbf{e}_{ij}$ is the edge connecting minutia $\mathbf{m}_i$ with minutia $\mathbf{m}_j$ in V_i; $\mathbf{e}_{ij}$ is labeled with a 5-tuple $(i, j, d(\mathbf{m}_i, \mathbf{m}_j), rc(\mathbf{m}_i, \mathbf{m}_j), \varphi_{ij})$, where $rc(\mathbf{m}_i, \mathbf{m}_j)$ is the ridge count between $\mathbf{m}_i$ and $\mathbf{m}_j$ and φ_{ij} is the angle subtended by the edge with the x-axis.

Figure 4.14 shows the star of a given minutia for two different values of d_{max}. During local minutiae matching, each star from **I** is matched against each star from **T**; given a starting edge pair, the matching between any two stars is performed by clockwise traversing the corresponding graphs in an increasing order of radial angles φ_{ij}. At the end of the first stage, a set TOP of best matching star pairs is returned, and during the consolidation stage, these pairs are checked for consistency: a pair of stars is consistent if their spatial relationships (distance and ridge count) with a minimum fraction of the remaining stars in TOP are consistent.

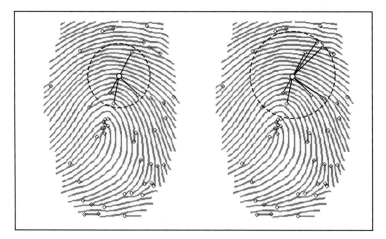

Figure 4.14. The stars of a given minutia for d_{max} = 70 (left) and d_{max} = 100 (right) (Ratha et al., 2000).

Variants of the Jiang and Yau (2000) and Ratha et al. (2000) two-stage approaches were introduced by Zhang and Wang (2002) and Lee, Choi, and Kim (2002). Zhang and Wang (2002) suggested using the core point as a reference point to speed up the initial local structure matching. Lee, Choi, and Kim (2002) argued that using more minutiae pairs (as reference pairs) to guide the consolidation step increases robustness when matching low-quality fingerprint images, where sometimes the best matching minutiae pair is unreliable; they also proposed normalizing the minutiae distance by the local ridge frequency to factor out the effect of local distortion.

Two quite atypical fingerprint matching approaches, classifiable as local minutiae matching, have been introduced by Maio and Maltoni (1995) and by Kovacs-Vajna (2000). Both these techniques operate asymmetrically; fingerprint enhancement and accurate minutiae extraction (which are time-consuming tasks) are performed only on the template fingerprint at enrollment time, resulting in the minutiae set **T**. During verification, the existence of a correspondence for each minutia in **T** is checked by locally searching the input fingerprint; this allows fingerprint verification to be executed very quickly.

Maio and Maltoni (1995) verified the minutiae existence by using their gray-scale-based minutiae detection algorithm (ref. Section 3.8); for each minutia in **T**; a neighborhood of the expected position in the input fingerprint is searched by tracking the ridge(s) in an attempt to establish a correspondence.

The Kovacs-Vajna (2000) method can be sketched as follows.

- the 16×16 gray-scale neighborhood of each minutia $\mathbf{m}_i$ of **T** is correlated with the gray-scale image **I** at all possible positions, and a list of *candidate positions* (i.e., those producing a very high correlation) is recorded;

- a triangular matching is carried out, where minutiae from **T** are incrementally matched with candidate positions from **I**. The matching starts by associating two minutiae from **T** with two candidate positions, and at each step, it is expanded by adding a pair (minutia, candidate position) that is compliant with the already created structure (Figure 4.15);

- the pairing obtained at the end of the above step is consolidated by checking the correspondence of gray-scale profiles between every pair of minutiae from **T** and the corresponding positions in **I**. Instead of explicitly computing the ridge count, Kovacs-Vajna (2000) matches gray-scale profiles via a dynamic time warping algorithm which is able to tolerate perturbations and small location errors.

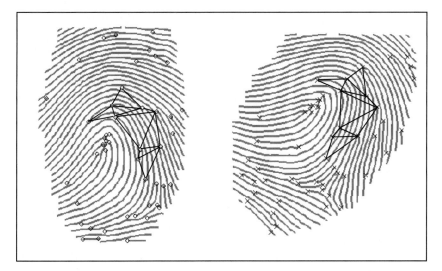

Figure 4.15. An example of partial triangular matching as proposed by Kovacs-Vajna (2000).

4.5 Dealing with Distortion

Non-linear distortion introduced when fingerprints are sensed is certainly one of the most critical intra-class variability. NIST Special Database 24 (Watson, 1998) contains videos of live-scan fingerprint data that clearly show the effect of distortion produced by users deliberately moving their fingers on the scanner surface once they are in contact.

Ratha and Bolle (1998) demonstrated that equipping a fingerprint scanner with a mechanical force sensor may help in controlling fingerprint acquisition and guiding the users toward a correct interaction with the sensor. Dorai, Ratha, and Bolle (2000) proposed an automatic method for detecting the presence of distortion from compressed fingerprint videos and rejecting the distorted frames. Unfortunately, most of the commercial acquisition devices do not mount force sensors and are not able to deliver images at a high frame rate and, therefore, the need for distortion-tolerant matchers is mandatory.

Although most of the matching algorithms discussed earlier incorporate ad hoc countermeasures to deal with distortion, few of them attempt to explicitly model fingerprint distortion. In general, distortion is dealt with by relaxing the spatial relationships between minutiae in the following ways.

- Global minutiae matching techniques use tolerance boxes (e.g., spheres), which allow pairing to be performed even if minutiae positions do not perfectly coincide. Unfortunately, because distortion may significantly alter the relative distance of two minutiae far away from the principal pair, large tolerance boxes need to be used. As a consequence, the probability of falsely matching fingerprints from different fingers increases.
- Tolerance boxes are defined in polar coordinates (sectors of circular annuluses) in the approaches by Jain et al. (1997) and Luo, Tian, and Wu (2000), where edit distance is used for matching pre-aligned minutiae. The size of the tolerance boxes is incrementally increased moving from the center toward the borders of the fingerprint area in order to compensate for the effect of distortion that spatially integrates.
- The local triangular matching proposed by Kovacs-Vajna (2000) allows only small local distortion but can tolerate large global distortion; in fact, the geometric aspect of the minutiae triangles that are incrementally constructed may differ only by a small percentage, but the spatial accumulation of small differences may result in a large correction.

A fingerprint matching technique that explicitly addresses the fingerprint distortion problem was proposed by Almansa and Cohen (2000). The authors introduced a 2D warping algorithm capable of mapping a fingerprint pattern into another one; the warping is controlled by an energy function that has to be minimized in order to find the optimal mapping. The first term of the energy function requires the two minutiae sets to spatially coincide, whereas the second term introduces a penalty that increases with the irregularity of the warping. Unfortunately, energy minimization is performed with a two-step iterative algorithm whose convergence may be critical and whose time complexity is high. For this reason, the authors suggest using their method to improve fingerprint minutiae matching once a coarse solution has been found through a simpler method.

The minutiae matching approach proposed by Bazen and Gerez (2002a) also attempts to find a smoothed mapping between the template and input minutiae. Minutiae pairing is initially computed through a local approach and a consolidation step; then the size of the tolerance boxes is reduced and a thin-plate spline model is used to deal with the non-linear distortions. Through an iterative procedure, which starts from the initial pairing, the minutiae in the input fingerprint are locally moved (according to the model smoothness constraints) to best fit the template minutiae. The authors report that they obtained a significant improvement when the distortion-tolerant matcher was used instead of the rigid matcher.

The most evident effect of distortion is the local compression/stretching of the fingerprint ridges and valley. To eliminate the undesired effects of distortion, Senior and Bolle (2001) proposed normalizing the fingerprint image to a *canonical* form by deriving a fingerprint representation where all the ridges are equally spaced. The fingerprint images are binarized and thinned, and ridge lines are approximated by spline curves. The average inter-ridge distance is then determined and two ridge dilatation maps are computed that encode the local deviation of the inter-ridge distance from the average one. Transformation into a canonical form is then performed by integration according to the two dilatation maps (Figure 4.16).

Figure 4.16. Transformation of a fingerprint skeleton (left) into canonical form (right) (Senior and Bolle, 2001). ©IEICE.

The canonical representation of a fingerprint is unaffected by distortion and a rigid matcher could, in principle, be used for direct comparison. In practice, the transformation into canonical representation and, in particular, a reliable estimation of the dilatation map can be quite critical in low-quality fingerprint images, and therefore a rigid matching technique is probably not the best choice. Furthermore, even though this approach can be adequate for a proprietary solution, such a canonical representation conflicts with efforts in establishing standard and interoperable fingerprint templates.

Another normalization technique was introduced by Lee, Choi, and Kim (2002). They normalized the minutiae distance during the matching stage instead of computing a canonical representation of the fingerprint. In particular, the distance between any two minutiae is normalized according to the local ridge frequency. Suppose that a portion of a fingerprint is distorted by a traction force that increases the distance between two minutiae; then the local ridge frequency decreases accordingly, and therefore, a simple normalization of the distance by the frequency results in a sort of distortion-tolerant distance. Lee, Choi, and Kim (2002) used normalized distances only for matching local minutiae arrangements; in fact, reliably estimating the ridge frequency profile between two minutiae that are far apart might introduce distance errors higher than those made by neglecting the effect of distortion.

Cappelli, Maio, and Maltoni (2001a) explicitly modeled skin distortion caused by non-orthogonal pressure of the finger against the sensor surface. By noting that the finger pressure against the sensor is not uniform but decreases from the center towards the borders, their distortion model defined three distinct regions (see Figure 4.17):

1. a close-contact region (a) where the high pressure and the surface friction do not allow any skin slippage;
2. an external region (c), whose boundary delimits the fingerprint visible area, where the light pressure allows the finger skin to be dragged by the finger movement;
3. a transitional region (b) where an elastic distortion is produced to smoothly combine regions a and c. The skin compression and stretching is restricted to region b, as points in a remain almost fixed and points in c rigidly move together with the rest of the finger.

The distortion model is defined by a mapping $\Re^2 \rightarrow \Re^2$ that can be viewed as an affine transformation (with no scale change) which is progressively "braked" as it moves from c towards a. Each point $\mathbf{v}$ is mapped into $distortion(\mathbf{v})$ such that:

$$distortion(\mathbf{v}) = \mathbf{v} + \Delta(\mathbf{v}) \cdot brake(shapedist_a(\mathbf{v}), k), \qquad (11)$$

where $\Delta(\cdot)$ specifies the affine transformation of a point of the external region c; $shapedist(\cdot)$ is a shape function describing the boundary of region a; $brake(\cdot)$ is a monotonically increasing function that rules the gradual transition from region a towards region c; the input parameter k regulates the skin plasticity. Figure 4.17.b shows some examples of distortion by varying the parameters.

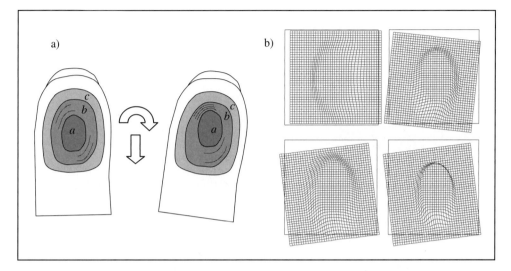

Figure 4.17. a) Bottom view of a finger before and after the application of traction and torsion forces. In both cases the fingerprint area detected by the sensor (i.e., the finger touching area) is delimited by the external boundary of region c. b) Distortions of a square mesh obtained by applying the above model with different parameter settings. The black square denotes the initial mesh position and its movement with respect to the mesh boundary indicates the amount of displacement and rotation that occurred. In the first row, two different transformations are shown: from left to right: a horizontal displacement ($\Delta x = 18$) and a combined displacement + rotation ($\Delta x = -6$, $\Delta y = 27$, $\theta = -6°$); the second row shows the effect of varying the skin plasticity coefficient k from 1.0 (left) and 0.5 (right) for a given transformation. Reprinted with permission from Cappelli, Maio, and Maltoni (2001a). ©Springer-Verlag.

Figure 4.18 shows an example of distortion recovery applied to fingerprint images; in the left column two distorted fingerprint images are shown and both their minutiae (denoted by small squares) and the corresponding minutiae (small circles) extracted from previous undistorted frames are superimposed. A displacement between pairs of corresponding minutiae is evident. In the central column, the same frames are shown, but now the minutiae from the non-distorted frames have been remapped by applying the distortion transformation. The good spatial minutiae matching obtained proves that the model is capable of dealing with such deformations. The model parameters have been manually adjusted and do not necessarily constitute the best choice. The corresponding mesh distortion is plotted in the third column and shows that, in the former case, the deformation is mainly caused by a vertical (downward) traction producing a compression at the top, whereas, in the latter, a (counterclockwise) torsion is the most evident cause. In this example, the ten parameters controlling the distortion model were manually adjusted to achieve optimal distortion recovery. The study of an effective and efficient optimization technique (eventually embedded into a minutiae matcher), which is capable of automatically deriving the deformation parameters, still remains a challenging research task.

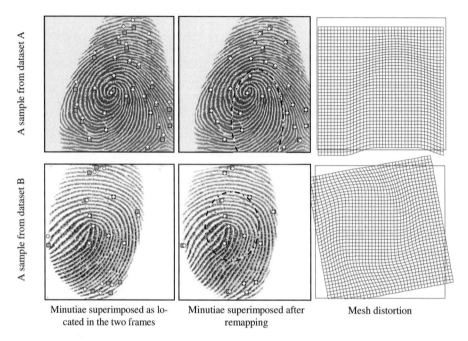

Figure 4.18. Minutiae correspondence before (first column) and after (second column) the distortion mapping. The third column shows the corresponding mesh distortion. Reprinted with permission from Cappelli, Maio, and Maltoni (2001a). ©Springer-Verlag.

4.6 Ridge Feature-based Matching Techniques

Three main reasons induce designers of fingerprint recognition techniques to search for other fingerprint distinguishing features, beyond minutiae:

- reliably extracting minutiae from poor quality fingerprints is very difficult. Although minutiae may carry most of the fingerprint discriminatory information, they do not always constitute the best tradeoff between accuracy and robustness;
- minutiae extraction is time consuming. This was a serious problem in the past, when the computational power of desktop computers was limited. Although computers are

much faster now, matching speed remains a concern because of the increasing interest in embedding fingerprint recognition algorithms in low-cost, standalone (embedded) systems. Furthermore, registering minutiae representation is very challenging;
minutiae-based matching algorithms are rather slow, especially for large-scale identification tasks;

- additional features may be used in conjunction with minutiae (and not as an alternative) to increase system accuracy and robustness.

The more commonly used alternative features are:

1. size of the fingerprint and shape of the external fingerprint silhouette;
2. number, type, and position of singularities;
3. spatial relationship and geometrical attributes of the ridge lines (Xiao and Bian
   (1986) and Kaymaz and Mitra (1992));
4. shape features (Takeda et al. (1990) and Ceguerra and Koprinska, 2002);
5. global and local texture information;
6. sweat pores (Stosz and Alyea, 1994);
7. fractal features (Polikarpova, 1996).

Features listed in 1) and 2) above are, in general, very unstable, and they vary depending on
which part of the finger touches the sensor. Sweat pores are undoubtedly highly discriminant
(as shown by Stosz and Alyea (1994)) but their detection requires high-resolution expensive
scanners.

The use of spatial relationship of ridges forms the basis of the structural methods proposed
by Moayer and Fu (1986) and Isenor and Zaky (1986). In the former, tree grammars are introduced to classify ridge line patterns after they are binarized and thinned. In the latter, incremental graph matching was carried out to compare a set of ridges arranged in graph structures
(ridges are the graph nodes and arches are defined according to ridge adjacency and visibility).

Ceguerra and Koprinska (2002) proposed shape-based features, where a compact one-
dimensional shape signature that encodes the general shape of the fingerprint is generated
from the two-dimensional fingerprint image using a reference axis (see also Takeda et al.
(1990)). Shape-based matching is then used together with the minutiae-based matching to
make the final matching decision.

Global and local texture information are important alternatives to minutiae- and texture-
based fingerprint matching is an active area of research. Textures are defined by spatial repetition of basic elements, and are characterized by properties such as scale, orientation, frequency, symmetry, isotropy, and so on. Fingerprint ridge lines (as discussed in Chapter 3) are
mainly described by smooth ridge orientation and frequency, except at singular regions. These
singular regions are discontinuities in a basically regular pattern and include the loop(s) and
the delta(s) at a coarse resolution and the minutiae points at a high resolution.

Coetzee and Botha (1993) and Willis and Myers (2001) proposed analyzing fingerprint
texture in the Fourier domain. Although ridges in the spatial domain transform to a fairly constant frequency (in the frequency domain), the distinguishing characteristics of a fingerprint
such as the specific ridge orientation and the minutiae manifest themselves as small deviations

from the dominant spatial frequency of the ridges. A "wedge-ring detector" is then used to perform the analysis in the frequency domain; the harmonics in each of the individual regions of the detector are accumulated, resulting in a fixed-length feature vector that is translation, rotation, and scale invariant. Global texture analysis fuses contributions from different characteristic regions into a global measurement and, as a result, most of the available spatial information is lost.

Local texture analysis has proved to be more effective than global feature analysis; although most of the local texture information is carried by the orientation and frequency images (ref. Sections 3.3 and 3.4), most of the proposed approaches extract texture by using a specialized bank of filters.

Jain et al. (2000) proposed a local texture analysis technique where the fingerprint area of interest is tessellated with respect to the core point (see Figure 4.19). A feature vector is composed of an ordered enumeration of the features extracted from the local information contained in each sector specified by the tessellation. Thus the feature elements capture the local texture information and the ordered enumeration of the tessellation captures the global relationship among the local contributions. The local texture information in each sector is decomposed into separate channels by using a Gabor filterbank (ref. Section 3.7); in fact, the Gabor filterbank is a well-known technique for capturing useful texture information in specific bandpass channels as well as decomposing this information into biorthogonal components in terms of spatial frequencies. In their experimentation, Jain et al. (2000) obtained good results by tessellating the area of interest into 80 cells (5 bands and 16 sectors), and by using a bank of 8 Gabor filters (8 orientations, 1 scale = 1/10 for 500 dpi fingerprint images). Therefore, each fingerprint is represented by a $80 \times 8 = 640$ fixed-size feature vector, called the *FingerCode*. The generic element V_{ij} of the vector ($i = 1..80$ is the cell index, $j = 1..8$ is the filter index) denotes the energy revealed by the filter j in cell i, and is computed as the average absolute deviation (AAD) from the mean of the responses of the filter j over all the pixels of the cell i:

$$V_{ij} = \frac{1}{n_i}\left(\sum_{C_i}\left| g(x, y : \theta_j, 1/10) - \overline{g_i}\right|\right),$$

where C_i is the ith cell of the tessellation, n_i is the number of pixels in C_i, the Gabor filter expression $g(.)$ is defined by Equation (5) in Section 3.7 and $\overline{g_i}$ is the mean value of g over the cell C_i. Matching two fingerprints is then translated into matching their respective FingerCodes, which is simply performed by computing the Euclidean distance between two FingerCodes.

From experimentation results over two fingerprint databases, Jain et al. (2000) concluded that although FingerCodes are not as distinctive as minutiae, they carry complementary information which, as they explicitly demonstrated, can be combined with minutiae to improve the overall matching accuracy.

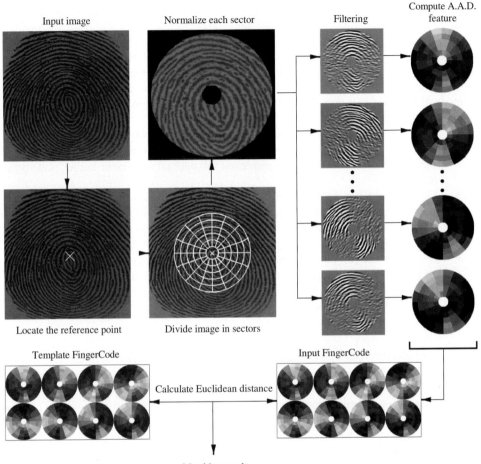

Figure 4.19. System diagram of Jain et al.'s (2000) FingerCode approach. ©IEEE.

One critical point in the above approach is the alignment of the grid defining the tessellation with respect to the core point. When the core point cannot be reliably detected, or it is close to the border of the fingerprint area, the FingerCode of the input fingerprint may be incomplete or incompatible with respect to the template. Jain, Ross, and Prabhakar (2001) and Ross, Jain, and Reisman (2002) propose variants of the above method, suitable for small-area capacitive sensors, where tessellation is performed over a square mesh grid after the two fingerprints have been aligned by using minutiae. A different way to overcome the critical core-based alignment is to use a feature-space correlation technique to simultaneously align and match the FingerCodes (Ross, Reisman, and Jain, 2002).

Two variants of the Jain et al. (2000) approach were introduced by Lee and Wang. In Lee and Wang (1999), instead of convolving the Gabor filters with all the pixels of each cell, the authors performed a sub-sampling at block level with the aim of improving efficiency. In Lee and Wang (2001), instead of recording the response of each filter at each sampling point, only the index of the filter that give the highest response was stored and used for subsequent fingerprint comparison.

Finally, other techniques based on local texture analysis were proposed as follows.

- Hamamoto (1999) applied Gabor filters at nine fixed positions around the core and used correlation between filter responses for optimal alignment during fingerprint matching;
- Tico, Kuosmanen, and Saarinen (2001) suggested using wavelet domain features, and claimed that their method achieved performance comparable with the Gabor-based one, but had the advantage of avoiding any pre-processing such as core point detection;
- Nilsson and Bigun (2001), computed the Linear Symmetry (LS) on a circle around each minutia, and classified minutiae according to the LS in their neighborhood. The minutiae classification was then exploited during fingerprint matching to simplify minutiae pairing and to increase minutiae distinctiveness.

4.7 Comparing the Performance of Matching Algorithms

Throughout this chapter several techniques for fingerprint matching have been surveyed and the pros and cons of different approaches have been highlighted. However, an explicit answer has not been provided to the question: what is the best algorithm for matching fingerprints? The two main reasons why it is difficult to assess the relative performance of the various matching algorithms are as follows.

- The performance of a fingerprint recognition method involves a tradeoff among different performance measures: accuracy (e.g., FMR and FNMR), efficiency (enrollment time, verification time), scalability to 1:N identification, template size, and so on. Different applications have different performance requirements. For example, an application may prefer a fingerprint matching algorithm that is lower in accuracy but has a small template size over an algorithm that is more accurate but uses a large template size;
- most of the scientific work published in the literature includes experimental results carried out on proprietary databases using different protocols, which are usually not shared with the research community. This makes it difficult to compare the results of

different methods; the performance measured is related to the "difficulty" of the benchmark.

Before the fingerprint verification competitions FVC2000 (Maio et al., 2002a) and FVC2002 (Maio et al., 2002b), the only large public domain fingerprint datasets were the National Institute of Standards and Technology (NIST) databases; although these databases constitute an excellent benchmark for AFIS development (Shen and Khanna, 1994) and fingerprint classification studies (ref. Chapter 5), they are not well suited for the evaluation of algorithms operating with live-scan (dab) images. In fact:

- NIST DB 4 (Watson and Wilson, 1992a), NIST DB 9 (Watson and Wilson, 1992b), NIST DB 10 (Watson, 1993b), and NIST DB 14 (Watson, 1993a) contain thousands of images scanned from rolled inked impressions on cards, which are quite different from live-scan dab images;
- NIST DB 24 (Watson, 1998) contains 100 live sequences (capture video) from ten individuals. In principle, static frames could be extracted from the videos and used for performance evaluation; on the other hand, most of the videos have been taken under particular conditions to study the effect of finger rotation and plastic distortion, and therefore are not well suited for overall system evaluations;
- NIST DB 27 (Garris and McCabe, 2000) was released to test the performance of latent fingerprint identification. Latent fingerprint images of varying quality were provided together with their corresponding rolled impressions taken from cards. Minutiae data manually extracted by human experts were also provided. NIST DB 27 is a valuable source of information for studying the difficult problems of latent fingerprint enhancement and matching.

FVC2000 and FVC2002 were organized with the aim of providing fingerprint databases to any interested researcher and to track performance of the state-of-the-art fingerprint matching algorithms. Fortunately, several authors now report the results of their experiments on these databases according to the proposed protocol, thus producing results that can be compared across the whole scientific community. It is hoped that this will become a common practice for scientists and practitioners in the field. For this purpose, we have included the four FVC2002, the four FVC2000 databases, and both the FVC2002 and FVC2000 reports in the DVD accompanying this book. The reader is invited to consult the reports where he will find all the details necessary to set up a test session identical to that performed in the two competitions.

Readers interested in measuring the performance of a biometric system (including fingerprints) in a real environment or specific application (see Section 1.5) should read the document "Best Practices in Testing and Reporting Performance of Biometric Devices" by UKBWG (2002). In fact, volunteer selection, operational conditions, and several other issues have to be taken into consideration when a test is performed in a laboratory or in the field. Other interesting readings on biometric system performance evaluation include Bradley (1981), Golfarelli, Maio, and Maltoni (1997), Jain, Prabhakar, and Ross (1999), Wayman (1999a, b), Phillips et al. (2000), Bolle, Ratha, and Pankanti (2000), and Pankanti, Ratha, and Bolle (2002).

To conclude this section, we caution practitioners against these common mistakes in evaluating the performance of their matching algorithms:

- avoid using the same dataset for training, validating, and testing an algorithm;
- do not compute performance on a very small dataset, and in particular abstain from claiming that a system has a very low error rate when the errors have been measured over a small dataset;
- avoid "cleaning" the database by removing samples that are either "rejected" or mis-classified by the system; in principle, by iteratively removing the fastidious samples, one could reach the desired level of accuracy;
- do not conclude that the accuracy of a system is better than that of a competing system when they were evaluated over different datasets;
- do not hide the weak points of an algorithm, but document its failures.

4.8 Summary

Different applications desire different properties in the fingerprint matching algorithms (e.g., template size, matching speed, memory requirements, etc.). The algorithms developed so far have taken a generalized approach (they have tried to optimize all the properties at the same time). With increasing interaction of the market and applications, it is likely that different matching algorithms will be developed for different applications. For example, embedded applications such as cell phones, PDA, and smartcards (match-on-card) will benefit from an algorithm with low computational complexity and eventually small template size. Similarly, mission-critical applications that may allow arbitrary resources but no matching errors will require extremely accurate response irrespective of computation and storage requirements.

Most of the fingerprint matching approaches introduced in the last four decades are minutiae-based, but recently correlation-based techniques are receiving renewed interest. New texture-based methods have been proposed and the integration of approaches relying on different features seems to be the most promising way to significantly improve the accuracy of fingerprint recognition systems.

Alignment of the input fingerprint representation with the database template representation remains a difficult problem, especially when the representations contain a large amount of errors (e.g., several false and missed minutiae due to poor image quality). Current fingerprint matching algorithms use rather ad hoc techniques to account for the non-linear distortion introduced in the fingerprint when a finger is pressed against the sensor surface. A complete understanding (and modeling) of distortion in fingerprint images and their association with human behavior (e.g., application of high or low pressure, shear, squirm, wiggle, etc.) will not only help in improving the matching accuracy but also in designing registration and user-training modules that provide "intelligent" feedback to the users (e.g., "apply less/more pressure," "do not wiggle," "move finger so that it is parallel to the sensor," "place the finger on the sensor by moving orthogonally to the sensor," etc.), which will be especially useful in fully automatic unattended fingerprint-based recognition systems.

5
Fingerprint Classification and Indexing

5.1 Introduction

The identification of a person requires a comparison of her fingerprint with all the fingerprints in a database. This database may be very large (e.g., several million fingerprints) in many forensic and civilian applications. In such cases, the identification typically has an unacceptably long response time. The identification process can be speeded up by reducing the number of comparisons that are required to be performed. Sometimes, information about sex, race, age, and other data related to the individual are available and the portion of the database to be searched can be significantly reduced; however, this information is not always accessible (e.g., criminal identification based on latent fingerprints) and, in the general case, information intrinsic to the biometric samples has to be used for an efficient retrieval. A common strategy to achieve this is to divide the fingerprint database into a number of bins (based on some predefined classes). A fingerprint to be identified is then required to be compared only to the fingerprints in a single bin of the database based on its class.

Fingerprint classification refers to the problem of assigning a fingerprint to a class in a consistent and reliable way. although fingerprint matching is usually performed according to local features (e.g., minutiae), fingerprint classification is generally based on global features, such as global ridge structure and singularities.

The first fingerprint classification rules were proposed in 1823 by Purkinje (Moenssens, 1971), who classified fingerprints into nine categories (transverse curve, central longitudinal stria, oblique stripe, oblique loop, almond whorl, spiral whorl, ellipse, circle, and double whorl) according to the global ridge configurations. The first in-depth scientific study on fingerprint classification was made by Francis Galton, who divided the fingerprints into three major classes (arch, loop, and whorl) and further divided each category into subcategories (Galton, 1892). Around the same time, Juan Vucetich, an Argentine police official, developed a different system of classification; the Vucetich classification system is still used in many Spanish-speaking countries. Vucetich was also the first to make a fingerprint identification of a suspect in 1892. Ten years later, Edward Henry refined Galton's classification by increasing the number of classes (Henry, 1900); the Galton–Henry classification scheme was adopted in several countries: in fact, most of the classification schemes currently used by law enforcement agencies worldwide are variants of the Galton–Henry classification scheme. Figure 5.1 shows the five most common classes of the Galton–Henry classification scheme (*arch, tented arch, left loop, right loop,* and *whorl*):

- an arch fingerprint has ridges that enter from one side, rise to a small bump, and go out the opposite side from which they entered. Arches do not have loops or deltas;
- a tented arch fingerprint is similar to the (plain) arch, except that at least one ridge exhibits a high curvature and one loop and one delta are present;
- a loop fingerprint has one or more ridges that enter from one side, curve back, and go out the same side they entered. A loop and a delta singularities are present; the delta is assumed to be south of the loop. Loops can be further subdivided: loops that have ridges that enter and leave from the left side are called left loops and loops that have ridges that enter and leave from the right side are called right loops;
- a whorl fingerprint contains at least one ridge that makes a complete 360-degree path around the center of the fingerprint. Two loops (or a whorl) and two deltas can be found in whorl fingerprints. The whorl class is quite complex and in some classification schemes, it is further divided into two categories: twin loop (or double loop) and plain whorl (see Figure 5.1).

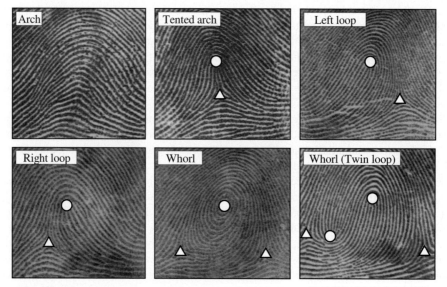

Figure 5.1. The five commonly used fingerprint classes: two whorl fingerprints are shown (a plain whorl and a twin loop, respectively).

Fingerprint classification is a difficult pattern recognition problem due to the small inter-class variability and the large intra-class variability in the fingerprint patterns (Figure 5.2). Moreover, fingerprint images often contain noise, which makes the classification task even more difficult (Figure 5.3). Several methods have been proposed for automatic fingerprint classification: Section 5.2 presents a survey of the main approaches in the literature; in Section 5.3, the performance of several classification approaches on some publicly available databases is summarized.

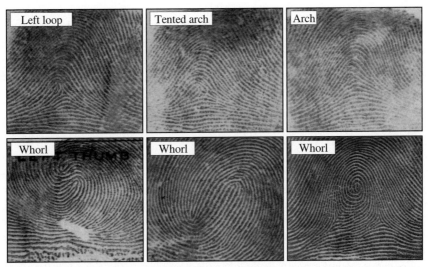

Figure 5.2. Top row: three fingerprints belonging to different classes that have similar appearance (small inter-class variability). Bottom row: three fingerprints belonging to the same class that have very different characteristics (large intra-class variability).

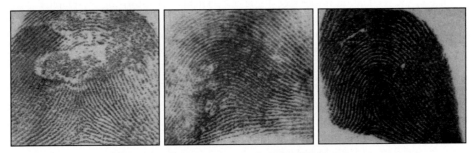

Figure 5.3. Examples of noisy fingerprint images.

The selectivity of classification-based techniques strongly depends on the number of classes and the natural distribution of fingerprints in these classes. Unfortunately, the number of classes used is often small and the fingerprints are non-uniformly distributed in these classes. For example, most automatic systems use five classes (i.e., arch, tented arch, left loop, right loop, and whorl) and the natural proportion of fingerprints in these classes is 3.7, 2.9, 33.8, 31.7 and 27.9%, respectively (Wilson, Candela, and Watson, 1994). Furthermore, there are many "ambiguous" fingerprints, whose exclusive membership cannot be reliably stated even by human experts. Nevertheless, exclusive classification allows the efficiency of the 10-print identification[1] to be improved, because knowledge of the classes of the 10 fingerprints can be used as a code for reducing the number of comparisons at minutiae level. On the other hand, a fingerprint classification approach does not offer sufficient selectivity for latent fingerprint searching.[2] For applications where there is no need to comply with an existing classification schema, some authors have proposed methods based on "continuous classification" or on other indexing techniques; these approaches are addressed in Section 5.4.

5.2 Classification Techniques

Fingerprint classification problem has attracted a significant amount of interest in the scientific community due to its importance and intrinsic difficulty, and a large number of papers have been published on this topic during the last 30 years. Although a wide variety of classification algorithms has been developed for this problem, a relatively small number of features extracted from fingerprint images have been used by most of the authors. In particular, almost all the methods are based on one or more of the following features (Figure 5.4): *ridge line flow, orientation image, singular points*, and *Gabor filter responses*. The ridge line flow is usually represented as a set of curves running parallel to the ridge lines; these curves do not necessarily coincide with the fingerprint ridges and valleys, but they exhibit the same local orientation. The ridge line flow can be traced by drawing curves locally oriented according to the orientation image (Candela et al., 1995). Most of the existing fingerprint classification approaches make use of the orientation image (see Table 5.1). This is not surprising inasmuch as such a feature, if computed with sufficient accuracy and detail, contains all the information required for the classification. Usually the orientation image is registered with respect to the core point (see Section 3.6) before being processed further. Furthermore, some authors (Cappelli et al. (1999) and Candela et al. (1995)) proposed specific enhancement techniques for the orientation image **D**, which allow higher accuracy to be achieved in the successive classification

---

1 Fingerprints from the ten fingers of an individual are compared with the corresponding fingerprints from known individuals (e.g., convicted criminals).

2 A latent fingerprint (typically lifted from a crime scene) is compared to all the fingerprints in a database.

stages; these techniques work by strengthening the orientation elements located in the most distinctive regions of the fingerprint image.

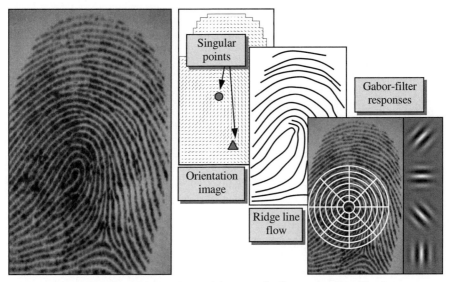

Figure 5.4. Most frequently used features for fingerprint classification.

In Cappelli et al. (1999), the enhancement is performed in two steps (Figure 5.5): the effects of noise (which affects the border elements significantly) is reduced through the application of a Gaussian-like attenuation function (*att*), which progressively reduces the magnitude of the elements $\mathbf{d}$ of $\mathbf{D}$ moving from the center towards the borders, thus obtaining the new elements $\mathbf{d}'$:

$$\mathbf{d}' = \mathbf{d} \cdot att(\mathbf{d}, \sigma_1), \qquad \text{where} \quad att(\mathbf{d}, \sigma) = \frac{1}{\sqrt{2\pi} \cdot \sigma} e^{-\left(distc(\mathbf{d})^2 / 2\sigma^2\right)}; \tag{1}$$

$distc(\mathbf{v})$ returns the distance of $\mathbf{d}$ from the center of the image and σ is the scale of the Gaussian function. Then, to increase the significance of the distinctive elements, the elements located in the irregular regions are strengthened by calculating, for each $\mathbf{d}'$:

$$str_{\mathbf{d}'} = 1 - \left| \sum_{\mathbf{d}' \in W_{5\times5}} \mathbf{d}' \right| / \sum_{\mathbf{d}' \in W_{5\times5}} |\mathbf{d}'|. \tag{2}$$

$str_{\mathbf{d}'}$ is a measure of irregularity of the 5×5 neighborhood of $\mathbf{d}'$ (denoted by $W_{5\times5}$). The final enhanced orientation image is made up of vectors $\mathbf{d}''$ such that:

$$\mathbf{d}'' = \mathbf{d}' \cdot \left(1 + R_m \cdot \overline{str_{\mathbf{d}'}} \cdot att\left(\mathbf{d}', \sigma_2\right)\right),$$ (3)

where R_m is a weighting factor and $\overline{str_{\mathbf{d}'}}$ is the local average of $str_{\mathbf{d}'}$ over a 3×3 window.

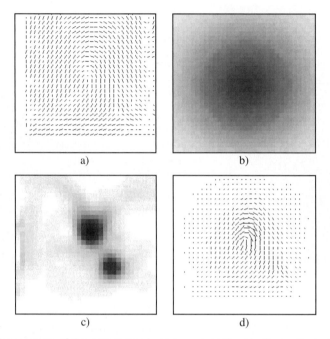

Figure 5.5. Enhancement of the orientation image as described in Cappelli et al. (1999): a) orientation image; b) Gaussian map obtained by applying the function *att*; c) irregularity map $str_{\mathbf{d}'}$; d) enhanced orientation image.

Most of the existing fingerprint classification methods can be coarsely assigned to one of these categories: *rule-based, syntactic, structural, statistical, neural network-based* and *multi-classifier* approaches. Table 5.1 highlights the features used and the classification strategy adopted by fingerprint classification methods published over the last 30 years. Fingerprint classification is one of the most representative pattern recognition problems; by observing the table, one can retrace the last three decades of research in the pattern recognition field: the interest in syntactical approaches in the 1970s/1980s, and the success of neural networks in the 1990s and of multiple classifier systems in recent years.

Fingerprint classification approach	Features				Classifier					
	O	S	R	G	Rb	Sy	Str	Sta	Nn	Mc
Moayer and Fu (1975)	√					√				
Moayer and Fu (1976)	√					√				
Rao and Balck (1980)	√					√				
Kawagoe and Tojo (1984)		√	√		√					
Hughes and Green (1991)	√								√	
Bowen (1992)	√	√							√	
Kamijo, Mieno, and Kojima (1992)	√								√	
Moscinska and Tyma (1993)	√				√				√	
Kamijo (1993)	√								√	
Wilson, Candela, and Watson (1994)	√								√	
Omidvar, Blue, and Wilson (1995)	√								√	
Candela et al. (1995)	√		√		√				√	√
Maio and Maltoni (1996)	√						√			
Halici and Ongun (1996)	√								√	
Karu and Jain (1996)		√			√					
Chong et al. (1997)			√		√					
Ballan, Sakarya, and Evans (1997)		√			√					
Senior (1997)			√				√			
Wei, Yuan, and Jie (1998)	√				√				√	√
Cappelli et al. (1999)	√						√			
Lumini, Maio, and Maltoni (1999)	√						√			
Jain, Prabhakar, and Hong (1999)				√				√	√	√
Hong and Jain (1999)		√	√		√					√
Cappelli, Maio, and Maltoni (1999)	√							√		
Cappelli, Maio, and Maltoni (2000a)	√							√		√
Cho et al. (2000)		√			√					
Bartesaghi, Fernández, and Gómez (2001)		√			√					
Bernard et al. (2001)	√								√	
Pattichis et al. (2001)	√				√				√	√
Marcialis, Roli, and Frasconi (2001)	√			√			√	√	√	√
Senior (2001)	√		√		√		√		√	√
Yao, Frasconi, and Pontil (2001)				√				√		√
Cappelli, Maio, and Maltoni (2002a)	√							√		√
Jain and Minut (2002)			√		√					

Table 5.1. A chronological review of several fingerprint classification methods: each work is labeled according to the features used (**O** = orientation image, **S** = singularities, **R** = ridge flow, **G** = Gabor) and the classification technique (**Rb** = rule-based, **Sy** = syntactic, **Str** = structural, **Sta** = statistical, **Nn** = neural network, **Mc** = multiple classifiers).

Rule-based approaches

A fingerprint can be simply classified according to the number and the position of the singularities (see Table 5.2 and Figure 5.1); this is the approach commonly used by human experts
for manual classification, therefore several authors proposed to adopt the same technique for
automatic classification.

Fingerprint class	Singular points
Arch	No singular points
Tented arch, Left loop, Right loop	One loop and one delta
Whorl	Two loops (or a whorl) and two deltas

Table 5.2. Singular points in the five fingerprint classes.

In Kawagoe and Tojo (1984), the Poincaré index (see Section 3.6) is exploited to find type
and position of the singular points and a coarse classification (according to Table 5.2) is derived. Then, a finer classification is obtained by tracing the ridge line flow. Discrimination
among tented arch, left loop, and right loop is performed according to the inclination of the
central trace (Figure 5.6). The authors also try to distinguish between plain whorl and twin
loop; for this purpose, two parameters (*twinness* and *flatness*) are calculated (see Figure 5.6)
and an empirical rule is adopted to make the final decision.

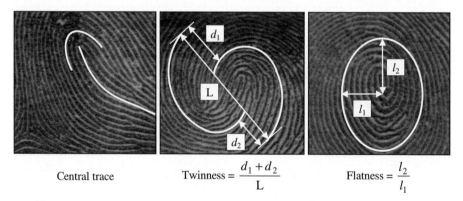

Central trace $\text{Twinness} = \dfrac{d_1 + d_2}{L}$ $\text{Flatness} = \dfrac{l_2}{l_1}$

Figure 5.6. Central trace, twinness, and flatness as defined by Kawagoe and Tojo (1984).

Although singularity-based methods are attractive for their simplicity, some problems arise
in the presence of noisy or partial fingerprints, where singularity detection can be extremely

difficult. In Karu and Jain (1996) an iterative regularization (by smoothing the orientation image with a 3×3 box filter) is carried out until a valid number of singular points are detected; this allows reducing noise and consequently improving classification accuracy. The criterion used to discriminate tented arches from loops consists of connecting the two singularities with a straight line and measuring the average difference between the local orientations along the line and the slope of the line itself. A fingerprint is classified as a tented arch if:

$$\frac{1}{n} \sum_{i=1}^{n} \sin(\alpha_i - \beta) \le 0.2 , \qquad (4)$$

where β is the slope of the line and α_i, $i = 1..n$, are the local orientations of elements lying along the straight line. Further discrimination between right and left loops is performed according to the relative position of the delta singularity with respect to the loop singularity.

Other classification strategies similar to the two described above can be found in Ratha et al. (1996), Ballan, Sakarya, and Evans (1997), and Bartesaghi, Fernández, and Gómez (2001). In Hong and Jain (1999) a more robust technique is proposed: the authors introduced a rule-based classification algorithm that uses the number of singularities together with the number of recurring ridges found in the image; the combination of these two distinct features leads to a performance better than that found in Karu and Jain (1996).

A further problem with the singularity-based approaches is that, although they may work reasonably well on *rolled* (nail-to-nail) fingerprint impressions scanned from cards, they are not suitable to be used on *dab* (live-scan) fingerprint images, because delta points are often missing in these types of images. Cho et al. (2000) propose a method that uses only the loop points and classifies fingerprints according to the curvature and orientation of the fingerprint area near the loop. Chong et al. (1997) and Jain and Minut (2002) propose rule-based approaches that do not search for any singularity: the classification is based on the geometrical shape of the ridge lines. In Chong et al. (1997), B-spline curves (Bartels, Beatty, and Barsky, 1987) are used to model fingerprint ridge lines, adjacent curves are merged to limit noise artifacts, and the classification is performed by tracing the resulting curves in order to detect turns (i.e., complete direction changes). In Jain and Minut (2002), for each class, a fingerprint kernel (which models the shape of fingerprints in that class) is defined; the classification is then performed by finding the kernel that best fits the orientation field of the given fingerprint.

Syntactic approaches

A syntactic method describes patterns by means of terminal symbols and production rules; a grammar is defined for each class and a parsing process is responsible for classifying each new pattern (Fu and Booth, 1986a, b).

In Moayer and Fu (1973) the authors proposed a syntactic approach where terminal symbols are associated with small groups of orientation elements within the fingerprint orientation image; a class of context-free grammars is used to describe the fingerprint patterns, which are divided into seven classes (see also Moayer and Fu (1975)). The same authors also experimented with other types of grammars: stochastic grammars (Moayer and Fu, 1976) and tree grammars (Moayer and Fu, 1986).

The approach introduced by Rao and Balck (1980) is based on the analysis of ridge line flow, which is represented by a set of connected lines (Figure 5.7). These lines are labeled according to the direction changes, thus obtaining a set of strings that are processed through ad hoc grammars or string-matching techniques to derive the final classification (Figure 5.7).

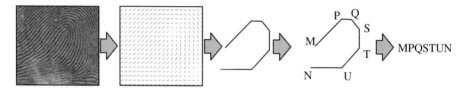

Figure 5.7. A schema of the string-construction approach in Rao and Balck (1980).

Other syntactic approaches were proposed by Tou and Hankley (1968) and Grasselli (1969), whose methods were based on context-free grammars and by Verma and Chatterjee (1989), who adopted regular grammars.

In general, due to the great diversity of fingerprint patterns, syntactic approaches require very complex grammars whose inference requires complicated and unstable approaches; for this reason, the use of syntactic methods for fingerprint classification has been almost abandoned, with a few exceptions (Chang and Fan, 2002).

Structural approaches

Structural approaches are based on the relational organization of low-level features into higher-level structures. This relational organization is represented by means of symbolic data structures, such as trees and graphs, which allow a hierarchical organization of the information (Bunke, 1993).

The orientation image is well suited for structural representation: in fact, it can be partitioned into connected regions that are characterized by "homogeneous" orientations; these regions and the relations among them contain information useful for classification. This is the basic idea of the method proposed by Maio and Maltoni (1996): the orientation image is partitioned into regions by minimizing a cost function that takes into account the variance of the element orientations within each region (Figure 5.8). An inexact graph matching technique is then used to compare the relational graphs with class-prototype graphs (see also Lumini, Maio, and Maltoni, 1999).

Although relational graph approaches have interesting properties (such as invariance to rotation and displacement, and the possibility of handling partial fingerprints), it is not easy to robustly partition the orientation image into homogeneous regions, especially in poor quality fingerprints. In Cappelli et al. (1999), a template-based matching is performed to guide the partitioning of the orientation images (Figure 5.9): the main advantage of the approach is that, because it relies only on global structural information, it is able to deal with partial fingerprints, where sometimes, singular points are not available, and it can also work on very noisy images.

Senior (1997) adopted a hidden Markov model classifier for fingerprint classification; the input features are the measurements taken at the intersection points between some horizontal and vertical "fiducial lines" and the ridge lines. At each intersection, the features extracted are: the local orientation of the ridge lines, the distance and the change in orientation since the last intersection, and the curvature of the ridge line at the intersection. Since hidden Markov models are inherently one-dimensional, the two-dimensional fingerprint pattern is linearized by nesting its rows, thus obtaining a unique sequence of observations.

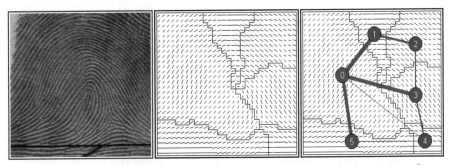

Figure 5.8. Classification approach of Maio and Maltoni (1996): from left to right: a fingerprint image, the partitioning of its orientation image, and the corresponding relational graph. ©IEEE.

Statistical approaches

In statistical approaches, a fixed-size numerical feature vector is derived from each fingerprint and a general-purpose statistical classifier is used for the classification.

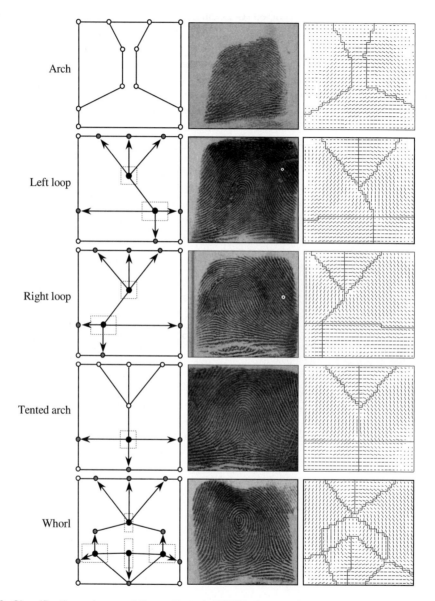

Figure 5.9. Classification scheme of Cappelli et al. (1999): the templates corresponding to the five classes and an example of application of each template to the orientation image of a fingerprint belonging to the corresponding class. ©IEEE.

One of the most widely adopted statistical classifiers is the k-nearest neighbor (Jain, Duin, and Mao, 2000); examples of its application in the fingerprint-classification domain can be found in Fitz and Green (1996), where wedge-ring features obtained from the hexagonal Fourier transform are used as input, and in Jain, Prabhakar, and Hong (1999), where the first step of a two-stage classification technique is performed by means of the k-nearest neighbor rule (see the following subsection "Multiple Classifier-based Approaches").

Many approaches directly use the orientation image as a feature vector, by simply nesting its rows (see, for instance, Cappelli, Maio, and Maltoni (1999) and Candela et al. (1995)). By encoding each element of the orientation image with the two components [$r \cdot \cos 2\theta$, $r \cdot \sin 2\theta$] (see Equation (1) in Section 3.3), a typical 30×30 orientation image results in a vector of 1800 elements. Training a classifier with such high-dimensional vectors would require large amounts of training data, memory, and computation time. For this reason, statistical dimensionality reduction techniques are often applied to reduce the dimensionality of the feature vector. The Karhunen–Loève (KL) transform (Jolliffe, 1986) is usually adopted for this purpose, as it guarantees a good preservation of Euclidean distances between vectors (see, for instance, Wilson, Candela, and Watson (1994) and Halici and Ongun (1996)).

The KL transform, besides being used for dimensionality reduction, can also be adopted for the classification itself. In Cappelli, Maio, and Maltoni (1999) and Cappelli, Maio, and Maltoni (2000a) a generalization of the KL transform called MKL (which was given in a more general context in Cappelli, Maio, and Maltoni (2001b)) was used for representing and classifying feature vectors derived from orientation images. The underlying idea of the approach was to find, for each class, one or more KL subspaces that were well suited to represent the fingerprints belonging to that class. These subspaces were created according to an optimization criterion that attempted to minimize the average mean square reconstruction error over a representative training set (Figure 5.10). The number of subspaces for each class was fixed a priori according to the class "complexity"; in particular, more subspaces were created for complex classes (e.g., whorl). The classification of an unknown fingerprint was performed according to its distances from all the KL subspaces. For example, in Figure 5.10, three KL subspaces (S_1, S_2, S_3) have been computed from a training set containing elements from the two classes A and B: subspaces S_1 and S_2 have been obtained from the elements in A, and S_3 has been obtained from those in B. Given a new vector $\mathbf{x}$, the distances from the three subspaces (d_1, d_2, and d_3) contain useful information for its classification. In Cappelli, Maio, and Maltoni (1999) the classification was simply performed according to the minimum distance from the MKL subspaces, whereas in Cappelli, Maio, and Maltoni (2000a) the results of both minimum distance and k-nearest neighbor classifiers were reported.

Neural network-based approaches

Most of the proposed neural network approaches are based on multilayer perceptrons and use the elements of the orientation image as input features (Hughes and Green (1991), Bowen

(1992), Kamijo, Mieno, and Kojima (1992), Kamijo (1993), and Pal and Mitra (1996)). Kamijo (1993) presents an interesting pyramidal architecture constituted of several multilayer perceptrons, each of which is trained to recognize fingerprints belonging to a different class. In Bowen (1992), the location of the singularities is used together with a 20×20 orientation image for the training of two disjoint neural networks, whose outputs are passed to a third one, which produces the final classification. Jain, Prabhakar, and Hong (1999) train 10 feed-forward neural networks to distinguish between each possible pair of classes (this method is described in more detail in the following subsection).

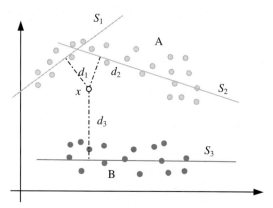

Figure 5.10. A two-dimensional example of the MKL transform (Cappelli, Maio, and Maltoni, 2001b), where two subspaces (S_1, S_2) and one subspace (S_3) are used to represent classes A and B, respectively.

One of the best-known neural network approaches to fingerprint classification was proposed by NIST researchers (Wilson, Candela, and Watson, 1994). This work was the result of previous studies aimed at: comparing different types of classifiers for fingerprint classification (Candela and Chellappa (1993) and Blue et al. (1993)), evaluating different fingerprint enhancement techniques (Watson, Candela, and Grother, 1994) and improving classification accuracy (Wilson et al., 1992). In Wilson, Candela, and Watson (1994) a multilayer perceptron is used for classification after reducing the dimensionality of the feature vector as explained in the previous subsection. Improved versions of this method are presented in Omidvar, Blue, and Wilson (1995), where specific changes and optimizations are introduced in the network architecture, and in Candela et al. (1995), which is described in the following subsection.

Finally, some researchers proposed the use of self-organizing neural networks: Moscinska and Tyma (1993), Halici and Ongun (1996), and Bernard et al. (2001). In Moscinska and Tyma (1993), a Kohonen map is trained to find delta points, and a rule-based approach is applied for the final classification; in Halici and Ongun (1996) a multilayer self-organizing map provides the classification.

Multiple classifier-based approaches

Different classifiers potentially offer complementary information about the patterns to be classified, which may be exploited to improve performance; in fact, in a number of pattern classification studies, it has been observed that different classifiers often misclassify different patterns (see Chapter 7 for an introduction to multiple classifiers). This motivates the recent interest in combining different approaches for the fingerprint classification task.

Several choices are possible for the selection of the component classifiers (e.g., different classifiers trained on the same data, the same classifier trained on different data, different input features) and for the combination strategy (from simple heuristic criteria of majority vote rule to more complex techniques that involve training an additional classifier for the final decision). Table 5.3 compares some fingerprint classification approaches that adopt different combination techniques.

	Distinct features	Distinct classifiers	Distinct training sets	Combination strategy
Candela et al. (1995)	Yes	Yes	No	Rule-based
Jain, Prabhakar, and Hong (1999)	No	Yes	No	Sequential (two stages)
Cappelli, Maio, and Maltoni (2000a)	No	Yes	Yes	Majority vote rule
Senior (2001)	Yes	Yes	No	Neural network
Marcialis, Roli, and Frasconi (2001)	Yes	Yes	No	k-nearest neighbor

Table 5.3. Some approaches based on multiple classifiers.

Candela et al. (1995) introduced PCASYS (Pattern-level Classification Automation SYStem): a complete fingerprint classification system based on the evolution of the methods proposed in Wilson, Candela, and Watson (1994). Figure 5.11 shows a functional schema of PCASYS: a probabilistic neural network (which replaced the multilayer perceptron used in Wilson, Candela, and Watson (1994)) is coupled with an auxiliary ridge tracing module, which determines the ridge flow in the bottom part of the fingerprint; this module is specifically designed to detect whorl fingerprints. PCASYS was a milestone for successive fingerprint classification studies because of its open source code and because it was one of the first studies that reported precise and reproducible results on publicly available databases (see Section 5.3). Wei, Yuan, and Jie (1998) proposed a feedback method based on a genetic algorithm to automatically select the best input parameters for PCASYS and achieved better accuracy. In Pattichis et al. (2001), a feature extraction method was adopted to improve PCASYS performance. Senior (2001) combined PCASYS with two other classifiers: the hidden Markov model classifier introduced in Senior (1997) and an approach based on ridge shape features classified by means of a decision tree.

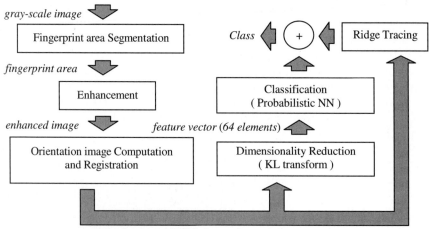

Figure 5.11. A functional scheme of PCASYS (Candela et al., 1995). Reprinted with permission from Cappelli et al. (1999). ©IEEE.

Jain, Prabhakar, and Hong (1999) adopt a two-stage classification strategy: a *k*-nearest neighbor classifier is used to find the two most likely classes from a FingerCode feature vector (see Section 4.6); then a specific neural network, trained to distinguish between the two classes, is exploited to obtain the final decision. A total of 10 neural networks is trained to distinguish between each possible pair of classes. In Figure 5.12, a graphical scheme of this sequential classification strategy is reported.

Cappelli, Maio, and Maltoni (2000a) trained two different types of classifiers (see subsection Statistical Approaches) on three disjoint training sets, thus obtaining a total of six classifiers that the authors combined using a majority vote rule (see also Cappelli, Maio, and Maltoni (2002a)). Very good results were reported on publicly available databases (see Section 5.3).

Other attempts at fingerprint classifier combinations can be found in Uchida et al. (1998), Marcialis, Roli, and Frasconi (2001), and Yao, Frasconi, and Pontil (2001). In Marcialis, Roli, and Frasconi (2001) a structural approach similar to Maio and Maltoni (1996) is combined with a neural network classifier that uses FingerCode feature vectors; in Yao, Frasconi, and Pontil (2001) the authors combine multiple Support Vector Machines trained to classify FingerCode feature vectors.

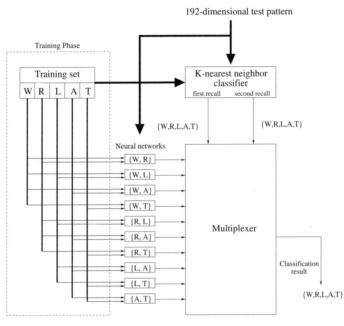

Figure 5.12. The classifier combination scheme proposed by Jain, Prabhakar, and Hong (1999). ©IEEE.

Miscellanea

Other approaches for fingerprint classification, in addition to those already described, were proposed by Shelman and Hodges (1973), Millard (1975), Rao (1976, 1978), Shelman (1976), Singh, Gyergyek, and Pavesic (1977), Shizume and Hefner (1978), Rabinowitz (1980), Lindh, Ford, and Boudreaux (1981), Nakamura, Goto, and Minami (1982), Fjetland and Robbins (1989), Geng and Shen (1997), and Sarbadhikari et al. (1998).

5.3 Performance of Fingerprint Classification Techniques

The performance of a fingerprint classification system is usually measured in terms of *error rate* or *accuracy*. The error rate is computed as the ratio between the number of misclassified fingerprints and the total number of samples in the test set; the accuracy is simply the percentage of correctly classified fingerprints:

$$\text{error rate} = \frac{\text{number of misclassified fingerprints} \times 100}{\text{total number of fingerprints}}\% \qquad (5)$$

$$\text{accuracy} = 100\% - \text{error rate}. \qquad (6)$$

The error rate of a classification system is generally reported as a function of the percentage of the database that the system has to search; this percentage is called *penetration rate* and can be simply computed as

$$\text{penetration rate} = \frac{\text{number of accessed fingerprints} \times 100}{\text{total number of fingerprints in the database}}\%. \qquad (7)$$

A more detailed analysis of the behavior of a classifier can be obtained by examining the *confusion matrix*. This matrix has a row for each true class and a column for each hypothesized class; each cell at row r and column c reports how many fingerprints belonging to class r are (in)correctly assigned to class c. Table 5.5 shows an example of confusion matrix.

Fingerprint images of poor quality are often difficult to classify, even for a human expert: in many applications it is desirable that a fingerprint classification algorithm rejects such images because this would be less damaging than a wrong decision. For this reason, several classification approaches include a rejection mechanism, which improves the accuracy at the cost of discarding some fingerprints (i.e., classifying them as "unknown"). A confidence value is usually assigned to the classifier decision or to the fingerprint itself: the rejection simply consists of discarding fingerprints whose confidence is lower than a fixed threshold. By taking into account the rejection rate, the performance of a fingerprint classifier can be described by a graph with the rejection rate on one axis and the error rate (or the accuracy) on the other (see Figure 5.13).

The early fingerprint classification systems proposed in the literature (years 1970 to 1990) were tested on small databases, usually collected by the authors themselves. Although the results reported on these internal databases provided an initial glimpse regarding the difficulty of the classification problem, a comparison among the various techniques was impossible and the results were not useful for tracking advances in the field. For example, in Moayer and Fu (1975) and Bowen (1992), the test sets used were two internally collected databases of 92 and 47 fingerprints, respectively: it is very difficult to deduce any conclusions from results reported on such small datasets.

In 1992 and 1993, NIST released two fingerprint databases well suited for development and testing of fingerprint classification systems: NIST Special Database 4 (Watson and Wilson, 1992a) and NIST Special Database 14 (Watson, 1993a), hereinafter named DB4 and DB14, respectively. Both databases consist of 8-bit grey-level images of rolled fingerprint impressions scanned from cards; two different fingerprint instances (F and S) are present for each finger. Each fingerprint was manually analyzed by a human expert and assigned to one of the five classes: Arch (A), Left loop (L), Right loop (R), Tented arch (T), and Whorl (W). Actually, in DB4, some ambiguous fingerprints (about 17%) have an additional reference to a "secondary" class and in DB14, there are a few fingerprints that the human expert was not able to classify. DB4 contains 2000 fingerprint pairs, uniformly distributed in the five classes; the images are numbered from F0001 to F2000 and from S0001 to S2000. DB14 contains 27,000 fingerprint pairs whose class distribution resembles natural fingerprint distribution: the images are numbered from F00001 to F27000 and from S00001 to S27000. NIST DB4 and DB14 became de facto standard benchmarks for fingerprint classification and most of the algorithms published in the last decade were tested on one of these databases. The following subsections report the performance of the main fingerprint classification approaches for which results on DB4 or DB14 are available.

Although DB4 and DB14 constitute very useful benchmarks for studies on fingerprint classification, they are not well suited for testing indexing/retrieval approaches using live-scan images. In fact, on-line impressions rarely contain all the fingerprint singularities (usually they do not cover the entire fingerprint area) and this may cause problems for methods using a global description of fingerprints (e.g., orientation image).

Results on NIST DB4

Table 5.4 reports the error rates on DB4 of 10 different approaches: most of them were obtained by using the 2000 images from the first 1000 fingers (F0001 to F1000 and S0001 to S1000) for the training and the remaining 2000 images for testing the system. Some rule-based methods (such as Karu and Jain (1996), Hong and Jain (1999), and Jain and Minut (2002)) were tested on the whole database; Senior (1997) reports results on 542 randomly selected fingerprints. All the results are reported at 0% rejection rate, with the exception of the approaches based on FingerCode feature vectors (Jain, Prabhakar, and Hong (1999), Marcialis, Roli, and Frasconi (2001), and Yao, Frasconi, and Pontil (2001)), where 1.8% fingerprints are rejected during the feature extraction stage. As to the ambiguous fingerprints with two class labels, the result is usually assumed correct if the class hypothesized by the classifier matches any of the two labels. Some authors, by noting that many errors are due to the misclassification of some tented arch fingerprints as arch (e.g., see the confusion matrix in Table 5.5) and considering that these two classes are not very common in nature (see Section 5.1), proposed to merge these two classes into a single class (four-class problem). When available, results of both the five-class and four-class problems are reported in Table 5.4. Furthermore, since DB4 contains an equal number of fingerprints for each class, some authors prefer to weight the results according to the natural class distribution (see Section 5.1): weighted results, when published by the authors themselves or derivable from the confusion matrices, are reported in Table 5.4 for both the five-class and four-class cases.

Method	Test set	5 classes		4 classes	
		%	Weighted (%)	%	Weighted (%)
Candela et al. (1995)	Second half	–	–	11.4	6.1
Karu and Jain (1996)	Whole DB	14.6	11.9	8.6	9.4
Senior (1997)	Random 542	–	–	–	8.4
Cappelli, Maio, and Maltoni (1999)	Second half	7.9	6.5	5.5	–
Hong and Jain (1999)	Whole DB	12.5	10.6	7.7	–
Jain, Prabhakar, and Hong (1999)	Second half	10.0	7.0	5.2	–
Marcialis, Roli, and Frasconi (2001)	Second half	12.1	9.6	–	–
Senior (2001)	Second half	–	–	–	5.1
Yao, Frasconi, and Pontil (2001)	Second half	10.7	9.0	6.9	–
Jain and Minut (2002)	Whole DB	–	–	8.8	9.3

Table 5.4. Error rates on NIST DB4. The results of the PCASYS system presented in Candela et al. (1995) were not reported in that work, but in Senior (2001).

True class	Hypothesized class				
	A	L	R	W	T
A	420	6	3	1	11
L	3	376	3	9	11
R	5	1	392	6	16
W	2	5	14	377	1
T	33	18	9	0	278

Table 5.5. Confusion matrix of the results on DB4 for the approach proposed in Cappelli, Maio, and Maltoni (1999): note that many errors are due to the misclassification of some tented arch fingerprints as arch.

Results on NIST DB14

Table 5.6 reports the error rates on DB14 of three published approaches; all the results were obtained using the last 2700 fingerprints (S24301 to S27000) as the test set.

The graph in Figure 5.13 shows how the accuracy of two of these approaches can be improved by including a rejection option. Two curves are drawn for the classifier proposed in Candela et al. (1995), to show the performance of the Probabilistic Neural Network alone (PNN only) and combined with the auxiliary Pseudo Ridge Tracing module (PNN + PRT). According to FBI specialists, the target error rate for automatic classification is 1% at a 20% rejection rate (Karu and Jain, 1996): the region where this requirement is met is displayed in gray in the graph.

Method	Error rate (%)
Candela et al. (1995)	7.8
Wei, Yuan, and Jie (1998)	6.0
Cappelli, Maio, and Maltoni (2000a)	5.6

Table 5.6. Error rates on NIST DB14.

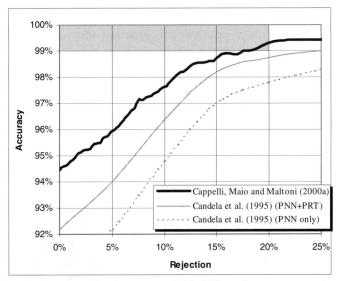

Figure 5.13. Accuracy versus rejection curves. PCASYS performance was manually sampled from the graph reported by Candela et al. (1995). The gray area denotes the target accuracy of automatic classification set by the FBI.

5.4 Fingerprint Indexing and Retrieval

The main problem of the classification schemes discussed in the previous sections (and of all the other commonly used schemes) is that the number of classes is small and fingerprints are unevenly distributed among them: more than 90% of the fingerprints belong to only three classes (loops and whorls). In 10-print identification (where an individual has to be identified using information from all of his 10 fingers), this does not compromise the efficiency too much, inasmuch as the knowledge of the classes of all the fingerprints can be used as a distinctive code for reducing the number of comparisons; on the other hand, when a single fingerprint has to be searched in a large database, the classification stage is not able to sufficiently narrow down the search. Furthermore, when classification is performed automatically, errors and rejected fingerprints are required to be handled gracefully. This problem can be addressed with two different approaches: *sub-classification* and *continuous classification*.

Fingerprint sub-classification

The goal of sub-classification is to further divide some of the classes into more specific categories. This approach has been typically adopted by human experts to perform manual fingerprint searching in forensic applications. For instance, the FBI defined (Federal Bureau of Investigation, 1984) a manual sub-classification procedure for loop and whorl fingerprints based on ridge counting (see Section 3.10); for right and left loop fingerprints, the number of ridges between the loop and delta singularities is determined: two sub-classes are defined according to the number of ridges. As to whorl fingerprints, the ridge just below the leftmost delta is traced until the position closest to the rightmost delta is reached; then the number of ridges between that point and the rightmost delta is counted (Figure 5.14).

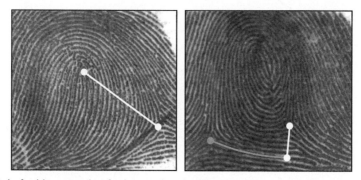

Figure 5.14. Left: ridge counting for loop sub-classification (the number of ridges between loop and delta is 16). Right: ridge tracing and counting for whorl sub-classification (the closest point is below the rightmost delta and number of the ridges is 5).

Three sub-classes are defined depending on the number of ridges and whether the traced ridge passes over the rightmost delta. Actually, the rules are quite complicated because the sub-classification criteria also vary according to the finger (thumb, index, middle, …).

Implementing a reliable automated fingerprint sub-classification is much more difficult than realizing a first-level classification into five classes. Therefore, it is not surprising that only a very limited number of algorithms have been proposed in the literature to address this problem (one of the very few examples is Drets and Liljenstrom (1998)).

Continuous classification and other indexing techniques

The intrinsic difficulties in automating fingerprint classification and sub-classification led some researchers to investigate fingerprint retrieval systems that are not based on human defined classes. In fact, for applications where there is no need to adhere to the Henry's classification scheme, and where the goal is purely to minimize the number of comparisons during retrieval, any technique able to characterize each fingerprint in a robust and stable manner (among different impressions of the same finger) may, in principle, be used.

An interesting approach is so-called "continuous classification" (Lumini, Maio, and Maltoni, 1997): in continuous classification, fingerprints are not partitioned into disjoint classes, but associated with numerical vectors summarizing their main features. These feature vectors are created through a similarity-preserving transformation, so that similar fingerprints are mapped into close points (vectors) in the multidimensional space. The retrieval is performed by matching the input fingerprint with those in the database whose corresponding vectors are close to the searched one. Spatial data structures (Samet, 1990) can be used for indexing very large databases. A continuous classification approach allows the problem of exclusive membership of ambiguous fingerprints to be avoided and the system efficiency and accuracy to be balanced by adjusting the size of the neighborhood considered (see the following subsection). Most of the continuous classification techniques proposed in the literature use the orientation image as an initial feature, but differ in the transformation adopted to create the final vectors and in the distance measure. In Lumini, Maio, and Maltoni (1997) and in Kamei and Mizoguchi (1998), the orientation image is aligned with respect to the core and treated as a single vector (by concatenating its rows); a dimensionality reduction (KL transform) is then performed to compute the final vectors. The similarity between two vectors is calculated with the Euclidean distance in Lumini, Maio, and Maltoni (1997) and with a more sophisticated approach, which also takes into account a quality index, in Kamei and Mizoguchi (1998). In Cappelli et al. (1999), the templates corresponding to the five classes (see Section 5.2) are used to create a numerical vector for continuous classification; the cost of the adaptation of each template to a given fingerprint is calculated and a five-dimensional vector is assembled by using the five normalized costs. The main advantage of this approach is that the orientation images do not need to be aligned with respect to a fixed point. In Cappelli, Maio, and Maltoni (2000a), the vector used for continuous classification is created by using the distances of the orientation image from all the MKL subspaces (see description of Cappelli, Maio, and Maltoni (2002a) in Section 5.2).

Some researchers proposed to index fingerprints using minutiae points (Germain, Califano, and Colville, 1997): exploiting the same feature for matching and indexing fingerprints is attractive, but care must be taken to construct an extremely redundant representation, inasmuch as only a subset of all the minutiae is always present in different impressions of the same finger. The algorithm proposed by Germain, Califano, and Colville (1997) first identifies all the minutiae triplets in a fingerprint. Each triplet defines a triangle whose geometric features are extracted: length of each side, the angles, and the ridge count between each pair of vertices. The similarity between two fingerprints is defined by the number of corresponding minutiae triplets that can be found under a rigid transformation; this method of defining fingerprint similarity has strong analogies with local minutiae-based matching described in Section 4.4. Instead of explicitly comparing the similarity between the input fingerprint and all the fingerprints in the database (which would be very time consuming), the authors use a geometric hashing technique: a hash table is built by quantizing all the possible triplets and, for each quantized triplet, a list of pointers (ID) to the fingerprints in the database containing that specific triplet is maintained. When a new fingerprint is inserted in the database, its triplets are extracted, and the hash table is updated by adding the fingerprint ID in the cell corresponding to the fingerprint triplets. At retrieval time, the triplets of the input fingerprint are computed and quantized and, for each triplet, the list of fingerprint IDs in which that triplet is present is retrieved together with the coordinate transformations that best map the input fingerprint into the database fingerprints. Intuitively, if the same fingerprint ID is hit by more triplets in the input (under consistent coordinate transformations), then it is more likely that the corresponding fingerprint is the searched one. A voting technique is then applied to obtain a final ranking, which is used for visiting the database in a convenient order. A variant of the above-described technique is presented in Bhanu and Tan (2001a), where more robust features are extracted from the minutiae triplets and some geometric constraints are introduced to more effectively filter the database.

Other indexing techniques are described in Shan, Shi, and Li (1994), Qun et al. (2002), and Maeda, Matsushita, and Sasakawa (2001); in particular, Maeda, Matsushita, and Sasakawa (2001) proposed a rather different approach, which is based only on the matching scores between fingerprints rather than on features extracted from the fingerprint images: a matrix containing all the matching scores between each pair of fingerprints in the database is maintained. During retrieval, as the input fingerprint is matched with database fingerprints, the resulting scores are incrementally used to find the maximum correlation with a column of the matrix and to select the next database fingerprint to be matched. The method is interesting, because it can be applied to any biometric identifier, inasmuch as it only relies on matching scores; on the other hand, it is not well suited for large databases (e.g., one million fingerprints) because the size of the matrix is quadratic with the number of fingerprints in the database and for each new insertion in the database (enrollment), the new fingerprint has to be matched with all the fingerprints currently stored in the database.

Finally, in some recent papers, different indexing techniques are combined to improve performance. In Cappelli, Maio, and Maltoni (2000a), the continuous classification technique proposed in Cappelli et al. (1999) is combined with an MKL-based approach: the distance measures produced by the two methods are fused by registering the different values according to their statistical distributions. In De Boer, Bazen, and Gerez (2001), two continuous classification techniques (the former similar to Lumini, Maio, and Maltoni (1997) and the latter using FingerCode feature vectors (Jain, Prabhakar, and Hong, 1999)) are combined with a simplified version of the minutiae-triplet approach proposed by Germain, Califano, and Colville (1997).

Retrieval strategies

Choosing an indexing technique alone is usually not sufficient: a retrieval strategy should also be defined according to the application requirements such as the desired accuracy and efficiency, the matching algorithm used to compare fingerprints, the presence of a human supervisor, and so on. In general, different strategies may be defined for the same indexing mechanism: for instance, the search may be stopped when a fixed portion of the database has been explored, or as soon as a matching fingerprint is found (in AFIS, this requires the presence of a human expert who visually examines the fingerprints that are considered sufficiently similar by the minutiae matcher and terminate the search when a true correspondence is found).

If an exclusive classification technique is used for indexing, these retrieval strategies can be used:

- *hypothesized class only*: only fingerprints belonging to the class to which the input fingerprint has been assigned, are retrieved. The search may be stopped as soon as a matching fingerprint is found, or extended to all the fingerprints of that class in the database;
- *fixed search order*: the search continues until a match is found, or the whole database has been explored; if a correspondence is not found within the hypothesized class, the search continues in another class, and so on. The optimal class visiting order can be a priori determined from the confusion matrix of a given fingerprint classifier (Lumini, Maio, and Maltoni, 1997). For example, if the input fingerprint is assigned to the arch class, the order could be: arch, tented arch, left loop, right loop, and whorl;
- *variable search order*: the different classes are visited according to the class likelihoods produced by the classifier for the input fingerprint. The search may be stopped as soon as a match is found, or when the likelihood ratio between the current class and the next to be visited is less than a fixed threshold (Senior, 2001).

Obviously, the first strategy (hypothesized class only) assumes no classification errors, which is quite unlikely for state-of-the-art automatic classifiers (see Section 5.3); the other strategies are more complex, but allow adjusting the accuracy of the system at the cost of speed. Each of the above three strategies may be combined with a rejection mechanism (see

Section 5.3): if the input fingerprint is rejected by the automatic classifier, it has to be either manually classified, or compared with all the fingerprints in the database.

If a continuous classification technique is used for indexing the database, these retrieval strategies may be used (Lumini, Maio, and Maltoni, 1997):

- *fixed radius*: given a prefixed tolerance ρ, the fingerprints considered are those whose corresponding vectors are inside the hypersphere with radius ρ centered at the point associated with the input fingerprint; the search may be halted as soon as a match is found, or when the whole portion of the database enclosed by the hypersphere has been explored;

- *incremental search*: fingerprints are visited according to the distance between their associated vectors and the input point; the search continues until a match is found (in the worst case, it is extended to the whole database).

Figure 5.15 shows an example of the above two strategies. The incremental search allows the corresponding fingerprint to be found in any case (if present), even if the indexing technique fails; on the other hand, it does not guarantee an upper bound on the retrieval time. Obviously, an intermediate approach is also possible, where fingerprints are incrementally searched until a match is found or a prefixed distance (or portion of the database) has been explored (Cappelli, Maio, and Maltoni, 2000c).

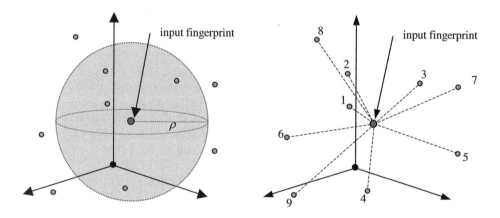

Figure 5.15. Retrieval strategies for continuous classification. On the left: the fingerprints whose corresponding vectors are inside the hypersphere are considered (*fixed radius*); on the right: the fingerprints are incrementally retrieved according to the distance of the corresponding vectors from the input point (*incremental search*).

Performance of fingerprint retrieval techniques

In Lumini, Maio, and Maltoni (1997), Cappelli et al. (1999), and Cappelli, Maio, and Maltoni (2000a), the performance of different retrieval strategies was measured both for continuous and exclusive classifications. The last 2700 fingerprint pairs of NIST Special Database 14 (see Section 5.3) were used as a benchmark: fingerprints F24301 to F27000 constituted the database and fingerprints S24301 to S27000 were used as input fingerprints. The graph in Figure 5.16 shows the performance of three continuous and one exclusive classification approach for strategies where retrieval errors are possible (i.e., where the fingerprint corresponding to the input may not be found): *fixed radius* and *hypothesized class* only. The performance of the exclusive classification approach is denoted by a single point, whereas performances of continuous classification approaches are reported for different operating points, as the speed/accuracy tradeoff depends on the chosen radius (ρ). For all the approaches, the search was not halted as soon as the corresponding fingerprint was found, but the whole portion of the database considered was explored.

Table 5.7 reports the performance of the same four approaches combined with strategies that do not allow any retrieval errors (i.e., the search can be extended to the whole database): *incremental search* and *fixed search order*. The advantage of continuous classification approaches is well evident: in the exclusive case, even if the hypothesized class is correct, half of the fingerprints belonging to that class have to be visited on average, whereas in the continuous case, if the features used are sufficiently selective, the portion of the database searched can be very small.

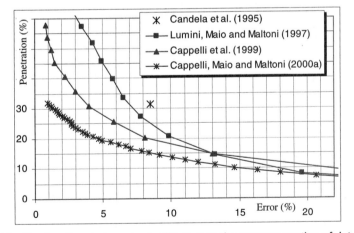

Figure 5.16. *Fixed radius* strategy: tradeoff between the average portion of database searched and the average retrieval error by varying the radius ρ. The point marked with "*" denotes the performance of an exclusive classification technique using the *hypothesized class only* strategy.

Average penetration rate (%)	
Candela et al. (1995)	18.9
Lumini, Maio, and Maltoni (1997)	7.1
Cappelli et al. (1999)	6.4
Cappelli, Maio, and Maltoni (2000a)	3.7

Table 5.7. Average penetration rate using the fixed search order strategy for the exclusive classification approach (Candela et al., 1995) and the incremental search strategy for the continuous classification approaches (Lumini, Maio, and Maltoni (1997), Cappelli et al. (1999), and Cappelli, Maio, and Maltoni (2000a)).

Other results have been published in the literature, where instead of using the NIST databases, the authors studied the effects of indexing/retrieval in the case of "smaller" live-scan dab images. Cappelli, Maio, and Maltoni (2000c) and De Boer, Bazen, and Gerez (2001) tested their retrieval systems on the second database (DB2) from FVC2000 (Maio et al., 2002a). The Cappelli, Maio, and Maltoni (2000c) method is based on MKL (see subsection "Statistical Approaches" in Section 5.2) and retrieves fingerprints by incrementally searching the database until a match is found or a maximum portion of the database is explored. The feature extraction and indexing are completely automatic and no manual quality control is performed. Figure 5.17 shows the retrieval error rate versus penetration rate graph.

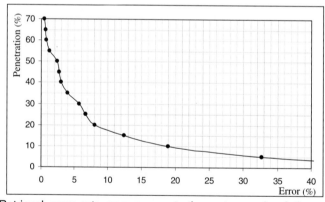

Figure 5.17. Retrieval error rate versus penetration rate graph of the automatic indexing/retrieval method proposed by Cappelli, Maio, and Maltoni (2000c).

As previously explained, De Boer, Bazen, and Gerez (2001) evaluated three indexing techniques based on orientation image, FingerCode, and minutiae triplets. Core detection (which is a crucial step for a reliable registration), was automatically performed but manually verified and corrected in 13% of the fingerprints; 1% of the fingerprints were also rejected because the core point could not be found. The retrieval error rate versus penetration rate graph obtained is reported in Figure 5.18. The two methods based on orientation image and FingerCode perform significantly better than that using minutiae triplets, and the performance of the minutiae trip-let method is substantially lower than those reported by Bhanu and Tan (2001a). Actually:

- the authors implemented a simplified version of the original triplet-based indexing (as introduced by Germain, Califano, and Colville (1997)), where the consistency of co-ordinate transformations was not taken into account in the computation of the final ranking;
- the semi-automatic core extraction significantly helps orientation image- and Finger-Code-based methods, and it is influential for the triplet-based method, which does not require any registration.

When combining the three methods at rank level, De Boer, Bazen, and Gerez (2001) obtained a significant improvement, as shown in Figure 5.18. The main advantage is due to the combination of the first two features (i.e., orientation image and FingerCode) and adding mi-nutiae triplets does not seem to improve the performance significantly. This is somewhat un-expected, because of the relatively high correlation between orientation image and FingerCode, and the low correlation between minutiae arrangements and texture information carried by the orientation image and FingerCode. The average portion of the database explored to find the query fingerprint for the three methods and their best combination is shown in Ta-ble 5.8.

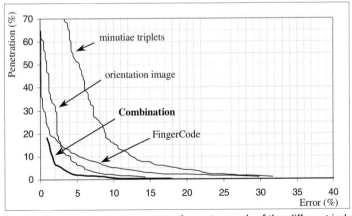

Figure 5.18. Retrieval error rate versus penetration rate graph of the different indexing/retrieval approaches evaluated by De Boer, Bazen, and Gerez (2001). These results are not directly comparable with those in Figure 5.17 because De Boer, Bazen, and Gerez (2001) manually assisted in the core detection stage.

Average penetration rate (%)	
Orientation image	2.58
FingerCode	2.40
Minutiae triplets	7.27
Combination	1.34

Table 5.8. Average penetration rate (with the incremental search strategy) in the indexing/retrieval approaches evaluated by De Boer, Bazen, and Gerez (2001).

5.5 Summary

Fingerprint classification has been the subject of several pattern recognition studies over the last three decades. Different solutions have been proposed and it is now possible to design classification systems that are able to meet the FBI requirement of 99% accuracy with a maximum rejection of 20%. However, it is unlikely that exclusive classification would make it possible to significantly reduce the effort of searching for a single fingerprint in the absence of other information (e.g., sex, age, race, etc.). Continuous classification and related indexing/retrieval strategies based on features extracted from fingerprints seem to be more promising alternatives for efficient implementations of the identification task in a variety of applications.

In AFIS and other semi-automatic civilian applications, the enrollment is supervised, the quality of the input fingerprint can be checked, and manual intervention is possible to correct feature extraction errors: this allows us to design indexing/retrieval mechanisms that achieve a relatively small retrieval error and a good penetration rate. On the other hand, the identification task in a completely automatic system, working with live-scan dab images, has more severe constraints: database templates and input fingerprint images are often low quality and provide only a partial impression of the finger, and the system response is usually expected within a few seconds. The development of such an automatic fingerprint-based identification system for large databases is a challenging task, due to both accuracy (see subsection "Identification System Errors" in Section 1.4) and speed issues. Multimodal systems (see Chapter 7), seem to be the most promising way to improve accuracy (De Boer, Bazen, and Gerez, 2001), and to derive sequential approaches that progressively refine the search when a large database has to be explored.

6
Synthetic Fingerprint Generation

Invited Chapter by
Raffaele Cappelli
University of Bologna

6.1 Introduction

Significant efforts are continuously being made in designing new fingerprint recognition algorithms both in academic and industrial environments. However, the accuracy of each algorithm is usually evaluated on relatively small proprietary databases. First, evaluation on small databases makes the accuracy estimates highly data dependent; as a result, they do not generalize well on fingerprint images captured in different applications and different environments. Second, when these small databases are proprietary, the accuracy of various fingerprint matching algorithms cannot be compared directly. A sharable large database of fingerprints (thousands or tens of thousands) is required to evaluate and compare various fingerprint recognition algorithms due to the very small error rates that have to be estimated. Unfortunately, collecting large databases of fingerprint images is: i) expensive both in terms of money and time; and ii) tedious for both the technicians involved and for the volunteers. Even if one is able to collect such a large fingerprint database, it is difficult to share it with others due to privacy legislation that often protects such personal data. Finally, publicly available databases of real fingerprints, such as those used in FVC2000 (Maio et al., 2002a) and FVC2002 (Maio et al., 2002b) technology evaluation, do not constitute lasting solutions for evaluating and comparing different algorithms because they expire once "used," and new databases have to be collected for future evaluations.

This chapter describes SFINGE, a synthetic fingerprint generation approach developed by Cappelli, Maio, and Maltoni (2000b, 2002b). SFINGE can be used to automatically create large databases of fingerprints, thus allowing fingerprint recognition algorithms to be effectively trained, tested, optimized, and compared. The artificial fingerprints emulate images acquired with electronic fingerprint scanners, because most commercial applications require online acquisition. In any case, impressions similar to those acquired by the traditional "ink-technique" can be generated with relatively few changes in the algorithm.

Few studies on synthetic fingerprint generation are available in the literature. In Sherstinsky and Picard (1994), a complex method, which employs a dynamic non-linear system called

"M-lattice," is introduced with the aim of binarizing a gray-scale fingerprint image. The method is based on the reaction–diffusion model first proposed by Turing in 1952 to explain the formation of various patterns observed on animal skin such as zebra stripes. Although this work does not address fingerprint synthesis, the ridge line model proposed could be used as a basis for synthetic fingerprint generation. Kosz of the Polish company Optel published some interesting results concerning artificial fingerprint generation based on a novel mathematical model of ridge patterns and minutiae; unfortunately, to protect the commercial exploitation of his idea, the author does not provide any technical details. Novikov and Glushchenko (1998) proposed a ridge generation technique operating in the frequency domain. For each pixel $[x,y]$ of an initial random image, the 2D Fourier spectrum of a local window, centered in $[x,y]$, is computed. The highest-energy harmonic (i.e., a pure two-dimensional sinusoid in the spatial domain) is chosen from the Fourier spectrum along the normal to the local ridge orientation at $[x,y]$ (according to an a priori artificially generated orientation image). All the sinusoids are summed and the result is binarized; the procedure is iteratively repeated until a sufficiently smooth image is obtained. This method has some analogies with the iterative application of Gabor filters in the spatial domain discussed in Section 6.3; in fact, the MTF of a Gabor filter is characterized by two symmetric peaks along the normal to the filter orientation (see Section 3.7). A constructive approach was proposed by Hill (2001) where a fingerprint pattern is generated starting from a given set of minutiae points; the work is aimed at proving that a masquerade attack can be carried out against a fingerprint-based biometric system, by "fraudulently" accessing and deciphering the content of a stored template and by recreating an artificial clone (either digital or synthetic). Unfortunately, the algorithm proposed to draw ridge patterns (starting from minutiae positions and then iteratively filling empty spaces) produces images that are visually non-realistic. Finally, Araque et al. (2002) introduced a synthetic generation technique whose main steps are similar to SFINGE, but which differs at some points: first, the orientation image synthesis is based on a new second-order model controlled by up to 11 complex coefficients, whose distributions are inferred from real data; second, the filters used for ridge pattern generation are simple binary masks instead of the Gabor filters used by SFINGE.

This chapter is organized as follows. Section 6.2 introduces the basic schema of the SFINGE approach including the different steps involved in the generation of a *master fingerprint* and its derived *fingerprint impressions*. A master fingerprint is a pattern that encodes the unique and immutable characteristics of a "synthetic finger" independently of the variations (displacement, rotation, pressure, skin condition, distortion, noise, etc.), that make the successive acquisitions different from each other. Sections 6.3 and 6.4 present the details of the generation of a master fingerprint and the derivation of fingerprint impressions, respectively. Section 6.5 introduces the evaluation performed to validate SFINGE and Section 6.6 briefly describes a software tool (included in the DVD that accompanies this book) that implements the SFINGE approach. Finally, Section 6.7 provides some concluding remarks.

6.2 The SFINGE Method

A typical fingerprint matching algorithm processes a fingerprint as summarized in Figure 6.1:

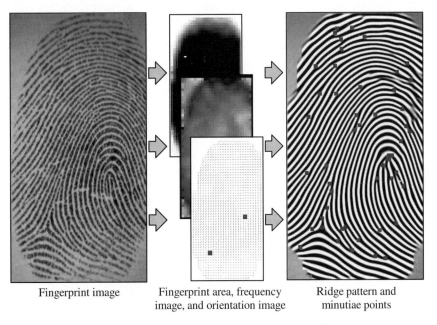

| Fingerprint image | Fingerprint area, frequency image, and orientation image | Ridge pattern and minutiae points |

Figure 6.1. A typical feature extraction process from a real fingerprint image.

the fingerprint is first segmented from the background; then the local frequency and orientation maps are estimated; finally, this information is exploited to enhance the ridge pattern and find the minutiae. In order to generate fingerprint images, SFINGE "inverts" some of the above operations (see Figure 6.2): a fingerprint area, an orientation image, and a frequency image, generated independently of each other, are the inputs of a ridge generation process; the resulting binary ridge pattern is then rendered by adding fingerprint-specific noise.

In order to generate multiple impressions of the same "synthetic finger," a more complicated schema has to be introduced: a *master fingerprint* (i.e., a ridge pattern that represents the unique and immutable characteristics of a "synthetic finger") is first generated; then several synthetic impressions can be derived from the master fingerprint by explicitly tuning displacement, rotation, distortion, skin condition, and noise (see Figure 6.3). Figure 6.4 shows the complete generation process: Steps 1 to 4 create a master fingerprint; Steps 5 to 10 are performed for each fingerprint impression derived from the master fingerprint.

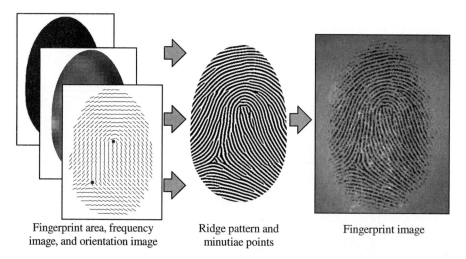

Fingerprint area, frequency   Ridge pattern and   Fingerprint image
image, and orientation image   minutiae points

Figure 6.2. The basic idea of the fingerprint generation method.

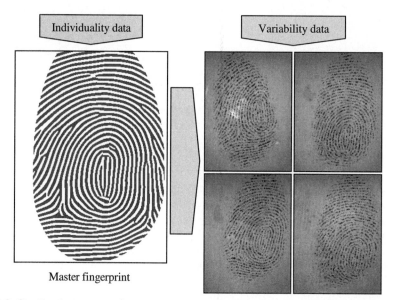

Figure 6.3. Starting from a set of parameters that represent the unique and immutable features of a "synthetic finger" (individuality data), SFINGE creates a master fingerprint; then a number of fingerprint impressions can be generated by changing several parameters that control the fingerprint appearance (variability data).

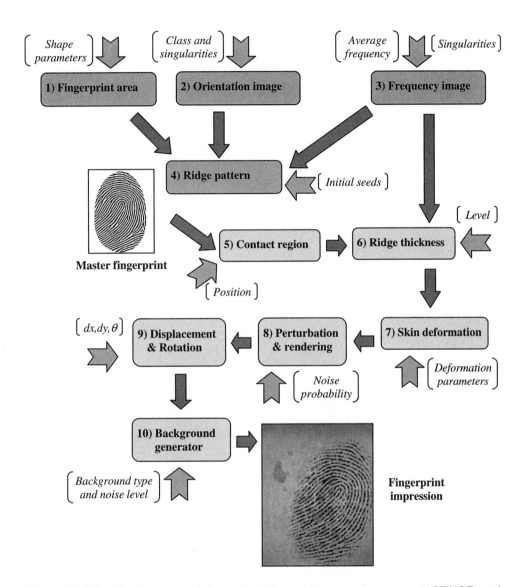

Figure 6.4. A functional schema of the synthetic fingerprint generation approach SFINGE: each rounded box represents a generation step; the main input parameters that control each step are reported between brackets. Steps 1 to 4 create a master fingerprint; Steps 5 to 9 derive a fingerprint impression from the master fingerprint and can be iterated to produce multiple impressions of the same finger.

6.3 Generation of a Master Fingerprint

Creating a master fingerprint involves the steps:
1.   fingerprint area generation,
2.   orientation image generation,
3.   frequency image generation, and
4.   ridge pattern generation.

Step 1 defines the external silhouette of the fingerprint; Step 2 starts from the positions of loop and delta singularities and exploits a mathematical flow model to generate a consistent orientation image. Step 3 creates a frequency image on the basis of some heuristic criteria inferred by visual inspection of a large number of real fingerprints. In Step 4, the ridge line pattern and the minutiae are created through a contextual iterative filtering; the output is a near-binary fingerprint image. A separate subsection is dedicated to the explanation of each of the above steps.

Fingerprint area generation

Depending on the finger size, position, and pressure against the acquisition sensor, the acquired fingerprint images have different sizes and external shapes (Figure 6.5).

Figure 6.5. Examples of fingerprint images with different sizes and shapes.

A visual examination of a large number of fingerprint images suggested that a simple model, based on four elliptical arcs and a rectangle and controlled by five parameters (see Figure 6.6), can handle most of the variations present in real fingerprint shapes. Figure 6.6 shows some examples of fingerprint shapes generated by this model by varying the five parameters.

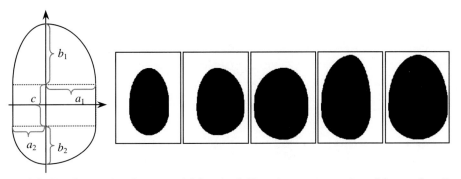

Figure 6.6. The fingerprint shape model (on the left) and some examples of fingerprint silhou-
ettes generated by this model (on the right).

Orientation image generation

 The orientation model proposed by Sherlock and Monro (1993) allows a consistent orientation
image to be computed from the knowledge of the position of fingerprint singularities (loops
and deltas) alone. In this model, the image is located in the complex plane and the local ridge
orientation is the phase of the square root of a complex rational function whose singularities
(poles and zeros) are located at the same place as the fingerprint singularities (loops and del-
tas). Let $\mathbf{ls}_i$, $i = 1..n_c$ and $\mathbf{ds}_i$, $i = 1.. n_d$ be the coordinates of the loops and deltas, respectively.
The orientation θ at each point $\mathbf{z} = [x,y]$ is calculated as

$$\theta = \frac{1}{2}\left[\sum_{i=1}^{n_d} arg(\mathbf{z} - \mathbf{ds}_i) - \sum_{i=1}^{n_c} arg(\mathbf{z} - \mathbf{ls}_i) \right], \tag{1}$$

where the function $arg(\mathbf{c})$ returns the phase angle of the complex number $\mathbf{c}$ (see Figure 6.7).
    Sherlock and Monro's model may be exploited for generating synthetic orientation images
as follows. First a fingerprint class is randomly chosen and then the positions of the singularities are randomly selected according to class-specific constraints (for instance, in a left loop,
the delta must be on the right side of the loop). Figure 6.8 shows some examples of orientation
images generated by this model. Unfortunately, the generation of synthetic orientation images
for arch type patterns that do not contain any singularities is not supported by this model, and
it must be considered separately. However, this does not pose a serious problem inasmuch as
arch orientation image generation is straightforward, and a simple sinusoidal function (whose
frequency and amplitude are tuned to control the arch curvature and aspect) adequately
approximates this pattern.

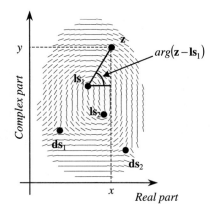

Figure 6.7. Each element of the orientation image is considered as a complex number (Sherlock and Monro, 1993).

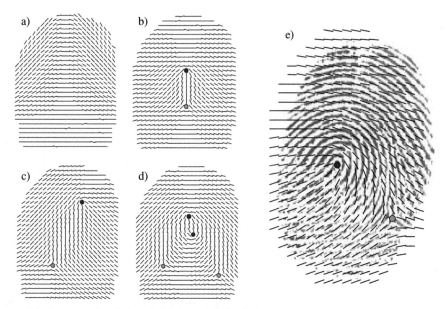

Figure 6.8. An example of a) arch, b) tented arch, c) right loop and d) whorl orientation image as generated by the Sherlock and Monro model. e) An example of a left loop orientation image superimposed over a left loop fingerprint with coincident singularity positions.

In nature, the ridge line flow cannot be completely determined by the singularity type and position. Hence, although the Sherlock and Monro model is a good starting point, it is not satisfactory. Figure 6.8.e shows a fingerprint image (belonging to the left loop class) and the orientation image generated by the Sherlock and Monro model, with the same position of loop and delta. Clear differences exist among the real ridge line orientations and the corresponding elements in the orientation image: in particular, the regions above the loop and between the loop and the delta are not well modeled.

Vizcaya and Gerhardt (1996) proposed a variant of the Sherlock and Monro model that introduces more degrees of freedom to cope with the orientation variability that may characterize orientation images with coincident singularities. The orientation θ at each point $\mathbf{z}$ is calculated as

$$\theta = \frac{1}{2} \left[\sum_{i=1}^{n_d} g_{\mathbf{ds}_i} \left(arg(\mathbf{z} - \mathbf{ds}_i) \right) - \sum_{i=1}^{n_c} g_{\mathbf{ls}_i} \left(arg(\mathbf{z} - \mathbf{ls}_i) \right) \right], \qquad (2)$$

where $g_k(\alpha)$, for $k \in \left\{ \mathbf{ls}_1, ..., \mathbf{ls}_{n_c}, \mathbf{ds}_1, ..., \mathbf{ds}_{n_d} \right\}$, are piecewise linear functions capable of locally correcting the orientation field with respect to the value given by the Sherlock and Monroe model:

$$g_k(\alpha) = \overline{g}_k(\alpha_i) + \frac{\alpha - \alpha_i}{2\pi/L} \left(\overline{g}_k(\alpha_{i+1}) - \overline{g}_k(\alpha_i) \right), \qquad (3)$$

for $\alpha_i \leq \alpha \leq \alpha_{i+1}$, $\alpha_i = -\pi + \frac{2\pi i}{L}$.

Each function $g_k(\alpha)$ is defined by the set of values $\left\{ \overline{g}_k(\alpha_i) \mid i = 0..L-1 \right\}$, where each value is the amount of correction of the orientation field at a given angle (in a set of L angles uniformly distributed between $-\pi$ and π). If $\overline{g}_k(\alpha_i) = \alpha_i \forall i \in \left\{ 0..L-1 \right\}$ (i.e., $g_k(\alpha)$ is the identity function), the model coincides with that of Sherlock and Monro (see Figure 6.9).

The aim of the Vizcaya and Gerhardt (1996) work is to approximate a real orientation image, given a specific fingerprint, and so the authors derive the values $\overline{g}_k(\alpha_i)$ through an optimization procedure. In SFINGE, the Vizcaya and Gerhardt model is not used to approximate the orientation image of a given fingerprint but instead, the additional degrees of freedom given by the Vizcaya and Gerhardt model are exploited to provide more variations. From the analysis of real fingerprints, Cappelli, Maio, and Maltoni (2000b) found that $L = 8$ is a reasonable value and derived appropriate ranges for the parameters $\overline{g}_k(\alpha_i)$ for each fingerprint class: during the orientation-image generation, random values are selected within such ranges. Actually, in order to produce realistic results, for each singularity k, only $\overline{g}_k(\alpha_0)$ and $\overline{g}_k(\alpha_4)$ are randomly selected: the other values are determined so that a smooth mapping function $g_k(\alpha)$ is obtained. Figure 6.10 shows the effect of changing the parameter $\overline{g}_{\mathbf{ls}_1}(\alpha_4)$ in a right loop fingerprint: the changes with respect to the Sherlock and Monro formulation

loop fingerprint: the changes with respect to the Sherlock and Monro formulation (see Figure 6.9) are highlighted in the corresponding orientation image.

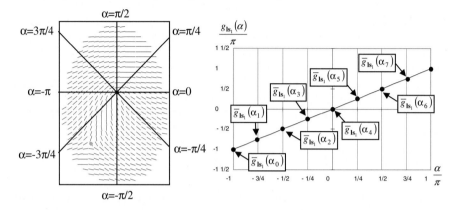

Figure 6.9. Definition of a function $g_k(\alpha)$ for the loop singularity of a right loop orientation image (Vizcaya and Gerhardt, 1996). In this case, $g_k(\alpha)$ is the identity function and the model coincides with that of Sherlock and Monro (1993).

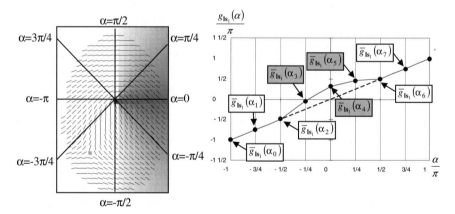

Figure 6.10. The effects of modifying the parameters that control a mapping function $g_k(\alpha)$ are highlighted in the corresponding orientation image (Vizcaya and Gerhardt, 1996).

Figures 6.11.a and b show two examples of orientation images generated according to the Vizcaya and Gerhardt model; these images are definitely more realistic than those in Figure

6.8. The superiority of the Vizcaya and Gerhardt model in approximating existing ridge patterns is also evident from the comparison between Figures 6.11.c and d.

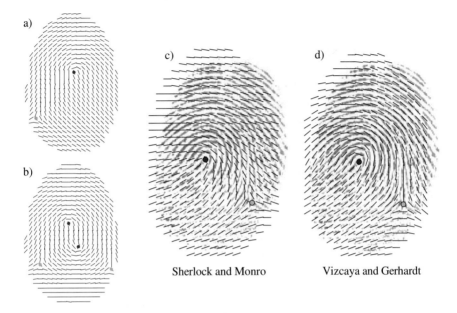

Sherlock and Monro   Vizcaya and Gerhardt

Figure 6.11. An example of a) right loop and b) whorl orientation images, as generated by the Vizcaya and Gerhardt model. In c) and d) the orientation images produced by the two models, for a given fingerprint, are compared.

Frequency image generation

Visual inspection of a large number of fingerprint images allows us to immediately discard the possibility of generating the frequency image in a completely random fashion. Quite often, in the regions above the northernmost loop and below the southernmost delta, the ridge line frequency is lower than in the rest of the fingerprint (see Figure 6.12). Therefore, frequency-image generation is performed:

1. a feasible overall frequency is randomly selected according to the distribution of ridge line frequency in real fingerprints; an average ridge/valley period of nine pixels is used: this simulates a 500 dpi sensor (see Section 3.1);
2. the frequency in the above-described regions is slightly decreased according to the positions of the singularities;

3.   the frequency image is randomly perturbed to improve its appearance;

4.   a local smoothing by a 3 × 3 averaging box filter is performed.

Figure 6.13 shows some examples of generated frequency images.

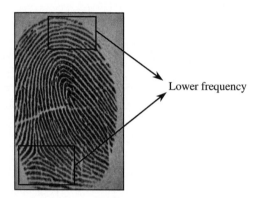

Figure 6.12. An example of a right loop fingerprint where the ridge line frequency is lower in the regions above the loop and below the delta.

Figure 6.13. Some examples of synthesized frequency images: light blocks denote higher frequencies.

Ridge pattern generation

Given an orientation image and a frequency image as an input, a deterministic generation of a ridge line pattern, including consistent minutiae, is not an easy task. One could try to fix a priori the number, the type, and the location of the minutiae, and by means of an explicit model, generate the gray-scale fingerprint image starting from the minutiae neighborhoods and expanding to connect different regions until the whole image is covered. Such a constructive approach would require several complex rules and "tricks" to be implemented in order to deal with the complexity of fingerprint ridge line patterns. A more elegant solution could be based on the use of a syntactic approach that generates fingerprints according to some starting symbols and a set of production rules.

The method used by SFINGE is very simple and at the same time powerful: by iteratively enhancing an initial image (containing one or more isolated points) through Gabor filters that are adjusted according to the local ridge orientation and frequency, a consistent and very realistic ridge line pattern gradually appears; in particular, fingerprint minutiae of different types (endings, bifurcations, islands, etc.) are automatically generated at random positions.

Gabor filters have been introduced in Chapter 3 as an effective tool for fingerprint enhancement; with respect to Equation (5) in Section 3.7, SFINGE uses equal values for the standard deviations of the Gaussian envelope along the x- and y-axes:

$$\sigma_x = \sigma_y = \sigma.$$

The filter applied at each pixel $[x,y]$ has the form:

$$g(x, y : \theta, f) = e^{-\left((x+y)^2 / 2\sigma^2\right)} \cdot \cos[2\pi \cdot f \cdot (x \cdot \sin\theta + y \cdot \cos\theta)], \qquad (4)$$

where θ and f are the corresponding local orientation and frequency, respectively. The parameter σ, which determines the bandwidth of the filter, is adjusted according to the local frequency so that the filter does not contain more than three effective peaks (as in Figure 3.28). In particular, the value of σ is determined by the solution of the following equation.

$$e^{-\left(\left(\frac{3}{2f}\right)^2 / 2\sigma^2\right)} = 10^{-3}. \qquad (5)$$

Although one could reasonably expect that iteratively applying "striped" filters to random images would simply produce striped images, very realistic minutiae are generated at random positions. Based on their experiments, Cappelli, Maio, and Maltoni (2000b) argue that minutiae primarily originate from the ridge line disparity produced by local convergence/divergence of the orientation field and by frequency changes. In Figures 6.14 and 6.15, some examples of the iterative ridge line generation process are shown. Cappelli, Maio, and Maltoni (2000b) experimentally found that increasing the number of initial points provides a more irregular ridge pattern richer in minutiae (see Figure 6.14): this is not surprising, because expanding distinct image regions causes interference where regions merge, thus favoring the creation of minutiae (see Figure 6.16).

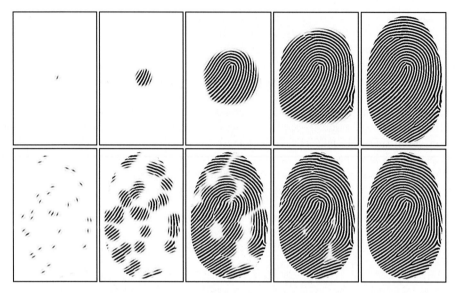

Figure 6.14. Some intermediate steps of a fingerprint generation process starting from a single central point (top row) and from a number of randomly located points (bottom row). Usually, increasing the number of initial points provides a more irregular ridge pattern richer in minutiae.

6.4 Generation of Synthetic Fingerprint Impressions

Several factors contribute to making the impressions of a given finger substantially different when captured by a live-scan scanner (see Chapter 2):

- displacement in the x- and y-directions and rotation;
- different touching areas;
- non-linear distortion produced by the non-orthogonal pressure of the finger against the sensor;
- variations in the ridge line thickness given by pressure intensity or by skin dampness (wet or dry);
- small cuts or abrasions on the fingertip;
- background noise and other random noise.

For each fingerprint impression to be generated from a given master fingerprint, SFINGE sequentially performs these steps (the numbering continues from Section 6.3 according to Figure 6.4):

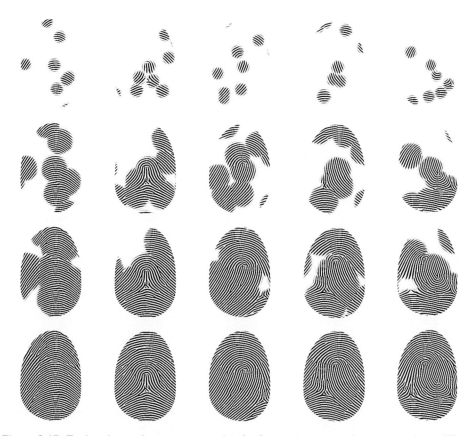

Figure 6.15. Each column shows an example of a fingerprint generation process for a different fingerprint class; from left to right: arch, tented arch, left loop, right loop, and whorl.

Figure 6.16. Genesis of a minutia point during the fusion of two regions created by two different initial points.

5. definition of the fingerprint portion that is in contact with the sensor (this is simply performed by shifting the fingerprint pattern with respect to the fixed external silhouette);
6. variation in the average thickness of the ridge (skin condition);
7. distortion;
8. perturbation;
9. global translation/rotation;
10. background generation.

Variation in the ridge thickness

Skin dampness and finger pressure against the sensor platen have similar effects on the acquired images: when the skin is dry or the pressure is low, ridges appear thinner, whereas when the skin is wet or the pressure is high, ridges appear thicker (see Figure 6.17).

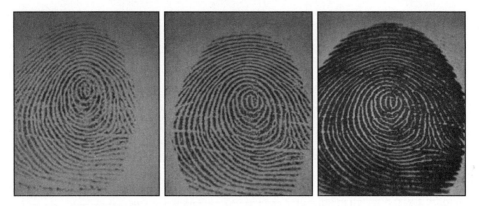

Figure 6.17. Three impressions of the same real finger as captured when the finger is dry, normal, and wet, respectively. Reprinted with permission from Cappelli, Maio, and Maltoni (2002b). ©IEEE.

Morphological operators (Gonzales and Woods, 1992) are applied to the master fingerprint to simulate different degrees of dampness/pressure. In particular, the erosion operator is applied to simulate low pressure or dry skin, and the dilation operator is adopted to simulate high pressure or wet skin (see Figure 6.18). The structuring element used is a square box; its size varies from 2×2 to 4×4, to modulate the magnitude of the ridge thickness variation.

Original image

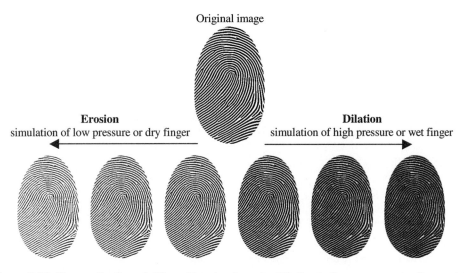

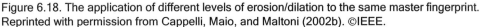

Erosion
simulation of low pressure or dry finger

Dilation
simulation of high pressure or wet finger

Figure 6.18. The application of different levels of erosion/dilation to the same master fingerprint. Reprinted with permission from Cappelli, Maio, and Maltoni (2002b). ©IEEE.

Fingerprint distortion

One of the main aspects that distinguishes different impressions of the same finger is the presence of non-linear distortions, mainly due to skin deformations according to different finger placements over the sensing element (see Figure 6.19). In fact, due to skin plasticity, the application of force, some of whose components are not orthogonal to the sensor surface, produces non-linear distortions (compression or stretching) in the acquired fingerprints (see Chapter 4).

SFINGE exploits the skin-distortion model introduced in Cappelli, Maio, and Maltoni (2001a). Unlike in fingerprint matching, where the function *distortion*(.) (see Section 4.5) is applied to re-map minutiae points in order to improve fingerprint matching, here the mapping has to be applied to the whole image, in order to simulate realistic distorted impressions. For this purpose, Lagrangian interpolation is employed to obtain smoothed gray-scale deformed images. Performing Lagrangian interpolation requires the inverse mapping function *distortion*$^{-1}$(.) to be computed, but unfortunately, this function cannot be analytically expressed. Therefore, for each pixel involved in the mapping, the Newton–Raphson method (Press et al., 1992) is used for numerically calculating the inverse. In Figure 6.20, a master fingerprint and a distorted impression of it are shown.

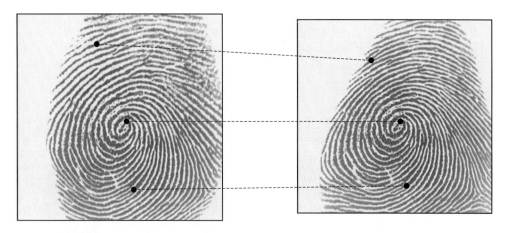

Figure 6.19. Two impressions of the same real finger where a few corresponding minutiae are marked to highlight the distortion. Reprinted with permission from Cappelli, Maio, and Maltoni (2002b). ©IEEE.

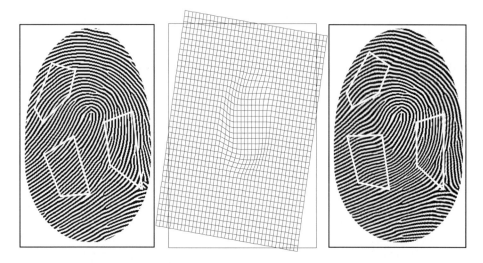

Figure 6.20. A master fingerprint (on the left) and a distorted impression (on the right); the equivalent distortion of a square mesh is shown in the middle. To better highlight the non-linear deformations, some corresponding minutiae are connected by white segments in both fingerprint images.

Perturbation and global translation/rotation

During fingerprint acquisition, several factors contribute to the deterioration of the original signal, thus producing a noisy gray-scale image: irregularity of the ridges and their different contact with the sensor surface, presence of small pores within the ridges, presence of very small prominence ridges, gaps, and cluttering noise due to non-uniform pressure of the finger against the sensor. Furthermore, the fingerprint is usually not perfectly centered in the image and can present a certain amount of rotation. The perturbation phase sequentially performs these steps:

1. isolate the white pixels associated with the valleys into a separate layer. This is simply performed by copying the pixels brighter than a fixed threshold to a temporary image;
2. add noise in the form of small white blobs of variable size and shape. The amount of noise increases with the inverse of the fingerprint border distance;
3. smooth the resulting image with a 3×3 averaging box filter;
4. superimpose the valley layer to the resulting image;
5. rotate and translate the image.

Steps 1 and 4 are necessary to avoid excessive overall image smoothing. Figure 6.21 shows an example where the intermediate images produced after Steps 2, 4, and 5 are reported.

Background generation

The output of the previous step is a fingerprint image that appears realistic, but the background is completely white. In order to generate backgrounds similar to those of fingerprint images acquired with a given sensor, a statistical model based on the KL transform (Jolliffe, 1986) is adopted. The model requires a set of background-only images as a training set (see Figure 6.22): a linear subspace that represents the main variations in the training backgrounds is calculated and then used to randomly generate new backgrounds. Formally, let $B = \{\mathbf{b}_1, \mathbf{b}_2, ..., \mathbf{b}_m\}$ be a set of m n-dimensional vectors (obtained from the background images simply by concatenating their rows) and let:

* $\overline{\mathbf{b}} = \dfrac{1}{m} \sum_{\mathbf{b} \in B} \mathbf{b}$ be their mean vector;

* $\mathbf{C} = \dfrac{1}{m} \sum_{\mathbf{b} \in B} (\mathbf{b} - \overline{\mathbf{b}})(\mathbf{b} - \overline{\mathbf{b}})^T$ be their covariance matrix;

* $\mathbf{\Phi} \in \mathfrak{R}^{n \times n}$ be the orthonormal matrix that diagonalizes $\mathbf{C}$; that is, $\mathbf{\Phi}^T \mathbf{C} \mathbf{\Phi} = \mathbf{\Lambda}$,

    $\mathbf{\Lambda} = Diag(\lambda_1, \lambda_2, ..., \lambda_n)$, $\mathbf{\Phi} = [\varphi_1, \varphi_2, ..., \varphi_n]$,

where λ_i and φ_i, $i = 1..n$ are the eigenvalues and the eigenvectors of $\mathbf{C}$, respectively.

Then, given a parameter k, $0 < k < \min(n,m)$, the k-dimensional subspace S_B is identified by the mean vector $\overline{\mathbf{b}}$ and by the projection matrix $\mathbf{\Phi}_k \in \mathfrak{R}^{n \times k}$, whose columns are the k columns of $\mathbf{\Phi}$ corresponding to the k largest eigenvalues:

$$\mathbf{\Phi}_k = \left[\boldsymbol{\varphi}_{i_1}, \boldsymbol{\varphi}_{i_2}, ..., \boldsymbol{\varphi}_{i_k} \right] \quad \text{with} \quad \lambda_{i_1} \geq \lambda_{i_2} \geq ... \lambda_{i_k} \geq ... \lambda_{i_n}.$$

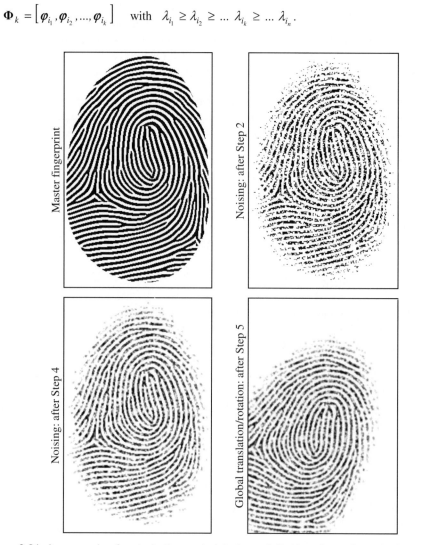

Figure 6.21. An example of perturbation and global translation/rotation, where the intermediate images produced after Steps 2, 4, and 5 are reported.

The generation of a new background is performed by selecting a point in the subspace S_B and by back projecting it in the original n-dimensional space:

1. a k-dimensional vector $\mathbf{y} = [y_1, y_2, ..., y_k]$ is randomly generated according to k normal distributions: $y_j = N\left(0, \lambda_{i_j}^{1/2}\right)$, $j = 1..k$;

2. the corresponding n-dimensional vector $\mathbf{b}$ is obtained as: $\mathbf{b} = \Phi_k \mathbf{y} + \overline{\mathbf{b}}$.

Figure 6.22 shows some examples of the background images (obtained from an optical scanner) used as a training set for the background generation step; Figure 6.23 reports three synthetic fingerprints with backgrounds generated according to the above model.

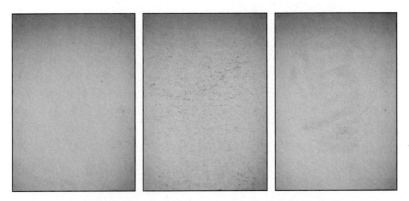

Figure 6.22. Examples of background-only images (acquired from an optical scanner) used for training the background generator.

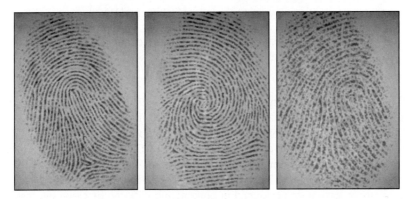

Figure 6.23. Three synthetic images with backgrounds generated according to the model (the parameters used for training are $m = 65$ and $k = 8$).

6.5 Validation of the Synthetic Generator

The fingerprint images generated by SFINGE appear very realistic (Figures 6.24 and 6.25 show some examples), but an in-depth analysis is necessary to understand if they can be a valid substitute for real fingerprints for testing and training fingerprint recognition algorithms. Some of the experiments that have been carried out to validate the images produced by SFINGE are described in the following.

Figure 6.24. Two synthetic fingerprint images (first row) are compared with two real fingerprints captured with a live-scan scanner (second row).

The first test was an experiment to determine if the synthetic fingerprints appeared visually similar to the real fingerprints. This test was performed during the Fifteenth International Conference on Pattern Recognition (September 2000), when about 90 people, most of them with some background in fingerprint analysis, were asked to find a synthetic fingerprint image among four images (three of which were real fingerprints) presented to them. Only 23% of subjects (refer to Figure 6.26 and Table 6.1) correctly identified the synthetic image.

Some extensive tests were performed in conjunction with the first two International Fingerprint Verification Competitions (FVC2000, Maio et al. (2002a) and FVC2002, Maio et al.

(2002b)). In both contests, four fingerprint databases were used. Three of the databases (DB1, DB2, and DB3) were acquired from real fingers through various live-scan scanners, and fingerprints in the fourth database (DB4) were synthetically generated by SFINGE. Not only did the participating algorithms exhibit very similar performance on DB4 as on the other databases, but the genuine/impostor distributions and the FMR/FNMR curves were also surprisingly close. Figure 6.27 shows the performance of the PA15 algorithm over the four databases of FVC2002. It is worth noting here that the graph computed on the synthetic database has a trend very similar to the other three graphs. This means that fingerprints generated by SFINGE are realistic from the point of view of the matching algorithm PA15.

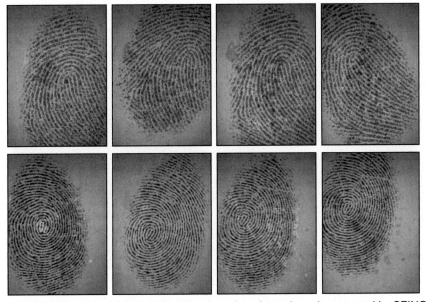

Figure 6.25. Two sets of fingerprint impressions (one in each row) generated by SFINGE.

In order to better support this claim and to consider all the algorithms evaluated in FVC2002, an analysis of the ranking distributions among all the participants over the four FVC2002 databases was performed. Let $R_{ik}^{(j)}$ be the ranking of participant i over database k according to performance indicator j (in FVC2002, the number of participants was 31 and four accuracy indicators were used to compare their performance: EER, ZeroFMR, FMR1000, and FMR100; see Section 1.4); let $RRD_i^{(j)}$ and $SRD_i^{(j)}$ be the average ranking difference of participant i according to indicator j, among the three real databases and between the synthetic database and each of the real ones, respectively:

$$RRD_i^{(j)} = \frac{\left|R_{i1}^{(j)} - R_{i2}^{(j)}\right| + \left|R_{i1}^{(j)} - R_{i3}^{(j)}\right| + \left|R_{i2}^{(j)} - R_{i3}^{(j)}\right|}{3} \tag{6}$$

$$SRD_i^{(j)} = \frac{\left|R_{i4}^{(j)} - R_{i1}^{(j)}\right| + \left|R_{i4}^{(j)} - R_{i2}^{(j)}\right| + \left|R_{i4}^{(j)} - R_{i3}^{(j)}\right|}{3}. \tag{7}$$

$RRD_i^{(j)}$ indicates how stable is the performance of participant i (according to indicator j) over the three databases; $SRD_i^{(j)}$ denotes the amount of variation between synthetic and real databases. Table 6.2 reports, for each indicator $j = 1..4$, some information about the distribution of $RRD_i^{(j)}$ and $SRD_i^{(j)}$ for $i = 1..31$; the results are somewhat unexpected: the ranking difference $SRD^{(j)}$ is often even lower than the corresponding $RRD^{(j)}$, thus indicating that the difference between the synthetic DB and the others is even smaller than the inter-difference among the three real databases; this proves that databases of synthetic fingerprints generated by SFINGE can be successfully used to measure the performance of matching algorithms.

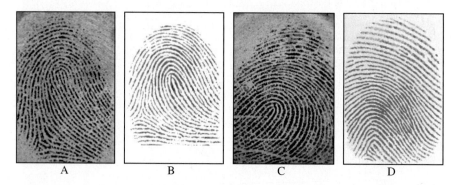

Figure 6.26. Three real fingerprints (B, C, and D), acquired with different sensors and a synthetic fingerprint (A).

Survey results (%)	
A	23
B	27
C	21
D	29

Table 6.1. For each fingerprint in Figure 6.26, the percentage of people (out of 90) that chose it as the synthetic one is reported.

	$RRD_i^{(1)}$	$SRD_i^{(1)}$	$RRD_i^{(2)}$	$SRD_i^{(2)}$	$RRD_i^{(3)}$	$SRD_i^{(3)}$	$RRD_i^{(4)}$	$SRD_i^{(4)}$
Average	2.84	2.65	3.14	2.74	2.58	2.58	2.69	2.59
Max	8.67	11.33	11.33	7.67	7.33	5.67	8.00	10.67
Min	0.00	0.00	0.67	0.33	0.00	0.33	0.00	0.33
St. Dev.	2.51	2.43	2.35	1.76	1.94	1.45	2.15	2.36

Table 6.2. Distributions of $RRD_i^{(j)}$ and $SRD_i^{(j)}$ over all the FVC2002 participants: the average, maximum, minimum values, and the standard deviations are reported for each indicator j.

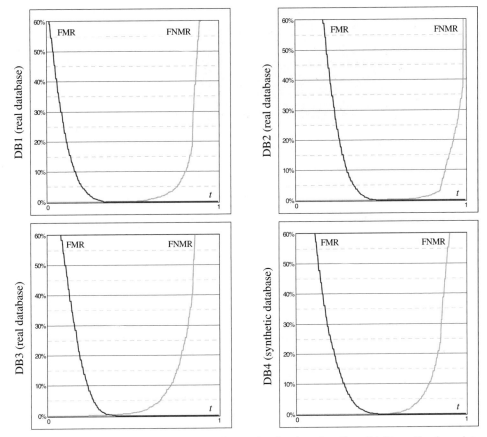

Figure 6.27. FVC2002: FMR versus FNMR graphs for the algorithm PA15 on the four databases.

6.6 The SFINGE Software Tool

BIOLAB, University of Bologna, Cesena, Italy has developed an automated software tool for generating fingerprint images according to the SFINGE method described in this chapter. A demo version of this tool is included in the DVD that accompanies this book. Figures 6.28 through 6.30 show the user interface of the software: for each step of the generation method, the user can adjust the main parameters and observe the corresponding effects on the synthetic fingerprint (Figure 6.30).

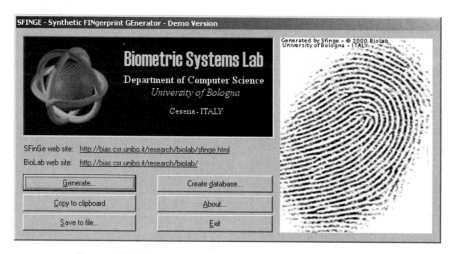

Figure 6.28. The main window of the SFINGE software tool.

The software also allows a database of synthetic fingerprints to be batch-generated, given a relatively small set of input parameters (see Figure 6.29): number of fingers, impressions per finger, image size, seed for the random number generator, maximum amount of translation/rotation, maximum amount of perturbation or noise, maximum amount of deformation, and global database difficulty. Although the code is not fully optimized, the fingerprint generation is quite fast: on a 1.5 GHz PC, a database of 10,000 fingerprints can be generated in about eight hours. Thus a large database of synthetic fingerprints can be generated in a reasonable amount of time at no additional cost! Furthermore, by using this software, two identical databases can be generated at different places by specifying the same pseudo random number and parameters; this allows the same test to be reproduced without exchanging huge amounts of test data.

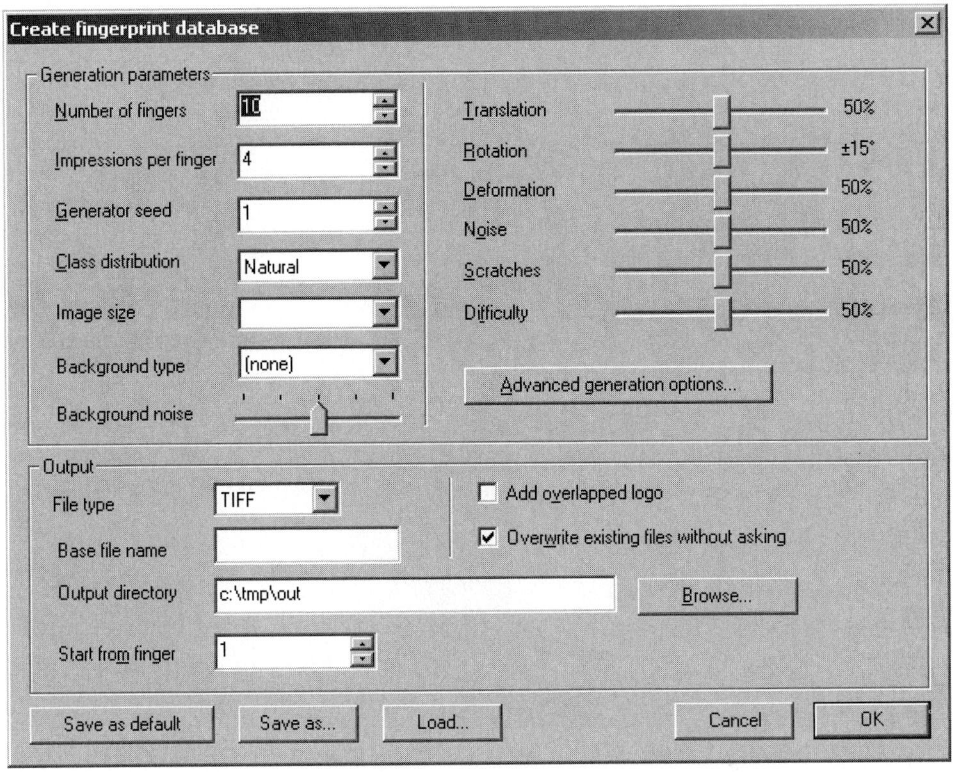

Figure 6.29. The batch generation options.

6.7 Summary

Synthetic fingerprint generation is an effective technique to overcome the problem of collecting large fingerprint databases for test purposes. Obviously, real fingerprint databases cannot be completely substituted, especially when the performance has to be measured with respect to a given real environment/application/demographics; on the other hand, synthetic fingerprints have proved to be well suited for technology evaluations like FVC2000 (Maio et al., 2002a) and FVC2002 (Maio et al., 2002b). The use of synthetic fingerprints is not only limited to the problem of performance evaluation. It can be also be used for these tasks:

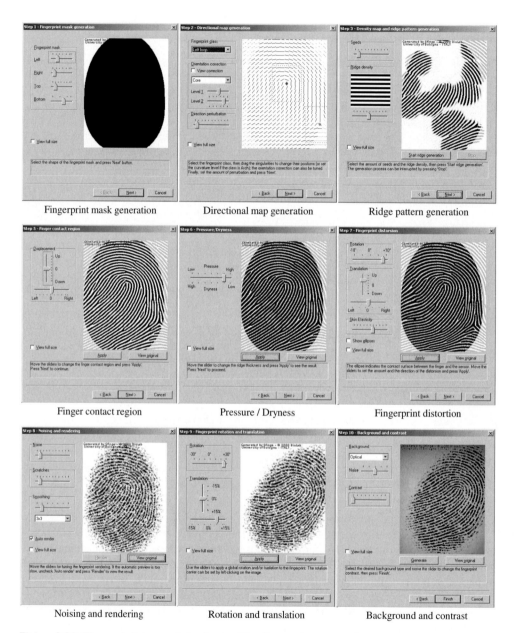

Figure 6.30. The main intermediate steps of the fingerprint generation, using the SFINGE software tool.

- many classifiers and pattern recognition techniques (i.e., neural networks, principal component analysis, Support Vector Machines, etc.) require a large training set for an accurate learning stage. Synthetic fingerprint images are very well suited for this purpose: in fact, the generator parameters allow explicit control of the type and features of the synthetic fingerprints (e.g., class, type of noise, distortion, etc.) and this can be exploited in conjunction with boosting techniques (Schapire (1990) and Freund and Schapire (1996)) to drive the learning process. For example, in Cappelli, Maio, and Maltoni (2000c), a large synthetic training set (generated by SFINGE) was successfully used to derive optimal MKL subspaces for fingerprint indexing;
- the synthetic fingerprints generated by SFINGE can be used to test the robustness of fingerprint verification systems against "Trojan horse" attacks at the sensor or the feature extractor module (see Section 9.5). SFINGE allows us to generate large sets of fingerprints whose features (e.g., minutiae distribution) can be varied independently of other fingerprint characteristics (e.g., orientation image) and, therefore, it is well suited to study the robustness against "hill-climbing" types of Trojan horse attacks.

The SFINGE method described here has some limitations:

- in SFINGE, the ridge thickness is constant throughout the fingerprint image; this is not true in nature, where this feature may vary across the same fingerprint;
- SFINGE distributes the noise uniformly over the entire fingerprint area (except for the borders where it gradually increases); in real fingerprints, the noise can be clustered in certain regions; both high quality and poor quality regions can be found in the same fingerprint (see Chapter 3);
- intra-ridge noise, which in nature is partially produced by finger pores, is randomly generated by SFINGE. Although this is not a problem when generating fingerprints from different fingers, this is not very realistic for impressions of the same finger, where a certain correlation should be taken into account.

Finally, further investigations are necessary to better understand how close synthetic fingerprints are to the real ones from an "individuality" point of view (ref. Chapter 8). Some experimentation in this direction has been performed to measure the intra-class and inter-class variation of the various fingerprint features (e.g., orientation image, frequency image, minutiae), showing that the parameters of the generator can be tuned to properly emulate the variations in real fingerprints. However, a more in-depth analysis is necessary to determine whether SFINGE is capable of generating all different types of minutiae with the frequencies found in nature.

7
Multimodal Biometric Systems

7.1 Introduction

A biometric system may use one or more instances of a single biometric identifier (e.g., multiple impressions of a finger) or it may utilize one or more instances of multiple biometric identifiers (e.g., fingerprint and face images) taken from an individual. Based on the nature of the input, a biometric system can be classified into one of the four categories:

- *unibiometric system* is a system that uses only a single biometric identifier;
- *unimodal biometric system* is a subset of a unibiometric system that uses a single instance (snapshot), a single representation, and a single matcher for a recognition decision;
- *multibiometric system* is a biometric system that uses more than one independent or weakly correlated biometric identifier taken from an individual (e.g., fingerprint and face of the same person, or fingerprints from two different fingers of a person, respectively);
- *multimodal biometric system* is a superset of a multibiometric system that may use more than one correlated biometric measurement. For example, a multimodal biometric system may be based on multiple impressions of a finger, multiple images of a face in a video, multiple representations of a single input, multiple matchers of a single representation, or any combination thereof.

Thus, the definition of a unimodal biometric system is the most restrictive and the definition of a multimodal biometric system is the most general. In this chapter, we discuss multimodal biometric systems involving fingerprints.

High-security verification applications typically have a very stringent performance requirement (e.g., very low FMR) that a unimodal biometric system is often unable to meet due to limited discriminatory information contained in each biometric. Golfarelli, Maio, and Maltoni (1997) have shown that the *information content* (number of distinguishable patterns) in two of the most commonly used representations of hand geometry and face are only of the order of 10^5 and 10^3, respectively. Therefore, hand geometry- and face-based systems are not expected to be sufficiently accurate for high-security applications. In addition, although fingerprint and iris possess much larger information content (see Chapter 8), the available fingerprint-based automatic verification systems are not always able to deal with poor quality images. As a result, they do not meet the high matching accuracy requirements of certain critical applications.

The limitations of a unimodal biometric system become more apparent if the system has to operate in the identification mode. As discussed in Section 1.4, the identification false match rate (FMR_N) increases linearly with the number N of the users in the database since $FMR_N \cong N \cdot FMR$, where FMR is the verification false match rate. For example, suppose that the FMR of a given system is 10^{-5} (i.e., just one false match in 100,000 matches); then, if the database size is 10^4 (i.e., $N = 10,000$), the probability of falsely matching a database template with an impostor input is $FMR_N = 10\%$. This suggests that an impostor has a good chance of "breaking" the security provided by the biometric system by using all 10 fingers of her two hands.

Combining biometrics with non-biometrics (knowledge or possession) based authentication schemes is an attractive choice. However, it reintroduces the security problems inherent in the knowledge- and possession-based techniques; that is, a password can be forgotten or guessed, a key may be lost or stolen, and both can be shared. On the other hand, a multimodal biometric system that combines more than one biometric modality can significantly improve the recognition accuracy of a verification/identification system, without reintroducing the problems associated with the non-biometric authentication techniques.

One of the important factors in selecting a biometric identifier is the universality property. But no biometric is truly universal. For example, fingerprints are supposedly universal, but there is a small fraction of the population that does not possess fingerprints due to hand-related disabilities, and yet another small fraction of the population (such as manual workers) that has have very poor quality fingerprints (due to cuts and bruises on the fingertips) that are unsuitable for automatic matching. Furthermore, a fingerprint sensor may not be able to acquire good quality fingerprint images from fingers that are very oily, dry, or devoid of any ridge structure. This results in non-zero failure to capture (FTC) and/or failure to enroll (FTE) errors. A multibiometric system may allow the users to choose a biometric of their preference, thus solving the parochiality of a single biometric. The resulting system is likely to be used by a larger target population and will be perceived as user friendly.

A multibiometric system may be more difficult to fool than a single biometric. For example, a system that combines fingerprint and voice not only leads to higher recognition accuracy, but it is also more difficult to circumvent such a multibiometric system. In this system, the fingerprint subsystem provides high accuracy and a challenge-response-based voice verification subsystem (Campbell, 1997) ensures higher fraud protection. In addition, a multibiometric system can request a user to present a subset of biometric traits in a random order to ensure that a "live" person is indeed present at the point of data acquisition. For example, a fingerprint-based biometric system may ask users to select a specific sequence of fingers at the time of enrollment. Suppose a user chooses the left index finger followed by the right middle finger, followed by the right index. At the time of verification, this user will be required to present three of his fingerprints in the same order. To fool this system, an adversary will not only need the fingerprints of the enrolled user, but also knowledge of the correct sequence of finger placement on the sensor. An arbitrarily long sequence of the 10 fingerprints of a person can be used to make the system increasingly difficult to circumvent and extremely accurate. In other schemes, a fingerprint verification system may enroll all the fingers of a user and prompt the user during the verification to present her fingerprints in an order that is randomly generated for each verification attempt.

There are, however, a few disadvantages of using a multimodal biometric system. First, a multimodal biometric system is more expensive and requires more computational and storage resources than a unimodal system. Second, when a multimodal system requires that more than one biometric be sensed, it causes some inconvenience to the user and requires additional verification time. For example, in a system that requires both fingerprint and retina images of a person, a user will not only need to touch the fingerprint sensor, but will also need to "peek" into the retinascope. This leads to longer enrollment as well as verification times. Furthermore, an effective fusion scheme is needed to combine the evidence from different modalities. If the multiple modalities are not properly combined, the combination may actually degrade system accuracy.

In designing a multimodal biometric system, a number of issues need to be considered: i) what is the main objective of utilizing multiple modalities? ii) what is the operational mode of the system (verification vs. identification)? iii) which biometrics should be integrated? iv) how many biometric identifiers are sufficient? The selection of the biometric identifiers depends upon the application requirement and the composition of the target population. Therefore the main challenge in designing a multimodal biometric system is the integration of individual modalities to improve the accuracy and speed of the recognition system.

7.2 Performance of a Multimodal Biometric System

Can the performance of a fingerprint recognition system be enhanced by involving other biometric modalities? It is well known in the pattern recognition literature that different classifiers[1] with essentially the same overall accuracy often misclassify different patterns (Ho, Hull, and Srihari (1994) and Kittler et al. (1998)). This suggests that different classifiers offer rather complementary information about a given classification task. Toussaint (1971), Cover (1974,

---

[1] Fingerprint verification and identification are essentially pattern classification problems. In fingerprint verification, the matcher classifies the input fingerprint feature vector into one of two classes ("genuine" and "impostor"). In fingerprint identification, the matcher classifies the input fingerprint feature vector into one of $N + 1$ classes ("user 1", "user 2", ..., "user N", and "impostor").

1977), Fang (1979), and Oh, Lee, and Suen (1999) have shown that a classifier using statistically independent features performs better than a classifier using correlated features. Kuncheva et al. (2000) and Kuncheva and Whitaker (2002) further show that the same reasoning is valid when combining different classifiers. Kuncheva et al. (2000) used synthetic data to demonstrate that the best improvement through classifier combination is achieved when the component classifiers are negatively correlated (when one classifier is wrong, the other is correct, and vice versa) and the amount of improvement is directly proportional to the degree of negative correlation.

Consider a two-class classification problem and a multiclassifier system consisting of NC classifiers (assume NC is odd); the majority vote rule classifies an input pattern as belonging to the class that obtains at least $K = (NC + 1)/2$ votes. If p is the probability that a single classifier performs correctly, then the probability that the multiclassifier system correctly classifies the input is given by the binomial equation:

$$P_{correct}(NC) = \sum_{m=K}^{NC} \binom{NC}{m} p^m (1-p)^{NC-m}.$$

If $p = 0.80$ (each individual classifier has a 20% error), then we obtain the following performance of the multiclassifier system for several values of NC.

$NC = 3$ $(K = 2) \rightarrow P_{correct} = 0.896,$

$NC = 5$ $(K = 3) \rightarrow P_{correct} = 0.942,$

$NC = 7$ $(K = 4) \rightarrow P_{correct} = 0.966,$

$NC = 9$ $(K = 5) \rightarrow P_{correct} = 0.980,$

$NC = 15$ $(K = 8) \rightarrow P_{correct} = 0.995,$

$NC = 21$ $(K = 11) \rightarrow P_{correct} = 0.999.$

The above formulation assumes that the classifiers themselves are statistically independent, which is not easy to justify in practice. Nevertheless, this analysis shows that a combination of multiple classifiers should be explored. Prabhakar and Jain (2002) demonstrated the improvement in matching accuracy from a combination of four different (not necessarily independent) fingerprint matchers.

According to Jain, Duin, and Mao (2000), there are several reasons why different classifiers may convey independent information for a given classification task. These reasons support the use of classifier combination to improve overall system performance. i) Different classifiers may be developed in different contexts for the same classification problem; for example, fingerprint and face information can be combined to establish the identity of a person. ii) When a classifier is trained on a small, often proprietary, training set collected at a certain time and in a certain environment, it may not generalize well on another data set collected at a different time and in a different environment. iii) Different classifiers trained on the same data differ in their performance in local regions as well as globally in the feature space. iv) Many classifiers provide different results with different (parameter) initializations. These classifiers (such as multilayer neural networks) can be combined to take advantage of various attempts to train a particular type of classifier. v) Multiple representations of the same biometric characteristic would lead to different matchers. For example, fingerprint matchers can be designed based on minutiae representation and filterbank features. In summary, different based on minutiae representation and filterbank features. In summary, different feature sets, different training sets, different classification methods, or different training sessions result in classifiers that misclassify different test patterns. The outputs from all these classifiers can be combined in the hope of improving the overall accuracy.

Note that not all the combination strategies may improve classification accuracy. Combining classifiers that are highly (positively) correlated may actually result in performance degradation, because no extra discriminatory information is available and errors may accumulate. This is related to the phenomenon of the "curse of dimensionality" (Jain and Chandrasekaran, 1982). To ensure that a combination results in performance improvement, Prabhakar and Jain (2002) have stressed that an automatic classifier selection (similar to feature selection methods proposed by Toussaint (1971) and Oh, Lee, and Suen (1999)) be first performed to eliminate highly correlated classifiers. In addition, how the classifier outputs are combined also plays an important role in the performance of the combined system; a poorly designed combination scheme can degrade classification accuracy in the same way as by including redundant classifiers. Typically, a combination scheme is designed based on certain assumptions (e.g., many schemes assume that the component classifiers are independent and identically distributed or the impostor and genuine distributions are "known"). A violation of these assumptions may result in the combination scheme actually decreasing system performance. Furthermore, a combination scheme may be sound from a theoretical point of view, but the training data may be either not representative or not sufficient (Jain and Chandrasekaran (1982) and Raudys and Jain (1991)). If the combination scheme is trained on a small sample size, it is not expected to generalize well. Finally, Prabhakar and Jain (2002) argue, in the context of fingerprint matching, combining two weak matchers is expected to result in a large improvement, combining two strong matchers is expected to result in a small improvement, and the two individually best matchers do not necessarily form the best pair.

7.3 Integration Strategies

Jain, Duin, and Mao (2000) summarized and categorized various classifier combination schemes based on the integration architecture, level of fusion, fusion strategy, and selection/training approaches of individual classifiers (also refer to Xu, Krzyzac, and Suen (1992), Dasarathy (1994), and Kittler et al. (1998)).

Architecture

The main architectures for classifier combination are: i) parallel, ii) cascading (or serial combination), and iii) hierarchical (treelike); see Figure 7.1.

In the parallel scheme, all the classifiers work independently of each other and the results from the individual classifiers are combined. In the cascading scheme, individual classifiers operate one after another in sequence.

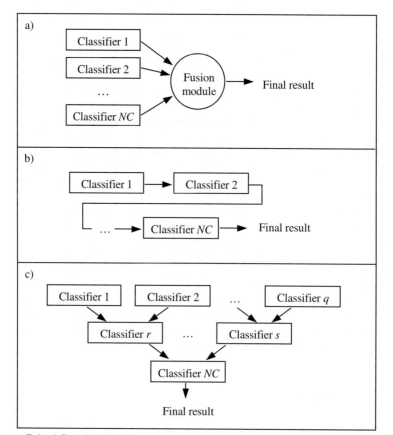

Figure 7.1. a) Parallel, b) serial, and c) hierarchical combination of *NC* classifiers.

The number of possible classes into which a given test pattern can be assigned is successively reduced as more classifiers in the sequence are invoked. For example, in a fingerprint
identification task involving a database of *N* templates, the first classifier in the multiclassifier
system may reduce the number of potential classes to, say 50; the second classifier can then
further reduce the number of possible classes from 50 to only 10, and so on. Typically, classifiers that are cheap (in terms of low computational and feature extraction costs) and have relatively low accuracy but small false non-match rate are used first, followed by more accurate
and expensive classifiers. In the hierarchical scheme, individual classifiers are combined in a
treelike structure.

Level of fusion

Different combination strategies expect different types of input from individual classifiers. These expectations can be grouped in the categories: i) *feature or measurement* values, ii) *confidence* values, iii) *rank* values, and iv) *abstract labels*. Refer to Figure 7.2 for schemes of fusion in a parallel architecture.

At the feature level, the features extracted from different modalities are combined. The new augmented feature space has a higher dimensionality (although feature reduction techniques can be applied) and it is hoped is more discriminative. The integration at the feature level assumes a strong interaction among the input measurements and such integration schemes are referred to as *tightly coupled integration* (Clark and Yuille, 1990). At the confidence level, a classifier outputs a numerical value for each class indicating the probability that the given input pattern belongs to that class. At the rank level, a classifier assigns a rank to each class with the highest rank being the first choice. Rank value should not be used in isolation because the highest rank does not necessarily mean a high confidence in the classification. At the abstract level, a classifier only outputs a unique label (e.g, accept or reject in a biometric system) or several class labels (in which case, the classes are equally good). A combined system based on the confidence or abstract level is called a *loosely coupled system* (Clark and Yuille, 1990). It assumes very little or no interaction among the biometric modalities (e.g., face and finger) and integration occurs at the output of relatively autonomous agents, each agent independently assessing the input from its own perspective. A major advantage of this combination is that it is easy to integrate different types of measurements or features (e.g., eigenface values and fingerprint minutiae).

It is generally believed that the earlier in a system a combination scheme is applied, the more effective it is. For example, an integration at the feature level typically results in more improvement than at the confidence level, followed by the abstract level. This is because feature representation conveys the richest information, followed by confidence value of a classifier, and the abstract labels contain the least amount of information about the decision being made. However, it is more difficult to combine classifiers at the feature level because the relationship between the feature spaces of different classifiers may not be known and the feature representations may not be compatible. Furthermore, the multimodal system may not have access to the feature values of individual modalities because of their proprietary nature. In such cases, the confidence or abstract level integrations are the only options. This is also reflected in the nature of the research dedicated to multimodal biometric systems; very few published papers report results on a combination at the feature level.

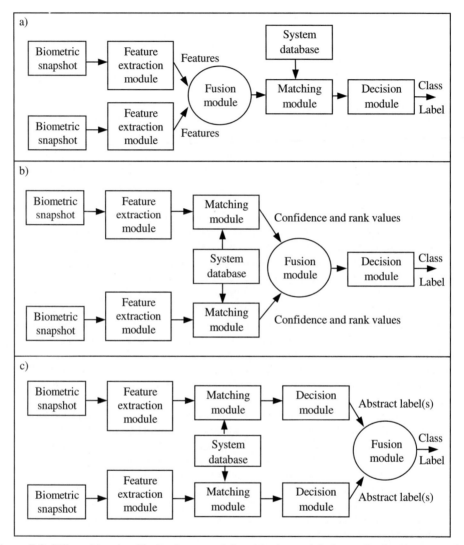

Figure 7.2. Different levels of fusion in a parallel architecture: a) fusion at the feature extraction level; b) fusion at confidence level or rank level; c) fusion at abstract level. In all the three cases the final class label is Accept or Reject when the biometric system is operating in the verification mode and the identity of the best matched user when operating in the identification mode. In c), the intermediate abstract label(s) could be Accept or Reject in a verification system or a subset of database users in an identification system.

Combination strategy

A *combination strategy* (also called *combination scheme*) is a technique used to combine the output of the individual classifiers. The most popular combination strategies at the abstract level are based on majority vote rules, which simply assign an input pattern to the most voted class (see Section 7.2). When two classifiers are combined, either a logical AND or a logical OR operator is typically used. When more than two classifiers are integrated, the AND/OR rules can be combined. For example, a biometric system may work on "fingerprint OR (face AND hand geometry)"; that is, it requires a user to present either a fingerprint or both face and hand geometry for recognition. Class set reduction, logistic regression, and *Borda* counts are the most commonly used approaches in combining classifiers based on the rank labels (Ho, Hull, and Srihari, 1994). In class set reduction, a subset of the classes is selected with the aim that the subset be as small as possible and still contain the true class. Multiple subsets from multiple modalities are typically combined using either a union or an intersection of the subsets. The logistic regression and Borda count methods are collectively called the class set reordering methods. The objective here is to derive a consensus ranking of the given classes such that the true class is ranked at the top. Rank labels are very useful for integration in an indexing/retrieval system. A biometric retrieval system typically outputs an ordered list of candidates (most likely matches). The top element of this ordered list is the most likely to be a correct match and the bottom of the list is the least likely match.

The most popular combination schemes for combining confidence values from multiple modalities are sum, mean, median, product, minimum, and maximum rules. Kittler et al. (1998) have developed a theoretical framework in an attempt to understand the underlying mathematical basis of these popular schemes. Their experiments demonstrated that the sum or mean scheme typically performs very well in practice. A problem in using the sum rule is that the confidences (or scores) from different modalities should be normalized. This normalization typically involves mapping the confidence measures from different modalities into a common domain. For example, a biometric system may output a distance score (the lower the score, the more similar the patterns) whereas another may output a similarity score (the higher the score, the more similar the patterns) and thus the scores cannot be directly combined using the sum rule. In its simplest form, this normalization may only include inverting the sign of distance scores such that a higher score corresponds to a higher similarity. In a more complex form, the normalization may be non-linear which can be learned from training data by estimating distributions of confidence values from each modality. The scores are then translated and scaled to have zero mean, unit variance, and then remapped to a fixed interval of (0,1) using a hyperbolic tangent function. Note that it is tempting to parameterize the estimated distributions for normalization. However, such parameterization of distributions should be used with care, because the error rates of biometric systems are typically very small and a small error in estimating the tails of the distributions may result in a significant change in the error estimates (see Figure 7.3). Another common practice is to compute different scaling factors (weights) for each modality from training data, such that the accuracy of the combined classifier is maximized. This weighted sum rule is expected to work better than the simple sum rule when the component classifiers have different strengths (i.e., different error rates).

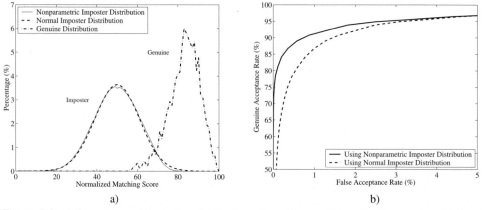

Figure 7.3. a) Genuine and impostor distributions for a fingerprint verification system (Jain et al., 2000) and a Normal approximation for the impostor distribution. Visually, the Normal approximation seems to be good, but causes significant decrease in performance compared to the non-parametric estimate as shown in the ROCs in b), where FMR is referred to as FAR (False Acceptance Rate) and (1-FNMR) as Genuine Acceptance Rate. ©Elsevier.

Some schemes to combine multiple modalities in biometric systems have also been studied from a theoretical point of view. Through a theoretical analysis, Daugman (1999b) showed that if a strong biometric and a weak biometric are combined with an abstract level combination using either the AND or the OR voting rules, the performance of the combination will be worse than the better of the two individual biometrics. Hong, Jain, and Pankanti's (1999) theoretical analysis that AND/OR voting strategies can improve performance only when certain conditions are satisfied confirmed Daugman's findings. Their analysis further showed that a confidence level fusion is expected to significantly improve overall performance even in the case of combining a weak and a strong biometric. Kittler et al. (1998) introduced a sensitivity analysis to explain why the sum (or average) rule outperforms the other rules. They showed that the sum rule is less sensitive than the other similar rules (such as the "product" rule) to the error rates of individual classifiers in estimating posterior probabilities (confidence values). They claim that the sum rule is the most appropriate for combining different estimates of the same posterior probabilities (e.g., resulting from different classifier initializations). Prabhakar and Jain (2002) compared the sum and the product rules with the Neyman–Pearson combination scheme and showed that the product rule is worse than the sum rule when combining correlated features and both the sum rule and the product rules are inferior to the Neyman–Pearson combination scheme when combining weak and strong classifiers.

Some of the well-known approaches for combining classifier outputs are compared in Table 7.1 based on a few properties.

Combination strategy	Information level	Architecture	Trainable	Adaptive	Comments
Voting, AND/OR	Abstract	Parallel	No	No	Assumes independent classifiers
Class set reduction	Rank confidence	Parallel cascading	Yes	No	Efficient
Borda count	Rank	Parallel	Yes	No	Converts ranks into confidences
Logistic Regression	Rank confidence	Parallel	Yes	No	Converts ranks into confidences
Sum, mean, median	Confidence	Parallel	No	No	Robust; assumes independent confidence estimators
Product, min, max	Confidence	Parallel	No	No	Assumes independent features
Dempster–Shafer	Rank confidence	Parallel	Yes	No	Fuses non-probabilistic confidences
Generalized ensemble	Confidence	Parallel	Yes	No	Considers error correlation
Adaptive weighting	Confidence	Parallel	Yes	Yes	Explores local expertise
Stacking	Confidence	Parallel	Yes	No	Good utilization of training data
Fuzzy integrals	Confidence	Parallel	Yes	No	Fuses non-probabilistic confidences
Mixture of local experts (MLE)	Confidence	Gated parallel	Yes	Yes	Explores local expertise; joint optimization
Hierarchical MLE	Confidence	Gated parallel hierarchical	Yes	Yes	Same as MLE; hierarchical
Associative switch	Abstract	Parallel	Yes	Yes	Same as MLE, but no joint optimization is done
Bagging	Confidence	Parallel	Yes	No	Needs many comparable classifiers
Boosting	Abstract	Parallel hierarchical	Yes	No	Improves margins; unlikely to overtrain; sensitive to mislabels; needs many comparable classifiers
Random subspace	Confidence	Parallel	Yes	No	Needs many comparable classifiers
Neural tree	Confidence	Hierarchical	Yes	No	Handles large number of classes

Table 7.1. Various classifier combination strategies are compared. Note that it is possible to train a new classifier by considering the outputs from the individual classifiers as a feature vector to this new classifier. Thus any reasonable classifier from the pattern recognition literature can be used for combining the classifiers.

Other combination schemes and strategies known in the pattern recognition literature, such as generalized ensemble, adaptive weighting, stacking, fuzzy integrals, mixture of local experts (MLE), hierarchical MLE, associative switch, bagging, boosting, random subspaces, neural trees, and so on. have also been used in the context of biometric systems, with the aim of combining various classifiers for classification/binning of databases in order to reduce computational efforts in identification systems.

In conclusion, a large number of combination strategies are available to system designers. A priori, it is not well understood which one of them works better than the others and if so, under what circumstances. Traditionally, selection of a particular combination scheme is based on either human intuition or on an experimental assessment of a set of schemes. The combination scheme that offers the best classification accuracy over a given set of test samples is finally chosen.

Training and adaptability

Different combination strategies can be distinguished from each other based on their trainability, adaptivity, and requirements on the outputs of individual classifiers. Some combination strategies such as voting (Lam and Suen, 1997), taking the average or sum (Kittler et al., 1998), and Borda count (Ho, Hull, and Srihari, 1994) are static and treat all the classifier outputs the same; these schemes do not require any training. The trainable combination strategies may lead to more improvement in classification accuracy than static ones, at the cost of additional training as well as the requirement of large training data. Other combination strategies are adaptive in the sense that they evaluate or weight the decisions of individual classifiers depending on the input. Adaptive combination schemes can further exploit the detailed error characteristics and expertise of individual classifiers. Examples of adaptive combination strategies include adaptive weighting (Tresp and Taniguchi, 1995), associative switch, mixture of local experts (MLE) (Jacobs et al., 1991), and hierarchical MLE (Jordan and Jacobs, 1994).

A classifier combination scheme is especially useful if the individual classifiers are largely independent. If this is not already guaranteed by the use of different training sets, various resampling techniques such as rotation and bootstrapping may be used to artificially create such differences. Here, modified training sets are formed by resampling from the original training set and the classifiers constructed using these training sets are then combined. Examples are stacking, bagging, and boosting (or ARCing). The main difference among these algorithms is the type of resampling technique used. In stacking (Wolpert, 1992), the training set is subsampled with replacement to train the individual classifiers and the outputs of the individual classifiers are used to train the "stacked" classifier. The final decision is made based on the outputs of the stacked classifier in conjunction with the outputs of individual classifiers. In bagging (Breiman, 1996), different datasets (called bootstrapped sets) are created by randomly subsampling the original dataset with replacement. A classifier is trained on each bootstrap set and various classifiers are combined using a fixed rule such as averaging. Boosting (Schapire (1990) and Freund and Schapire (1996)) is another resampling technique for generating a sequence of training data sets. In boosting, weights are attached to each element of the training set and the subsequent training sets are generated from the original set by re-weighting the misclassified samples. As a result, the individual classifiers are trained hierarchically to learn to discriminate more complex regions in the feature space.

7.4 What to Integrate?

Now that we know how to integrate multiple classifiers, let us focus on what information can be combined in order to improve the performance of a biometric recognition system. Multi-modal biometric systems can be designed to operate in one of the following scenarios (see Figure 7.4).

1. *Multiple sensors*: The information obtained from different sensors for the same biometric are combined. For example, optical, solid-state, and ultrasound based sensors are available to capture fingerprints.

2. *Multiple biometrics*: Multiple biometrics such as fingerprint and face are combined. These systems will necessarily contain more than one sensor but each sensor will sense a different biometric. In a verification system, the multiple biometrics are typically used to improve system accuracy and the matching speed of an identification system can also be improved with a proper combination scheme (e.g., face matching which is typically fast but not very accurate can be used for retrieving the top M matches and fingerprint matching which is slower but more accurate can be used for making the final identification decision).

3. *Multiple units of the same biometric*: Fingerprints from two or more fingers of a person may be combined, or one image each from the two irises of a person may be combined.

4. *Multiple snapshots of the same biometric*: More than one instance of the same biometric is used for the enrollments and/or recognition. For example, multiple impressions of the same finger, multiple samples of the voice, or multiple images of the face may be combined.

5. *Multiple representations and matching algorithms for the same biometric*: This involves combining different approaches to feature extraction and matching of fingerprints. This could be used in two cases: a verification or an identification system can use such a combination scheme to make a recognition decision; and an identification system may use such a combination scheme for indexing.

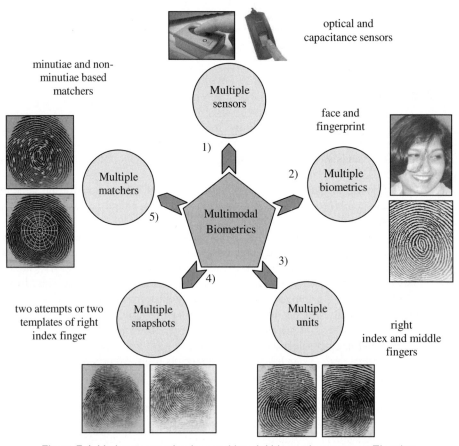

Figure 7.4. Various scenarios in a multimodal biometric system. ©Elsevier.

In the first scenario, multiple sensors are used to sense the same biometric identifier whereas the second scenario uses multiple sensors to sense different biometric identifiers. An example of the first scenario may be the use of multiple cameras mounted to capture different views of a person's face. An example of the second scenario is to use a camera for capturing the face and an optical sensor to capture a fingerprint. Scenario 1 combines moderately independent information and Scenarios 2 and 3 combine completely independent (or weakly dependent) information and are expected to result in the largest improvement in accuracy. However, this improvement comes at the cost of inconvenience to the user in providing multiple cues and a longer acquisition time. In Scenario 4, only a single input is acquired during recognition that is matched with several stored templates acquired during the one-time enrollment process; alternatively, more data acquisitions are made at recognition time and used to consolidate the matching against a single/multiple template. Scenario 5 combines different representation and matching algorithms to improve system accuracy. In our opinion, Scenarios 4 and 5 combine strongly correlated measurements and are expected to result in a smaller improvement in system accuracy than Scenarios 2 and 3, but they are more cost effective than Scenario 2 and more convenient than Scenario 3. Scenarios 4 and 5 do require more computational and storage resources than a unimodal system but, in principle, different feature extractors and matchers can work in parallel and, so, the overall response time of the system is limited by the slowest individual feature extractor and/or matcher. Finally, a combination of more than one of these scenarios may also be used.

7.5 Examples of Multimodal Biometric Systems

Sensor fusion has been used in a variety of pattern recognition applications such as remote sensing, scene interpretation, and target recognition for more than two decades (Dasarathy (1994) and Iyengar and Brooks (1997)). Classifier combination has become extremely popular after its remarkable success in handwriting and optical character recognition applications (Xu, Krzyzak, and Suen (1992) and Ho, Hull, Srihari (1994)). In this section, we review some examples of successful multimodal biometric recognition systems and summarize them in Table 7.2.

   To our knowledge, the first successful application of classifier combination in biometric identification was demonstrated by Brunelli and Falavigna (1995). They combined two classifiers based on acoustic features (static and dynamic) and three classifiers based on face features (eyes, nose, and mouth). The acoustic classifiers provided distance values between the input and the template and the face classifiers provided similarity scores. The distances were converted to similarity scores so that they were compatible with those resulting from face features. The location and scale parameters of the similarity scores from the five individual classifiers were first estimated (μ_{tanh} and σ_{tanh}, respectively) from the training data using the hyperbolic tangent function (tanh). The authors claim that these estimators are more robust than the commonly used *mean-variance* and *median-absolute deviation from the median* estimators. The normalized scores $\{S_i' \mid S_i' \in [0,1], \ i = 1..5\}$ for a person were then computed from the raw scores $\{S_i \mid i = 1..5\}$ as

$$S_i' = \frac{1}{2}\left[\tanh\left(0.01\frac{(S_i - \mu_{\text{tanh}})}{\sigma_{\text{tanh}}}\right) + 1\right].$$

The five normalized scores (sorted by decreasing values) were then combined using a weighted geometric average:

$$S = \left(\prod_i S_i'^{w_i} \right)^{1/\sum_i w_i},$$

where the weights w_i, $i = 1..5$ were estimated from the score dispersion in the right tail of the corresponding distributions. Under the assumption that normalized scores are equivalent to probabilities and the five classifiers are independent, the geometric average yields the product of the individual probabilities and is used to make the final decision. The accuracies of the five individual classifiers were 77, 71, 80, 77, and 83% for static acoustic, dynamic acoustic, eyes, nose, and mouth classifiers, respectively, on a database of 89 users. The accuracy of the combination of these five classifiers was 98% which indicates a significant improvement over the performance of the individual classifiers. The authors further used an integration of ranks and scores by means of an artificial neural network. Finally, they used a hierarchical combination to reduce the retrieval time of their identification system. In the first stage, the acoustic and face features were extracted at a coarse resolution and a candidate list was extracted from the full database. At each subsequent stage, the resolution was increased and the candidate list was shortened. The final stage used the features at full resolution and output the best match.

Bigun et al. (1997) (see also Duc et al., 1997) combined face and speech in their recognition system. Assume that $X_i \in [0,1]$ is the score from the ith expert for a claimed identity and Y is the ground truth decision about this identity claim (0 for false and 1 for true) which is independent of the expert. Then the *miss-identification score* (the verification error) Z_i is given by $Z_i = Y - X_i$. Under the assumption that Z_i is distributed normally and the opinions provided by different experts and different training samples are independent, the bias parameters (mean μ_i, variance v_i) of each expert (modality) are computed using the Bayes rule. In the verification phase, the scores X_1 and X_2 from the face and the speech experts, respectively, are converted from [0,1] to [-∞,∞], resulting in new scores S_1 and S_2; (the transformation known as "odds of X" is used for the conversion:

$$S_i = \log \frac{X_i}{1 - X_i}.$$

The scores from the two modalities are normalized by the bias of each expert that was computed during the training stage, and combined using a weighted average (the weight being the inverse of normalized variance bias of the experts):

$$S = \frac{\sum_{i=1}^{2} \frac{S_i}{v_i}}{\sum_{i=1}^{2} \frac{1}{v_i}}.$$

On a database of 37 users, the total error rate (false match rate + false non-match rate) of the face and speech experts alone was 11.0 and 6.7%, respectively, when trained on 2664 impostor and genuine matches and tested on 7992 impostor and genuine matches. The total error rate from their combination methodology was 0.5% as compared to a total error rate of 3.3% when a simple mean of the scores was used for the combination. Kittler et al. (1998) combined frontal face, face profile, and voice verification systems using the sum, product, maximum, median, and minimum rules and reported best improvement in performance from the sum rule.

Hong and Jain (1998) combined face and fingerprint in an identification system. The face identification system was based on the eigenface approach (Turk and Pentland, 1991) and given an input face, the output is the top n matches from the face database arranged in the increasing order of DFFS (Distance From Feature Space); the smaller the DFFS value, the more likely it is that the match is correct. Let I_1, I_2, ..., I_n denote the n possible identities established by face identification and let $\{X_1, X_2, ..., X_n\}$ denote the corresponding n DFFSs. The probability that one of the retrieved top n matches is incorrect is different for different ranks and different Relative DFFS (RDFFS) values (RDFFS: $\Delta_i = X_{i-1} - X_i$). The fingerprint verification subsystem matches the input fingerprint with the n fingerprint templates corresponding to the top n matches from the face identification subsystem and yields n verification scores. Let $\{Y_1, Y_2, ..., Y_n\}$ denote the n fingerprint matching scores corresponding to the top n face matches. Hong and Jain (1998) argued that an estimate of the impostor distributions from the face and fingerprint matching scores should be available for performing multibiometric combination and that a very large database of representative samples is needed to estimate these impostor distributions. So they assumed that $\{X_1, X_2, ..., X_n\}$ followed a Gaussian distribution with unknown mean and variance and derived a parametric impostor distribution $F_i(\Delta)P_{order}(i)$ for face matching as a function of the rank i and RDFFS. Similarly, under the assumption that minutiae are randomly distributed in a fingerprint, they derived a theoretic parametric impostor distribution $G(Y)$ for fingerprint matching scores as a function of the number of matching minutiae. Under the assumption that the face and the fingerprint impostor distributions are independent, the composite impostor distribution is the product of the two distributions:

$$H_i(\Delta, Y) = F_i(\Delta)P_{order}(i)G(Y).$$

The final decision, $ID(I)$, for a given individual I is determined by the criterion:

$$ID(I) = \begin{cases} I_k & \text{if} \begin{pmatrix} H_k(\Delta_k, Y_k) < \text{FMR}_0, \text{ and} \\ H_k(\Delta_k, Y_k) = \min\{H_1(\Delta_1, Y_1), ..., H_n(\Delta_n, Y_n)\} \end{pmatrix}, \\ \text{impostor} & \text{otherwise}, \end{cases}$$

where individual I is identified as I_k if his distance score H_k is the minimum among those of all the individuals in the database and H_k is smaller than the desired false match rate (FMR_0). The impostor distributions for the face and fingerprint matches were learned from 542 face images and 640 fingerprint images, respectively, and the performance was evaluated on an independent database of 86 individuals. The face identification retrieved the top five matches ($n = 5$) in decreasing order of similarity with the corresponding RDFFS values. The fingerprint verification was then applied to each of the top five matches resulting in five fingerprint matching scores and the final decision was made by decision fusion. The accuracy results are shown in Figure 7.5. The face recognition took 0.9 seconds and the fingerprint verification took 3.2 seconds on a Sun Sparc 20 workstation. The decision fusion was extremely fast and thus the identification system took a total of 4.1 seconds for making an identification from a database of 560 identities.

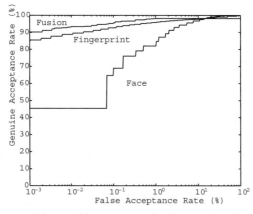

Figure 7.5. The improvement in matching accuracy is shown when face recognition and finger-print verification systems are combined in an identification system developed by Hong and Jain (1998). In the graphic, FMR is referred to as FAR (False Acceptance Rate) and (1–FNMR) as Genuine Acceptance Rate. ©IEEE.

Jain, Hong, and Kulkarni (1999) combined fingerprint, face, and speech in a verification system using the Neyman–Pearson rule (Rice, 1995). Let X_1, X_2, and X_3 be the random variables used to indicate the similarity between the input and a template for fingerprint verification, face verification, and speaker verification, respectively. Let c_1 and c_2 denote the genuine and impostor classes, respectively. Let $p\ (X_j|c_i)$, where $j = 1,2,3$ and $i = 1,2$, be the class-conditional probability density function of X_j. They assumed that X_1, X_2, and X_3 are statistically independent, and so the joint probability density function of X_1, X_2, and X_3, has the form:

$$p(X_1, X_2, X_3 | c_i) = \prod_{j=1}^{3} p(X_j | c_i), \qquad i = 1,2 .$$

According to the Neyman–Pearson rule, a test observation $X^0 = \{X^0_1, X^0_2, X^0_3\}$ is classified as

$$\left(X^0_1, X^0_2, X^0_3\right) \in \begin{cases} c_1 & \text{if } \dfrac{p\left(x^0_1, x^0_2, x^0_3 | c_1\right)}{p\left(x^0_1, x^0_2, x^0_3 | c_2\right)} > \lambda, \\ c_2 & \text{otherwise,} \end{cases} .$$

The value of λ is based on the pre-specified false match rate (FMR$_0$) and is determined in the following way. First, R_1, the decision region associated with class c_1 is empirically determined as per the equation:

$$\text{FMR}_0 = \int_{R_1} p(X_1, X_2, X_3 \mid c_2) \cdot dX_1 dX_2 dX_3 \ .$$

Then, a pattern, (X_1^*, X_2^*, X_3^*) lying on (or close to) the boundary between R_1 and R_2, where R_2 is the decision region associated with class c_2, is found empirically. The value of λ is then determined as follows:

$$\lambda = \frac{p\left(X_1^*, X_2^*, X_3^* \middle| c_1\right)}{p\left(X_1^*, X_2^*, X_3^* \middle| c_2\right)} \ .$$

Jain, Hong, and Kulkarni (1999) estimated the densities $p(X_j|c_i)$, for $j = 1,2,3$ and $i = 1,2$ from the training data and reported a significant improvement in performance from the combination of fingerprint, face, and speech.

Ben-Yacoub (1999), Ben-Yacoub et al. (1999) and Ben-Yacoub, Abdeljaoued and Mayoraz (1999) combined face and speech verification systems using a large number of combination schemes based on general-purpose pattern recognition classifiers, such as Support Vector Machines, tree classifiers, neural networks, the Fisher linear discriminant, and the naïve Bayes classifier. They also compared the results of these combinations with the maximum, minimum, median, average, and product rules. The best performance was achieved with a combination using the naïve Bayes classifier on a database of 295 subjects. Choudhury et al. (1999) also reported an improvement in performance from a combination of face and speech verification systems using the naïve Bayes classifier.

Dieckmann, Plankensteiner, and Wagner (1997) and Frischholz and Dieckmann (2000) combined face, voice, and lip movement for their verification system using a "2 out of 3" (voting) and a weighted sum rule. Verlinde, Chollet, and Acheroy (2000) combined frontal face, face profile, and voice verification systems using a large number of classifiers that included the maximum likelihood method, naïve Bayes classifier, logistic regression, quadratic classifier, linear classifier, voting rule (AND and OR), k-nearest neighbor using vector quantization, and binary decision tree. The validation results showed that the naïve Bayes and logistic regression classifiers yielded the best improvement in performance.

Ross, Jain, and Qian (2001) combined face, fingerprint, and hand geometry verification systems using the sum rule, decision trees, and Fisher linear discriminant. The sum rule resulted in the best improvement in performance. They also suggested a combination of PCA-based face features (Turk and Pentland, 1991) and texture-based fingerprint features (Jain et al., 2000) at the feature level. Both the PCA-based face features and the texture-based fingerprint features are in the Euclidean space, and so a feature level combination is achieved in a rather straightforward manner by concatenating the face and feature vectors into a higher dimensional feature vector. The face and the fingerprint features were separately normalized to a unit norm before concatenation. Their initial results indicated that this feature-level combination performed better than the confidence-level combination using the sum rule. In the same combination of face, fingerprint, and hand geometry verification systems, Jain and Ross (2002a) further demonstrated that the weighted sum rule, where different weights are learned for each individual user performs better than the simple sum rule. A disadvantage in learning user-specific weights is that a large number of training samples are required for every user. Because it is inconvenient for a user to provide a large number of samples during the enrollment phase, the weights need to be learned over a period of time.

Jain, Prabhakar, and Chen (1999) used the logistic regression transform and Prabhakar and Jain (2002) used the Neyman–Pearson rule to combine the confidence values obtained from four different fingerprint matching algorithms. Marcialis, Roli, and Loddo (2002) also reported an improvement in performance from a logistic transform-based combination of multiple fingerprint matchers. Prabhakar and Jain (2002) further combined two templates per finger and two different fingers of a person. They argued that a combination may not necessarily result in an improvement in performance, especially when the information sources to be combined are highly correlated and therefore an automatic classifier selection should be performed before the combination. They also did not make any assumption about the independence of the various classifiers (unlike the naïve Bayes approach) and estimated the multidimensional genuine and impostor densities using the Parzen window estimator (Duda, Hart, and Stork, 2001) (see Figure 7.6.a). The performance of this combination strategy was better than the simple combination schemes such as the sum and the product rules, but suffers from the disadvantage that a large amount of training data is required to obtain reasonable estimates of the multidimensional distributions. The results of their combinations are shown in Figure 7.6.

Table 7.2 summarizes the characteristics of the multimodal biometric systems described in this section.

Finally, notice that most of the best performing fingerprint classification/retrieval algorithms (see Chapter 5) use a combination of classifiers and perform better than the fingerprint classification algorithms based on any single classifier. For example, Jain, Prabhakar, and Hong (1999) used a combination of a k-nearest neighbor and 10 neural networks to classify fingerprint images into five classes based on a texture representation of fingerprints. Senior (2001) combined three fingerprint classifiers based on three different types of fingerprint representations using a neural network. Cappelli, Maio, and Maltoni (2002a) combined six classifiers based on two different fingerprint representations and three disjoint training sets by using a majority vote for an exclusive fingerprint classification. They also combined (at the confidence level) two different classifiers based on different fingerprint representations by using a weighted average of normalized scores for continuous fingerprint classification. See Chapter 5 for more details.

7.6 Summary

Multimodal biometrics systems are gaining popularity among system designers due to their proven capability in improving system performance. A combination in a verification system is typically used to improve system accuracy, whereas a combination in an identification system is used to improve system speed as well. Moreover, the multiple modalities that are combined in a verification system are chosen based on their verification accuracies and they are typically combined in parallel. On the other hand, in an identification system, the first modality that is chosen is based on the matching speed rather than its accuracy and is combined with subsequent modalities that are slower but more accurate in a serial combination.

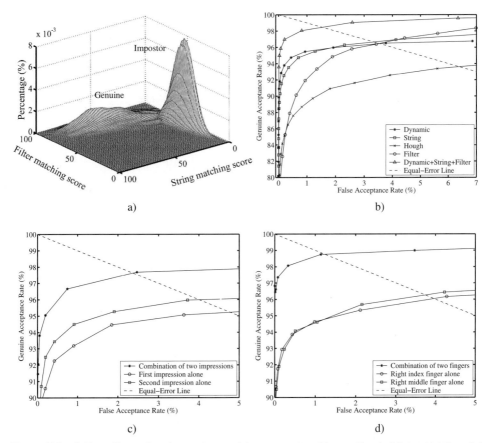

Figure 7.6. a) Two dimensional genuine and impostor densities estimated from training data using the Parzen window estimator. The ROCs in b), c), and d) show the improvement in verification performance from a combination of four fingerprint matching algorithms, a combination of two templates per finger, and a combination of two fingers of a person, respectively, at a confidence level using the Neyman–Pearson rule (Prabhakar and Jain, 2002). In the graphics, FMR is referred to as FAR (False Acceptance Rate) and (1–FNMR) as Genuine Acceptance Rate. ©Elsevier.

Author(s)	Biometrics	N	Accuracy	Archit.	Level	Scheme
Brunelli and Falavigna (1995)	Speaker, face	5	ID: 17→2 (TE)	Parallel	Confidence	Weighted geometric average
Duc et al. (1997)	Speaker, face	2	VER: 6.7→0.5 (TE)	Parallel	Confidence	Naïve Bayes
Kittler et al. (1998)	Speaker, face	3	VER: 1.4→0.7 (EER)	Parallel	Confidence	Sum
Hong and Jain (1998)	Face, fingerprint	2	ID: 6.9→4.54 (FNMR at 0.1% FMR)	Serial	Rank and confidence	Naïve Bayes
Jain, Hong, and Kulkarni (1999)	Speaker, face, fingerprint	3	VER: ~15→~3 (FNMR at 0.1% FMR)	Parallel	Confidence	Neyman-Pearson
Ben-Yacoub, Abdeljaoued, and Mayoraz (1999)	Speaker, face	3	VER: ~4→0.5 (EER)	Parallel	Confidence	Naïve Bayes
Choudhury et al. (1999)	Speaker, face	3	ID: 16.5→6.5 (TE)	Parallel	Confidence	Naïve Bayes
Verlinde, Chollet, and Acheroy (2000)	Speaker, face	3	VER: 3.7→0.1 (TE)	Parallel	Confidence	Naïve Bayes
Ross, Jain, and Qian (2001)	Face, fingerprint, hand geometry	3	VER: ~16→~2 (FNMR at 0.1% FMR)	Parallel	Confidence	Sum
Prabhakar and Jain (2002)	Fingerprint	4	VER: 3.5→1.4 (EER)	Parallel	Confidence	Neyman-Pearson

Table 7.2. Various classifier combination examples in Section 7.5 are tabulated for a comparison. In the third column, N denotes the total number of classifiers combined; the fourth column shows the improvement in VER (verification) or ID (identification) errors from the most accurate component classifier. TE denotes the total error (FNMR + FMR) and EER denotes the equal error rate.

It is well known that the independence of classifiers plays a very important role in the amount of improvement when combining multiple modalities. A combination of uncorrelated modalities (e.g., fingerprint and face, two fingers of a person, etc.) is expected to result in a better improvement in performance than a combination of correlated modalities (e.g, different impressions of the same finger, different fingerprint matchers, etc.). Furthermore, a combination of uncorrelated modalities can significantly reduce the failure to enroll rate as well as provide more security against fraud. However, such a combination requires the users to provide multiple identity cues, which may cause inconvenience. The convenience factor remains one of the biggest barriers in the use of such multibiometrics systems in civilian applications. We anticipate that the very high security applications, large-scale systems, and negative identification applications will increasingly use multimodal systems, and the personal low-cost civilian applications will probably continue striving to improve unimodal systems.

8
Fingerprint Individuality[1]

8.1 Introduction

Fingerprint-based recognition is routinely used in forensic laboratories and identification units around the world and it has been accepted in courts of law for nearly a century. A few years after Galton (1892) and Henry (1900) published the first extensive studies on fingerprints, the popular press claimed that fingerprints were truly unique (Cole 2001b):

> "Only once during the existence of our solar system will two human beings be born with similar finger markings." – *Harper's* headline, 1910.

> "Two like fingerprints would be found only once every 10^{48} years" – *Scientific American,* 1911.

The uniqueness of fingerprints has been accepted over time because of a lack of contradiction and relentless repetition. As a result, fingerprint-based recognition has been regarded as a perfect system of person recognition. However, some questions have been raised recently about the uniqueness of fingerprints.

> "They left a mark – on criminology and culture. But what if they're not what they seem?" – Simon Cole, 2001.

The 1993 case of Daubert vs. Merrell Dow Pharmaceuticals, Inc. (113 S. Ct. 2786), where the US Supreme Court ruled that the reliability of expert scientific testimony must be established, may have a profound impact on the admissibility of the latent fingerprint examiner's testimony in courts. The Court stated that when assessing the admissibility of any *scientific* testimony, these factors should be considered:

---

[1] Portions reprinted with permission from *IEEE Transactions on Pattern Analysis and Machine Intelligence*, vol. 24, no. 8, pp. 1010–1025, 2002. © 2002 IEEE.

1. the particular technique or methodology in question has been subject to a statistical hypothesis testing,
2. its error rate has been established,
3. the standards controlling the technique's operations exist and have been maintained,
4. it has been peer reviewed and published, and
5. it has a general widespread acceptance.

Subsequently, handwriting recognition was challenged under *Daubert* in several cases between the years 1995 and 2001. It was claimed that handwriting recognition does not meet the scientific evidence criteria established in the Daubert case. For an empirical study on the individuality of handwriting, see Srihari et al. (2001). Several courts have now ruled that handwriting recognition does not meet the *Daubert* criteria.

Fingerprint recognition was first challenged by defense lawyers under *Daubert* in the 1999 case of USA vs. Byron Mitchell (Criminal Action No. 96-407, US District Court for the Eastern District of Pennsylvania) on the basis that the fundamental premise of fingerprint *uniqueness* has not been objectively tested and the potential error rate in fingerprint matching is unknown. The defense motion to exclude fingerprint evidence and testimony was denied. On January 7, 2002, a federal court judge ruled that, without the credible (peer-reviewed) published estimates of matcher accuracies, fingerprint experts cannot testify with certainty whether two fingerprint impressions originated from the same finger (Cr. No. 98-362-10, 11, 12 in the US District Court of the Eastern District of Pennsylvania). However, the same judge then vacated this ruling on March 13, 2002.

The two fundamental premises on which fingerprint recognition is based are: fingerprint details are permanent, and fingerprints of an individual are unique. The validity of the first premise has been established by empirical observations as well as based on the anatomy and morphogenesis of friction ridge skin. It is the second premise that is being challenged in court cases. The notion of fingerprint individuality has been widely accepted based on a manual inspection (by experts) of millions of fingerprints. However, the underlying scientific basis of fingerprint individuality has not been rigorously studied or tested. In March 2000, the US Department of Justice admitted that no such testing has been done and acknowledged the need for such a study (www.ojp.usdoj.gov). In response to this, the National Institute of Justice identified the following two main topics of basic research: measure the amount of detail in a single fingerprint that is available for comparison, and measure the amount of detail in correspondence between two fingerprints.

What is meant by fingerprint individuality? Most human experts and automatic fingerprint identification systems declare that the fingerprints originate from the same source if they are "sufficiently" similar. How similar should the two fingerprints be before we can claim that they are from the same finger? The fingerprint individuality problem can be formulated in many different ways, depending on which one of these aspects of the problem is under examination: i) the individuality problem may be cast as determining the probability that any two or more individuals may have sufficiently similar fingerprints in a given target population; ii) given a sample fingerprint, determine the probability of finding a sufficiently similar fingerprint in a target population; iii) given two fingerprints from two different fingers, determine the probability that they are sufficiently similar (*probability of a false correspondence*); when the comparison is made by an automatic system, the probability of false correspondence coincides with the false match rate (FMR). Formulation iii) is more general as its solution would also provide solutions to the other two formulations (Rice, 1995). A reliable statistical estimate of the matching error in fingerprint comparison can determine the admissibility of fingerprint recognition in courts of law as an evidence of identity. Furthermore, it can establish an upper bound on the performance of automatic fingerprint recognition systems.

In order to solve the individuality problem, one needs to define a priori the representation of the fingerprint and the metric used for computing the similarity. Fingerprints can be represented by several different features, including the overall ridge flow pattern, ridge frequency, number and position of singularities (loops and deltas), type, direction, and location of minutiae points, ridge counts between pairs of minutiae, and location of pores. All these features contribute to fingerprint individuality. In this chapter, we have focused on minutiae representation of the fingerprints (refer to Chapter 4) because it is utilized by forensic experts, it has been demonstrated to be highly stable, and it has been adopted by most of the commercially available automatic fingerprint matching systems. Note that forensic experts use several other features in addition to minutiae when matching fingerprints. Moreover, neither the minutiae-based representation nor the simple similarity metric model considered in this chapter completely captures the complexity of the fingerprint expert matching process. Perhaps the individuality estimates are a reasonable first-order approximation of most of the discriminatory information that is consistently available to the expert across the impressions.

Given a representation scheme and a similarity metric, there are two approaches for determining the individuality of the fingerprints. In the empirical approach, representative samples of fingerprints are collected and, using a typical fingerprint matcher (automatic or human), the accuracy of the matcher is calculated which provides an indication of the uniqueness of the fingerprint with respect to the matcher. There are known problems (and costs) associated with collection of the representative samples. In addition, even if a large database of fingerprints such as the FBI database which contains over 200 million fingerprints is used for an empirical evaluation of fingerprint individuality, it would take approximately 1270 years to match all the fingerprints in the database with each other using a processor with a speed of one million matches per second ($200 \times 10^6 \times 200 \times 10^6 / (10^6 \times 60 \times 60 \times 24 \times 365) \cong 1270$)! In a theoretical approach to individuality estimation, one models all realistic phenomena affecting inter-class and intra-class fingerprint pattern variations. Given the similarity metric, one could then theoretically estimate the probability of a false correspondence. Theoretical approaches are often limited by the extent to which the assumed models conform to reality. In this chapter, we give a brief survey of the existing work on fingerprint individuality. The individuality model introduced by Pankanti, Prabhakar, and Jain (2002) is described in detail. We also juxtapose the probabilities obtained from this individuality model with the empirical results obtained using a state-of-the-art automatic fingerprint matcher (Jain et al., 1997).

The total number of degrees-of-freedom of the minutiae configuration space does not directly relate to the discriminability of different fingers. The effective estimation of discriminatory information can only be achieved by taking into account intra-pattern variations. There are several sources of variability in the multiple impressions of a finger (see Section 4.1). This variability in multiple impressions of a finger manifests itself into i) detection of spurious minutiae or missing genuine minutiae, ii) displacement/disorientation (also called deformation) of the genuine minutiae, and iii) transformation of the type of minutiae (connective ambiguity). This entails designing a similarity metric (matcher) that accommodates these intra-class variations.

Most of the approaches to fingerprint individuality do not explicitly account for these intra-class variabilities in their models (see Stoney and Thornton (1986) for a critical review of several models) and, therefore, overestimate fingerprint individuality (give a smaller probability of false correspondence). Furthermore, because most of the existing models of individuality do not address the problems associated with the occurrence of spurious minutiae or missing genuine minutiae, they do not provide a systematic framework to address issues related to a partial representational match between two fingerprints (e.g., what is the probability of finding 7 matched minutiae in two fingerprints with 18 and 37 minutiae, respectively?). This is very important in an automatic fingerprint matching system where the feature extraction algorithms are not always correct and in matching latent fingerprints. Although, in a manual fingerprint matching procedure, the likelihood of detecting false minutiae is significantly smaller than that in an automatic system, the prints imaged from different portions of a finger may give rise to variability in the number of detected minutiae. The approach described in Pankanti, Prabhakar, and Jain (2002) not only explicitly models the situation of partial representational match, but also incorporates constraints on the configuration space due to intra-class variations (e.g., number of minutiae, minutia position/orientation, image area) based on empirical estimates derived from the ground truth data marked on fingerprints obtained in a realistic environment.

8.2 Background

Fingerprint individuality studies have typically focused on minutiae-based representations; some studies explicitly factored in fingerprint class (e.g., right loop, left loop, whorl, arch, tented arch, etc.) information. The type, direction, and location of minutiae are the most commonly used features in these individuality studies. See Table 8.1 for a comparison of the features used in various fingerprint individuality models. The types of minutiae used vary from one study to another: some studies used 2 minutiae types (termination and bifurcation) whereas others (e.g., Osterburg (1964) and Osterburg et al. (1977)) used as many as 13 types of events (empty cell, ridge termination, ridge bifurcation, island, dot, broken ridge, bridge, spur, enclosure, delta, double bifurcation, trifurcation, and multiple events). Subsequent models considered additional features (e.g., ridge counts (Stoney, 1985) or sweat pores (Roddy and

Stosz, 1997)) to determine the probability of occurrence of a particular fingerprint configuration.

Most of the early individuality studies have examined the distinctiveness of a portion/feature of the fingerprint. By assuming that events (e.g., placement of minutiae) are independent and identically distributed, these studies estimated the distinctiveness of the entire fingerprint (total pattern variation) by collating the distinctiveness in the features extracted from fingerprints (total feature variation). We refer to these total pattern variation-based fingerprint individuality estimates as the *probability of fingerprint configuration*. A summary of these studies is presented in Table 8.1.

Author	Fingerprint features
Galton (1892)	Ridges, minutiae types
Pearson (1930, 1933)	Ridges, minutiae types
Henry (1900)	Minutiae locations, types, core-to-delta ridge count
Balthazard (1911) (cf. Stoney and Thornton, 1986)	Minutiae locations, two types, and two directions
Bose (1917) (cf. Stoney and Thornton, 1986)	Minutiae locations and three types
Wentworth and Wilder (1918)	Minutiae locations
Cummins and Midlo (1943)	Minutiae locations and types, core-to-delta ridge count
Gupta (1968)	Minutiae locations and types, fingerprint types, ridge count
Roxburgh (1933)	Minutiae locations, two minutiae types, two orientations, fingerprint and core types, number of positionings, area, fingerprint quality
Amy (1948) (cf. Stoney and Thornton, 1986)	Minutiae locations, number, types, and orientation
Trauring (1963)	Minutiae locations, two types, and two orientations
Kingston (1964)	Minutiae locations, number, and types
Osterburg et al. (1977)	Minutiae locations and types
Stoney and Thornton (1986)	Minutiae locations, distribution, orientation, and types, variation among prints from the same source, ridge counts, and number of alignments
Pankanti, Prabhakar, and Jain (2002)	Minutiae locations, number, and direction

Table 8.1. Fingerprint features used in different individuality models.

The fingerprint individuality problem was first addressed by Galton in 1892 (Galton 1892), who considered a square region spanning six-ridges in a given fingerprint. He assumed that, on average, a full fingerprint can be covered by 24 such six-ridge wide independent square regions. Galton estimated that he could correctly reconstruct any of the regions with a probability of 1/2, by looking at the surrounding ridges (see Figure 8.1). Accordingly, the probability of a specific fingerprint configuration, given the surrounding ridges, is $(1/2)^{24}$. Galton multiplied this conditional (on surrounding ridges) probability with the probability of finding the surrounding ridges to obtain the probability of occurrence of a fingerprint as

$$P(\text{Fingerprint Configuration}) = \frac{1}{16} \times \frac{1}{256} \times \left(\frac{1}{2}\right)^{24} = 1.45 \times 10^{-11}, \tag{1}$$

where 1/16 is the probability of occurrence of a specific fingerprint type (such as arch, tented arch, left loop, right loop, double loop, whorl, etc.) and 1/256 is the probability of occurrence of the correct number of ridges entering and exiting each of the 24 regions. Equation (1) gives the probability that a particular fingerprint configuration in an average size fingerprint (containing 24 regions defined by Galton) will be observed in nature.

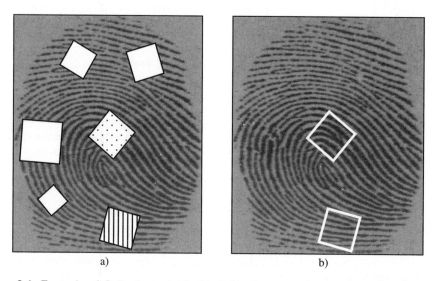

a)   b)

Figure 8.1. Example of Galton's method of individuality estimation. Galton laid out enlargements of the fingerprints on the floor. He then dropped different sized squares such that they fell randomly on the enlarged fingerprint. Galton sought that size of paper square where he could correctly guess the ridge structure hidden underneath with a probability of 1/2. For example, one can easily guess the ridges hidden by the six-ridge wide square marked with dots in a) by looking at the surrounding ridges around the square. On the other hand, one cannot correctly guess the ridge structure hidden by the six-ridge wide square marked with vertical stripes in a). The hidden areas for these two squares are shown in b).

Roxburgh (1933), Pearson (1930, 1933), and Kingston (1964) objected to Galton's assumption that the probability of occurrence of any particular ridge configuration in a six-ridge square is 1/2 and claimed that Equation (1) grossly underestimates fingerprint individuality (i.e., overestimates the probability of occurrence). Pearson (1930, 1933) argued that there could be 36 (6 × 6) possible minutiae locations within one of Galton's six-ridge-square regions, leading to a probability of occurrence of a particular fingerprint configuration of

$$\text{P(Fingerprint Configuration)} = \frac{1}{16} \times \frac{1}{256} \times \left(\frac{1}{36}\right)^{24} = 1.09 \times 10^{-41}. \tag{2}$$

A number of subsequent models (Henry (1900), Balthazard (1911) (cf. Stoney and Thornton, 1986), Bose (cf. Stoney and Thornton, 1986), Wentworth and Wilder (1918), Cummins and Midlo (1943), and Gupta (1968)) are interrelated and are based on a fixed probability p for the occurrence of a minutia. They compute the probability of a particular n-minutiae fingerprint configuration as

$$\text{P(Fingerprint Configuration)} = p^n. \tag{3}$$

In the following, we provide the values of p used in these studies. In most cases, the authors do not present any details on how they arrived at their choice of p.

- Henry (1900) chose $p = 1/4$ and added 2 to the number of minutiae n if the fingerprint type and core-to-delta ridge count could be determined from the given (latent) fingerprint.
- Balthazard (1911) (cf. Stoney and Thronton, 1986) also set $p = 1/4$, under the assumption that there are four types of equally likely minutiae events: bifurcation to the right, bifurcation to the left, termination to the right, and termination to the left.
- Bose (cf. Stoney and Thornton, 1986) adopted $p = 1/4$, under the assumption that there are four possibilities in each square region of one ridge interval width in a fingerprint: a dot, a bifurcation, a termination, and a continuous ridge.
- Wentworth and Wilder (1918) chose 1/50 as the value of p.
- Cummins and Midlo (1943) adopted the same value of p as Wentworth and Wilder, but introduced a multiplicative constant of 1/31 to account for the variation in fingerprint pattern type.
- Gupta (1968) estimated the value of p as 1/10 for bifurcations and terminations, and 1/100 for the less commonly occurring minutiae types, based on 1000 fingerprints. He also used a fingerprint type factor of 1/10 and correspondence in ridge count factor of 1/10.

Because of the widely varying values of p used in the above studies, the probability of a given fingerprint configuration also dramatically varies from one model to the other. Roxburgh (1933) proposed a more comprehensive analysis to compute the probability of a fingerprint configuration. His analysis was based on considering a fingerprint as a pattern with concentric circles, one ridge interval apart, in a polar coordinate system. Roxburgh also incorporated a quality measure of the fingerprint into his calculations. He computed the probability of a particular n-minutiae fingerprint configuration to be:

$$\text{P(Fingerprint Configuration)} = \left(\frac{C}{P}\right) \times \left(\frac{Q}{RT}\right)^n, \tag{4}$$

where P is the probability of encountering a particular fingerprint type and core type, Q is a measure of quality ($Q = 1.5$ for an average quality print, and $Q = 3.0$ for a poor quality print), R is the number of semicircular ridges in a fingerprint ($R = 10$), T is the corrected number of minutiae types ($T = 2.412$), and C is the number of possible positions for the configuration ($C = 1$). Amy (1948) (cf. Stoney and Thornton, 1986) considered the variability in minutiae type, number, and position in his model for computing the probability of a fingerprint configuration. He further recognized that K multiple comparisons of the fingerprint pair (e.g., each hypothesized orientation alignment and each reference point correspondence) increase the possibility of false association which is given by

$$\text{P(False Association)} = 1 - \left(1 - \text{P(Fingerprint Configuration)}\right)^K. \tag{5}$$

Kingston's (1964) model, which is very similar to Amy's model, computes the probability of a fingerprint configuration based on the probabilities of the observed number of minutiae, observed positions of minutiae, and observed minutiae types as follows.

$$\text{P(Fingerprint Configuration)} = \left(e^{-y}\right)\left(y^n / n!\right)\left(P_1\right)\prod_{i=2}^{n}\left(P_i\right)\frac{(0.082)}{[S - (i-1)(0.082)]}, \tag{6}$$

where y is the expected number of minutiae in a region of given size S (in mm^2) and P_i is the probability of occurrence of a particular minutiae type in the ith minutia.

Most of the models discussed above implicitly assume that fingerprints are being matched manually. The probability of observing a given fingerprint feature is estimated by manually extracting the features from a small number of fingerprint images. Champod and Margot (1996) used an AFIS to extract minutiae from 977 fingerprint images scanned at a relatively high resolution of 800 dpi. They generated frequencies of minutiae occurrence and minutiae densities after manually verifying the thinned ridges produced by the AFIS to ensure that the feature extraction algorithm did not introduce errors. They considered minutiae only in concentric bands (five ridges wide) above the core and acknowledged that their individuality estimates were conservative (i.e., provided an upper bound). As an example, they estimated the probability of occurrence of a seven-minutiae configuration (five terminations and two bifurcations) as 2.25×10^{-5}.

Osterburg et al. (1977) divided fingerprints into discrete cells of size 1 mm $\times$ 1 mm. They computed the frequencies of 13 types of minutiae events (including an empty cell) from 39 fingerprints (8591 cells) and estimated the probability that 12 ridge terminations will match between two fingerprints based on an average fingerprint area of 72 mm^2 as 1.25×10^{-20}. Sclove (1979) modified Osterburg et al.'s model by incorporating the observed dependence of minutiae occurrence in cells and came up with an estimate of probability of fingerprint configuration that is slightly higher than that obtained by Osterburg et al.; Stoney and Thornton (1986) criticized Osterburg et al.'s and Sclove's models because these models did not consider the fingerprint ridge structure, distortions, and the uncertainty in the positioning of the grid. Stoney and Thornton (1986) critically reviewed earlier fingerprint individuality models and proposed a detailed set of fingerprint features that should be taken into consideration. These features included ridge structure and description of minutiae location, ridge counts between pairs of minutiae, description of minutiae distribution, orientation of minutiae, variation in minutiae type, variation among fingerprints from the same source, number of positions (different translations and rotations of the input fingerprint), and number of comparisons performed with other fingerprints for identification.

Stoney's (1985) model is different from other models in that it attempts to characterize a significant component of pairwise minutiae dependence. Stoney (1985) and Stoney and Thornton (1986) studied probabilities of occurrences of various types of minutiae, their orientation, number of neighboring minutiae, and distances/ridge counts to the neighboring minutiae. Given a minutiae set, they calculated the probability of a minutiae configuration by conjoining the probabilities of the individual events in the configuration. For instance, they proposed a linear ordering of minutiae in a minutiae configuration and recursively estimated the probability of an n-minutiae configuration from the probability of an $(n-1)$-minutiae configuration and the occurrence of a new minutia of certain type/orientation at a particular distance/ridge counts from its nearest minutia within the $(n-1)$-minutiae configuration. The model also incorporated constraints due to connective ambiguity and due to minutiae-free areas. The model corrected for the probability of false association by accounting for the various possible linear orderings that could initiate/drive the search for correspondence. A sample calculation for computing the probability of a false association using Stoney's model is given below.

$$
\begin{aligned}
\text{P(False Association)} &= 1 - \left(1 - 0.6 \times \left(0.5 \times 10^{-3}\right)^{(n-1)}\right)^{\lfloor n/5 \rfloor} \\
&\approx \frac{n}{5} \times 0.6 \times \left(0.5 \times 10^{-3}\right)^{(n-1)}.
\end{aligned}
\tag{7}
$$

For the sake of simplicity, we have considered only a rudimentary version of Stoney's model for the above computation; it is arbitrarily assumed that the probability of a typical *starting* minutia is 0.6, a typical neighboring minutia places an additional constraint on the probability, and there are no constraints due to connective ambiguity, minutiae-free areas, or minutiae-free borders. Finally, it is (arbitrarily) assumed that one in every five minutiae can potentially serve as a starting point for a new search. Stoney and Thornton identified weaknesses in their model and acknowledged that one of the most critical requirements (i.e., consideration of variation among prints from the same finger) was not sufficiently addressed. Their tolerances for minutiae position were derived from successive printings under ideal conditions and are far too low to be applicable in actual fingerprint comparisons.

The models discussed above (including Amy's model of false association due to multiple comparisons) focused mainly on measuring the amount of detail in a single fingerprint (i.e., estimation of the probability of a fingerprint configuration). These models did not emphasize the intra-class variations in multiple impressions of a finger. We refer to the quantifications of fingerprint individuality that explicitly consider the intra-class variations as the *probability of correspondence*. Trauring (1963) was the first to concentrate explicitly on measuring the amount of detail needed to establish a correspondence between two prints from the same finger (intra-class variation) using an AFIS and observed that corresponding fingerprint features in impressions of the same finger could be displaced from each other by as much as 1.5 times the inter-ridge distance. He further assumed that i) minutiae are distributed randomly, ii) there are only two types of minutiae (termination and bifurcation), iii) the two types of minutiae are equally likely, iv) the two possible orientations of minutiae are equally likely, and v) minutiae type, orientation, and position are independent variables. Trauring computed the probability of a coincidental correspondence of n minutiae between two fingerprints from different fingers to be:

$$P(\text{Fingerprint Correspondence}) = (0.1944)^n. \tag{8}$$

Stoney and Thornton's (1986) criticism of the Trauring model is that he did not consider ridge count, connective ambiguity, and correlation among minutiae location. Furthermore, they claim that Trauring's assumption that the minutiae types and orientations are equally probable is not correct. The probabilities of observing a particular minutiae configuration from different models are compared in Table 8.2.

There have been few studies that empirically estimate the probability of finding a fingerprint in a large database that successfully matches the input fingerprint. Meagher et al. (1999) matched about 50,000 rolled fingerprints belonging to the same fingerprint class (left loop) with each other, to compute the impostor distribution. However, the genuine distribution was computed by matching each fingerprint image with itself; this ignores the variability present in different impressions of the same finger. Furthermore, they assumed that the impostor and the genuine distributions follow a Gaussian distribution and computed the probability of a false correspondence to be 10^{-97}. This model grossly underestimates the probability of a false correspondence because it does not consider realistic intra-class variations in impressions of a finger.

Daugman (1999a) analyzed the probability of a false match in an iris recognition system based on an empirical impostor distribution of the IrisCode matching scores from 340 irises. Under the assumption that the impostor and the genuine distributions follow a binomial distribution, he concluded that irises are extremely individual (false match rate of 10^{-12} at false non-match rate of 8.5×10^{-5}). Golfarelli, Maio, and Maltoni (1997) formulated the optimum Bayesian decision criterion for a biometric verification system; assuming the data distributions to be multinormals, they derived two statistical expressions for theoretically calculating the false match and false non-match rates. By inferring the model parameters from real prototypes, they obtained a theoretical equal error rate of 1.31×10^{-5} for a hand-geometry-based verification system and of 2×10^{-3} for a face-based verification system.

Author	P(Fingerprint configuration)	Probability values for $n=36, G=24, B=72$ $(n=12, G=8, B=24)$
Galton (1892)	$(1/16)\times(1/256)\times(1/2)^{G}$	1.45×10^{-11} (9.54×10^{-7})
Pearson (1930, 1933)	$(1/16)\times(1/256)\times(1/36)^{G}$	1.09×10^{-41} (8.65×10^{-17})
Henry (1900)	$(1/4)^{n+2}$	1.32×10^{-23} (3.72×10^{-9})
Balthazard (1911) (cf. Stoney and Thornton, 1986)	$(1/4)^{n}$	2.12×10^{-22} (5.96×10^{-8})
Bose (1917) (cf. Stoney and Thornton, 1986)	$(1/4)^{n}$	2.12×10^{-22} (5.96×10^{-8})
Wentworth and Wilder (1918)	$(1/50)^{n}$	6.87×10^{-62} (4.10×10^{-22})
Cummins and Midlo (1943)	$(1/31)\times(1/50)^{n}$	2.22×10^{-63} (1.32×10^{-22})
Gupta (1968)	$(1/10)\times(1/10)\times(1/10)^{n}$	1.00×10^{-38} (1.00×10^{-14})
Roxburgh (1933)	$(1/1000)\times(1.5/24.12)^{n}$	3.75×10^{-47} (3.35×10^{-18})
Trauring (1963)	$(0.1944)^{n}$	2.47×10^{-26} (2.91×10^{-9})
Osterburg et al. (1977)	$(0.766)^{B-n}(0.234)^{n}$	1.33×10^{-27} (1.10×10^{-9})
Stoney (1985)	$(n/5)\times0.6\times(0.5\times10^{-3})^{n-1}$	1.20×10^{-80} (3.50×10^{-26})

Table 8.2. Comparison of probability of a particular fingerprint configuration using different models. For a fair comparison, we do not distinguish between minutiae types. By assuming that an average size fingerprint has 24 regions ($G = 24$) as defined by Galton, 72 regions ($B = 72$) as defined by Osterburg et al., and has 36 minutiae on average ($n = 36$), we compute the probability of observing a given fingerprint configuration in the last column of the table. The probability of observing a fingerprint configuration with $n = 12$ and, equivalently, $G = 8$ and $B = 24$, is also given in braces in the third column. Note that all probabilities represent a full (n minutiae) match as opposed to a partial match (see Table 8.3).

8.3 A Model for Fingerprint Individuality

Pankanti, Prabhakar, and Jain (2002) developed a fingerprint individuality model in an attempt to obtain a realistic and more accurate probability of correspondence between fingerprints. They compared the probabilities obtained using this model against empirical values using an automatic fingerprint matching system (Jain et al., 1997). To estimate the probability of correspondence, the following assumptions were made by Pankanti, Prabhakar, and Jain (2002).

1. Only ridge terminations and ridge bifurcation minutiae features are considered, because the occurrence of other minutiae types such as islands, dots, enclosures, bridges, double bifurcations, trifurcations, and so on is relatively rare. Because minutiae can reside only on ridges that follow certain overall patterns in a fingerprint, the

minutiae directions are not completely independent of the minutiae locations. The statistical dependence between minutiae directions and locations is implicitly modeled.

2.   A uniform distribution of minutiae in a fingerprint is assumed with the restriction that two minutiae cannot be very close to each other. Although minutiae locations are not uniformly distributed, this assumption approximates the slightly overdispersed uniform distribution found by Stoney (1988).

3.   Correspondence of a minutiae pair is an independent event and each correspondence is equally important. It is possible to weigh spatially diverse correspondences more than all correspondences localized in a narrow spatial neighborhood.

4.   Fingerprint image quality is not explicitly taken into account in the individuality determination. It is very difficult to reliably assign a quality index to a fingerprint because image quality is a subjective concept.

5.   Ridge widths are assumed to be the same across the population and spatially uniform in the same finger. This assumption is justified because pressure variations could make non-uniform ridge variations uniform and vice versa.

6.   The analysis of matching of different impressions of the same finger binds the parameters of the probability of matching minutiae in two fingerprints from different fingers.

7.   It is assumed that there exists one and only one (correct) alignment between the template and the input minutiae sets. The fingerprint correspondence problem involves matching two fingerprints: the template (stored in the system) and the *input* (which needs to be verified/identified). It is assumed that a reasonable *alignment* has been established between the template and the input.

Given an input fingerprint containing n minutiae, Pankanti, Prabhakar, and Jain (2002) computed the probability that an arbitrary fingerprint (template in a database of fingerprints) containing m minutiae will have exactly q corresponding minutiae with the input. Because they only considered fingerprint minutiae that were defined by their location, $[x,y]$ coordinates, and by the angle of the ridge on which they reside θ, the template and the input minutiae sets $\mathbf{T}$ and $\mathbf{I}$, respectively, were defined as

$$\mathbf{T} = \{\{x_1, y_1, \theta_1\}, \{x_2, y_2, \theta_2\}, ..., \{x_m, y_m, \theta_m\}\}. \tag{9}$$
$$\mathbf{I} = \{\{x_1', y_1', \theta_1'\}, \{x_2', y_2', \theta_2'\}, ..., \{x_n', y_n', \theta_n'\}\}. \tag{10}$$

A minutia j in the input fingerprint is considered as "corresponding" or "matching" to the minutia i in the template, if and only if

$$\sqrt{(x_i' - x_j)^2 + (y_i' - y_j)^2} \le r_0, \quad \text{and} \tag{11}$$
$$min\left(|\theta_i' - \theta_j|, 360° - |\theta_i' - \theta_j|\right) \le \theta_0, \tag{12}$$

where r_0 is the tolerance in distance and θ_0 is the tolerance in angle. Both manual and automatic fingerprint matches are based on some tolerance in minutiae location and angle to account for the variations in different impressions of the same finger (see Section 4.3). Equation (12) computes the minimum of $|\theta'_i - \theta_j|$ and $360° - |\theta'_i - \theta_j|$ because the angles are mod $360°$ (the difference between angles of $2°$ and $358°$ is only $4°$).

Let A be the total area of overlap between the input and the template fingerprints after a reasonable alignment has been achieved (see Figure 8.2). The probabilities that an arbitrary minutia in the input will match an arbitrary minutia in the template, only in terms of location, and only in terms of direction, are given by Equations (13) and (14), respectively. Equation (13) assumes that $[x,y]$ and $[x',y']$ are independent and Equation (14) assumes that θ and θ' are independent.

$$P\left(\sqrt{(x'-x)^2 + (y'-y)^2} \le r_0\right) = \frac{\text{area of tolerance}}{\text{total area of overlap}} = \frac{\pi r_0^2}{A} = \frac{C}{A}, \tag{13}$$

$$P\left(min\left(|\theta' - \theta|, 360 - |\theta' - \theta|\right) \le \theta_0\right) = \frac{\text{angle of tolerance}}{\text{total angle}} = \frac{2\theta_0}{360}. \tag{14}$$

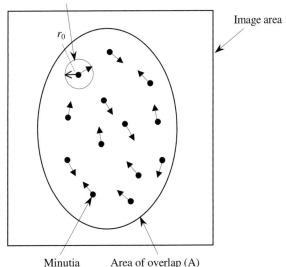

Figure 8.2. The area of the input fingerprint image that overlaps with the template and the input minutiae within the overlap area are shown. In addition, tolerance (in area) for minutia matching for one particular minutia is illustrated.

First consider the fingerprint correspondence model when only minutiae locations are matched; minutiae angles are introduced later in the formulation. If the template contains m minutiae, the probability that only one minutia in the input will correspond to any of the m template minutiae is given by mC/A. Note that this and the subsequent location-based probability estimates are based on the assumption that the minutiae in fingerprints follow a slightly overdispersed uniform distribution (Stoney, 1988); that is, only one template and one input minutia can occur in a single tolerance area (C). If this assumption is violated, mC/A could become greater than one and the model cannot tolerate this elegantly. Now, given two input minutiae, the probability that only the first one corresponds to one of the m template minutiae is the product of the probabilities that the first input minutia has a correspondence (mC/A) and the second minutia does not have a correspondence $(A - mC)/(A - C)$. Thus the probability that exactly one of the two input minutiae matches any of the m template minutiae is $2 \times (mC/A) \times (A - mC)/(A - C)$, as either the first input minutia alone may have a correspondence or the second input minutia alone may have a correspondence. If the input fingerprint has n minutiae, the probability that exactly one input minutia matches one of the m template minutiae is

$$p(A,C,m,n) = \binom{n}{1}\left(\frac{mC}{A}\right)\left(\frac{A-mC}{A-C}\right).$$
(15)

The probability that there are exactly ρ corresponding minutiae, *given* n input minutiae, m template minutiae, the area of overlap (A), and area of tolerance (C) is:

$$p(\rho \mid A,C,m,n) = \binom{n}{\rho}\underbrace{\left(\frac{mC}{A}\right)\left(\frac{(m-1)C}{A-C}\right)\cdots\left(\frac{(m-\rho-1)C}{A-(\rho-1)C}\right)}_{\rho \text{ terms}} \times$$

$$\underbrace{\left(\frac{A-mC}{A-\rho C}\right)\left(\frac{A-(m-1)C}{A-(\rho+1)C}\right)\cdots\left(\frac{A-(m-(n-\rho+1)C}{A-(n-1)C}\right)}_{n-\rho \text{ terms}}.$$
(16)

The first ρ terms in Equation (16) denote the probability of matching ρ minutiae between the template and the input; and remaining $(n - \rho)$ terms express the probability that $(n - \rho)$ minutiae in the input do not match any minutiae in the template. Dividing the numerator and denominator of each term in Equation (16) by C, replacing A/C with M, and assuming that M is an integer (which is a realistic assumption because A is much greater than C), one can write the above equation in a compact form as (Rice, 1995)

$$p(\rho \mid M,m,n) = \frac{\binom{m}{\rho}\binom{M-m}{n-\rho}}{\binom{M}{n}}.$$
(17)

Equation (17) defines a hyper-geometric distribution of ρ with parameters m, M, and n (Rice, 1995). To get an intuitive understanding of the probability model for the minutiae correspondence in two fingerprints, imagine that the overlapping area of the template and the input fingerprints is divided into M non-overlapping cells. The shape of the individual cells does not matter, just the number of cells. Now consider a deck of cards containing M distinct cards. Each card represents a cell in the overlapping area. There is one such deck of M cards for the template fingerprint and an identical deck of M cards for the input fingerprint. If m cards are drawn from the first (template) deck without replacement, and n cards are drawn from the second (input) deck without replacement, the probability of matching exactly ρ cards among the cards drawn is given by the hyper-geometric distribution in Equation (17) (Rice, 1995).

The above analysis considers a minutiae correspondence based solely on the minutiae location. Minutiae patterns are generated by the underlying fingerprints which are smoothly flowing oriented textures. The orientations of nearby minutiae points are strongly correlated. The orientations of minutiae points are also correlated with the location of the minutiae point in the fingerprint depending on the fingerprint type. Thus the configuration space spanned by the minutiae pattern is smaller than that spanned by a pattern of (directed) random points. This typically implies that the probability of finding sufficiently similar prints from two different fingers is higher than that of finding sufficiently similar sets of random (directed) point patterns.

To account for the dependence between θ and θ', let l be such that $P(\min(|\theta' - \theta|, 360° - |\theta' - \theta|) \leq \theta_0) = l$ in Equation (14). Given n input and m template minutiae, the probability of minutiae falling into *similar* positions can be estimated by Equation (17). Once ρ minutiae positions are matched, the probability that q ($q \leq \rho$) minutiae among them have similar directions is given by

$$\binom{\rho}{q} (l)^q (1-l)^{\rho-q},$$

where l is the probability of two position-matched minutiae having a similar direction and $1 - l$ is the probability of two position-matched minutiae taking different directions. This analysis assumes that the ridge direction information/uncertainty can be completely captured by $P(\min(|\theta' - \theta|, 360° - |\theta' - \theta|) \leq \theta_0)$. Therefore, the probability of matching q minutiae in both position as well as direction, *given M, m, and n* is:

$$p(q \mid M, m, n) = \sum_{\rho=q}^{min(m,n)} \left(\frac{\binom{m}{\rho}\binom{M-m}{n-\rho}}{\binom{M}{n}} \times \binom{\rho}{q}(l)^q(1-l)^{\rho-q} \right). \tag{18}$$

The above formulation has assumed that the minutiae locations are uniformly distributed within the *entire* fingerprint area. A is the area of overlap between the template and the input fingerprints, therefore the ridges occupy approximately $A/2$ of the area and the other half is occupied by the valleys. Assume that the number (or the area) of ridges across all fingerprint types is the same. Because the minutiae can lie only on ridges (i.e., along a curve of length A/w, where w is the ridge period), the value of M in Equation (18) should, therefore, be changed from $M = A/C$ to $M = (A/w)/2r_0$, where $2r_0$ is the length tolerance in minutiae location (see Figure 8.3).

Parameter estimation

The individuality model of Pankanti, Prabhakar, and Jain (2002) has several parameters, namely, r_0, l, w, A, m, n, and q. The value of l further depends on θ_0. They estimated values of r_0, θ_0, l, and w for a given sensor resolution. To compare the probabilities obtained from the theoretical model with the empirical results, the values of A, m, and n were estimated from two different databases as described in the next section.

Pankanti, Prabhakar, and Jain (2002) estimated the value of r_0 to account for the variations in different impressions of the same finger (intra-class variation). However, inasmuch as the spatial tolerance is dependent upon the scale at which the fingerprint images are scanned, r_0 should be estimated for a specific sensor resolution. For this, they used a database (called GT) consisting of 450 mated pairs of fingerprints using a high-quality optical scanner, manufactured by Identicator, at a resolution of 500 dpi.

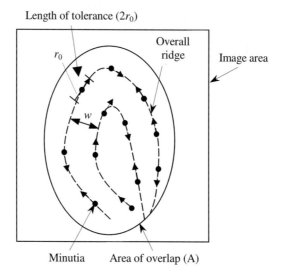

Figure 8.3. The area of the input fingerprint image that overlaps with the template and the input minutiae within the overlap area are shown. In addition, the overall ridge flow is shown and the tolerance (in length) for minutia matching for one particular minutia is illustrated.

The second print in the mated pair was acquired at least a week after the first print. The minutiae were manually extracted from the prints by a fingerprint expert. The expert also determined the correspondence information for the detected minutiae. Using the ground truth correspondence information between two pairs of corresponding minutiae, a rigid transformation between the mated pair was determined. The overall rigid transformation between the mated pair was determined using a least square approximation of the candidate rigid transformations estimated from each duplex pair of the corresponding minutiae. After aligning a given mated pair of fingerprints using the overall transformation, the spatial difference $(x' - x, y' - y)$ for each corresponding minutiae pair was computed; distances between all minutiae pairs in all mated fingerprint pairs were pooled to obtain an empirical distribution (see Figure 8.4). The smallest value of r_0 is sought for which:

$$P\left(\sqrt{(x' - x)^2 + (y' - y)^2} \le r_0 \right) \ge 0.975 \ ,$$

that is, the value of r_0 that accounts for at least 97.5% of variation in the minutiae position of genuine fingerprint matches. Thus r_0 is determined from the distribution shown in Figure 8.4 and is found to be 15 pixels for fingerprint images scanned at 500 dpi resolution under the assumption that the matcher uses a rigid transformation. Note that if the matcher can correctly model the non-linear distortion in fingerprints, the value of r_0 may be smaller (Bazen and Gerez, 2002a).

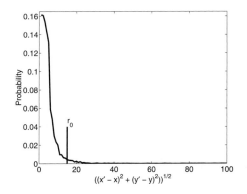

Figure 8.4. Distribution of minutiae distance differences for the genuine fingerprint pairs in the GT database.

To estimate the value of l, Pankanti, Prabhakar, and Jain (2002) first estimated the value of θ_0 using the database GT. After aligning a given mated pair of fingerprints using the overall transformation, that value of θ_0 is sought that accounts for 97.5% variation in the minutiae angles in the genuine fingerprint matches; that is, find the value of θ_0 for which $P(\min(|\theta' - \theta|, 360° - |\theta' - \theta|) \le \theta_0) \ge 0.975$. The distribution $P(\min(|\theta' - \theta|, 360° - |\theta' - \theta|))$ for the genuine fingerprint matches in GT is shown in Figure 8.5.a. The smallest value of θ_0 for which $P(\min(|\theta' - \theta|, 360° - |\theta' - \theta|) \leq \theta_0) \geq 0.975$ is found to be $\theta_0 = 22.5°$. In the second step, the distribution $P(\min(|\theta' - \theta|, 360° - |\theta' - \theta|))$ for the impostor fingerprint matches is determined. Because the GT database does not have correspondences marked by an expert between impostor fingerprint pairs, an automatic fingerprint matcher (Jain et al., 1997) is used to establish correspondences between minutiae in impostor pairs. Thus, the estimation of l depends on the automatic fingerprint matcher used. The distribution $P(\min(|\theta' - \theta|, 360° - |\theta' - \theta|))$ estimated by using this matcher on the GT database is shown in Figure 8.5.b from which it is determined that $P(\min(|\theta' - \theta|, 360° - |\theta' - \theta|) \leq 22.5°) = 0.267$; that is, $l = 0.267$. Note that under the assumption that minutiae directions are uniformly distributed and the directions for the minutiae that match in their location (θ' and θ) are independent, $l = (2 \times 22.5)/360 = 0.125$. If minutiae orientations were considered instead of directions, the estimated value of l would be 0.417 as opposed to a value of $(2 \times 22.5)/180 = 0.25$ determined under the assumption stated above.

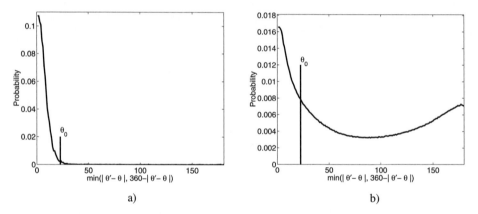

a)   b)

Figure 8.5. Distribution of minutiae angle differences for the a) genuine fingerprint pairs using the ground truth and b) impostor matches using the automatic fingerprint matcher.

Pankanti, Prabhakar, and Jain (2002) used the same value of w as reported by Stoney (1988). Stoney estimated the value of the ridge period as 0.463 mm/ridge from a database of 412 fingerprints. For fingerprint sensors with a resolution of 500 dpi, the ridge period converts to ~9.1 pixels/ridge. Thus $w \sim 9.1$. This value is also in close agreement with the values reported by Cummins, Waits, and McQuitty (1941), Cummins and Midlo (1943), and Kingston (1964).

8.4 Experimental Evaluation

In order to evaluate their individuality model, Pankanti, Prabhakar, and Jain (2002) used two fingerprint databases (called MSU_DBI and MSU_VERIDICOM). The MSU_DBI database contains fingerprint images of 167 subjects using an optical FTIR sensor manufactured by Digital Biometrics, Inc. (image size = 508 × 480, resolution = 500 dpi). Four impressions of the right index, right middle, left index, and left middle fingers for each subject are available that were captured over an interval of six weeks. The database contains a total of 2672 (167 × 4 × 4) fingerprint images. The MSU_VERIDICOM database was collected following the same protocol, but using a solid-state capacitive fingerprint sensor manufactured by Veridicom, Inc. (image size = 300 × 300, resolution = 500 dpi).

A large number of impostor matches (over 4,000,000) were generated using the automatic fingerprint matcher of Jain et al. (1997). The mean values of m and n for impostor matches were estimated as 46 for the MSU_DBI database and as 26 for the MSU_VERIDICOM database from the distributions of m and n (Figures 8.6.a and b). The average values of A for the MSU_DBI and the MSU_VERIDICOM databases are 67,415 pixels and 28,383 pixels, respectively. Pankanti, Prabhakar, and Jain (2002) estimated the value of the overall effective area A in the following fashion. After the template and the input fingerprints were aligned using the estimated transformation, a bounding box A_i of all the corresponding minutiae in the input fingerprint was computed in a common coordinate system. Similarly, a bounding box A_t of all the corresponding minutiae in the template fingerprint was also computed in the common coordinate system. The intersection A of these two bounding boxes A_i and A_t for each matching was then estimated. The estimates of A for all the matches performed in the database were pooled to obtain a distribution for A (see Figures 8.7.a and b). An arithmetic mean of the distribution was used to arrive at an estimate of A.

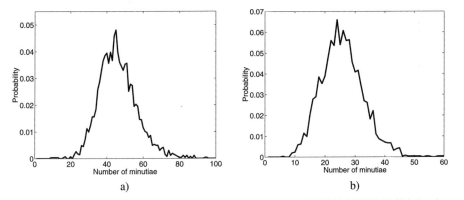

a)   b)

Figure 8.6. Distribution of m and n for a) MSU_DBI database, b) MSU_VERIDICOM database.

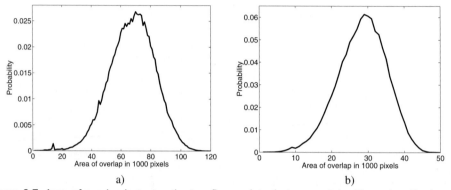

a)   b)

Figure 8.7. Area of overlap between the two fingerprints that are matched based on the bounding boxes of the minutiae features for a) MSU_DBI database, b) MSU_VERIDICOM database.

The probabilities of a fingerprint correspondence obtained for different values of M, m, n, and q are given in Table 8.3. The values shown in Table 8.3 obtained based on the model of Pankanti, Prabhakar, and Jain (2002) can be compared with values obtained from the other models in Table 8.2 for $m = 36$, $n = 36$, and $q = 36, 12$.

M, n, m, q	P(Fingerprint correspondence)
104, 26, 26, 26	5.27×10^{-40}
104, 26, 26, 12	3.87×10^{-9}
176, 36, 36, 36	5.47×10^{-59}
176, 36, 36, 12	6.10×10^{-8}
248, 46, 46, 46	1.33×10^{-77}
248, 46, 46, 12	5.86×10^{-7}
70, 12, 12, 12	1.22×10^{-20}

Table 8.3. Fingerprint correspondence probabilities obtained from the individuality model of Pankanti, Prabhakar, and Jain (2002) for different sizes of fingerprint images containing 26, 36, or 46 minutiae. The entry (70, 12, 12, 12) corresponds to the 12-point guideline. The value of M for this entry was computed by estimating typical print area manifesting 12 minutiae in a 500 dpi optical fingerprint scan.

Typically, a match consisting of 12 minutiae points (the 12-*point guideline*) is considered as sufficient evidence in many courts of law. Assuming that an expert can correctly glean all the minutiae in a latent, a 12-point match with the full-print template (see the first row, last column entry in Table 8.4) is an overwhelming amount of evidence, provided that there is no contradictory minutiae evidence in the overlapping area. The value of A was computed for 500 dpi fingerprint images from the minutiae density of 0.246 minutiae/mm^2 estimated by Kingston (1964) from 100 fingerprints; thus $M = 70$ was used for all the entries in Table 8.4. Because latent prints are typically of very poor quality, it is possible that there could be an error in judgment regarding the existence of minutiae in the latent or their possible match to the minutiae in the template print. The effect of such misjudgments on the probability of a false correspondence is certainly not negligible. For instance, two incorrect minutiae match judgments increases the probability of a false correspondence from 1.22×10^{-20} (entry $n = 12$, $q = 12$ in Table 8.4) to 1.96×10^{-14} (entry $n = 12$, $q = 10$ in Table 8.4) and ignoring two genuine minutiae present in the input (latent) print increases the probability from 1.22×10^{-20} (entry $n = 12$, $q = 12$ in Table 8.4) to 1.11×10^{-18} (entry $n = 14$, $q = 12$ in Table 8.4). Thus a false minutiae match has significantly more impact than that of missing genuine minutiae in the input latent print.

		q				
		8	9	10	11	12
	12	6.19×10^{-10}	4.88×10^{-12}	1.96×10^{-14}	3.21×10^{-17}	**1.22×10^{-20}**
	13	1.58×10^{-9}	1.56×10^{-11}	8.42×10^{-14}	2.08×10^{-16}	1.58×10^{-19}
n	14	3.62×10^{-9}	4.32×10^{-11}	2.92×10^{-13}	9.66×10^{-16}	1.11×10^{-18}
	15	7.63×10^{-9}	1.06×10^{-10}	8.68×10^{-13}	3.60×10^{-15}	5.53×10^{-18}
	16	1.50×10^{-8}	2.40×10^{-10}	2.30×10^{-12}	1.45×10^{-14}	2.21×10^{-17}

Table 8.4. The adverse effects of the fingerprint expert/matcher misjudgments in using the 12-point guideline. The source of error could be in underestimating the number of actual minutiae in the latent print (n) or overestimating the number of matched minutiae (q). The value of m is 12 for all entries in this table. The entry ($n = 12$, $q = 12$) represents the probability of a false correspondence when the 12-point guideline is correctly applied by a fingerprint examiner. Except for the ($n = 12$, $q = 12$) entry, all other entries represent incorrect judgments by the fingerprint expert to arrive at a decision that exactly 12 minutiae in the latent print matched 12 corresponding minutiae in the template print. For instance, the entry ($n = 14$, $q = 8$) in the table represents an estimate of probability of a false correspondence due to two misjudgments by the examiner: the fingerprint examiner detected 12 minutiae in the latent print although there were in fact 14 minutiae in the latent print; that is, the examiner overlooked 2 latent print minutiae; furthermore, although he associated all 12 minutiae he detected in the latent print to the 12 minutiae in the template print, only 8 of those correspondences were indeed genuine correspondences (4 incorrect minutiae match judgments).

Figures 8.8.a and b show the distributions of the number of matching minutiae computed from the MSU_DBI and MSU_VERIDICOM databases using the matcher of Jain et al. (1997), respectively. These figures also show the theoretical distributions obtained from the model of Pankanti, Prabhakar, and Jain (2002), described in Section 8.3, for the average values of M, m, and n computed from the databases. The empirical distribution is to the right of the theoretical distribution. This is because the theoretical model deviates from the Jain et al.'s (1997) matcher at several places. First, the theoretical model assumes that the "true" alignment between the input and the template is known although the automatic fingerprint matcher of Jain et al. (1997) is estimating the alignment between the two fingerprints based on the minutiae information alone. For example, if there is only one minutia in the input fingerprint, the matcher will establish an alignment such that this minutia matches with a minutia in the template with a probability of 1. Thus the theoretical probability estimate of (mC/A) for $n = 1$ is a gross underestimate for this matcher. In addition, the matcher is seeking that alignment which maximizes the number of minutiae correspondences. Thus it may find an alignment that is wrong but results in a large number of minutiae correspondences. Moreover, the matcher tests a large number of alignment hypotheses and, consequently, the probability of a false correspondence increases significantly according to Equation (5). Second, the theoretical model assumes that two minutiae cannot be closer than the tolerance distance of $2r_0$ both in the input and the template fingerprints. However, the automatic matcher does not enforce this requirement and both the input and the template minutiae sets contain minutiae that are closer than the tolerance. This difference between the theoretical model and the automatic matcher becomes wider in the case of poor quality fingerprint images where the matcher detects close clusters of spurious minutiae. Finally, as explained in Table 8.4, any spurious minutiae detected by the matcher increase the probability of a false correspondence.

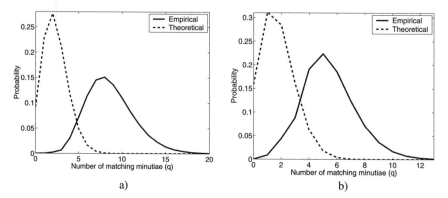

Figure 8.8. Comparison of experimental and theoretical probabilities of false correspondence: a) MSU_DBI database, b) MSU_VERIDICOM database.

Table 8.5 shows the empirical probabilities of matching 10 and 15 minutiae in the MSU_VERIDICOM and MSU_DBI databases, respectively. The typical values of m and n

were estimated from their distributions by computing the arithmetic means. The probabilities of false correspondence for these values of m, n, and q are reported in the third column of Table 8.5 (note that Table 8.5 reports the probabilities of matching exactly q minutiae). The probabilities for matching "q or more" minutiae are 3.0×10^{-2} and 3.2×10^{-2} for the MSU_VERIDICOM and MSU_DBI databases, respectively; that is, they are of the same order. The probabilities of false match (FMR) obtained on these databases are consistent with those obtained on similar databases by several other state-of-the-art automatic fingerprint verification systems reported in the FVC2002 fingerprint verification competition (Maio et al., 2002b). On the other hand, the performance claims by several fingerprint verification system vendors vary over a large range (a false match rate of 10^{-9} to 10^{-3}) due to the absence of standardized testing protocols and databases. The probabilities of a false fingerprint correspondence from the proposed theoretical model obtained for different values of M, m, n, and q given in Table 8.3 are several orders of magnitude lower than the corresponding empirical probabilities given in Table 8.5.

Database	m, n, q	P(False correspondence)
MSU_VERIDICOM	26, 26, 10	1.7×10^{-2}
MSU_DBI	46, 46, 15	1.4×10^{-2}

Table 8.5. False correspondence probabilities obtained from matching impostor fingerprints using an automatic matcher (Jain et al., 1997) for the MSU_VERIDICOM and MSU_DBI databases. The probabilities given in the table are for matching "exactly q" minutiae. The average values for A, m, and n are 28383, 26, and 26 for the MSU_VERIDICOM database and 67415, 46, and 46 for the MSU_DBI database, respectively.

8.5 Summary

Estimating fingerprint individuality essentially involves determining the discriminatory information in fingerprint images to resolve the identities of the people. The empirical and theoretical methods of estimating individuality serve complementary goals. Empirical observations lead us to characterize the constraints on the discriminatory information across different fingers as well as the invariant information among the different impressions of the same finger; the theoretical modeling/generalization of these constraints permits prediction of the bounds on the performance and facilitates development of constructive methods for an independent empirical validation. Historically, there has been a disconnect in the performance evaluations of practical fingerprint systems and theoretical performance predictions. Furthermore, the results of the data-dependent empirical performance evaluations themselves have varied quite dramatically.

Although the individuality information derived from the minutiae representation based on the model of Pankanti, Prabhakar, and Jain (2002) is lower than the previous estimates, it indicates that the likelihood of an adversary guessing someone's fingerprint pattern (e.g., requiring matching 20 or more minutiae from a total of 36) is significantly lower than a hacker being able to guess a six-character alphanumeric case-sensitive (most probably weak) password by social engineering techniques (most common passwords are based on birthday, spouse's name, etc.) or by brute force (the probability of guessing such a password by brute force is $(1 / (26 + 26 + 10))^6 = 1.76 \times 10^{-11}$). Obviously, more stringent conditions on matching will provide better cryptographic strength at the risk of increasing the false non-match error rate.

Although there is a huge amount of "inherent" discriminatory information available in minutiae representation, the observed matching performance of the state-of-the art automatic matching systems is several orders of magnitude lower than the theoretical performance because of the noise in sensing fingerprints, errors in locating minutiae, and fragility of the matching algorithms. In addition, present understanding of fingerprint feature (minutiae) detection and invariance as implemented in the automatic fingerprint matching system is too simplistic to accomplish significantly better accuracies. If a typical full dab fingerprint contains 46 minutiae, there is an overwhelming amount of information present in the minutiae representation of fingerprints for manual recognition (the probability of a false correspondence between two fingerprints from different users containing 46 minutiae each is 1.33×10^{-77}). However, an automatic system that makes its decision based on 12 minutiae correspondences is utilizing only limited information (the probability of a false correspondence for matching 12 minutiae between two fingerprints from different users containing 46 minutiae each is 5.86×10^{-7}). Given this liberal operating point of an automatic matcher, it may be desirable to explore additional complementary representations of fingerprints for automatic matching (see Section 4.6).

9
Securing Fingerprint Systems

9.1 Introduction

Consider that a facility is secured with a lock. Usually, the sturdier the lock, the higher is the perceived level of security. However, even if a facility is equipped with the strongest possible lock, it is not absolutely certain that the facility cannot be broken into. For example, instead of trying to break the lock, a burglar may break the door, chainsaw a wall, smash windows, disguise himself as a policeman, or rob key holders at gunpoint to gain entry. Thus a stronger lock does not necessarily mean better security. In fact, no matter what type of security system is installed, no system is absolutely secure or foolproof. Given the right circumstances and plenty of time and resources, any security system can be broken.

This is not to say that a system designer should not try her best to guard against all possible security threats. What it implies is that the type of security needed depends upon the requirements of the application. A *threat model* for an application can be defined based on what needs to be protected and from whom. Threat models are almost always tied to the expected attack (e.g., resources available, intent, and expertise of the attacker). Unless a threat model is clearly defined for a system, it is very difficult to decide if the proposed security solution is adequate. The typical threats in an application may include the following.

- *Denial of service* (*DoS*): An adversary damages the system such that legitimate users can no longer access the system.
- *Circumvention*: An unauthorized user illegitimately gains access to the system and data. Circumvention could either be a privacy attack or a subversive attack. In a privacy attack, the intruder gets access to data that he may not be authorized to access. In a subversive attack, an intruder may manipulate the system to use it for illegal activities. For example, an intruder may break into a person's bank account and withdraw/transfer all the money.
- *Repudiation*: A legitimate user denies having accessed the system. For example, in a government welfare benefits distribution, an authorized user may first receive a bene-

fit, and then later deny having received any benefits and receive the benefits again (also called double dipping).

- *Contamination or covert acquisition*: It is possible that the means of recognition could be compromised without the knowledge of a legitimate user and be subsequently abused. For instance, an adversary can lift the latent fingerprint of a legitimate user, make a three-dimensional mold of the fingerprint and use it to gain access. A fingerprint acquired for one application may also be used in another application for which it was not intended.

- *Collusion*: In any application, some users of the system will have a super-user status that allows them to bypass the recognition component and to overrule the decision made by the system. This facility is incorporated in the system workflow to permit handling of exceptional situations, for example, processing of individuals with no fingers in a fingerprint-based recognition system. This could potentially lead to an abuse of the system by way of collusion between the super-users and the other users. It is often mentioned that the easiest way to break a security system is to compromise the system administrator.

- *Coercion*: The genuine users could be potentially coerced (forced) to identify themselves to the system. The recognition measurements could be forcibly extracted from a genuine user to gain access to the system with concomitant privileges. For instance, an ATM user could be forced to give away her ATM card and PIN at gunpoint. It is desirable to reliably detect instances of coercion without endangering the lives of genuine users.

In this chapter, we focus only on the methods available to secure the fingerprint recognition process and leave out the details of implementations in various application scenarios. Depending upon the threat model of an application, an impostor may invest varying degree of time and resources in launching such an attack. For example, in a remote and unattended recognition application that requires recognition from a remote server, a hacker may have the opportunity and plenty of time to make a large number of attacks or even physically violate the integrity of a client system. We also consider both unintentional and intentional attacks on a fingerprint recognition system. Note that although this chapter discusses security of a fingerprint verification system, the discussions are also applicable to other biometric systems as well as both verification and identification problems. In addition, we compare the specific security methods used in a fingerprint verification system with their equivalent methods used in traditional knowledge- and possession-based systems whenever possible.

We first compare traditional knowledge- and possession-based methods with biometrics-based recognition methods in general terms. Most people set their passwords based on words or numbers that they can easily remember, such as names and birthdays of family members, favorite movie or music star, and dictionary words. This makes these passwords easy to crack by guessing or a simple brute force dictionary attack. Although it is possible and even advisable to keep different passwords for different applications, most people use the same password across different applications. If a single password is compromised, it may open many doors.

Long and random passwords are more secure but harder to remember, which prompts some users to write them down in accessible locations (e.g., under the keyboard). Strong (difficult to remember) passwords also result in more system help desk calls for forgotten or expired passwords. Cryptographic techniques such as encryption can provide very long passwords that are not required to be remembered but that are in turn protected by simple passwords, thus defeating their purpose. Furthermore, a hacker needs to break the password of only one employee to gain access to a company's Intranet and thus a single weak password compromises the overall security of the system. Therefore, the security of the entire system is only as good as the weakest link (weakest password). Finally, when a password is shared with a colleague, there is no way for the system to know who the actual user is. Similarly, there are many problems with possession-based authentication. For example, keys and tokens can be shared, duplicated, lost, or stolen. When keys are misplaced, lost, or stolen, the system administrator either revokes the old key and issues a new one or allows access without the key/token. On the other hand, it is significantly more difficult to copy, share, and distribute fingerprints with as much ease as passwords and tokens. Fingerprints cannot be lost or forgotten and fingerprint-based recognition requires the person to be present at the point of authentication. It is difficult to forge fingerprints and unlikely for a user to repudiate having used the system. All the users of the system will have a relatively equal security level and one "password" is no easier to break (e.g., through "social engineering" methods) than any other. The main advantage of a fingerprint recognition system is the convenience it provides the users while maintaining sufficiently high accuracy.

The above-mentioned advantages make fingerprints a very attractive choice for person recognition applications. However, fingerprint-based recognition has some disadvantages as well (Schneier, 1999). Although fingerprints are distinctive identifiers, they are not secret. People leave latent fingerprints on everything that they touch. Furthermore, a compromised token or password can be cancelled and a new token or password can be issued as often as desired. On the other hand, people have only 10 fingerprints on two hands and if a fingerprint is compromised (a communication channel snooper may get hold of a user's fingerprint image/template), it cannot be replaced. Finally, in principle, a fingerprint template stolen from one application may be used in another application. However, most of these disadvantages can be alleviated in a proper system design. In this chapter, we discuss the various methods that can be used to secure the process of fingerprint recognition.

9.2 Points of Attack

Many of the possible attacks in fingerprint recognition systems were identified and systematically documented by Bolle, Connell, and Ratha (2002). A number of other types of attack points have been documented by Anderson (1994) and Schneier (1998). Anderson (1994) studied the technical aspect of fraud involved in using ATMs and found that most of the failures were due to poor design and administration. Schneier (1998) pointed out a number of system vulnerabilities due to errors in design, implementation, and installation. Figure 9.1 shows the major modules and the dataflow paths in a fingerprint verification system. The eight potential attack points are also marked in Figure 9.1 and are elaborated below.

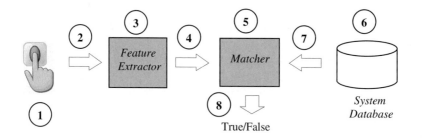

Figure 9.1. The design of a fingerprint verification system is shown to illustrate the possible security attack points which are marked with numbers from 1 to 8. Note that similar attack points exist during the fingerprint enrollment process as well but are not shown here to avoid redundancy. Any of the communication channels (2, 4, 7, and 8) could isolate the corresponding modules in a network.

1. *Attack at the scanner*: There are several types of attacks that can be launched against a fingerprint scanner. First, the surface or the sensor can be physically destroyed in a denial-of-service attack. Second, a fake fingerprint, such as a latent fingerprint lifted on a paper, a fingerprint image printed/copied on a paper, a thin rubber membrane containing an impression of a fingerprint, or a three-dimensional plastic, rubber, or gelatin mold of a fingerprint could be presented to a scanner as input. Third, an image could be injected between the sensing element (e.g., a silicon chip) and the rest of the scanner electronics (e.g., A/D converter, microprocessor, interface module, etc.).

2. *Attack on the channel between the scanner and the feature extractor*: The channel between the scanner and the feature extractor can be intercepted for a digital fingerprint image of a legitimate user originating from the scanner. This fingerprint image can be replayed at a later time to the feature extractor by bypassing the scanner.

3. *Attack on the feature extraction module*: A Trojan horse[1] program can disguise itself as the feature extractor, bypass the feature extractor, and submit artificially generated fingerprint features to the matcher.

---

[1] A Trojan horse program, named after the wooden artifact from Greek mythology that contained more than could be seen on the surface, refers to an executable code that is not a translation of the original

4. *Attack on the channel between the feature extractor module and the matcher module*: The channel between the feature extractor and matcher can be snooped for the fingerprint feature set of a legitimate user and stored. This feature set can be replayed at a later time on the channel.

5. *Attack on the matcher module*: A Trojan horse program can disguise itself as a matcher, bypass the matcher, and submit an artificially generated matching score or yes/no decision to the application requesting authentication. If this program always generated a high matching score (or a "yes" response), it would result in a circumvention attack. If this program always generated a low matching score (or a "no" response), it would result in a denial-of-service attack.

6. *Attack on the system database*: A Trojan horse program can disguise itself as the system database, bypass the system database, and submit an artificially generated database record (typically containing fingerprint template, user name, access privileges, etc.). This attack could be launched during enrollment time, during verification time, or directly on the database at any time. In a smartcard application where the template resides on the card that is carried by the user, a lost card, if not adequately protected, could give the impostor access to the template.

7. *Attack on the channel between the system database and matcher module*: The channel between the system database and the matcher can be snooped to steal the record of a legitimate user that can be replayed at a later time on the channel.

8. *Attack on the channel between the matcher module and the application requesting verification*: The channel between the matcher and the application requesting verification can be snooped to access the response of a previous verification and stored. This response can be replayed at a later time in the channel.

Note that attacks 2, 4, 7, and 8 are launched against communication channels; they are similar in nature and can be collectively called "replay" attacks. The attacks 1, 3, 5, and 6 are launched against system modules; they are also similar in nature and can be collectively called Trojan horse attacks. Furthermore, the replay attacks are similar to those present in token- and knowledge-based authentication systems whereas the fake finger attack is unique to the fingerprint recognition system.

9.3 Denial-of-service Attacks at the Scanner

There are a number of fingerprint scanners based on different technologies such as optical, solid-state, and so on (see Chapter 2). These scanners differ from one another not only in fingerprint image size, image quality, number of gray-levels, resolution, and the like, but also in

program but was added later, usually maliciously, and comes into the system disguised as the original program.

durability and ruggedness. Ruggedness of a fingerprint sensor is the most important property to guard against unintentional (such as due to extreme weather conditions) or intentional (such as breaking or scratching the sensor surface) denial of service. The desired ruggedness of a fingerprint sensor also depends upon the recognition application. For example, a keyless car entry application requires a more rugged sensor than an e-Commerce application because the weather conditions around an automobile are more fluctuating and severe than in an office environment. A fragile fingerprint scanner for keyless entry application may result in an unintentional denial of service. A border control application may require a more rugged scanner than an ATM application because a criminal may intentionally break the fingerprint scanner at the border in order to escape recognition. The glass/plastic surface of optical sensors can be easily broken. Optical sensors also typically have a conformal (e.g., silicone) coating on them to facilitate imaging of dry prints. This coating can easily be damaged by scratching the sensor surface. Chip-based sensors can be damaged by electrostatic discharge and contact with sharp metal objects. Depending on the level of ruggedness desired by an application, the fingerprint sensor surface and housing can be designed to resist or to be more robust against denial-of-service attacks. For example, most chip-based sensors contain grounding mechanisms to avoid damage from electrostatic discharge and a surface coating to avoid damage from moisture and sharp objects. Optical sensors use certain types of thick glass that are more rugged than plastic. A metallic housing is more rugged than the more commonly used plastic housing.

9.4 Fake Finger Attacks

The most common method of launching a fake finger attack is to build an accurate three-dimensional model of a fingerprint from a latent fingerprint of a legitimate user. Latent fingerprints are formed when the fingers leave a thin layer of sweat and grease on the surface that they touch, due to the presence of sweat pores in our fingertips. These impressions can be colored with a dye and then "lifted" with adhesive tape or glue. A three-dimensional mold (such as a rubber membrane, glue impression, or gelatin finger) can then be made from this latent fingerprint that duplicates the ridge characteristics of the lifted fingerprint, thus creating a fake finger. Although it may be possible to fool a fingerprint recognition system using a fake finger, the relevance of a fake finger attack depends on the application's threat model. First of all, either a latent fingerprint of a legitimate user or a willing/coerced legitimate user who allows the use of his fingers is required to create a fake finger. For lifting a latent fingerprint, one needs to know the whereabouts of the legitimate user and the surfaces he has touched. It is not easy to lift a latent fingerprint of good quality in practice because most latent fingerprints are incomplete, wrapped around irregular surfaces, or partially cancelled by the finger slipping. Building an accurate three-dimensional model (Figure 9.2) (remember that a simple two-dimensional fingerprint image cannot easily deceive optical or solid-state sensors) requires expertise and laboratory equipment such as a high resolution video-entry system, a three-dimensional printing device (e.g., stereolithography), and so on. Putte and Keuning (2000) and Matsumoto et al. (2002) have documented in detail several methods of creating a fake finger from silicone and gelatin that is able to fool many commercially available fingerprint scanners. Although producing a gummy clone of an available real fingerprint is relatively simple, the reconstruction of a fake finger from latent fingerprints remains quite complicated.

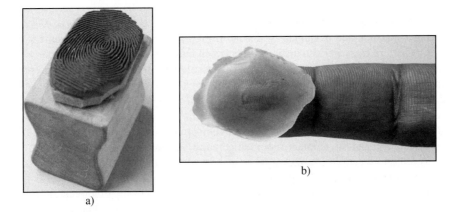

a)
b)

Figure 9.2. Fake finger examples: a) a rubber stamp is made from a fingerprint image; b) a wa-fer-thin plastic sheet containing a three-dimensional replication of a fingerprint.

In another scenario, a fingerprint image can be either intercepted on the communication channel or requested by a Trojan horse server and used to make a three-dimensional mold. Hill (2001) argued that a two-dimensional fingerprint image can be synthesized from a fingerprint minutiae template and used to make a three-dimensional mold. Even if the images synthesized by Hill (2001) are visually not realistic and, in principle, a fingerprint image cannot be completely reconstructed from the minutiae template, Hill (2001) proved that some commercial fingerprint recognition systems can be fooled by using such surrogates. However, in all these cases, the knowledge of the specific target (user) is required to launch a fake finger attack. A single fake finger cannot be used to launch attacks against multiple users. Finally, creating a fake finger is as difficult the second or the third time as it is the first time, and thus there are no "economies of scale" in repeating the attack.

As mentioned earlier, the severity of a fake finger attack depends upon the application. For example, in a network access application, a fake finger attack on a fingerprint recognition system is much less damaging than an attack on a password authentication system. This is because, in a password-based network authentication application, a hacker may launch an attack remotely without knowing any of the users. Also, the same password (e.g., a dictionary word) can be used to launch an attack against all the enrolled users at no extra cost. Thus, in our opinion, the threat from a fake finger attack on a fingerprint-based recognition system is considerably lower than a remote network attack on a password-based authentication system. Security can be further improved by utilizing additional credentials such as a token or a password with the fingerprint recognition system. On the other hand, for many applications (e.g., high-security access control), the fake finger attacks are of considerable concern. This threat can be addressed by building *vitality* detection mechanisms in the fingerprint recognition system hardware and software.

The finger vitality detection problem, stated from a technical standpoint, is to differentiate a live finger that is made of human epidermis from a finger that is made of some synthetic material. A pattern classifier can distinguish between the human epidermis and other synthetic material by measuring the thermal, electric, and optical properties of the material presented to the fingerprint scanner. A classifier that distinguishes a dead finger from a live finger can be based on measuring one or more of the vitality signs of a finger such as the pulse, blood pressure, or sweating process.

At normal room temperatures (~20° C), the temperature of the epidermis is typically 8 to 10 degrees higher than the ambient room temperature. A fake finger made of synthetic material is expected to be cooler. In fact, a fake finger made of silicone rubber is about 2 degrees cooler than a live finger. This temperature difference could be used as a feature to distinguish between live human epidermis and a fake finger. However, due to the temperature variations in operating environments (e.g., due to air-conditioning or a person holding a cold soda can), and the possibility of simply artificially heating the fake finger, thermal measurements are not very reliable.

The conductivity of human tissue differs from conductivity of many other synthetic materials such as silicone rubber and gelatin. The conductivity of the material presented to the fingerprint sensor can be measured to differentiate a live finger from a fake finger. However, the conductivity of live fingers varies a lot depending on weather conditions such as humidity and temperature. If water or saliva is added to a fake finger, its conductivity may be indistinguishable from that of a live finger. Relative dielectric constant (RDC) is also influenced by the humidity of the finger and thus will not be very effective in distinguishing a live finger from a fake. Moreover, simply applying alcohol on a fake finger changes its RDC significantly and thus can make it indistinguishable from live fingers.

Optical fingerprint sensors typically have the inherent capability to reject any two-dimensional reproductions of a fingerprint. Human skin has different optical properties than many other synthetic materials and optical fingerprint sensors may incorporate mechanisms to measure the optical properties of the material presented to the sensor to distinguish between a live finger and a fake finger. The optical properties that may be measured include the absorption, reflection, scattering, and refraction properties under different lighting conditions (such as red, blue, green, infrared, laser lights). However, it is not difficult to find materials that have optical properties close to those of a live finger. For example, a fake finger made from gelatin has optical properties close to a live human finger.

Certain solid-state fingerprint sensors can detect the pattern of ridges and valleys underneath the epidermis. For example, ultrasonic sensors can image the pattern underneath the epidermis based on the property that the layer under the epidermis is softer than the epidermis. Electric field sensors can image the pattern underneath the epidermis based on the property that the layer under the epidermis has a higher electric conductivity than the epidermis. It is claimed that these fingerprint sensors cannot be fooled by fake fingers (Putte and Keuning (2000) and Putte (2001)). However, once it is known which property a sensor is using, a silicone rubber fake finger with suitable properties can be created together with a silicone rubber fake finger with properties similar to the epidermis. These two silicone rubber fake fingers can be overlapped and together they will exactly duplicate the two layers of fingerprint patterns on live fingers.

By learning a skin deformation model when a human live finger is pressed on the sensor surface, fake fingers that are either made from material that does not deform like fingertips or cannot be applied on the sensor surface to produce that deformation can be rejected. For example, if users are required to place a finger twice on the sensor, or to move it once it is in contact with the sensor surface, there will be some non-linear distortions between the two fingerprint impressions. If a fake finger made from rubber is placed twice or moved on the sensor surface, there may only be a rigid transformation between the two fingerprint impressions. However, if a wafer-thin silicone rubber glued to a real finger is applied on the sensor surface, it will produce non-linear deformations that may be quite similar to those produced by a real finger.

One of the most common methods of preventing paper currency counterfeiting is to design the currency with complicated patterns and very fine details. Similarly, if a fingerprint sensor images a finger at a very high resolution, then it may be able to capture certain fingerprint details (such as the sweat pores) that may be difficult to reproduce in a synthetically made fake finger. By simply checking for the existence of fingerprint sweat pores, it may be possible to reject those replications that do not explicitly duplicate the fingerprint pores on the fake finger as well. Actually, experiments performed by Matsumoto et al. (2002) showed that a coarse reproduction of intra-ridge pores is feasible with gummy fingers and therefore, very high-quality scanners should be used to capture pore positions and shape.

Derakhshani et al. (2002) proposed a method to differentiate live fingers from fingers of human cadavers and fake fingers made from play dough using a rubber-based cast. Their method is based on measurements of the sweating process of a live finger in a video acquired during the acquisition of a fingerprint impression from the fingerprint scanner. Their results showed no errors on a very small database of 18 live, 18 cadaver, and 18 fake fingers. However, this method is not expected to work very well for people with perspiration disability. Furthermore, it will have difficulty in dealing with varying amounts of moisture content occurring in live human fingers.

Other biomedical methods of finger vitality determination include measurements of pulse and blood pressure in the fingers. However, the pulse rate in the finger varies significantly from one person to another. In addition, pulse rate also varies depending on physical activity and emotional state of the person at the time of acquisition. Furthermore, finger pressure on the sensor surface can also change the measurement of the pulse quite dramatically and a single pulse measurement may take up to five seconds. Finally, if a wafer-thin silicone rubber is glued to a real finger, the heartbeat of the underlying finger will result in the detection of a pulse. Blood pressure and electrocardiogram sensors also have similar advantages and disadvantages.

Developments in cryptographic systems have demonstrated that any security solution based on the secrecy of an algorithm/method (sometimes referred to as "security by obscurity") does not provide satisfactory results over a period of time. This is because the secret needs to be broken only by a single person and once this happens (it eventually always does), the entire solution immediately falls apart. Therefore, we should assume that the characteristics/phenomena that a fingerprint scanner is using to determine the vitality of a finger are available in the public domain. Based on this knowledge, it is easy to envision the design of a fake finger that will circumvent the fingerprint scanner. For example, if it is known that a fingerprint device measures the pulse to check finger vitality, one could design a three-dimensional mold of a finger that has a fingerprint on its outer surface and a pulse generating device inside it. Some characteristics may be easier to simulate (such as thermal or optical property of human skin) than others (such as the sweating process). Matsumoto et al. (2002) argue that many scanners can be fooled by flashing a light against the fingerprint scanner, or by heating up, cooling down, humidifying, impacting on, or vibrating the scanner outside its environmental tolerances. When a large number of vital characteristics are measured by a fingerprint device (e.g., a vitality detection system may check for fingerprint sweat pores as well as the pulse) and combined for vitality detection, it becomes increasingly difficult (but not impossible) to fool the system. We argue that although scanner manufacturers should build multiple vitality detection mechanisms into their fingerprint scanners to make it increasingly difficult to fool their devices, a fake finger that will pass all these measures and will be accepted by a fingerprint scanner can still be built given enough resources.

In our opinion, the best method of vitality verification should not be based on a characteristic that is common to all people (such as pulse), but rather is unique to each individual and is not easily available to an adversary to copy. For starters, a fingerprint-based recognition system may use the impression of the tip of a finger for recognition but match a side impression (near the nail) of the same finger with the enrolled side impression of the finger as a check for vitality. This may be a satisfactory solution in many applications because the sides of the fingerprints are typically not found in latent fingerprints. A combination of several fingers of the same person in conjunction with a specific order in which they are required to be presented to a fingerprint system can also enhance security. These solutions come at a relatively low cost, as no other sensor is required and any existing fingerprint verification system can be easily adopted to handle multiple fingerprint impressions. Such a multibiometric solution for vitality detection can also improve the verification system performance at the cost of longer acquisition and processing times. A more secure solution may involve combining palm print, hand vein, hand geometry, or finger thermogram with the fingerprint recognition system. These biometric identifiers may not be as accurate as biometric identifiers may not be as accurate as fingerprint recognition, but may provide sufficient individuality for a liveness check and are more difficult to acquire covertly. Note that almost all the solutions to fake finger detection come at the additional cost of increasing scanner hardware price, higher false reject rate, and longer fingerprint acquisition time.

9.5 Trojan Horse Attacks

A Trojan horse attack can be launched at the scanner (e.g., a sensor emulator), feature extractor, matcher, or the system database. These attacks are launched against "entities." A Trojan horse program can disguise itself as one or more of these modules and generate false results (such as a fingerprint image, a fingerprint template, or a matching score). A Trojan horse attack at the feature extractor (see Figure 9.3) is almost the same as the attack on the system database and very similar to the attacks at the scanner and matcher. We discuss these attacks collectively.

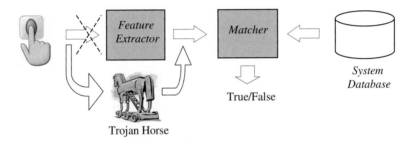

Figure 9.3. A Trojan horse attack against the feature extraction module is shown. A Trojan horse is a program that disguises itself as something else (fingerprint feature extraction module in this case). The fingerprint device will not know that it is sending the fingerprint image to the Trojan horse instead of the real feature extraction module and the matcher module will not know that the input is not coming from the real feature extraction module.

First of all, it is extremely important that the feature extraction, matcher, and system database reside at a secure and trusted location. Furthermore, the fingerprint scanner should be trustworthy and have some security capability (such as encryption) built into it. The trust between the scanner and the server should be established both ways (i.e., server trusts the scanner and the scanner trusts the server). In a remote recognition application, a client cannot always be trusted and it only acts as a medium that passes the encrypted fingerprint image from the scanner to the server for feature extraction and matching (see Figure 9.8). A two-way mutual trust is established when the scanner authenticates the server and the server authenticates the scanner that is necessary in a network environment. Maio and Maltoni (1999a) envisaged an electronic commerce system based on fingerprint recognition and encryption techniques. They proposed that, in the case where both the seller and buyer cannot trust each other, the fingerprint matching be performed by a trusted third party "certifier," which also manages the fingerprint template database. When the seller is a trusted entity, it can perform the fingerprint matching and store the fingerprint template database at its site.

Smartcards have received much attention from developers/integrators of fingerprint recognition systems because of their internally protected storage and computational resources. In fact, embedding a fingerprint recognition system inside a smartcard is an effective way to prevent unauthorized users from installing Trojan horses and to avoid eavesdropping of critical information in transit. Although an entire fingerprint recognition system can be implemented onto a smartcard (including sensing element, feature extraction, matching and template database), most of the solutions proposed to date (e.g., Ishida, Mimura, and Seta (2001)) implement only some parts of the recognition system "on-card," due to the limited computational power of the onboard CPU. For example, if the templates are stored on-card and the fingerprint feature extraction and matching is performed on-card, the user's fingerprint template is never allowed to leave the card and, therefore, makes it practically impossible to intercept it. The computational power of smartcards is continuously and rapidly increasing. As a result, it will be possible in the future to implement very sophisticated and reliable algorithms on-card.

Enterprise environments often require multiple applications and access locations where a user can register and use his fingerprints to gain access to services. It would be time consuming and expensive to require users to re-enroll their fingerprints for several different template databases. A distributed system can solve this problem, but all the locations where the fingerprint data can be processed ("hosts") need to first establish a trust relationship. This can be achieved by using a *Certificate Authority* (CA). CA is an independent third party that everyone trusts and whose responsibility is to issue certificates. When the host is installed onto a computer, it generates a key pair (public-key cryptography is discussed in the next section) and signs all outgoing data with its private key. Every host can administratively choose to trust the data coming from other hosts by using the other host's public key. A host, after being certified as a trusted certificate authority, can in turn certify other hosts. The CA typically sits on top of a network operating system security model (see Figure 9.4). Thus, in a commercial fingerprint-based recognition system, it will be extremely difficult for a hacker to gain access to the feature extractor, matcher, or database modules. However, because many manufacturers offer Software Developers' Kits (SDKs) in addition to fully integrated recognition solutions, one could possibly get access to the same feature extraction, matching, and database modules in an independent standalone SDK that is also being used in an installed recognition application.

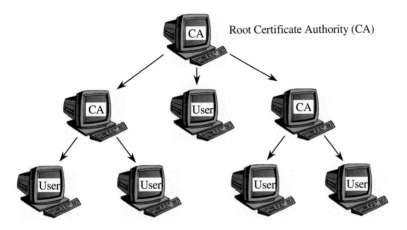

Figure 9.4. Distributed certificate authority based on hierarchical trust model.

Note that the Trojan horse attacks on a fingerprint recognition system have a very strong resemblance to such attacks on password-based systems. Consider that a PIN/password-based system accepts only four-digit numbers. Each of these four digits can take a value from 0 to 9. Thus there are a total of 10,000 (10^4) possible combinations resulting from a four-digit PIN. Let us assume that a user chooses her PIN completely randomly. This PIN is stored in the system database. If the representation/encryption is known, a Trojan horse program can replace this PIN with another PIN. If the PIN for the user is known in advance, then the Trojan horse can simply replace the PIN with this known PIN. If the PIN is not known in advance, then a hacker may try all 10,000 four-digit combinations one after another. This is called a *brute force attack*.

To launch a Trojan horse attack against a fingerprint recognition system, the fingerprint representation must be known: not only the type of features used, but also their digital representation, quantization, spatial reference, ordering, and so on (Hill, 2001). If the fingerprint of the user is known in advance, a set of fingerprint features can be reproduced by this program in the required format; otherwise the program may generate all possible configurations (brute force attack). If a minutiae representation is used, this Trojan horse program may generate the minutiae points randomly in an oval area contained inside a fingerprint (Stoney and Thornton (1987) have reported that minutiae are distributed more or less uniformly in a fingerprint). If a fingerprint recognition system uses the gray-scale fingerprint image as the feature (such as those based on correlation), then a synthetic fingerprint generator program (such as the one described in Chapter 6) may be used to launch a brute force attack. Actually, a synthetic fingerprint generator program can also be used to attack a minutiae-based system. In this scenario, the minutiae will be extracted from synthetically generated fingerprints to launch an attack. This scenario may be more effective in a brute force attack on a minutiae-based system than a randomly generated minutiae set because the fingerprints generated by the synthetic fingerprint generator program produce a more realistic minutiae distribution than a randomly generated point pattern set. In any case, the knowledge of fingerprint representation is necessary to launch an effective brute force attack. Thus, in principle, a fingerprint recognition system that uses a proprietary representation scheme/format and system architecture is less likely to be broken by a brute force attack. One could also argue that fingerprint template standardization attempts (e.g., Higgins (1995), ANSI (1986, 2000), NIST (1991, 1994), and Common Biometric Exchange File Format (CBEFF)) somewhat weaken the security of a system by publishing the basic format of stored template data. Similarly, by making the functionality and interface public, common API systems such as BioAPI may become more prone to hacker attacks than the systems designed with unknown software architecture. Actually, once again, security by obscurity is certainly not a lasting solution and the secrecy of a proprietary template coding (or interface) could be easily broken by an attacker with adequate resources. Therefore security standards such as ANSI standard X.94 are being developed to ensure that the known software API structure is minimally exposed to adverse hacking attacks (e.g., through encryption).

In the four-digit PIN authentication system discussed earlier, it is certain that one of the 10^4 possible attack attempts will succeed. In a fingerprint-based recognition system, the number of attempts required for success depends upon the invariant information in fingerprints and the system operating point (i.e., FMR and FNMR tradeoff). One difference between a brute force attack on a PIN/password system and a fingerprint recognition system is that an exact match is required for a PIN to be accepted. In contrast, an input fingerprint need only be "sufficiently similar" to the template to result in a match. A longer PIN/password (assuming that users will choose them randomly) has a higher *information content*. On the other hand, a fingerprint containing more numbers of minutiae does not necessarily have a higher information content (Ratha, Connell, and Bolle, 2001a).

A brute force attack may also be optimized using a strategy such as *hill climbing* if feedback (such as the matching score) is offered by the fingerprint matching module. Soutar (2002) first described this hill climbing attack in the context of a fingerprint recognition system based on BioAPI and proposed a solution to lower the chance of success of this type of attack. A hill climbing Trojan horse program first provides an input to the fingerprint matcher (Figure 9.5) and notes its response (matching score). The program then perturbs the first input, resubmits it to the fingerprint matcher and monitors the matching score. If the matching score is higher than the matching score in the previous iteration, the changes to the input are kept; otherwise, they are discarded. Thus, in each iteration where the matching score is higher than before, the input signal moves closer to the template. The procedure is repeated until the matching score exceeds the threshold and the false representation is accepted by the recognition system.

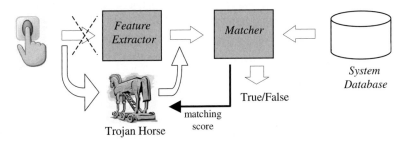

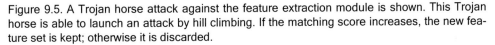

Figure 9.5. A Trojan horse attack against the feature extraction module is shown. This Trojan horse is able to launch an attack by hill climbing. If the matching score increases, the new feature set is kept; otherwise it is discarded.

Just like the brute force attack, the hill climbing attack can also be launched against any known fingerprint representation (e.g., gray-scale image- or minutiae-based). In particular, using a synthetic fingerprint generation technique (see Chapter 6), the feasibility of a hill climbing attack could be enhanced: suppose the attacker has an idea of the overall structure of the fingerprint he wants to imitate, then he may fix some parameters (e.g., fingerprint class and coarse singularity positions) and iteratively generate fingerprints having the same overall structure but different minutiae. The feedback received by the matcher would give him useful information for the iterative generation.

Soutar (2002) proposed increasing the granularity of the matching score as a solution to the hill climbing attack. He argues that if the matching scores are granular (e.g., reported in steps of 10 for a matching score in the range [0,100]), then the hill climbing attack would require a huge number of attempts before observing a change in score and thus the total number of attempts required for the matching score to exceed the threshold would become prohibitively large. One way to deal with a large number of attacks against a single user is to accept no more than a prespecified number of recognition attempts (e.g., three) in a given period of time. However, there are ways to get around this as well. For example, a hacker may attack a large number of accounts with the same fingerprint instead of attacking a single user with a large number of attempts.

Note that in the case of fingerprint-based recognition, the number of attempts (the probability of a false match) required in a brute force or a hill climbing attack in order to get accepted by the recognition system can be arbitrarily increased at the expense of increasing the false non-match rate of the system (by increasing the value of the decision threshold). As a general rule, applications should avoid providing matching scores or other information that could be exploited to carry out smart hill climbing attacks. In fact, if the complexity of a brute force attack is prohibitive in practical cases, well-designed hill climbing techniques could be quite effective in breaking weak systems.

The challenge-response and encryption technologies (described in the next section) used in a fingerprint recognition system make it more difficult to implement a Trojan horse attack.

9.6 Replay Attacks

In addition to safeguarding a fingerprint recognition system against fake finger attacks and Trojan horse attacks, protection against any replay attack is required to ensure data integrity and non-repudiation. Let us assume that the fingerprint scanner can reject fake fingers, it can be trusted, has some security capability, and the feature extraction, matcher, and system database reside at a trusted and secure location. It is further necessary to secure the communication links in the recognition system: between the scanner and the feature extractor, between the feature extractor and matcher, between system database and matcher, and between matcher and the application requesting authentication. In other words, the integrity of the data transmission must be secure all the way from the scanner to the application. This is typically achieved by cryptographic methods. In particular, encryption, digital signature, and challenge-response provide sufficient security for data integrity, non-repudiation, and replay attacks, respectively. It is therefore required that the fingerprint scanner be capable of setting up a challenge-response, encrypted, and digitally signed link with the trusted authentication server. These techniques are well established and are briefly discussed here as they relate to a fingerprint recognition system. A more detailed treatment can be found in Schneier (1996). We only focus on some techniques available for securing a communication channel; discussion of implementations in various applications and network environments is beyond the scope of this chapter.

Encryption and digital signatures

There are two types of key-based encryption algorithms: symmetric and public key. A *key* is typically a string of bits and the longer the length of the string, the harder it is to break the encrypted message, but the longer it takes to encrypt and decrypt a message. *Symmetric cryptography* uses a single secret key for both encrypting and decrypting a message. Let $E(m,k)$ and $D(m,k)$, respectively, be the functions that allow a message m to be encrypted or decrypted through a key k.

$D(E(m,k),k) = m$.

The advantage of this type of encryption is that a large number of fast and effective algorithms are available and the secrecy of the key guarantees a high level of security. The disadvantage of symmetric encryption lies in the difficulty of key distribution. The receiver and the sender need to first exchange a key secretly before they can begin to communicate. The key must remain secret; if the secrecy of the key is compromised, the encrypted message can be easily decrypted by an impostor who has possession of the key. As a result, the keys are often hand-carried by couriers to their destinations. The Data Encryption Standard (DES) is the best known symmetric cryptography algorithm based on a 56-bit key, and one of its variants (triple-DES) is currently being used by most encryption systems. A new algorithm called AES (Advanced Encryption Standard) has been selected by NIST to become the successor of DES.

Public-key cryptography uses a pair of keys for each entity that takes part in the communication. Here the key that is used to encrypt a message is different from the key used to decrypt the message (and hence the key pair is called "asymmetric"). Furthermore, the encryption and decryption keys cannot be derived from each other, even if a large amount of messages encrypted from a public or a private key is available. One of the keys of the pair is called the *private key* that is held by a specific person and kept secret. The other key is called the *public key* and is made known to everybody who wants to communicate with this specific person. Anybody who wants to communicate with a subject, say *A*, can send her messages encrypted by means of *A*'s public key and only *A* will be able to decrypt these messages with her private key, inasmuch as she is the only one who knows her private key (see Figure 9.6).

$$D(E(m,k_{A-pub}),k_{A-pri}) = m \quad \text{and conversely,}$$
$$D(E(m,k_{A-pri}),k_{A-pub}) = m.$$

Figure 9.6. Public-key cryptography method based on a pair of keys (public and private). A's private and public keys are denoted by "*A-pri*" and "*A-pub*," respectively.

The advantage of public-key cryptography over symmetric cryptography is that key management becomes easier. The main disadvantage is that it is several orders of magnitude slower than symmetric cryptography (Schneier, 1996). Rivest–Shamir–Adleman (RSA) is the most popular public-key algorithm. These symmetric and asymmetric encryption techniques can be used to secure a communication link for data integrity. However, they do not solve the non-repudiation problem. *Digital signature* is the technology that can ensure/certify that a message has been sent by a specific person who cannot deny having sent the message. The popular RSA public-key algorithm itself is a straightforward way to digitally sign and encrypt a message (see Figure 9.7). Suppose that *A* wants to send a message *m* to *B* that is digitally signed. For this purpose, A first encrypts the message m with his private key (something only A can do) and then with B's public key (something that only B can decrypt) and sends the resulting message m' to B.

$$m' = E(E(m,k_{A\text{-}pri}),k_{B\text{-}pub}).$$

When B receives m', she first decrypts it with her private key and then applies A's public key to verify A's signature (thus ensuring that only A could have sent the message).

$$m = D(D(m',k_{B\text{-}pri}),k_{A\text{-}pub}).$$

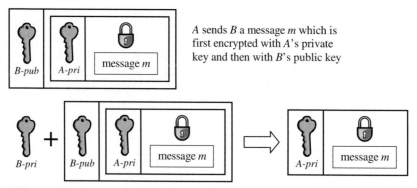

A sends B a message m which is first encrypted with A's private key and then with B's public key

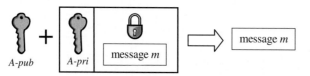

Figure 9.7. Digital signature using public-key cryptography is shown. A's private, A's public, B's private, and B's public keys are denoted by "$A\text{-}pri$," "$A\text{-}pub$," "$B\text{-}pri$," and "$B\text{-}pub$," respectively. A is sure that only B can decipher his message; on the other hand, B is sure that A is the sender of message m.

Although public-key cryptography is most desirable for its proven performance in encryption and digital signatures, it is computationally expensive. Therefore, in practice, other optimization schemes are used without sacrificing the security that public-key cryptography offers. For example, public-key cryptography is used only to exchange (session) symmetric keys. A symmetric encryption algorithm is then used to carry out the rest of the data transfer for that session. Similarly, the use of public-key cryptography is expensive for digital signatures and therefore, *one-way hash functions* (H) are used for optimization (Schneier, 1996).

$m = E(H(m),k_{A\text{-}pri})$.

The Digital Signature Algorithm (DSA) is another popular method based on public-key encryption that can only be used for digital signatures and not for encryption.

Timestamp and challenge-response

Encryption solves the problem of data integrity and digital signatures solve the problem of non-repudiation. However, a digitally signed encrypted message from A to B can still be "sniffed" from a communication channel and replayed at a later time. The receiver, B, will not be able to know that this replayed message did not come from A or was not intended for B. A simple solution to this problem requires that the recipient store all the previous messages it has received and compare a new message against them to ascertain that the new message is not a copy of a previously received message. This approach requires the recipient to have a very large amount of storage space and a fast comparison algorithm. An optimization of this approach may involve storing hashes of the messages instead of the entire messages and comparing the hash of a new message with them. However, the storage and comparison time required in this solution are still prohibitive. Therefore the most popular solutions to the replay attacks involve building either a *timestamp* or a *challenge-response* mechanism in the communication link.

In a timestamp-based scheme, when A wants to communicate with B, she sends B an encrypted and signed request message that includes a timestamp taken from her internal clock. When B receives the request, he decrypts it and checks the timestamp and compares it with his internal clock. If the difference in time is within a threshold (typically computed based on the expected time of message transfer), B responds to A by sending her the requested data and his timestamp in an encrypted form. Upon receiving the response from B, A decrypts the message and checks the timestamp. This solution requires that the clocks of the sender and receiver be synchronized, which is difficult to achieve in practice.

The popular challenge-response schemes are based either on *nonce* or *session keys*. These schemes do not require the use of timestamps. In the nonce-based scheme, if A wants to communicate with B, she sends B an encrypted and signed request message that includes a random number (called the nonce). B responds to A by sending her the requested data and the nonce in an encrypted form. Upon receiving the response from B, A decrypts the message and the nonce and compares the received nonce with the one she had sent. A challenge-response link can also be established by using one-time encryption key (i.e., the session key) for each communication session. In Figure 9.8, a client-server architecture is shown where the client system, which is directly connected to the fingerprint scanner, is used only to route images/features to a remote server, which securely exchanges information with the fingerprint scanner through a channel-response mechanism. Attacks against the client are not effective, because the client cannot decipher information in transit.

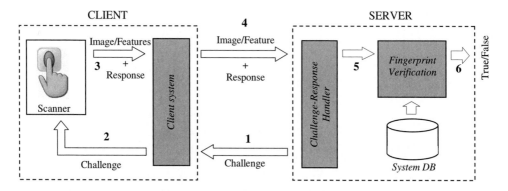

Figure 9.8. A client-server communication model with challenge-response link. The server generates a challenge and sends it to the fingerprint scanner (1,2). The fingerprint scanner sends a fingerprint image (or certain fingerprint features) together with a challenge-based response back to the server (3,4,5), where the user verification takes place (6). The client cannot decipher information in transit.

Digitally signing fingerprint images/features

A few image-based techniques similar to digital signatures (where the key is constant) and challenge-response (when a different key is sent by the server before each verification) have also been proposed specifically for fingerprints. Digital watermarking (Hartung and Kutter, 1999) is a technique that hides a secret digital pattern (called a digital watermark) in a digital image or data. A digital watermark may be visible or invisible. In a visible watermark, a visible pattern or image is embedded in the original image, but the invisible watermark does not change the visual appearance of the image. The existence of an invisible watermark can be determined only through a watermark extraction or detection algorithm. Furthermore, a digital watermarking algorithm may be robust (the watermark can withstand attacks such as compression and enhancement of an image) or fragile (the watermark is "broken" under the slightest change to the image). Typically, robust watermarking is used for copyright protection and fragile watermarking is used for data integrity. Yeung and Pankanti (2000) proposed a fragile invisible digital watermarking of fingerprint images based on a verification key that does not affect the recognition or retrieval accuracy in a fingerprint identification system. The fingerprints captured by the scanner are watermarked by the scanner and any tampering of the image data can be detected by the server using this method. Gunsel, Uludag, and Tekalp (2002) proposed a robust invisible watermarking of fingerprint images where the watermark can be verified even if the fingerprint image is cropped. Jain and Uludag (2002) argued that when the feature extractor sends the fingerprint features to the matcher over an unsecure link, it should hide the fingerprint features in a host (i.e., cover) image whose only purpose is to carry the fingerprint feature data. The pixel locations of the host image that are modified depend on a secret key and the scheme is robust to cropping of the fingerprint image because of redundancy. Jain, Uludag, and Hsu (2002) proposed that, in a multibiometric system, the secret key that is hidden in the fingerprint image could be the face image of the user.

Ratha, Connell, and Bolle (2001b) have introduced an image-based nonce scheme where the nonce sent by the application contains a set of random pixel locations and the scanner returns the values of the pixel intensities at these locations together with the fingerprint image as response. This ensures that the image was acquired by the scanner only after receiving the challenge. Ratha, Connell, and Bolle (2001b) also proposed a data hiding method, where the fingerprint scanner returns the nonce sent by the application hidden in the Wavelet Scale Quantization (WSQ) compressed fingerprint image. This technique involves slightly altering certain Discrete Wavelet Transform (DWT) coefficients at the locations specified by the nonce, such that there is no degradation in the quality of the fingerprint image when it is uncompressed.

Although the standard cryptographic techniques (i.e., symmetric cryptography, public-key cryptography, one-way hash functions, and digital signatures) have been proven to be secure in an information-theoretic sense, the security of image-based techniques designed for fingerprints has not yet been established and it is debatable whether they provide any benefit over standard cryptographic techniques.

9.7 Cancelable/private Biometrics

Schneier (1999) pointed out that one of the most problematic vulnerabilities of biometrics is that once a biometric image or template (i.e., fingerprint image or fingerprint template) is stolen, it is stolen forever and cannot be reissued, updated, or destroyed. Comparing a password-based system with a biometrics-based recognition system, Schneier (1999) further noted that it is desirable for a user to have a different password (and a different encryption key) for each account/service/application. Although ignoring the impracticality of maintaining different, complex, and changing passwords (most people use simple passwords or same password across different systems and never change their passwords), this does bring up an interesting matter from the point of view of security. Is it possible to design biometric systems such that if the template in an application is compromised, the biometric information is not lost forever and a new biometric template can be reissued? In addition, different applications are not able to use the same biometric template, thus preserving privacy. Only limited research has been carried out in this direction. Ratha, Connell, and Bolle (2001b) used the term *cancelable biometrics* and Davida, Frankel, and Matt (1998) used the term *private biometrics* to denote the use of application-specific biometric templates. The purpose of designing a cancelable biometrics has many objectives. First, a cancelable template stored in a database of certain application cannot be used as a template in another application. Second, if a database record (e.g., fingerprint template and other user credentials) is compromised, a new database record can be issued (just like a new password or card can be issued in a knowledge- or token-based authentication, respectively). Finally, altering a database record (e.g., replacing a fingerprint template) is unfeasible because the template can be digitally signed by the issuer, or some privileged information (e.g., an encryption key) can be stored in the template in such a way that it can be released only through biometric recognition. Here, we discuss only general techniques that can be used to build cancelable biometrics in security applications, because the implementation details depend on application requirements.

Conceptually, a cancelable/private template can be produced by transforming either the fingerprint image or the fingerprint features into another representation space by using a *non-invertible transform*. The most popular non-invertible transform is a one-way hash function, $H(x) = c$ which is used together with a verification function $V(x,c) \Rightarrow \{True, False\}$. This pair has the properties: *collision avoidance* (i.e., $V(x,c)$ and $V(y,c)$ cannot both be true if $x \neq y$); and *information hiding* (i.e., if an adversary has access to a hashed code c^* as well as the hashing function $H(x)$ the only way to determine the data x^* corresponding to the hashed code c^* is to exhaustively search over x (brute force attack)). Thus the security (cryptographic strength) provided by the one-way hash function is largely dependent on the information content of the data x.

Hashing techniques have been extensively used in password-based authentication systems. Passwords are hashed (non-invertible transformed) and stored in the database during user enrollment (see Figure 9.9.a). When an input password is received, it is also hashed and compared with the hashed password stored in the database. If the transformation is invertible, the knowledge of transformation and/or its parameters can be used to recover the original password. However, if the transformation is non-invertible (in a cryptographic sense), the original password cannot be recovered even if the exact transformation/parameters, as well as transformed password, are known. A different transform (or its parameters) is used during enrollment for each application and thus a single database template (containing the non-invertible transformed password) cannot be used across multiple applications.

The same concept can be applied to fingerprints. Instead of maintaining a database of fingerprint templates, the hashes of the templates are stored; at each verification attempt, the input fingerprint is also hashed and the matching is performed in the non-invertible transformed space (Figure 9.9.b). Although there is an analogy between password and fingerprint hashing, a significant difference exists between the two cases. Passwords are exactly the same during different authentication attempts, but fingerprint images are rarely identical during various acquisitions, and this prevents the same hash from being obtained from different instances of the same fingerprint. Therefore a "soft" comparison/matching needs to be performed in the non-invertible transformed space which is considerably more difficult in the case of biometrics than in the case of passwords.

Password enrollment

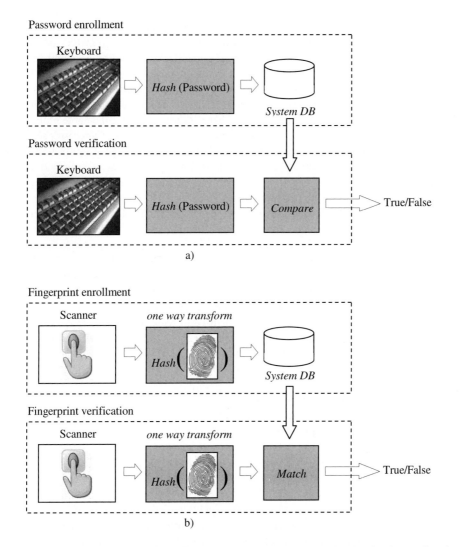

a)

b)

Figure 9.9. Hashing techniques. a) Passwords are typically stored in the database after they are hashed; when a new password is received, it is hashed and compared with the hashed enrollment. If a person has access to the database of hashed passwords, a password is not compromised. In b), a similar analogy is applied to fingerprint recognition. Only one-way transformed representation is stored and thus, if an adversary has an access to a database, the biometric information is not compromised.

The main reason for the difficulty in using cancelable fingerprints is that it is easier to recover an alignment between two fingerprints in the feature space than in the non-invertible transformed space. One method to alleviate this difficulty is to pre-align (register) the fingerprint images or features before the transformation is applied (e.g., based on core and delta in the fingerprints). Another method is to design the transformation in such a way that it results in an alignment invariant representation. Furthermore, an error-correction mechanism is typically built into the fingerprint matcher to account for the various intra-class variations in fingerprints (e.g., missed and spurious minutiae). The security provided by cancelable biometrics depends on the system module where the transformation is applied (e.g., fingerprint scanner, client, server, or third party certifier) and the location where the fingerprint template resides (e.g., client, server, third party certifier, or smartcard). Cancellation can be simply done by destroying an old template and re-enrolling the user by applying a different transform (or different parameters of a transform) to her fingerprints.

In principle, if a perfect one-way hash function could be designed such that different instances of the same finger were mapped into the same string (eventually using error-correction mechanisms), then this string could be directly used as a key for encrypting messages, and it would not be necessary to store any template at all (not even hashed templates). The finger itself would act as a key capable of ciphering and deciphering messages. Some attempts have been made in this direction, and there is substantial research ongoing on this topic.

Davida, Frankel, and Matt (1998) and Davida et al. (1999) proposed a method where a biometric template stored in the database cannot be used to reconstruct the original biometric information. They used IrisCode (Daugman, 1999a), which is a translation and rotation invariant texture-based feature set used for iris recognition. The individual features in the IrisCode are binary. They set up an algebraic (N,K,D) error-correcting code (Morelos-Zaragoza, 2002), where:

- N is the length of the codewords;
- K is the length of the IrisCode template ($\mathbf{T}$);
- D is the minimum distance between any two codewords (such a code can correct $(D-1)/2$ errors).

Given an enrollment template $\mathbf{T}$, a codeword E is generated using check digits C. During enrollment, $Sig(Hash(NAME, ATTR, E), NAME, ATTR$, and C for an individual are stored in a database record, where Sig applies a digital signature, $Hash$ is a one-way hashing function, $NAME$ is the user's name or ID, and $ATTR$ is other public attributes such as issuing location and user's access control list. During verification, an input IrisCode $\mathbf{I}$ is acquired, error correction is performed using the stored C to obtain E', and $Sig(Hash(NAME,ATTR,E')$ is compared with the stored $Sig(Hash(NAME,ATTR,E)$ for verification. Because only a hash of the biometric features and the error-correcting digits are stored in the database record, the original biometric cannot be reconstructed, even if an attacker has acquired the database record and the Hash function. Furthermore, if a database record is compromised, a new one can be reissued by using a differing Hash function (or its parameters).

Soutar et al. (1998a, b) have also used a similar idea for producing a cancelable fingerprint template in the context of an optical correlation-based fingerprint verification system. During enrollment, their technique first encrypts some data using a key derived from the fingerprint features and then hashes them to produce an "identification code, id_0." During verification, another key is derived from the input fingerprint (under error correction). This key is then used to encrypt the same data (as during enrollment) and the result is hashed to produce identification code, id_1. If id_0 and id_1 are identical, a successful match is declared. In this technique too, the original fingerprint is not stored, only a hash of some data that have been encrypted by the key derived from the fingerprint together with error-correcting information is stored. A compromised database record can be discarded and a new one can be issued by using a different hash function (or its parameters). Ratha, Connell, and Bolle (2001b) proposed that a high-order polynomial function can be used as a non-invertible transform for fingerprint minutiae features. Juels and Sudan (2002) used cryptographic one-way hash functions for obtaining cancelable/private fingerprint templates.

Traditionally, a fingerprint verification system outputs a binary (yes/no) decision, which could be trapped and altered by a malicious program. Hence, in certain applications, it is beneficial that the fingerprint verification release a stronger secret (e.g., cryptographic key) instead of the simple "yes" output upon a successful fingerprint match. An application can then use this released secret as a cryptographic key, thus alleviating the problem of key management (see Figure 9.10).

In its most simple (and most insecure) form, a key may be stored as part of a user's database record, together with the user name, fingerprint template, access privileges, and the like, which may be released upon a successful match. This provides convenience in key management, however, it is secure only when the database record is located and the matching is performed at a trusted location. A better solution is to hide a cryptographic key within the enrollment template itself (e.g., via a trusted and secret bit-replacement algorithm that can replace the least significant bits of the pixel values/features with the secret). Upon a successful fingerprint match, the correct secret is extracted from the fingerprint database template and released into the system. The security of this method is dependent on the secrecy of the key hiding and retrieval algorithms. If the key hiding and retrieval algorithms are deterministic (e.g., they always hide the key at the same locations), they can be easily compromised. For example, an attacker may enroll several people in the system using identical keys and locate the bits with common information across the enrolled templates. Therefore, it is useful that the secret be bounded with the fingerprint template in the stored database in such a way that it cannot be revealed without a successful fingerprint match. This binding is required to have properties similar to encryption, where the fingerprint is used as a key to lock the secret.

Yamazaki and Komatsu (2001) proposed to extract a cryptographic key from a user's handwriting. However, the key extracted from a person's handwriting is always the same. Thus, if a cryptographic key is ever compromised, it is not possible to cancel the old key and reissue a new key (see Figure 9.11). To overcome this limitation, parametric hashing algorithms may be adjusted (by varying parameters) to produce different strings (keys) for the same input.

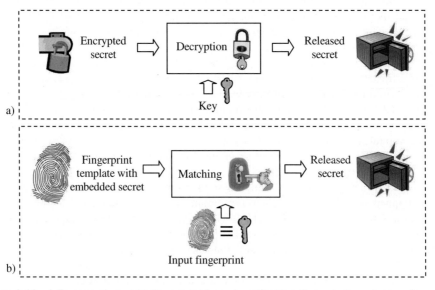

a)

b)

Figure 9.10. a) Password- and b) fingerprint-based verification through the release of a secret instead of the traditional true/false answer.

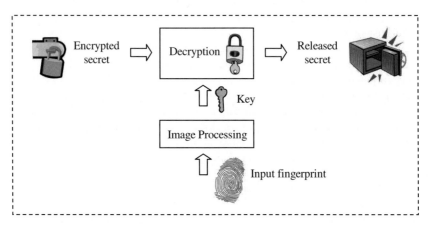

Figure 9.11. When an encryption key is exacted from the fingerprint itself, it is not possible to cancel the old key and reissue a new key.

Soutar et al. (1998a, b) proposed a solution in the context of an optical correlation based fingerprint matcher where a secret is linked with the fingerprint during enrollment, and is later retrieved only upon a successful fingerprint match. They used secrets that are completely independent of the fingerprint data so that a secret can be easily modified or updated at a later time. In addition, if a secret is ever compromised, it does not reveal the fingerprint. To achieve this goal, they combined the fingerprint features with random data in the stored template. However, their technique is applicable only in an optical correlation-based fingerprint matching system, is expensive, and has not been proven secure. Monrose, Reiter, and Wetzel (1999) and Monrose et al. (2001) proposed a key generation method from keystroke dynamics and voice, respectively. The security of their scheme is based on the computational hardness of small polynomial reconstruction. Juels and Sudan (2002) proposed a scheme called *fuzzy vault* that is designed with similar goals with proven security. In the fuzzy vault scheme, the secret k is locked by a user's biometric (set A) using a probabilistic LOCK function, resulting in a vault V_A. The corresponding decryption algorithm UNLOCK takes as input a vault V_A, and a decryption biometric (set B) and outputs k if B is close enough to A, or null, otherwise. Juels and Sudan (2002) argue that in a minutiae-based fingerprint matching system, if a minutiae template is augmented with a large number of "chaff" points that constitute random noise, the secrecy of the fingerprint features as well as the secret k is strengthened. Note that the biometric template size increases several fold as a result of introduction of a large number of false features and the accuracy of the fingerprint recognition might be affected. This may be undesirable in certain applications that require small template size. Another disadvantage of their approach is that the chaff points are added only to the enrollment fingerprint template. During verification, the chaff points are not added to the input fingerprint representation. As a result, although the fingerprint templates in the system database are secure, a Trojan horse matcher can build a dictionary that maps secrets to verification features (which could be used to reconstruct fingerprint image) by intercepting fingerprint features during verification.

9.8 Coercion

Genuine users could be potentially coerced (forced) to identify themselves to a fingerprint-based recognition system. Coercion cannot be detected either by cryptographic techniques or by fake finger detection. However, depending on the application, a mechanism can be built into the recognition system for coercion detection. We briefly describe a scenario that can be implemented in a fingerprint-based recognition system in an ATM application; similar methods can also be used in other authentication systems (e.g., password) and other applications. Consider that a user registers two of his fingers in a banking application. He registers one finger (e.g., right middle) as his "default" finger and another finger (e.g., right index) as his "panic" finger. The fingerprint recognition system matches his input with both his registered fingers and determines which finger was used for a transaction. At an ATM, if this user is withdrawing money willfully, he will use his "default" finger for recognition; if he is being coerced, he will use his "panic" finger for the withdrawal. On recognizing the user's "panic" finger, the ATM may dispense currency marked with special invisible ink that can later be identified, acquire a digital surveillance video of the transaction, and inform the local law enforcement agency about the location of the ATM, a video of the transaction, and the name and photograph of the user from the bank files. In this way, instances of coercion can be detected without endangering the lives of genuine users.

9.9 Summary

With large-scale deployments of biometric systems in various commercial and government applications, security issues related to the biometric system itself are becoming ever more important. Commercial fingerprint system vendors are rapidly building fake finger rejection features in their products. The public-key cryptography infrastructure is also being rapidly adopted to build end-to-end security in fingerprint verification products. The public is (rightfully) concerned about the privacy of biometric data. Cancelable biometrics could solve this problem, but this approach requires new efficient and robust techniques that allow a tolerant match to be performed in the hash space; unfortunately, the design of such algorithms seems to rely on fingerprint pre-alignment (registration). This is a difficult problem and any error in registration will result in a decrease in the verification performance of the fingerprint recognition system. More research is necessary in this direction to develop cancelable biometrics that do not compromise verification accuracy.

Finally, it is important to understand that *foolproof* personal recognition systems simply do not exist and perhaps never will. Security is a risk management strategy that identifies, controls, eliminates, or minimizes uncertain events that may adversely affect system resources and information assets. The security requirements of a system depend on the requirements (threat model) of an application and the cost–benefit analysis. Therefore, in addition to cryptographic techniques and mechanisms, it is also essential to conduct a security risk assessment and evaluation of the systems and products. Best practices guidelines for such assessments are being developed by Common Criteria (www.commoncriteria.org). Security standards are necessary, especially because certain biometrics systems are required to interoperate whereas interoperability between others is strictly prohibited. The ANSI X.9.84 Biometric Information Management and Security standard (www.x9.org) sets the requirements for managing and securing biometric information (mainly for use in the financial industry). This standard identifies the digital signature and encryption to provide integrity and privacy of biometric data. The standard also provides a comprehensive set of control objectives suitable for use by the professional audit practitioner to validate a biometric system. X.9.84 was developed in conjunction with other standards such as Biometric Application Programming Interface (BioAPI; www.bioapi.org) and NIST Common Biometric Exchange File Format (CBEFF;

www.nist.gov/cbeff) and has been submitted to ISO Technical Committee 68 for international standardization.

Bibliography

Abdelmalek et al. (1984). Abdelmalek N., Kasvand T., Goupil D., and Otsu N., "Fingerprint Data Compression," in *Proc. Int. Conf. on Pattern Recognition (7th)*, pp. 834–836, 1984.

Abutaleb and Kamel (1999). Abutaleb A.S. and Kamel M., "A Genetic Algorithm for the Estimation of Ridges in Fingerprints," *IEEE Transactions on Image Processing*, vol. 8, no. 8, pp. 1134–1138, 1999.

Almansa and Cohen (2000). Almansa A. and Cohen L., "Fingerprint Image Matching by Minimization of a Thin-Plate Energy Using a Two-Step Iterative Algorithm with Auxiliary Variables," in *Proc. Workshop on Applications of Computer Vision*, pp. 35–40, 2000.

Almansa and Lindeberg (1997). Almansa A. and Lindeberg T., "Enhancement of Fingerprint Images Using Shape-Adapted Scale-Space Operators," in *Gaussian Scale-Space Theory*, J. Sporring, M. Nielsen, L. Florack, and P. Johansen (Eds.), pp. 21–30, Kluwer, New York, 1997.

Almansa and Lindeberg (2000). Almansa A. and Lindeberg T., "Fingerprint Enhancement by Shape Adaptation of Scale-Space Operators with Automatic Scale Selection," *IEEE Transactions on Image Processing*, vol. 9, no. 12, pp. 2027–2042, 2000.

Anderson (1994). Anderson R.J., "Why Cryptosystems Fail," *Communications of the ACM*, vol. 37, no. 11, pp. 32–40, 1994.

Anderson et al. (1991). Anderson S., Bruce W., Denyer P., Renshaw D., and Wang G., "A Single Chip Sensor & Image Processor for Fingerprint Verification," in *Proc. IEEE Custom Integrated Circuits Conf.*, pp. 12.1.1–12.1.4, 1991.

Ansari, Chen, and Hou (1992). Ansari N., Chen M.H., and Hou E.S.H., "A Genetic Algorithm for Point Pattern Matching," in *Dynamic Genetic and Chaotic Programming*, B. Souckec and IRIS group (Eds.), Wiley, New York, 1992.

ANSI (1986). ANSI, "Fingerprint Identification — Data Format for Information Interchange," American International Standards Institute, New York, 1986.

ANSI (2000). ANSI, "Data Format for the Interchange of Fingerprint, Facial, Scar Mark, Tattoo (SMT) Information," ANSI/NIST-CSL ITL 1–2000; NIST Special Public Report 500–245, American National Standards Institute, New York, 2000.

Araque et al. (2002). Araque J., Baena M., Chalela B., Navarro D., and Vizcaya P., "Synthesis of Fingerprint Images," in *Proc. Int. Conf. on Pattern Recognition (16th)*, vol. 2, pp. 422–425, 2002.

Arcelli and Baja (1984). Arcelli C. and Baja G.S.D., "A Width Independent Fast Thinning Algorithm," *IEEE Transactions on Pattern Analysis and Machine Intelligence*, vol. 4, no. 7, pp. 463–474, 1984.

Asai et al. (1975). Asai K., Hoshino Y., Yamashita N., and Hiratsuka S., "Fingerprint Identification System," in *Proc. Second US-Japan Computer Conference*, pp. 30–35, 1975.

Ashbaugh (1999). Ashbaugh D.R., *Quantitative-Qualitative Friction Ridge Analysis: An Introduction to Basic and Advanced Ridgeology*, CRC Press, Boca Raton, FL, 1999.

Aushermann et al. (1973). Aushermann D.A., Fairchild R.C., Moyers R.E., Hall W.D, and Mitchel R.H., "A Proposed Method for the Analysis of Dermatoglyphics Patterns," *Proc. SPIE*, vol. 40, 1973.

Babler (1991). Babler W.J., "Embryologic Development of Epidermal Ridges and Their Configuration," *Birth Defects Original Article Series*, vol. 27, no. 2, 1991.

Bahuguna and Corboline (1996). Bahuguna R.D. and Corboline T., "Prism Fingerprint Sensor that Uses a Holographic Element," *Applied Optics*, vol. 35, no. 26, pp. 5242–5245, 1996.

Baird (1984). Baird H., *Model Based Image Matching Using Location*, MIT Press, Cambridge, MA, 1984.

Baldi and Chauvin (1993). Baldi P. and Chauvin Y., "Neural Networks for Fingerprint Recognition," *Neural Computation*, vol. 5, no. 3, pp. 402–418, 1993.

Ballan, Sakarya, and Evans (1997). Ballan M., Sakarya F.A., and Evans B.L., "A Fingerprint Classification Technique Using Directional Images," in *Proc. Asilomar Conf. on Signals Systems and Computers*, 1997.

Ballard (1981). Ballard D.H., "Generalizing the Hough Transform to Detect Arbitrary Shapes," *Pattern Recognition*, vol. 3, no. 2, pp. 110–122, 1981.

Banner and Stock (1974). Banner C.B. and Stock R.M., "Finder, the FBI's Approach to Automatic Fingerprint Identification," in *Proc. Conf. on Science of Fingerprints*, pp. 15–49, 1974.

Banner and Stock (1975a). Banner C.B. and Stock R.M., "The FBI's Approach to Automatic Fingerprint Identification (Part I)," U.S. Government Publication, FBI Law Enforcement Bulletin, vol. 44, no. 1, Jan. 1975.

Banner and Stock (1975b). Banner C.B. and Stock R.M., "The FBI's Approach to Automatic Fingerprint Identification (Part II)," U.S. Government Publication, FBI Law Enforcement Bulletin, vol. 44, no. 2, Feb. 1975.

Bartels, Beatty, and Barsky (1987). Bartels R.H., Beatty J.C., and Barsky B.A., *An Introduction to Splines for Use in Computer Graphics and Geometric Modeling*, Morgan-Kauffmann, San Mateo, CA, 1987.

Bartesaghi, Fernández, and Gómez (2001). Bartesaghi A., Fernández A., and Gómez A., "Performance Evaluation of an Automatic Fingerprint Classification Algorithm Adapted to a Vucetich Based Classification System," in *Proc. Int. Conf. on Audio- and Video-Based Biometric Person Authentication (3rd)*, pp. 259–265, 2001.

Baruch (1988). Baruch O., "Line Thinning by Line Following," *Pattern Recognition Letters*, vol. 8, no. 4, pp. 271–276, 1988.

Bazen and Gerez (2001a). Bazen A.M. and Gerez S.H., "An Intrinsic Coordinate System for Fingerprint Matching," in *Proc. Int. Conf. on Audio- and Video-Based Biometric Person Authentication (3rd)*, pp. 198–204, 2001.

Bazen and Gerez (2001b). Bazen A.M. and Gerez S.H., "Segmentation of Fingerprint Images," in *Proc. Workshop on Circuits Systems and Signal Processing (ProRISC 2001)*, pp. 276–280, 2001.

Bazen and Gerez (2002a). Bazen A.M. and Gerez S.H., "Elastic Minutiae Matching by Means of Thin-Plate Spline Models," in *Proc. Int. Conf. on Pattern Recognition (16th)*, vol. 2, pp. 985–988, 2002.

Bazen and Gerez (2002b). Bazen A.M. and Gerez S.H., "Systematic Methods for the Computation of the Directional Fields and Singular Points of Fingerprints," *IEEE Transactions on Pattern Analysis and Machine Intelligence*, vol. 24, no. 7, pp. 905–919, 2002.

Bazen et al. (2000). Bazen A.M., Verwaaijen G.T.B., Gerez S.H., Veelenturf L.P.J., and van der Zwaag B.J., "A Correlation-Based Fingerprint Verification System," in *Proc. Workshop on Circuits Systems and Signal Processing (ProRISC 2000)*, pp. 205–213, 2000.

Beleznai et al. (2001). Beleznai C., Ramoser H., Wachmann B., Birchbauer J., Bischof H., and Kropatsch W., "Memory-efficient Fingerprint Verification," in *Proc. IEEE Int. Conf. on Image Processing*, pp. 463–466, 2001.

Ben-Yacoub (1999). Ben-Yacoub S., "Multi-Modal Data Fusion for Person Verification Using SVM," in *Proc. Int. Conf. on Audio- and Video-Based Biometric Person Authentication (2nd)*, pp. 25–30, 1999.

Ben-Yacoub et al. (1999). Ben-Yacoub S., Luettin J., Jonsson K., Matas J., and Kittler J., "Audio-Visual Person Verification," in *Proc. IEEE Conf. Computer Vision and Pattern Recognition*, vol. 1, pp. 580–585, 1999.

Ben-Yacoub, Abdeljaoued, and Mayoraz (1999). Ben-Yacoub S., Abdeljaoued Y., and Mayoraz E., "Fusion of Face and Speech Data for Person Identity Verification," *IEEE Transactions on Neural Networks*, vol. 10, no. 5, pp. 1065–1074, 1999.

Berdan and Chiralo (1978). Berdan L. and Chiralo R., "Adaptive Digital Enhancement of Latent Fingerprints," in *Proc. Int. Carnahan Conf. on Electronic Crime Countermeasures*, pp. 131–135, 1978.

Bergengruen (1994). Bergengruen O., "Preprocessing of Poor Quality Fingerprint Images," in *Proc. Int. Conf. of the Chilean Computer Science Society (14th)*, 1994.

Bernard et al. (2001). Bernard S., Boujemaa N., Vitale D., and Bricot C., "Fingerprint Classification Using Kohonen Topologic Map," in *Proc. Int. Conf. on Image Processing*, vol. 3, pp. 230–233, 2001.

Bernard et al. (2002). Bernard S., Boujemaa N., Vitale D., and Bricot C., "Fingerprint Segmentation Using the Phase of Multiscale Gabor Wavelets," in *Proc. Asian Conf. Computer Vision*, 2002.

Besl and McKay (1992). Besl P.J. and McKay N.D., "A Method for Registration of 3-D Shapes," *IEEE Transactions on Pattern Analysis and Machine Intelligence*, vol. 14, no. 2, pp. 239–256, 1992.

Beyer, Lake, and Lougheed (1993). Beyer J., Lake C., and Lougheed R., "Ridge Flow Determination in Fingerprint Images," in *Proc. Conf. Artificial Intelligence Pattern Recognition*, pp. 32–43, 1993.

Bhanu and Tan (2001a). Bhanu B. and Tan X., "A Triplet Based Approach for Indexing of Fingerprint Database for Identification," in *Proc. Int. Conf. on Audio- and Video-Based Biometric Person Authentication (3rd)*, pp. 205–210, 2001.

Bhanu and Tan (2001b). Bhanu B. and Tan X., "Learned Templates for Feature Extraction in Fingerprint Images," in *Proc. IEEE Conf. Computer Vision and Pattern Recognition*, vol. 2, pp. 591–596, 2001.

Bhanu, Boshra, and Tan (2000). Bhanu B., Boshra M., and Tan X., "Logical Templates for Feature Extraction in Fingerprint Images," in *Proc. Int. Conf. on Pattern Recognition (15th)*, vol. 2, pp. 850–854, 2000.

Bicz et al. (1999). Bicz W., Banasiak D., Bruciak P., Gumienny S., Gumulinski Z., Kosz D., Krysiak A., Kuczynski W., Pluta M., and Rabiej G., "Fingerprint Structure Imaging Based on an Ultrasound Camera," *Instrumentation Science and Technology*, vol. 27, pp. 295–303, 1999.

Bigun and Granlund (1987). Bigun J. and Granlund G.H., "Optimal Orientation Detection of Linear Symmetry," in *Proc. Int. Conf. on Computer Vision (1st)*, pp. 433–438, 1987.

Bigun et al. (1997). Bigun E.S., Bigun J., Duc B., and Fischer S., "Expert Conciliation for Multi Modal Person Authentication Systems by Bayesian Statistics," in *Proc. Int. Conf. on Audio- and Video-Based Biometric Personal Authentication (1st)*, pp. 291–300, 1997.

Blue et al. (1993). Blue J.L., Candela G.T., Grother P.J., Chellappa R., Wikinson R., and Wilson C., "Evaluation of Pattern Classifiers for Fingerprint and OCR Applications," Tech. Report: NIST TR 3162, 1993.

Bolle at al. (2002). Bolle R.M., Serior A.W., Ratha N.K., and Pankanti S., "Fingerprint Minutiae: A Constructive Definition," in *Proc. Workshop on Biometric Authentication (in ECCV 2002)*, LNCS 2359, pp. 58–66, Springer Verlag, New York, 2002.

Bolle, Connell, and Ratha (2002). Bolle R.M., Connell J.H., and Ratha N.K., "Biometric Perils and Patches," *Pattern Recognition*, vol. 35, no. 12, pp. 2727–2738, 2002.

Bolle, Ratha, and Connell (1998). Bolle R.M., Ratha N.K., and Connell J., "Image Mosaicing for Rolled Fingerprint Construction," in *Proc. Int. Conf. on Pattern Recognition (14th)*, vol. 2, pp. 1651–1653, 1998.

Bolle, Ratha, and Pankanti (1999). Bolle R.M., Ratha N.K., and Pankanti S., "Evaluating Authentication Systems Using Bootstrap Confidence Intervals," in *Proc. Workshop on Automatic Identification Advanced Technologies*, pp. 9–13, 1999.

Bolle, Ratha, and Pankanti (2000). Bolle R.M., Ratha N.K., and Pankanti S., "Evaluation Techniques for Biometrics-Based Authentication Systems," in *Proc. Int. Conf. on Pattern Recognition (15th)*, vol. 2, pp. 835–841, 2000.

Bolle, Ratha, and Pankanti (2001). Bolle R.M., Ratha N.K., and Pankanti S., "Confidence Interval Measurement in Performance Analysis of Biometrics Systems Using the Bootstrap," in *Proc. Workshop on Empirical Evaluation Methods in Computer Vision*, CD no. 1 — Pre-Conference Workshops, IEEE Conference on Computer Vision and Pattern Recognition, 2001.

Bowen (1992). Bowen J., "The Home Office Automatic Fingerprint Pattern Classification Project," in *Proc. IEE Colloquium on Neural Networks for Image processing Applications*, 1992.

Bradley (1981). Bradley R., "Performance Estimates for Personnel Access Control System," in *Proc. Int. Carnahan Conf. on Electronic Crime Countermeasures*, pp. 23–27, 1981.

Bradley, Brislawn, and Hopper (1992). Bradley J.N., Brislawn C.M., and Hopper T., "The FBI Wavelet/Scalar Quantization Standard for Grayscale Fingerprint Image Compression," *Proc. of SPIE (Visual Info. Proc. II)*, pp. 293–304, 1992.

Breiman (1996). Breiman L., "Bagging Predictors," *Machine Learning*, vol. 24, no. 2, pp. 123–140, 1996.

Brin (1998). Brin D., *The Transparent Society: Will Technology Force Us to Choose Between Privacy and Freedom?*, Addison-Wesley, Reading, MA, 1998.

Brislawn et al. (1996). Brislawn C.M., Bradley J.N., Onyshczak R.J., and Hopper T., "The FBI Compression Standard for Digitized Fingerprint Images," *Proc. of SPIE (Applications of Digital Image Processing XIX)*, vol. 2847, 1996.

Brooks and Iyengar (1997). Brooks R.R. and Iyengar S.S., *Multi-Sensor Fusion: Fundamentals and Applications with Software*, Prentice-Hall, Upper Saddle River, NJ, 1997.

Brown (1992). Brown L.G., "Image Registration Techniques," *ACM Computing Surveys*, vol. 24, no. 4, pp. 326–376, 1992.

Brunelli and Falavigna (1995). Brunelli R. and Falavigna D., "Personal Identification Using Multiple Cues," *IEEE Transactions on Pattern Analysis and Machine Intelligence*, vol. 17, no. 10, pp. 955–966, 1995.

Bunke (1993). Bunke H., "Structural and Syntactic Pattern Recognition," in *Handbook of Pattern Recognition & Computer Vision*, C.H. Chen et al. (Eds.), World Scientific, River Edge, NJ, 1993.

Campbell (1997). Campbell J., "Speaker Recognition: A Tutorial," *Proceedings of the IEEE*, vol. 85, no. 9, pp. 1437–1462, 1997.

Candela and Chellappa (1993). Candela G.T. and Chellappa R., "Comparative Performance of Classification Methods for Fingerprints," Tech. Report: NIST TR 5163, Apr. 1993.

Candela et al. (1995). Candela G.T., Grother P.J., Watson C.I., Wilkinson R.A., and Wilson C.L., "PCASYS — A Pattern-Level Classification Automation System for Fingerprints," Tech. Report: NIST TR 5647, Aug. 1995.

Cappelli et al. (1999). Cappelli R., Lumini A., Maio D., and Maltoni D., "Fingerprint Classification by Directional Image Partitioning," *IEEE Transactions on Pattern Analysis and Machine Intelligence*, vol. 21, no. 5, pp. 402–421, 1999.

Cappelli, Maio, and Maltoni (1999). Cappelli R., Maio D., and Maltoni D., "Fingerprint Classification Based on Multi-space KL," in *Proc. Workshop on Automatic Identification Advanced Technologies*, pp. 117–120, 1999.

Cappelli, Maio, and Maltoni (2000a). Cappelli R., Maio D., and Maltoni D., "Combining Fingerprint Classifiers," in *Proc. Int. Workshop on Multiple Classifier Systems (1st)*, pp. 351–361, 2000.

Cappelli, Maio, and Maltoni (2000b). Cappelli R., Maio D., and Maltoni D., "Synthetic Fingerprint-Image Generation," in *Proc. Int. Conf. on Pattern Recognition (15th)*, vol. 3, pp. 475–478, 2000.

Cappelli, Maio, and Maltoni (2000c). Cappelli R., Maio D., and Maltoni D., "Indexing Fingerprint Databases for Efficient 1:N Matching," in *Proc. Int. Conf. on Control Automation Robotics and Vision (6th)*, 2000.

Cappelli, Maio, and Maltoni (2001a). Cappelli R., Maio D., and Maltoni D., "Modelling Plastic Distortion in Fingerprint Images," in *Proc. Int. Conf. on Advances in Pattern Recognition (2nd)*, pp. 369–376, 2001.

Cappelli, Maio, and Maltoni (2001b). Cappelli R., Maio D., and Maltoni D., "Multi-Space KL for Pattern Representation and Classification," *IEEE Transactions on Pattern Analysis and Machine Intelligence*, vol. 23, no. 9, pp. 977–996, 2001.

Cappelli, Maio, and Maltoni (2002a). Cappelli R., Maio D., and Maltoni D., "A Multi-Classifier Approach to Fingerprint Classification," *Pattern Analysis and Applications (special Issue on Fusion of Multiple Classifiers)*, vol. 5, no. 2, pp. 136–144, 2002.

Cappelli, Maio, and Maltoni (2002b). Cappelli R., Maio D., and Maltoni D., "Synthetic Fingerprint-Database Generation," in *Proc. Int. Conf. on Pattern Recognition (16th)*, vol. 3, pp. 744–747, 2002.

Ceguerra and Koprinska (2002). Ceguerra A. and Koprinska I., "Integrating Local and Global Features in Automatic Fingerprint Verification," in *Proc. Int. Conf. on Pattern Recognition (16th)*, vol. 3, pp. 347–350, 2002.

Champod and Margot (1996). Champod C. and Margot P.A., "Computer Assisted Analysis of Minutiae Occurrences on Fingerprints," in *Proc. Int. Symp. on Fingerprint Detection and Identification*, J. Almog and E. Spinger (Eds.), Israel National Police, Jerusalem, pp. 305, 1996.

Chang (1980). Chang T., "Texture Analysis of Digitized Fingerprints for Singularity Detection," in *Proc. Int. Conf. on Pattern Recognition (5th)*, pp. 478–480, 1980.

Chang and Fan (2001). Chang J.H. and Fan K.C., "Fingerprint Ridge Allocation in Direct Gray-Scale Domain," *Pattern Recognition*, vol. 34, no. 10, pp. 1907–1925, 2001.

Chang and Fan (2002). Chang J.H. and Fan K.C., "A New Model for Fingerprint Classification by Ridge Distribution Sequences," *Pattern Recognition*, vol. 35, no. 6, pp. 1209–1223, 2002.

Chang et al. (1997). Chang S.H., Cheng F.H., Hsu W.H., and Wu G.Z., "Fast Algorithm for Point Pattern-Matching: Invariant to Translations, Rotations and Scale Changes," *Pattern Recognition*, vol. 30, no. 2, pp. 311–320, 1997.

Chapel (1971). Chapel. C., *Fingerprinting — A Manual of Identification*, Coward McCann, New York, 1971.

Chen and Kuo (1991). Chen Z. and Kuo C.H., "A Topology-Based Matching Algorithm for Fingerprint Authentication," in *Proc. Int. Carnahan Conf. on Security Technology (25th)*, pp. 84–87, 1991.

Chen and Kuo (1995). Chen W.S. and Kuo C.L., "Apparatus for Imaging Fingerprint or Topographic Relief Pattern on the Surface of an Object," US Patent 5448649, 1995.

Cheng, Tian, and Zhang (2002). Cheng J., Tian J., and Zhang T., "Fingerprint Enhancement with Dyadic Scale-Space," in *Proc. Int. Conf. on Pattern Recognition (16th)*, vol. 1, pp. 200–203, 2002.

Cho et al. (2000). Cho B.H., Kim J.S., Bae J.H., Bae I.G., and Yoo K.Y., "Core-Based Fingerprint Image Classification," in *Proc. Int. Conf. on Pattern Recognition (15th)*, vol. 2, pp. 863–866, 2000.

Chong et al. (1992). Chong M., Gay R., Tan H., and Liu J., "Automatic Representation of Fingerprints for Data Compression by B-Spline Functions," *Pattern Recognition*, vol. 25, no. 10, pp. 1199–1210, 1992.

Chong et al. (1997). Chong M.M.S., Ngee T.H., Jun L., and Gay R.K.L., "Geometric Framework for Fingerprint Image Classification," *Pattern Recognition*, vol. 30, no. 9, pp. 1475–1488, 1997.

Choudhury et al. (1999). Choudhury T., Clarkson B., Jebara T., and Pentland A., "Multimodal Person Recognition Using Unconstrained Audio and Video," in *Proc. Int. Conf. on Audio- and-Video-Based Biometric Person Authentication (2nd)*, pp. 176–181, 1999.

CJIS (1999). Criminal Justice Information Services, "Electronic Fingerprint Transmission Specification," Int. Report. CJIS-RS-0010 (V7), 1999, available at: http://www.fbi.gov/hq/cjisd/iafis/efts70/cover.htm .

Clark and Yuille (1990). Clark J. and Yuille A., *Data Fusion for Sensory Information Processing Systems*, Kluwer Academic, Boston, 1990.

Coetzee and Botha (1990). Coetzee L. and Botha E.C., "Fingerprint Recognition with a Neural-net Classifier," in *Proc. South African Workshop on Pattern Recognition (1st)*, vol. 1, pp. 33–40, Nov 1990.

Coetzee and Botha (1993). Coetzee L. and Botha E.C., "Fingerprint Recognition in Low Quality Images," *Pattern Recognition*, vol. 26, no. 10, pp. 1441–1460, 1993.

Cole (2001). Cole S., "The Myth of Fingerprints," *The New York Times*, May 13, 2001.

Cole (2001a). Cole S.A., "What Counts for Identity?" *Fingerprint Whorld*, vol. 27, no. 103, pp. 7–35, 2001.

Cole (2001b). Cole S.A., *Suspect Identities: A History of Fingerprint and Criminal Identification*, Harvard University Press, Cambridge, MA, 2001.

Colins (1992). Colins M.W., *Realizing the Full Value of Latent Prints*, California Identification Digest, 1992.

Cormen, Leiserson, and Rivest (1990). Cormen T.H., Leiserson C.E., and Rivest R.L., *Introduction to Algorithms*, McGraw-Hill, New York, 1990.

Costello (1999). Costello D., "Families: The Perfect Deception: Identical Twins," *Wall Street Journal*, Feb 12, 1999.

Costello, Gunawardena, and Nadiadi (1994). Costello B.D, Gunawardena C.A., and Nadiadi Y.M., "Automated Coincident Sequencing for Fingerprint Verification," in *Proc. IEE Colloquium on Image Processing for Biometric Measurement*, pp. 3/1–3/5, 1994.

Cover (1974). Cover T.M., "The Best Two Independent Measurements Are Not the Two Best," *IEEE Transactions on Systems, Man, and Cybernetics*, vol. 4, no. 1, pp. 116–117, 1974.

Cover (1977). Cover T.M., "On the Possible Ordering in the Measurement Selection Problem," *IEEE Transactions on Systems, Man, and Cybernetics*, vol. 9, pp. 657–661, 1977.

Cowger (1983). Cowger J., *Friction Ridge Skin: Comparison and Identification of Fingerprints*, Elsevier, New York, 1983.

Crouzil, Massip-Pailhes, and Castan (1996). Crouzil A., Massip-Pailhes L., and Castan S., "A New Correlation Criterion Based on Gradient Fields Similarity," in *Proc. Int. Conf. on Pattern Recognition (13th)*, pp. 632–636, 1996.

Cummins and Midlo (1943). Cummins H. and Midlo C., *Fingerprints, Palms and Soles*, Dover, New York, 1943.

Cummins and Midlo (1961). Cummins H. and Midlo C., *Fingerprints, Palms and Soles: An Introduction to Dermatoglyphics*, Dover, New York, 1961.

Cummins, Waits, and McQuitty (1941). Cummins H., Waits W.J., and McQuitty J.T., "The Breadths of Epidermal Ridges on the Fingertips and Palms: A Study of Variations," *American Journal of Anatomy*, vol. 68, pp. 127–150, 1941.

Danielsson and Ye (1988). Danielsson P. and Ye Q., "Rotation-Invariant Operators Applied to Enhancement of Fingerprints," in *Proc. Int. Conf. on Pattern Recognition (9th)*, pp. 329–333, 1988.

Dasarathy (1994). Dasarathy B.V., *Decision Fusion*, IEEE Computer Society Press, Los Alamitos, CA, 1994.

Daugman (1985). Daugman J., "Uncertainty Relation for Resolution in Space, Spatial-Frequency, and Orientation Optimized by Two-dimensional Visual Cortical Filters," *Journal Optical Society American*, vol. 2, pp. 1160–1169, 1985.

Daugman (1999a). Daugman J., "Recognizing Persons by Their Iris Patterns," in *Biometrics: Personal Identification in a Networked Society*, A.K. Jain, R. Bolle, and S. Pankanti (Eds.), Kluwer Academic, New York, 1999.

Daugman (1999b). Daugman J., "Biometric Decision Landscapes," Tech Report: TR482, University of Cambridge Computer Laboratory, 1999, available at: http://www.cl.cam.ac.uk/users/jgd1000/ .

Davida et al. (1999). Davida G., Frankel Y., Matt B.J., and Peralta R., "On the Relation of Error Correction and Cryptography to an Offline Biometric Based Identification Scheme," in *Proc. Workshop on Coding and Cryptography*, 1999.

Davida, Frankel, and Matt (1998). Davida G.I., Frankel Y., and Matt B.J., "On Enabling Secure Applications Through Off-Line Biometric Identification," in *Proc. Symp. on Privacy and Security*, pp. 148–157, 1998.

De Boer, Bazen, and Gerez (2001). De Boer J., Bazen A.M., and Gerez S.H., "Indexing Fingerprint Databases Based on Multiple Features," in *Proc. Workshop on Circuits Systems and Signal Processing (ProRISC 2001)*, pp. 300–306, 2001.

Derakhshani et al. (2002). Derakhshani D., Schuckers S.A.C., Hornak L. A., and O'Gorman L., "Determination of Vitality from a Non-Invasive Biomedical Measurement for Use in Fingerprint Scanners," *Pattern Recognition*, vol. 36, no. 2, pp. 383–396, 2003.

Deriche, Kasaei, and Bouzerdoum (1999). Deriche M., Kasaei S., and Bouzerdoum A., "A Novel Fingerprint Image Compression Technique Using the Wavelet Transform and Piecewise Uniform Pyramid Lattice Vector Quantization," in *Proc. Int. Conf. on Image Processing*, vol. 3, pp. 359–363, 1999.

Dickinson et al. (2000). Dickinson A., McPherson R., Mendis S., and Ross P.C., "Capacitive Fingerprint Sensor with Adjustable Gain," US Patent 6049620, 2000.

Dieckmann, Plankensteiner, and Wagner (1997). Dieckmann U., Plankensteiner P., and Wagner T., "SESAM: A Biometric Person Identification System Using Sensor Fusion," *Pattern Recognition Letters*, vol. 18, pp. 827–833, 1997.

Doddington et al. (1998). Doddington G., Ligget W., Martin A., Przybocki M., and Reynolds D., "Sheeps, Goats, Lambs, Wolves: An Analysis of Individual Differences in Speaker Recognition Performance," in *Proc. Int. Conf. on Speech and Language Processing*, 1998.

Domeniconi, Tari, and Liang (1998). Domeniconi C., Tari S., and Liang P., "Direct Gray Scale Ridge Reconstruction in Fingerprint Images," in *Proc. Int. Conf. on Acoustic Speech and Signal Processing*, 1998.

Donahue and Rokhlin (1993). Donahue M.L and Rokhlin S.I., "On the use of Level Curves in Image Analysis," *CVGIP: Image Understanding*, vol. 57, no. 2, pp. 185–203, 1993.

Dorai, Ratha, and Bolle (2000). Dorai C., Ratha N.K., and Bolle R.M., "Detecting Dynamic Behavior in Compressed Fingerprint Videos: Distortion," in *Proc. IEEE Conf. Computer Vision and Pattern Recognition*, vol. 2, pp. 320–326, 2000.

Dowling and Knowlton (1988). Dowling Jr. R.F. and Knowlton K.L., "Fingerprint Acquisition System with a Fiber Optic Block," US Patent 4785171, 1988.

Drets and Liljenstrom (1998). Drets G. and Liljenstrom H., "Fingerprint Sub-Classification and Singular Point Detection," *International Journal of Pattern Recognition and Artificial Intelligence*, vol. 12, no. 4, pp. 407–422, 1998.

Driscoll (1994). Driscoll D., "Fingerprint Identification Systems: Going Multimedia & Portable," *Advanced Imaging*, vol. 9, no. 5, 1994.

Duc et al. (1997). Duc B., Bigun E.S., Bigun J., Maitre G., and Fischer S., "Fusion of Audio and Video Information for Multi Modal Person Authentication," *Pattern Recognition Letters*, vol. 18, no. 9, pp. 835–843, 1997.

Duda, Hart, and Stork (2001). Duda R.O., Hart P.E., and Stork D.G., *Pattern Classification*, 2nd edition, Wiley, New York, 2001.

Edwards (1984). Edwards D.G., "Fingerprint Sensor," US Patent 4429413, 1984.

Eleccion (1973). Eleccion M., "Automatic Fingerprint Identification," *IEEE Spectrum*, vol. 10, pp. 36–45, Sept. 1973.

Erol, Halici, and Ongun (1999). Erol A., Halici U., and Ongun G., "Feature Selective Filtering for Ridge Extraction," in *Intelligent Biometric Techniques in Fingerprint & Face Recognition*, L.C. Jain, U. Halici, I. Hayashi, and S.B. Lee (Eds.), CRC Press, Boca Raton, FL, 1999.

Ersoy, Ercal, and Gokmen (1999). Ersoy I., Ercal F., and Gokmen M., "A Model-Based Approach for Compression of Fingerprint Images," in *Proc. Int. Conf. on Image Processing*, vol. 2, pp. 973–977, 1999.

Fan, Liu, and Wang (2000). Fan K.C., Liu C.W., and Wang Y.K., "A Randomized Approach with Geometric Constraints to Fingerprint Verification," *Pattern Recognition*, vol. 33, no. 11, pp. 1793–1803, 2000.

Fang (1979). Fang G.S., "A Note on Optimal Selection of Independent Observables," *IEEE Transactions on Systems, Man, and Cybernetics*, vol. 9, no. 5, pp. 309–311, 1979.

Farina, Kovacs-Vajna, and Leone (1999). Farina A., Kovacs-Vajna Z.M., and Leone A., "Fingerprint Minutiae Extraction from Skeletonized Binary Images," *Pattern Recognition*, vol. 32, no. 5, pp. 877–889, 1999.

Federal Bureau of Investigation (1984). Federal Bureau of Investigation, "The Science of Fingerprints: Classification and Uses," U.S. Government Publication, Washington, DC, 1984.

Federal Bureau of Investigation (1991). Federal Bureau of Investigation, "The FBI Fingerprint Identification Automation Program: Issues and Options," U.S. Government Publication, U.S. Congress, Office of Technology Assessment, Washington, DC, 1991.

Fielding, Homer, and Makekau (1991). Fielding K., Homer J., and Makekau C., "Optical Fingerprint Identification by Binary Joint Transform Correlation," *Optical Engineering*, vol. 30, no. 12, pp. 1958, 1991.

Fitz and Green (1996). Fitz A.P. and Green R.J., "Fingerprint Classification Using Hexagonal Fast Fourier Transform," *Pattern Recognition*, vol. 29, no. 10, pp. 1587–1597, 1996.

Fjetland and Robbins (1989). Fjetland R. and Robbins C., "The AFIS Advantage: A Milestone in Fingerprint Identification Technology," *The Police Chief*, vol. 56, no. 6, pp. 20, 1989.

Freund and Schapire (1996). Freund Y. and Schapire R., "Experiments with a New Boosting Algorithm," in *Proc. Int. Conf. Machine Learning*, pp. 148–156, 1996.

Frischholz and Dieckmann (2000). Frischholz R.W. and Dieckmann U., "BioId: A Multimodal Biometric Identification System," *IEEE Computer*, pp. 64–68, Feb. 2000.

Fu and Booth (1986a). Fu K.S. and Booth T.L., "Grammatical Inference: Introduction and Survey: Part I," *IEEE Transactions on Pattern Analysis and Machine Intelligence*, vol. 8, no. 3, pp. 343–360, 1986.

Fu and Booth (1986b). Fu K.S. and Booth T.L., "Grammatical Inference: Introduction and Survey: Part II," *IEEE Transactions on Pattern Analysis and Machine Intelligence*, vol. 8, no. 3, pp. 360–376, 1986.

Fujieda, Ono, and Sugama (1995). Fujieda I., Ono Y., and Sugama S., "Fingerprint Image Input Device Having an Image Sensor with Openings," US Patent 5446290, 1995.

Galton (1892). Galton F., *Finger Prints*, McMillan, London, 1892.

Gamble, Frye, and Grieser (1992). Gamble F.T., Frye L.M., and Grieser D.R., "Real-Time Fingerprint Verification System," *Applied Optics*, vol. 31, no. 5, pp. 652–655, 1992.

Garris and McCabe (2000). Garris M.D. and McCabe R.M., "NIST Special Database 27, Fingerprint Minutiae from Latent and Matching Tenprint Images," U.S. National Institute of Standards and Technology, 2000.

Geng and Shen (1997). Geng Z.J. and Shen W.C., "Fingerprint Classification Using Fuzzy Cerebellar Model Arithmetic Computer Neural Networks," *Journal of Electronic Imaging*, vol. 6, no. 3, pp. 311–318, 1997.

Germain, Califano, and Colville (1997). Germain R., Califano A., and Colville S., "Fingerprint Matching Using Transformation Parameters," *IEEE Computational Science and Engineering*, vol. 4, no. 4, pp. 42–49, 1997.

Ghosal et al. (2000a). Ghosal S., Ratha N.K., Udupa R., and Pankanti S., "Hierarchical Partitioned Least Squares Filter-Bank for Fingerprint Enhancement," in *Proc. Int. Conf. on Pattern Recognition (15th)*, pp. 334–337, 2000.

Ghosal et al. (2000b). Ghosal S., Udupa R., Pankanti S., and Ratha N.K., "Learning Partitioned Least Squares Filters for Fingerprint Enhancement," in *Proc. Workshop on Applications of Computer Vision*, pp. 2–7, 2000.

Gokmen and Jain (1997). Gokmen M. and Jain A.K., "λ–τ Representation of Image and Generalized Edge Detection," *IEEE Transactions on Pattern Analysis and Machine Intelligence*, vol. 19, no. 6, pp. 545–563, 1997.

Gokmen, Ersoy, and Jain (1996). Gokmen M., Ersoy I., and Jain A.K., "Compression of Fingerprint Images Using Hybrid Image Model," in *Proc. Int. Conf. on Image Processing*, vol. 3, pp. 395–398, 1996.

Gold and Rangarajan (1996). Gold S. and Rangarajan A., "A Graduated Assignment Algorithm for Graph Matching," *IEEE Transactions on Pattern Analysis and Machine Intelligence*, vol. 18, no. 4, pp. 377–388, 1996.

Goldberg (1989). Goldberg D., *Genetic Algorithms in Search, Optimization and Machine Learning*, Addison-Wesley, Reading, MA, 1989.

Golfarelli, Maio, and Maltoni (1997). Golfarelli M., Maio D., and Maltoni D., "On the Error-Reject Tradeoff in Biometric Verification Systems," *IEEE Transactions on Pattern Analysis and Machine Intelligence*, vol. 19, no.7, pp. 786–796, 1997.

Gonzales and Woods (1992). Gonzales R.C. and Woods R.E., *Digital Image Processing*, Addison-Wesley, Reading, MA, 1992.

Gowrishankar (1989). Gowrishankar T.R., "Fingerprint Identification on a Massively Parallel Architecture," in *Proc. Symp. on Frontiers of Massively Parallel Computation (2nd)*, pp. 331–334, 1989.

Grasselli (1969). Grasselli A., "On the Automatic Classification of Fingerprints," in *Methodologies of Pattern Recognition*, S. Watanabe (Ed.), Academic, New York, 1969.

Greenberg et al. (2000). Greenberg S., Aladjem M., Kogan D., and Dimitrov I., "Fingerprint Image Enhancement Using Filtering Techniques," in *Proc. Int. Conf. on Pattern Recognition (15th)*, vol. 3, pp. 326–329, 2000.

Grycewicz (1995). Grycewicz T.J., "Fingerprint Identification with Joint Transform Correlator Using Multiple Reference Fingerprints," *Proc. of SPIE (Optical Pattern Recognition VI)*, vol. 2237, pp. 249–254, 1995.

Grycewicz (1996). Grycewicz T.J., "Fingerprint Recognition Using Binary Nonlinear Joint Transform Correlators," *Optoelectronic Devices and Systems for Processing*, Critical Review, vol. CR65., 1996.

Grycewicz and Javidi (1996). Grycewicz T.J. and Javidi B., "Experimental Comparison of Binary Joint Transform Correlators Used for Fingerprint Identification," *Optical Engineering*, vol. 35, pp. 2519–2525, 1996.

Gunawardena and Sagar (1991). Gunawardena C.A. and Sagar V.K., "Fingerprint Verification Using Coincident Sequencing and Thinning," in *Proc. Conf. of the IEEE Industrial Electronics Society (IECON)*, pp. 1917–1922, 1991.

Gunsel, Uludag, and Tekalp (2002). Gunsel B., Uludag B., and Tekalp A.M., "Robust Watermarking of Fingerprint Images," *Pattern Recognition*, vol. 35, no. 12, pp. 2739–2748, 2002.

Gupta (1968). Gupta S.R., "Statistical Survey of Ridge Characteristics," *Int. Criminal Police Review*, vol. 218, no. 130, 1968.

Halici and Ongun (1996). Halici U. and Ongun G., "Fingerprint Classification Through Self Organizing Feature Maps Modified to Treat Uncertainties," *Proceedings of the IEEE*, vol. 84, no. 10, pp. 1497–1512, 1996.

Hamamoto (1999). Hamamoto Y., "A Gabor Filter-Based Method for Fingerprint Identification," in *Intelligent Biometric Techniques in Fingerprint & Face Recognition*, L.C. Jain, U. Halici, I. Hayashi, and S.B. Lee (Eds.), CRC Press, Boca Raton, FL, 1999.

Hartung and Kutter (1999). Hartung F. and Kutter M., "Multimedia Watermarking Techniques," *Proceedings of the IEEE*, vol. 87, no. 7, pp. 1079–1107, 1999.

Hase and Shimisu (1984). Hase M. and Shimisu A., "Entry Method of Fingerprint Image Using a Prism," *Trans. Institute Electron. Commum. Eng. Jpn.*, vol. J67-D, pp. 627–628, 1984.

Hatano et al. (2002). Hatano T., Adachi T., Shigematsu S., Morimura H., Onishi S., Okazaki Y., and Kyuragi H., "A Fingerprint Verification Algorithm Using the Differential Matching Rate," in *Proc. Int. Conf. on Pattern Recognition (16th)*, vol. 3, pp. 799–802, 2002.

Henry (1900). Henry E., *Classification and Uses of Finger Prints*, Routledge, London, 1900.

Higgins (1995). Higgins P.T., "Standards for the Electronic Submission of Fingerprint Cards to the FBI," *Journal of Forensic Identification*, vol. 45, no. 4, pp. 409–418, 1995.

Hill (2001). Hill C.J., "Risk of Masquerade Arising from the Storage of Biometrics," Bachelor of Science Thesis — The Department of Computer Science, Australian National University, Nov. 2001.

Ho, Hull, and Srihari (1994). Ho T.K., Hull J.J., and Srihari S.N., "Decision Combination in Multiple Classifier Systems," *IEEE Transactions on Pattern Analysis and Machine Intelligence*, vol. 16, no. 1, pp. 66–75, 1994.

Hollingum (1992). Hollingum J., "Automated Fingerprint Analysis Offers Fast Verification," *Sensor Review*, vol. 12, no. 3, pp. 12, 1992.

Hong and Jain (1996). Hong L. and Jain A.K., "On-Line Fingerprint Verification," in *Proc. Int. Conf. on Pattern Recognition (13th)*, pp. 596–600, 1996.

Hong and Jain (1998). Hong L. and Jain A.K., "Integrating Faces and Fingerprints for Personal Identification," *IEEE Transactions on Pattern Analysis and Machine Intelligence*, vol. 20, no. 12, pp. 1295–1307, 1998.

Hong and Jain (1999). Hong L. and Jain A.K., "Classification of Fingerprint Images," in *Proc. Scandinavian Conf. on Image Analysis (11th)*, 1999.

Hong and Tan (1988). Hong J. and Tan X., "A New Approach to Point Pattern Matching," in *Proc. Int. Conf. on Pattern Recognition (9th)*, pp. 82–84, 1988.

Hong et al. (1996). Hong L., Jain A.K., Pankanti S., and Bolle R., "Fingerprint Enhancement," in *Proc. Workshop on Applications of Computer Vision*, pp. 202–207, 1996.

Hong, Jain, and Pankanti (1999). Hong L., Jain A.K., and Pankanti S., "Can Multibiometrics Improve Performance ?" in *Proc. Workshop on Automatic Identification Advanced Technologies*, pp. 59–64, 1999.

Hong, Wan, and Jain (1998). Hong L., Wan Y., and Jain A.K., "Fingerprint Image Enhancement: Algorithms and Performance Evaluation," *IEEE Transactions on Pattern Analysis and Machine Intelligence*, vol. 20, no. 8, pp. 777–789, 1998.

Hopper and Preston (1991). Hopper T. and Preston F., "Compression of Grey-Scale Fingerprint Images," in *Proc. Data Compression Conf.*, pp. 309–318, 1991.

Hopper, Brislawn, and Bradley (1993). Hopper T., Brislawn C., and Bradley J., "WSQ GrayScale Fingerprint Image Compression Specification," Federal Bureau of Investigation, Washington, DC, Feb. 1993.

Hoshino et al. (1980). Hoshino Y., Asai K., Kato Y., and Kiji K., "Automatic Reading and Matching for Single-Fingerprint Identification," in *Proc. Int. Conf. Association for Identification (65th)*, pp. 1–7, 1980.

Hrechak and McHugh (1990). Hrechak A. and McHugh J., "Automated Fingerprint Recognition Using Structural Matching," *Pattern Recognition*, vol. 23, no. 8, pp. 893–904, 1990.

Hughes and Green (1991). Hughes P. and Green A., "The Use of Neural Networks for Fingerprint Classification," in *Proc. Int. Conf. on Neural Networks (2nd)*, pp. 79–81, 1991.

Hung (1993). Hung D.C.D., "Enhancement and Feature Purification of Fingerprint Images," *Pattern Recognition*, vol. 26, no. 11, 1661–1671, 1993.

Hung and Huang (1996). Hung. D.C.D. and Huang C., "A Model for Detecting Singular Points of a Fingerprint," in *Proc. Florida Artificial Intelligence Research Symposium (9th)*, pp. 444–448, 1996.

Huvanandana, Kim, and Hwang (2000). Huvanandana S., Kim C., and Hwang J.N., "Reliable and Fast Fingerprint Identification for Security Applications," in *Proc. Int. Conf. on Image Processing*, vol. 2, pp. 503–506, 2000.

Igaki et al. (1992). Igaki S., Eguchi S., Yamagishi F., Ikeda H., and Inagaki T., "Real-Time Fingerprint Sensor Using a Hologram," *Applied Optics*, vol. 31, no. 11, pp. 1794–1802, 1992.

Ikeda et al. (2002). Ikeda N., Nakanishi M., Fujii K., Hatano T., Shigematsu S., Adachi T., Okazaki Y., and Kyuragi H., "Fingerprint Image Enhancement by Pixel-Parallel Processing," in *Proc. Int. Conf. on Pattern Recognition (16th)*, vol. 3, pp. 752–755, 2002.

Inglis et al. (1998). Inglis C., Manchanda L., Comizzoll R., Dickinson A., Martin E., Mandis S., Silveman P., Weber G., Ackland B., and O'Gorman L., "A Robust, 1.8 V, 250 mW, Direct Contact 500 dpi Fingerprint Sensor," in *Proc. IEEE Solid-State Circuits Conf.*, pp. 284–285, 1998.

Isenor and Zaky (1986). Isenor D.K. and Zaky S.G., "Fingerprint Identification Using Graph Matching," *Pattern Recognition*, vol. 19, pp. 113–122, 1986.

Ishida, Mimura, and Seta (2001). Ishida S., Mimura M., and Seta Y., "Development of Personal Authentication Techniques Using Fingerprint Matching Embedded in Smart Cards," *IEICE Transactions on Information and Systems (Special Issue on Biometrics)*, vol. E84-D, no. 7, pp. 812–818, 2001.

Iyengar and Brooks (1997). Iyengar S. and Brooks R.R., *Multi-Sensor Fusion: Fundamentals and Applications with Software*, Prentice-Hall, Englewood Cliffs, NJ, 1997.

Jacobs et al. (1991). Jacobs R.A., Jordan M.I., Nowlan S.J., and Hinton G.E., "Adaptive Mixtures of Local Experts," *Neural Computation*, vol. 3, pp. 79–87, 1991.

Jain and Chandrasekaran (1982). Jain A.K. and Chandrasekaran B., "Dimensionality and Sample Size Considerations in Pattern Recognition Practice," in *Handbook of Statistics*, vol. II, P.R. Krishnaiah and L.N. Kanal (Eds.), North-Holland, Amsterdam, pp. 835–855, 1982.

Jain and Farrokhnia (1991). Jain A.K. and Farrokhnia F., "Unsupervised Texture Segmentation Using Gabor Filters," *Pattern Recognition*, vol. 24, no. 12, pp. 1167–1186, 1991.

Jain and Minut (2002). Jain A.K. and Minut S., "Hierarchical Kernel Fitting for Fingerprint Classification and Alignment," in *Proc. Int. Conf. on Pattern Recognition (16th)*, vol. 2, pp. 469–473, 2002.

Jain and Pankanti (2000). Jain A.K. and Pankanti S., "Fingerprint Classification and Recognition," in *Image and Video Processing Handbook*, A. Bovik (Ed.), pp. 821–836, Academic, New York, 2000.

Jain and Pankanti (2001). Jain A.K. and Pankanti S., "Automated Fingerprint Identification and Imaging Systems," in *Advances in Fingerprint Technology*, 2nd edition, H.C. Lee and R.Gaensslen (Eds.), CRC Press, Boca Raton, FL, 2001.

Jain and Pankanti (2001b). Jain A.K. and Pankanti S., "Biometrics Systems: Anatomy of Performance," *IEICE Transactions on Information and Systems (Special Issue on Biometrics)*, vol. E84-D, no. 7, pp. 788–799, 2001.

Jain and Ross (2002a). Jain A.K. and Ross A., "Learning User-Specific Parameters in a Multibiometric System," in *Proc. Int. Conf. on Image Processing*, vol. 1, pp. 57–60, 2002.

Jain and Ross (2002b). Jain A.K. and Ross A., "Fingerprint Mosaicking," in *Proc. Int. Conf. on Acoustic Speech and Signal Processing*, vol. 4, pp. 4064–4067, 2002.

Jain and Uludag (2002). Jain A.K. and Uludag U., "Hiding Fingerprint Minutiae in Images," in *Proc. Workshop on Automatic Identification Advanced Technologies*, pp. 97–102, 2002.

Jain et al. (1997). Jain A.K., Hong L., Pankanti S., and Bolle R., "An Identity Authentication System Using Fingerprints," *Proceedings of the IEEE*, vol. 85, no. 9, pp. 1365–1388, 1997.

Jain et al. (1999). Jain L.C., Halici U., Hayashi I., and Lee S.B., *Intelligent Biometric Techniques in Fingerprint and Face Recognition*, CRC Press, Boca Raton, FL, 1999.

Jain et al. (2000). Jain A.K., Prabhakar S., Hong L., and Pankanti S., "Filterbank-Based Fingerprint Matching," *IEEE Transactions on Image Processing*, vol. 9, pp. 846–859, 2000.

Jain et al. (2001). Jain A.K., Pankanti S., Prabhakar S., and Ross A., "Recent Advances in Fingerprint Verification," in *Proc. Int. Conf. on Audio- and Video-Based Biometric Person Authentication (3rd)*, pp. 182–191, 2001.

Jain, Bolle, and Pankanti (1999). Jain A.K., Bolle R., and Pankanti S. (Eds.), *Biometrics: Personal Identification in Networked Society*, Kluwer Academic, New York, 1999.

Jain, Duin, and Mao (2000). Jain A.K., Duin P.W., and Mao J., "Statistical Pattern Recognition: a Review," *IEEE Transactions on Pattern Analysis and Machine Intelligence*, vol. 22, no. 1, pp. 4–37, 2000.

Jain, Hong, and Bolle (1997). Jain A.K., Hong L., and Bolle R., "On-line Fingerprint Verification," *IEEE Transactions on Pattern Analysis and Machine Intelligence*, vol. 19, no. 4, pp. 302–313, 1997.

Jain, Hong, and Kulkarni (1999). Jain A.K., Hong L., and Kulkarni Y., "A Multimodal Biometric System Using Fingerprint, Face, and Speech," in *Proc. Int. Conf. on Audio- and-Video-Based Biometric Person Authentication (2nd)*, pp. 182–187, 1999.

Jain, Hong, and Pankanti (2000). Jain A.K., Hong L., and Pankanti S., "Biometrics: Promising Frontiers for Emerging Identification Market," *Communications of the ACM*, pp. 91–98, Feb. 2000.

Jain, Prabhakar, and Chen (1999). Jain A.K., Prabhakar S., and Chen S., "Combining Multiple Matchers for a High Security Fingerprint Verification System," *Pattern Recognition Letters*, vol. 20, no. 11–13, pp. 1371–1379, 1999.

Jain, Prabhakar, and Hong (1999). Jain A.K., Prabhakar S., and Hong L., "A Multichannel Approach to Fingerprint Classification," *IEEE Transactions on Pattern Analysis and Machine Intelligence*, vol. 21, no. 4, pp. 348–359, 1999.

Jain, Prabhakar, and Pankanti (2002). Jain A.K., Prabhakar S., and Pankanti S., "On the Similarity of Identical Twin Fingerprints," *Pattern Recognition*, vol. 35, no. 12, pp. 2653–2663, 2002.

Jain, Prabhakar, and Ross (1999). Jain A.K., Prabhakar S., and Ross A., "Fingerprint Matching: Data Acquisition and Performance Evaluation," Tech. Report: MSU TR99–14, 1999.

Jain, Ross, and Prabhakar (2001). Jain A.K., Ross A., and Prabhakar S., "Fingerprint Matching Using Minutiae and Texture Features," in *Proc. Int. Conf. on Image Processing*, pp. 282–285, 2001.

Jain, Uludag, and Hsu (2002). Jain A.K., Uludag U., and Hsu R.L., "Hiding a Face in a Fingerprint Image," in *Proc. Int. Conf. on Pattern Recognition (16th)*, vol. 3, pp. 756–759, 2002.

Jiang (2000). Jiang X., "Fingerprint Image Ridge Frequency Estimation by Higher Order Spectrum," in *Proc. Int. Conf. on Image Processing*, vol. 1, pp. 462–465, 2000.

Jiang (2001). Jiang X., "A Study of Fingerprint Image Filtering," in *Proc. Int. Conf. on Image Processing*, vol. 3, pp. 238–241, 2001.

Jiang and Yau (2000). Jiang X. and Yau W.Y., "Fingerprint Minutiae Matching Based on the Local and Global Structures," in *Proc. Int. Conf. on Pattern Recognition (15th)*, vol. 2, pp. 1042-1045, 2000.

Jiang, Yau, and Ser (1999). Jiang X., Yau W.Y., and Ser W., "Minutiae Extraction by Adaptive Tracing the Gray Level Ridge of the Fingerprint Image," in *Proc. Int. Conf. on Image Processing*, vol. 2, pp. 852–856, 1999.

Jiang, Yau, and Ser (2001). Jiang X., Yau W.Y., and Ser W., "Detecting the Fingerprint Minutiae by Adaptive Tracing the Gray-Level Ridge," *Pattern Recognition*, vol. 34, no. 5, pp. 999–1013, 2001.

Johannesen et al. (1996). Johannesen F.R., Raaschou S., Larsen O.V., and Jurgensen P., "Using Weighted Minutiae for Fingerprint Identification," in *Proc. Advances in Structural and Syntactical Pattern Recognition*, pp. 289–99, 1996.

Jolliffe (1986). Jolliffe I.T., *Principle Component Analysis*, Springer-Verlag, New York, 1986.

Jordan and Jacobs (1994). Jordan M.I. and Jacobs R.A., "Hierarchical Mixtures of Experts and the EM Algorithm," *Neural Computation*, vol. 6, pp. 181–214, 1994.

Juels and Sudan (2002). Jules A. and Sudan M., "A Fuzzy Vault Scheme," in *Proc. Int. Symp. on Information Theory*, pp. 408–408, 2002.

Jung et al. (1999). Jung S., Thewes R., Scheiter T., Goser K.F., and Weber W., "A Low-Power and High-Performance CMOS Fingerprint Sensing and Encoding Architecture," *IEEE Journal of Solid-State Circuits*, vol. 34, no. 7, pp. 978–984, 1999.

Kamei and Mizoguchi (1995). Kamei T. and Mizoguchi M., "Image Filter Design for Fingerprint Enhancement," in *Proc. Int. Symp. on Computer Vision*, pp. 109–114, 1995.

Kamei and Mizoguchi (1998). Kamei T. and Mizoguchi M., "Fingerprint Preselection Using Eigenfeatures," in *Proc. IEEE Conf. Computer Vision and Pattern Recognition*, pp. 918–923, 1998.

Kamijo (1993). Kamijo M., "Classifying Fingerprint Images Using Neural Network: Deriving the Classification State," in *Proc. Int. Conf. on Neural Networks*, vol. 3, pp. 1932–1937, 1993.

Kamijo, Mieno, and Kojima (1992). Kamijo M., Mieno H., and Kojima K., "Classification of Fingerprint Images Using a Neural Network," *Systems and Computers in Japan*, vol. 23, pp. 89–101, 1992.

Karu and Jain (1996). Karu K. and Jain A.K., "Fingerprint Classification," *Pattern Recognition*, vol. 29, no. 3, pp. 389–404, 1996.

Kasaei, Deriche, and Boashash (1997). Kasaei S., Deriche M., and Boashash B., "An Efficient Quantization Technique for Wavelet Coefficients of Fingerprint Images," *Signal Processing*, vol. 62, no. 3, pp. 361–366, 1997.

Kass and Witkin (1987). Kass M. and Witkin A., "Analyzing Oriented Patterns," *Computer Vision, Graphics, and Image Processing*, vol. 37, no. 3, pp. 362–385, 1987.

Kawagoe and Tojo (1984). Kawagoe M. and Tojo A., "Fingerprint Pattern Classification," *Pattern Recognition*, vol. 17, pp. 295–303, 1984.

Kaymaz and Mitra (1992). Kaymaz E. and Mitra S., "Analysis and Matching of Degraded and Noisy Fingerprints," *Proc. of SPIE (Applications of Digital Image Processing XV)*, vol. 1771, pp. 498–508, 1992.

Kaymaz and Mitra (1993). Kaymaz E. and Mitra S., "A Novel Approach to Fourier Spectral Enhancement of Laser-Luminescent Fingerprint Images," *Journal of Forensic Sciences*, vol. 38, no. 3, pp. 530, 1993.

Kim, Kim, and Park (2002). Kim B.G., Kim H.J., and Park D.J., "New Enhancement Algorithm for Fingerprint Images," in *Proc. Int. Conf. on Pattern Recognition (16th)*, vol. 3, pp. 879–892, 2002.

Kim, Lee, and Kim (2001). Kim S., Lee D., and Kim J., "Algorithm for Detection and Elimination of False Minutiae in Fingerprint Images," in *Proc. Int. Conf. on Audio- and Video-Based Biometric Person Authentication (3rd)*, pp. 235–240, 2001.

Kingston (1964). Kingston C., "Probabilistic Analysis of Partial Fingerprint Patterns," Ph.D. Thesis, University of California, Berkeley, 1964.

Kittler et al. (1998). Kittler J., Hataf M., Duin R.P.W., and Matas J., "On Combining Classifiers," *IEEE Transactions on Pattern Analysis and Machine Intelligence*, vol. 20, no. 3, pp. 226–238, 1998.

Kittler, Messer, and Sadeghi (2001). Kittler J., Messer K., and Sadeghi M., "Model Validation for Model Selection," in *Proc. Int. Conf. on Advances in Pattern Recognition (2nd)*, pp. 240–249, 2001.

Knapp (1994). Knapp A.G., "Fingerprint Sensing Device and Recognition System Having Predetermined Electrode Activation," US Patent 5325442, 1994.

Kobayashi and Toyoda (1999). Kobayashi Y. and Toyoda H., "Development of an Optical Joint Transform Correlation System for Fingerprint Recognition," *Optical Engineering*, vol. 38, no. 7, pp. 1205–1210, 1999.

Kohonen et al. (1992). Kohonen T., Kangas J., Laaksonen J., and Torkkola K., "LVQ_PAQ: A Program Package for the Correct Application of Learning Vector Quantization Algorithms," in *Proc. Int. Joint Conf. On Neural Network*, pp. 1725–1730, 1992.

Koo and Kot (2001). Koo W.M and Kot A., "Curvature-Based Singular Points Detection," in *Proc. Int. Conf. on Audio- and Video-Based Biometric Person Authentication (3rd)*, pp. 229–234, 2001.

Kovacs-Vajna (2000). Kovacs-Vajna Z.M., "A Fingerprint Verification System Based on Triangular Matching and Dynamic Time Warping," *IEEE Transactions on Pattern Analysis and Machine Intelligence*, vol. 22, pp. 1266–1276, 2000.

Kovacs-Vajna, Rovatti, and Frazzoni (2000). Kovacs-Vajna Z.M., Rovatti R., and Frazzoni M., "Fingerprint Ridge Distance Computation Methodologies," *Pattern Recognition*, vol. 33, no. 1, pp. 69–80, 2000.

Kuncheva and Whitaker (2002). Kuncheva L.I. and Whitaker C.J., "Measure of Diversity in Classifier Ensembles," *Machine Learning*, vol. 51, pp. 181–207, 2003.

Kuncheva et al. (2000). Kuncheva L.I., Whitaker C.J., Shipp C.A., and Duin R.P.W., "Is Independence Good for Combining Classifiers," in *Proc. Int. Conf. on Pattern Recognition (15th)*, vol. 2, pp. 168–171, 2000.

Lam and Suen (1997). Lam L. and Suen C.Y., "Application of Majority Voting to Pattern Recognition: An Analysis of Its Behavior and Performance," *IEEE Transactions on Systems, Man, and Cybernetics*, vol. 27, no. 5, pp. 553–568, 1997.

Lam, Lee, and Suen (1992). Lam L., Lee S.W., and Suen C.Y., "Thinning Methodologies: A Comprehensive Survey," *IEEE Transactions on Pattern Analysis and Machine Intelligence*, vol. 14, no. 9, pp. 869–885, 1992.

Landy, Cohen, and Sperling (1984). Landy M.S., Cohen Y., and Sperling G., "Hips: A Unix-Based Image Processing System," *Computer Vision, Graphics, and Image Processing*, vol. 25, no. 3, pp. 331–347, 1984.

Lee and Gaensslen (2001). Lee H.C. and Gaensslen R.E., *Advances in Fingerprint Technology*, 2nd edition, Elsevier, New York, 2001.

Lee and Wang (1999). Lee C.J. and Wang S.D., "Fingerprint Feature Extraction Using Gabor Filters," *Electronics Letters*, vol. 35, no. 4, pp. 288–290, 1999.

Lee and Wang (2001). Lee C.J. and Wang S.D., "Fingerprint Feature Reduction by Principal Gabor Basis Function," *Pattern Recognition*, vol. 34, no. 11, pp. 2245–2248, 2001.

Lee et al. (1999). Lee J.W., Min D.J., Kim J., and Kim W., "A 600 dpi Capacitive Fingerprint Sensor Chip and Image Synthesis Technique," *IEEE Journal of Solid-State Circuits*, vol. 34, no. 4, pp. 469–475, 1999.

Lee, Choi, and Kim (2002). Lee D., Choi K., and Kim J., "A Robust Fingerprint Matching Algorithm Using Local Alignment," in *Proc. Int. Conf. on Pattern Recognition (16th)*, vol. 3, pp. 803–806, 2002.

Leung et al. (1991). Leung W.F., Leung S.H., Lau W.H., and Luk A., "Fingerprint Recognition Using Neural Network," in *Proc. Workshop Neural Network for Signal Processing*, pp. 226–235, 1991.

Leung, Engeler, and Frank (1990). Leung M, Engeler W., and Frank P., "Fingerprint Image Processing Using Neural Network," in *Proc. IEEE Region 10 Conf. on Computer and Comm. Systems*, 1990.

Levi and Sirovich (1972). Levi G. and Sirovich F., "Structural Description of Fingerprint Images," *Information Sciences*, pp. 327–355, 1972.

Li and Zhang (1984). Li Z. and Zhang D., "A Fingerprint Recognition System with Micro-Computer," in *Proc. Int. Conf. on Pattern Recognition (7th)*, pp. 939–941, 1984.

Lin and Dubes (1983). Lin W. and Dubes R., "A Review of Ridge Counting in Dermatoglyphics," *Pattern Recognition*, vol. 16, pp. 1–8, 1983.

Lin et al. (1982). Lin C.H., Liu J.H., Ostenberg J.W., and Nicol J.D., "Fingerprint Comparison I: Similarity of Fingerprints," *Journal of Forensic Sciences*, vol. 27, no. 2, pp. 290–304, 1982.

Lindh, Ford, and Boudreaux (1981). Lindh T.K., Ford F.A., and Boudreaux N.A., "An Automated Fingerprint Retrieval System," in *Proc. Int. Carnahan Conf. on Electronic Crime Countermeasures*, pp. 71–75, 1981.

Liu et al. (1982). Liu J.H., Lin C.H., Osterburg J.W., and Nichol J.D., "Fingerprint Comparison II: On the Development of a Single Fingerprint Filing and Searching System," *Journal of Forensic Sciences*, vol. 27, no. 2, pp. 305–317, 1982.

Liu, Huang, and Chan (2000). Liu J., Huang Z., and Chan K., "Direct Minutiae Extraction from Gray-Level Fingerprint Image by Relationship Examination," in *Proc. Int. Conf. on Image Processing*, vol. 2, pp. 427–430, 2000.

Lumini, Maio, and Maltoni (1997). Lumini A., Maio D., and Maltoni D., "Continuous vs. Exclusive Classification for Fingerprint Retrieval," *Pattern Recognition Letters*, vol. 18, no. 10, pp. 1027–1034, 1997.

Lumini, Maio, and Maltoni (1999). Lumini A., Maio D., and Maltoni D., "Inexact Graph Matching for Fingerprint Classification," *Machine Graphics & Vision (Special Issue on Graph Transformations in Pattern Generation and CAD)*, vol. 8, no. 2, pp. 231–248, 1999.

Luo and Tian (2000). Luo X. and Tian J., "Knowledge Based Fingerprint Image Enhancement," in *Proc. Int. Conf. on Pattern Recognition (15th)*, vol. 4, pp. 783–786, 2000.

Luo, Tian, and Wu (2000). Luo X., Tian J., and Wu Y., "A Minutia Matching Algorithm in Fingerprint Verification," in *Proc. Int. Conf. on Pattern Recognition (15th)*, vol. 4, pp. 833–836, 2000.

Maeda, Matsushita, and Sasakawa (2001). Maeda T., Matsushita M., and Sasakawa K., "Identification Algorithm Using a Matching Score Matrix," *IEICE Transactions on Information and Systems (Special Issue on Biometrics)*, vol. E84-D, no. 7, pp. 819–824, 2001.

Mainguet, Pegulu, and Harris (1999). Mainguet J.G., Pegulu M., and Harris J.B., "Fingerchip: Thermal Imaging and Finger Sweeping in a Silicon Fingerprint Sensor," in *Proc. Workshop on Automatic Identification Advances Technologies*, pp. 91–94, 1999.

Maio and Maltoni (1995). Maio D. and Maltoni D., "An Efficient Approach to On-Line Fingerprint Verification," in *Proc. Int. Symp. on Artificial Intelligence (8th)*, pp. 132–138, 1995.

Maio and Maltoni (1996). Maio D. and Maltoni D., "A Structural Approach to Fingerprint Classification," in *Proc. Int. Conf. on Pattern Recognition (13th)*, 1996.

Maio and Maltoni (1997). Maio D. and Maltoni D., "Direct Gray-Scale Minutiae Detection in Fingerprints," *IEEE Transactions on Pattern Analysis and Machine Intelligence*, vol. 19, no. 1, 1997.

Maio and Maltoni (1998a). Maio D. and Maltoni D., "Ridge-Line Density Estimation in Digital Images," in *Proc. Int. Conf. on Pattern Recognition (14th)*, pp. 534–538, 1998.

Maio and Maltoni (1998b). Maio D. and Maltoni D., "Neural Network Based Minutiae Filtering in Fingerprints," in *Proc. Int. Conf. on Pattern Recognition (14th)*, pp. 1654–1658, 1998.

Maio and Maltoni (1999a). Maio D. and Maltoni D., "A Secure Protocol for Electronic Commerce Based on Fingerprints and Encryption," in *Proc. World Conf. on Systems Cybernetics and Informatics*, vol. 4, pp. 519–525, 1999.

Maio and Maltoni (1999b). Maio D. and Maltoni D., "Minutiae Extraction and Filtering from Gray-scale Images," in *Intelligent Biometric Techniques in Fingerprint & Face Recognition*, L.C. Jain, U. Halici, I. Hayashi, and S.B. Lee (Eds.), CRC Press, Boca Raton, FL, 1999.

Maio et al. (2000). Maio D., Maltoni D., Cappelli R., Wayman J.L., and Jain A.K., "FVC2000: Fingerprint Verification Competition," Tech. Report: DEIS, University of Bologna, Sept. 2000.

Maio et al. (2002a). Maio D., Maltoni D., Cappelli R., Wayman J.L., and Jain A.K., "FVC2000: Fingerprint Verification Competition," *IEEE Transactions on Pattern Analysis and Machine Intelligence*, vol. 24, no. 3, pp. 402–412, 2002.

Maio et al. (2002b). Maio D., Maltoni D., Cappelli R., Wayman J.L., and Jain A.K., "FVC2002: Second Fingerprint Verification Competition," in *Proc. Int. Conf. on Pattern Recognition (16th)*, vol. 3, pp. 811–814, 2002.

Marcialis, Roli, and Frasconi (2001). Marcialis G.L., Roli F., and Frasconi P., "Fingerprint Classification by Combination of Flat and Structural Approaches," in *Proc. Int. Conf. on Audio- and Video-Based Biometric Person Authentication (3rd)*, pp. 241–246, 2001.

Marcialis, Roli, and Loddo (2002). Marcialis G.L., Roli F., and Loddo P., "Fusion of Multiple Matchers for Fingerprint Verification," in *Proc. Workshop on Machine Vision and Perception*, Siena, Italy, 2002.

Mardia et al. (1997). Mardia K.V., Baczkowski A.J., Feng X., and Hainsworth T.J., "Statistical Methods for Automatic Interpretation of Digitally Scanned Finger Prints," *Pattern Recognition Letters*, vol. 18, no. 11–13, pp. 1197–1203, 1997.

Marr and Hildreth (1980). Marr D. and Hildreth E.C., "Theory of Edge Detection," *Proc. Royal Society London*, B 207, pp. 187–217, 1980.

Matsumoto et al. (2002). Matsumoto T., Matsumoto H., Yamada K., and Hoshino S., "Impact of Artificial "Gummy" Fingers on Fingerprint Systems," *Proc. of SPIE*, vol. 4677, pp. 275–289, Feb 2002.

McGinity (2000). McGinity M., "Body of Technology," *Communications of the ACM*, vol. 43, pp. 17–19, Sept. 2000.

McMahon et al. (1975). McMahon D., Johnson G.L., Teeter S.L., and Whitney C.G., "A Hybrid Optical Computer Processing Technique for Fingerprint Identification," *IEEE Transactions on Computers*, C-24, pp. 358–369, 1975.

Meagher et al. (1999). Meagher S.B., Buldowle B., and Ziesig D., "50K Fingerprint Comparison Test," United States of America vs. Byron Mitchell — U.S. District Court Eastern District of Philadelphia. Government Exhibits 6–8 and 6–9 in Daubert Hearing before Judge J. Curtis Joyner, July 8–9, 1999.

Mehtre (1993). Mehtre B.M., "Fingerprint Image Analysis for Automatic Identification," *Machine Vision and Applications*, vol. 6, no. 2–3, pp. 124–139, 1993.

Mehtre and Chatterjee (1989). Mehtre B.M. and Chatterjee B., "Segmentation of Fingerprint Images — A Composite Method," *Pattern Recognition*, vol. 22, no. 4, pp. 381–385, 1989.

Mehtre and Chatterjee (1991). Mehtre B.M. and Chatterjee B., "Automatic Fingerprint Identification," *Journal of the Institution of Electronics and Telecommunication Engineers (Special Issue on Pattern Recognition)*, vol. 37, no. 5–6, pp. 493–499, 1991.

Mehtre and Murthy (1986). Mehtre B.M. and Murthy N.N., "A Minutia Based Fingerprint Identification System," in *Proc. Int. Conf. on Avances in Pattern Recognition and Digital Techniques (2nd)*, 1986.

Mehtre et al. (1987). Mehtre B.M., Murthy N.N., Kapoor S., and Chatterjee B., "Segmentation of Fingerprint Images Using the Directional Image," *Pattern Recognition*, vol. 20, no. 4, pp. 429–435, 1987.

Millard (1975). Millard K., "An Approach to Automatic Retrieval of Latent Fingerprints," in *Proc. Int. Carnahan Conf. on Electronic Crime Countermeasures*, pp. 45–51, 1975.

Millard (1983). Millard K., "Developments on Automatic Fingerprint Recognition," in *Proc. Int. Carnahan Conf. on Security Technology (17th)*, pp. 173–178, 1983.

Miller (1994). Miller B., "Vital Signs of Identity," *IEEE Spectrum*, pp. 22–30, Feb. 1994.

Moayer and Fu (1973). Moayer B. and Fu K., "A Syntactic Approach to Fingerprint Pattern Recognition," in *Proc. Int. Joint Conf. on Pattern Recognition*, 1973.

Moayer and Fu (1975). Moayer B. and Fu K., "A Syntactic Approach to Fingerprint Pattern Recognition," *Pattern Recognition*, vol. 7, pp. 1–23, 1975.

Moayer and Fu (1976). Moayer B. and Fu K., "An Application of Stochastic Languages to Fingerprint Pattern Recognition," *Pattern Recognition*, vol. 8, pp. 173–179, 1976.

Moayer and Fu (1986). Moayer B. and Fu K., "A Tree System Approach for Fingerprint Pattern Recognition," *IEEE Transactions on Pattern Analysis and Machine Intelligence*, vol. 8, no. 3, 376–388, 1986.

Moenssens (1971). Moenssens A., *Fingerprint Techniques*, Chilton, London, 1971.

Monrose et al. (2001). Monrose F., Reiter M.K., Li Q., and Wetzel S., "Cryptographic Key Generation from Voice," in *Proc. Symp. on Security and Privacy*, pp. 202–213, 2001.

Monrose, Reiter, and Wetzel (1999). Monrose F., Reiter M.K., and Wetzel S., "Password Hardening Based on Keystroke Dynamics," in *Proc. Computer and Communications Security Conf. (6th)*, 1999.

Morelos-Zaragoza (2002). Morelos-Zaragoza R.H., *The Art of Error Correcting Coding*, Wiley, New York, 2002.

Moscinska and Tyma (1993). Moscinska K. and Tyma G., "Neural Network Based Fingerprint Classification," in *Proc. Int. Conf. on Artificial Neural Networks (3rd)*, 1993.

Mulvhill (1969). Mulvhill J.J., "The Genesis of Dematoglyphics," *The Journal of Pediatrics*, vol. 75, no. 4, pp. 579–589, 1969.

Murty (1992). Murty K.G., *Network Programming*, Prentice-Hall, Englewood Cliffs, NJ, 1992.

Nakamura, Goto, and Minami (1982). Nakamura O., Goto K., and Minami T., "Fingerprint Classification by Directional Distribution Patterns," *System Computer Controls*, vol. 13, pp. 81–89, 1982.

Nakamura, Nagaoka, and Minami (1986). Nakamura O., Nagaoka Y., and Minami T., "A Restoration Algorithm of Fingerprint Images," *Systems and Computers in Japan*, vol. 17, no. 6, p. 31, 1986.

Nilsson and Bigun (2001). Nilsson K. and Bigun J., "Using Linear Symmetry Features as a Pre-processing Step for Fingerprint Images," in *Proc. Int. Conf. on Audio- and Video-Based Biometric Person Authentication (3rd)*, pp. 247–252, 2001.

Nilsson and Bigun (2002a). Nilsson K. and Bigun J., "Complex Filters Applied to Fingerprint Images Detecting Prominent Symmetry Points Used for Alignment," in *Proc. Workshop on Biometric Authentication (in ECCV 2002)*, LNCS 2359, pp. 39–47, Springer-Verlag, New York, 2002.

Nilsson and Bigun (2002b). Nilsson K. and Bigun J., "Prominent Symmetry Points as Landmarks in Fingerprint Images for Alignment," in *Proc. Int. Conf. on Pattern Recognition (16th)*, vol. 3, pp. 395–398, 2002.

Nissenbaum (2001). Nissenbaum H., "New Computer System Embody Values," *IEEE Computer Magazine*, pp. 120, March 2001.

NIST (1991). National Institute of Standards and Technology, "Data Format for the Interchange of Fingerprint Information," U.S. Government Publication, Washington, DC, Dec 1991.

NIST (1994). National Institute of Standards and Technology, "Guideline for the Use of Advanced Authentication Technology Alternatives," Federal Information Processing Standards Publication 190, 1994.

Novikov and Glushchenko (1998). Novikov S.O. and Glushchenko G.N., "Fingerprint Ridges Structure Generation Models," *Proc. of SPIE (Int. Workshop on Digital Image Processing and Computer Graphics (6th): Applications in Humanities and Natural Sciences)*, vol. 3346, pp. 270–274, 1998.

Novikov and Kot (1998). Novikov S.O. and Kot V.S., "Singular Feature Detection and Classification of Fingerprints Using Hough Transform," *Proc. of SPIE (Int. Workshop on Digital Image Processing and Computer Graphics (6th): Applications in Humanities and Natural Sciences)*, vol. 3346, pp. 259–269, 1998.

O'Gorman and Nickerson (1988). O'Gorman L. and Nickerson J.V., "Matched Filter Design for Fingerprint Image Enhancement," in *Proc. Int. Conf. on Acoustic Speech and Signal Processing*, pp. 916–919, 1988.

O'Gorman and Nickerson (1989). O'Gorman L. and Nickerson J.V., "An Approach to Fingerprint Filter Design," *Pattern Recognition*, vol. 22, no. 1, pp. 29–38, 1989.

Oh, Lee, and Suen (1999). Oh I.S., Lee J.S., and Suen C.Y., "Analysis of Class Separation and Combination of Class-Dependent Features for Handwriting Recognition," *IEEE Transactions on Pattern Analysis and Machine Intelligence*, vol. 21, no. 10, pp. 1089–1094, 1999.

Omidvar, Blue, and Wilson (1995). Omidvar O.M., Blue J.L., and Wilson C.L., "Improving Neural Network Performance for Character and Fingerprint Classification by Altering Network Dynamics," in *Proc. World Congress on Neural Networks*, pp. 151–158, 1995.

Osterburg (1964). Osterburg J.W., "An Inquiry into the Nature of Proof: The Identity of Fingerprints," *Journal of Forensic Sciences*, vol. 9, pp. 413–427, 1964.

Osterburg et al. (1977). Osterburg J., Parthasarathy T., Raghaven T., and Sclove S., "Development of a Mathematical Formula for the Calculation of Fingerprint Probabilities Based on Individual Characteristic," *Journal American Statistic Association*, vol. 72, pp. 772–778, 1977.

Overton and Richardson (1991). Overton W. and Richardson M., "The Key to Capture. Automated Fingerprint Identification Systems (AFISs) Are Revolutionizing the Way Fingerprints Are Processed for Identifying and Apprehending Criminals," *Security Management*, vol. 35, no. 1, pp. 54, 1991.

Pal and Mitra (1996). Pal S.K. and Mitra S., "Noisy Fingerprint Classification Using Multilayer Perceptron with Fuzzy Geometrical and Textural Features," *Fuzzy Sets and Systems*, vol. 80, no. 2, pp. 121–132, 1996.

Pankanti et al. (2002). Pankanti S., Haas N., Ratha N.K., and Bolle R.M., "Quantifying Quality: A Case Study in Fingerprints," in *Proc. Workshop on Automatic Identification Advanced Technologies*, 2002.

Pankanti, Bolle, and Jain (2000). Pankanti S., Bolle R., and Jain A.K., *Special Issue on Biometrics*, IEEE Computer Magazine, Feb 2000.

Pankanti, Prabhakar, and Jain (2002). Pankanti S., Prabhakar S., and Jain A.K., "On the Individuality of Fingerprints," *IEEE Transactions on Pattern Analysis and Machine Intelligence*, vol. 24, no. 8, pp. 1010–1025, 2002.

Pankanti, Ratha, and Bolle (2002). Pankanti S., Ratha N., and Bolle R., "Structure in Errors: A Case Study in Fingerprint Verification," in *Proc. Int. Conf. on Pattern Recognition (16th)*, vol. 3, pp. 440–443, 2002.

Park and Smith (2000). Park S.I. and Smith M., "Fingerprint Enhancement Based on the Directional Filter Bank," in *Proc. Int. Conf. on Image Processing*, vol. 3, pp. 793–796, 2000.

Pattichis et al. (2001). Pattichis M.S., Panayi G., Bovik A.C., and Hsu S.P., "Fingerprint Classification Using an AM-FM Model," *IEEE Transactions on Image Processing*, vol. 10, no. 6, pp. 951–954, 2001.

Pearson (1930). Pearson K., *The Life and Letters of Francis Galton*, vol. IIIA, University Press, Cambridge, 1930.

Pearson (1933). Pearson K., "Galton's Work on Evidential Value of Fingerprints," *Sankhya: Indian Journal of Statistics*, vol. 1, no. 50, 1933.

Penrose (1965). Penrose L.S., "Dermatoglyphic Topology," *Nature*, vol. 205, pp. 545–546, 1965.

Pernus, Kovacic, and Gyergyek (1980). Pernus F., Kovacic S., and Gyergyek L., "Minutiae Based Fingerprint Recognition," in *Proc. Int. Conf. on Pattern Recognition (5th)*, pp. 1380–1382, 1980.

Perona (1998). Perona P., "Orientation Diffusions," *IEEE Transactions on Image Processing*, vol. 7, no. 3, pp. 457–467, 1998.

Petillot, Guibert, and de Bougrenet (1996). Petillot Y., Guibert L., and de Bougrenet J.L., "Fingerprint Recognition Using a Partially Rotation Invariant Composite Filter in a FLC Joint Transform Correlator," *Optics Communications*, vol. 126, pp. 213–219, 1996.

Phillips et al. (2000). Phillips P.J., Martin A., Wilson C.L., and Przybocki M., "An Introduction to Evaluating Biometric Systems," *IEEE Computer Magazine*, Feb. 2000.

Polikarpova (1996). Polikarpova N., "On the Fractal Features in Fingerprint Analysis," in *Proc. Int. Conf. on Pattern Recognition (13th)*, vol. 3, pp. 591–595, 1996.

Prabhakar and Jain (2002). Prabhakar S. and Jain A.K., "Decision-Level Fusion in Fingerprint Verification," *Pattern Recognition*, vol. 35, pp. 861–874, 2002.

Prabhakar and Rao (1989). Prabhakar R.V.S.N. and Rao K., "A Parallel Algorithm for Fingerprint Matching," in *Proc. Tencon Conf.*, pp. 373–376, 1989.

Prabhakar et al. (2000). Prabhakar S., Jain A.K., Wang J., Pankanti S., and Bolle R., "Minutiae Verification and Classification for Fingerprint Matching," in *Proc. Int. Conf. on Pattern Recognition (15th)*, vol. 1, pp. 25–29, 2000.

Pradenas (1997). Pradenas R., "Directional Enhancement in the Frequency Domain of Fingerprint Images," *Proc. of SPIE*, vol. 2932, pp. 150–160, 1997.

Press et al. (1992). Press W.H., Teukolsky S.A., Vetterling W.T., and Flannery B.P., *Numerical Recipes in C*, Cambridge University Press, Cambridge, UK, 1992.

Putte (2001). Putte T.v.d., "Forging Ahead," *Biometric Technology Today*, no. 10, pp. 9–11, 2001.

Putte and Keuning (2000). Putte T.v.d. and Keuning J., "Biometrical Fingerprint Recognition: Don't Get Your Fingers Burned," in *Proc. Working Conf. on Smart Card Research and Advanced Applications (4th)*, Proc. IFIP TC8/WG8.8, pp. 289–303, 2000.

Quek, Tan, and Sagar (2001). Quek. C., Tan K.B., and Sagar V.K., "Pseudo-Outer Product Based Neural Network Fingerprint Verification System," *Neural Networks*, vol. 14, pp. 305–323, 2001.

Qun et al. (2002). Qun R., Jie T., Yuliang H., and Jiangang C., "Automatic Fingerprint Identification Using Cluster Algorithm," in *Proc. Int. Conf. on Pattern Recognition (16th)*, vol. 2, pp. 398–401, 2002.

Rabinowitz (1980). Rabinowitz A., "Fingerprint Card Search Result with Ridge-contour Based Classification," in *Proc. Int. Conf. on Pattern Recognition (5th)*, pp. 475–477, 1980.

Rämö et al. (2001). Rämö P., Tico M., Onnia V., and Saarinen J., "Optimized Singular Point Detection Algorithm for Fingerprint Images," in *Proc. Int. Conf. on Image Processing*, vol. 3, pp. 242–245, 2001.

Ramoser, Wachmann, and Bischof (2002). Ramoser H., Wachmann B., and Bischof H., "Efficient Alignment of Fingerprint Images," in *Proc. Int. Conf. on Pattern Recognition (16th)*, vol. 3, pp. 748–751, 2002.

Ranade and Rosenfeld (1993). Ranade A. and Rosenfeld A., "Point Pattern Matching by Relaxation," *Pattern Recognition*, vol. 12, no. 2, pp. 269–275, 1993.

Rao (1976). Rao M., "Feature Extraction for Fingerprint Classification," *Pattern Recognition*, vol. 8, pp. 599–605, 1976.

Rao (1978). Rao C.V.K., "On Fingerprint Pattern Recognition," *Pattern Recognition*, vol. 10, pp. 15–18, 1978.

Rao (1990). Rao A.R., *A Taxonomy for Texture Description and Identification*, Springer-Verlag, New York, 1990.

Rao and Balck (1978). Rao K. and Balck K., "Finding the Core Point in a Fingerprint," *IEEE Transactions on Computers*, C-27, pp. 78–81, 1978.

Rao and Balck (1980). Rao K. and Balck K., "Type Classification of Fingerprints: A Syntactic Approach," *IEEE Transactions on Pattern Analysis and Machine Intelligence*, vol. 2, no. 3, pp. 223–231, 1980.

Rao, Prasad, and Sharma (1974). Rao K., Prasad B., and Sharma K., "Automatic Fingerprint Classification System," in *Proc. Int. Conf. on Pattern Recognition (2nd)*, pp. 180–184, 1974.

Ratha and Bolle (1998). Ratha N.K. and Bolle R.M., "Effect of Controlled Image Acquisition on Fingerprint Matching," in *Proc. Int. Conf. on Pattern Recognition (14th)*, vol. 2, pp. 1659–1661, 1998.

Ratha et al. (1996). Ratha N.K., Karu K., Chen S., and Jain A.K., "A Real-Time Matching System for Large Fingerprint Databases," *IEEE Transactions on Pattern Analysis and Machine Intelligence*, vol. 18, no. 8, pp. 799–813, 1996.

Ratha et al. (1999). Ratha N.K., Bolle R., Senior A., and Pankanti S., "Common Minutiae Template Representation," in *Proc. Workshop on Automatic Identification Advanced Technologies*, pp. 74–77, 1999.

Ratha et al. (2000). Ratha N.K., Pandit V.D., Bolle R.M., and Vaish, V., "Robust Fingerprint Authentication Using Local Structural Similarity," in *Proc. Workshop on Applications of Computer Vision*, pp. 29–34, 2000.

Ratha, Chen, and Jain (1995). Ratha N.K., Chen S.Y., and Jain A.K., "Adaptive Flow Orientation-Based Feature Extraction in Fingerprint Images," *Pattern Recognition*, vol. 28, no. 11, pp. 1657–1672, 1995.

Ratha, Connell, and Bolle (1999). Ratha N.K., Connell J., and Bolle R., "Secure Biometric Authentication," in *Proc. Workshop on Automatic Identification Advances Technologies*, 1999.

Ratha, Connell, and Bolle (2001a). Ratha N.K., Connell J.H., and Bolle R.M., "An Analysis of Minutiae Matching Strength," in *Proc. Int. Conf. on Audio- and Video-Based Biometric Person Authentication (3rd)*, pp. 223–228, 2001.

Ratha, Connell, and Bolle (2001b). Ratha N.K., Connell J., and Bolle R., "Enhancing Security and Privacy in Biometrics-Based Authentication Systems," *IBM Systems Journal*, vol. 40, no. 3, pp. 614–634, 2001.

Ratha, Rover, and Jain (1995). Ratha N.K., Rover D., and Jain A.K., "An FPGA-Based Point Pattern Matching Processor with Application to Fingerprint Matching," in *Proc. Conf. Computer Architectures for Machine Perception*, Italy, pp. 394–401, 1995.

Ratha, Rover, and Jain (1996). Ratha N.K., Rover D., and Jain A.K., "Fingerprint Matching on Splash 2," in *Splash 2: FPGAS in a Custom Computing Machine*, D. Buell, J. Arnold, and W. Kleinfolder (Eds.), pp. 117–140, IEEE Computer Society Press, Los Alamitos, CA, 1996.

Raudys and Jain (1991). Raudys S. and Jain A.K., "Small Sample Size Effects in Statistical Pattern Recognition: Recommendations for Practitioners," *IEEE Transactions on Pattern Analysis and Machine Intelligence*, vol. 13, no. 3, pp. 252–264, 1991.

Reed and Meier (1990). Reed T. and Meier R., "Taking Dermatogyphic Prints: A Self-instruction Manual," *American Dermatoglyphics Association Newsletter: Supplement*, vol. 9, pp. 18, 1990.

Rerkrai and Areekul (2000). Rerkrai K. and Areekul V., "A New Reference Point for Fingerprint Recognition," in *Proc. Int. Conf. on Image Processing*, vol. 2, pp. 499–502, 2000.

Rhodes (1956). Rhodes H.T.F., *Alphonse Bertillon: Father of Scientific Detection*, Abelard-Schuman, New York, 1956.

Rice (1995). Rice J.A., *Mathematical Statistics and Data Analysis*, 2nd edition, Duxbury Press, CA, 1995.

Riganati (1977). Riganati J., "An Overview of Algorithms Employed in Automated Fingerprint Processing," in *Proc. Int. Carnahan Conf. on Electronic Crime Countermeasures*, pp. 125–131, 1977.

Roddy and Stosz (1997). Roddy A. and Stosz J., "Fingerprint Features: Statistical-Analysis and System Performance Estimates," *Proceedings of the IEEE*, vol. 85, no. 9, pp. 1390–1421, 1997.

Rodolfo, Rajbenbach, and Huignard (1995). Rodolfo J., Rajbenbach H., and Huignard J., "Performance of a Photo-Refractive Joint Transform Correlator for Fingerprint Identification," *Optical Engineering*, vol. 34, no. 4, pp. 1166–1171, 1995.

Rosenfeld and Kak (1976). Rosenfeld A. and Kak A., *Digital Picture Processing*, Academic, New York, 1976.

Ross, Jain, and Qian (2001). Ross A., Jain A.K., and Qian J., "Information Fusion in Biometrics," in *Proc. Int. Conf. on Audio- and Video-Based Biometric Person Authentication (3rd)*, pp. 354–359, 2001.

Ross, Jain, and Reisman (2002). Ross A., Jain A.K., and Reisman J., "A Hybrid Fingerprint Matcher," in *Proc. Int. Conf. on Pattern Recognition (16th)*, vol. 3, pp. 795–798, 2002.

Ross, Reisman, and Jain (2002). Ross A., Reisman J., and Jain A.K., "Fingerprint Matching Using Feature Space Correlation," in *Proc. Workshop on Biometric Authentication (in ECCV 2002)*, LNCS 2359, pp. 48–57, Springer-Verlag, New York, 2002.

Roxburgh (1933). Roxburgh T., "On Evidential Value of Fingerprints," *Sankhya: Indian Journal of Statistics*, vol. 1, pp. 189–214, 1933.

Samet (1990). Samet H., *The Design and Analysis of Spatial Data Structures*, Addison-Wesley, Reading, MA, 1990.

Sarbadhikari et al. (1998). Sarbadhikari S.N., Basak J., Pal S.K., and Kundu M.K., "Noisy Fingerprints Classification with Directional FFT Based Features Using Mlp," *Neural Computing and Applications*, vol. 7, no. 2, pp. 180–191, 1998.

Sasakawa, Isogai, and Ikebata (1990). Sasakawa K., Isogai F., and Ikebata S., "Personal Verification System with High Tolerance of Poor Quality Fingerprints," *Proc. of SPIE*, vol. 1386, pp. 265–272, 1990.

Schapire (1990). Schapire R.E., "The Strength of Weak Learnability," *Machine Learning*, vol. 5, pp. 197–227, 1990.

Schneider and Wobschall (1991). Schneider J. and Wobschall D., "Live Scan Fingerprint Imagery Using High Resolution C-SCAN Ultrasonography," in *Proc. Int. Carnahan Conf. on Security Technology (25th)*, pp. 88–95, 1991.

Schneier (1996). Schneier B., *Applied Cryptography*, Wiley, New York, 1996.

Schneier (1998). Schneier B., "Security Pitfalls in Cryptography," in *Proc. CardTech/SecueTech Conf.*, pp. 621–626, 1998.

Schneier (1999). Schneier B., "Inside Risks: The Uses and Abuses of Biometrics," *Communications of the ACM*, vol. 42, pp. 136, Aug. 1999.

Sclove (1979). Sclove S.L., "The Occurrence of Fingerprint Characteristics as a Two Dimensional Process," *Journal of American Statistical Association*, vol. 74, no. 367, pp. 588–595, 1979.

Scott (1951). Scott W., *Fingerprint Mechanics — A Handbook*, C. Thomas, Springfield, IL, 1951.

Seigo, Shin, and Takashi (1989). Seigo I., Shin E., and Takashi S., "Holographic Fingerprint Sensor," *Fujitsu Scientific & Technical Journal*, vol. 25, no. 4, pp. 287, 1989.

Senior (1997). Senior A., "A Hidden Markov Model Fingerprint Classifier," in *Proc. Asilomar Conf. on Signals Systems and Computers (31st)*, pp. 306–310, 1997.

Senior (2001). Senior A., "A Combination Fingerprint Classifier," *IEEE Transactions on Pattern Analysis and Machine Intelligence*, vol. 23, no. 10, pp. 1165–1174, 2001.

Senior and Bolle (2001). Senior A.W. and Bolle R., "Improved Fingerprint Matching by Distortion Removal," *IEICE Transactions on Information and Systems (Special Issue on Biometrics)*, vol. E84-D, no. 7, pp. 825–832, 2001.

Setlak (1999). Setlak D.R., "Electric Field Fingerprint Sensor Apparatus and Related Methods," US Patent 5963679, 1999.

Setlak et al. (2000). Setlak D.R., VanVonno N.W., Newton M., and Salatino M.M., "Fingerprint Sensor Including an Anisotropic Dielectric Coating and Associated Methods," US Patent 6088471, 2000.

Shan, Shi, and Li (1994). Shan Y., Shi P., and Li J., "Fingerprint Preclassification Using Key-Points," in *Proc. International Symp. on Speech Image Proc. and Neural Network*, vol. 1, no. 308–311, 1994.

Shelman (1976). Shelman C., "Fingerprint Classification — Theory and Application," in *Proc. Int. Carnahan Conf. on Electronic Crime Countermeasures*, pp. 131–138, 1976.

Shelman and Hodges (1973). Shelman C.B. and Hodges D., "A Decimal Henry System," in *Proc. Int. Carnahan Conf. on Electronic Crime Countermeasures*, pp. 213–220, 1973.

Shen and Khanna (1994). Shen W. and Khanna R., "Automated Fingerprint Identification System (AFIS) Benchmarking Using the National Institute of Standards and Technology (NIST) Special Database 4," in *Proc. Int. Carnahan Conf. on Security Technology (28th)*, pp. 88–95, 1994.

Shen and Khanna (1997). Shen W. and Khanna R., "Special Issue on Biometrics," *Proceedings of the IEEE*, vol. 85, no. 9, 1997.

Shen, Kot, and Koo (2001). Shen L., Kot A., and Koo W.M., "Quality Measures of Fingerprint Images," in *Proc. Int. Conf. on Audio- and Video-Based Biometric Person Authentication (3rd)*, pp. 266–271, 2001.

Sherlock and Monro (1993). Sherlock B.G. and Monro D.M., "A Model for Interpreting Fingerprint Topology," *Pattern Recognition*, vol. 26, no. 7, pp. 1047–1055, 1993.

Sherlock, Monro, and Millard (1992). Sherlock B.G., Monro D.M., and Millard K., "Algorithm for Enhancing Fingerprint Images," *Electronics Letters*, vol. 28, no. 18, pp. 1720, 1992.

Sherlock, Monro, and Millard (1994). Sherlock B.G., Monro D.M., and Millard K., "Fingerprint Enhancement by Directional Fourier Filtering," *IEE Proceedings Vision Image and Signal Processing*, vol. 141, no. 2, pp. 87–94, 1994.

Sherstinsky and Picard (1994). Sherstinsky A. and Picard R.W., "Restoration and Enhancement of Fingerprint Images Using M-Lattice — A Novel Non-Linear Dynamical System," in *Proc. Int. Conf. on Pattern Recognition (12th)*, vol. 2, pp. 195–200, 1994.

Sherstinsky and Picard (1996). Sherstinsky A. and Picard R.W., "M-Lattice: From Morphogenesis to Image Processing," *IEEE Transactions on Image Processing*, vol. 5, no. 7, pp. 1137–1150, 1996.

Shigematsu et al. (1999). Shigematsu S., Morimura H., Tanabe Y., and Machida K., "A Single-Chip Fingerprint Sensor and Identifier," *IEEE Journal of Solid-State Circuits*, vol. 34, no. 12, pp. 1852–1859, 1999.

Shizume and Hefner (1978). Shizume P.K. and Hefner C.G., "A Computer Technical Fingerprint Search System," in *Proc. Int. Carnahan Conf. on Electronic Crime Countermeasures*, pp. 121–129, 1978.

Shumurun et al. (1994). Shumurun A., Bjorn V., Tam S., and Holler M., "Extraction of Fingerprint Orientation Maps Using a Radial Basis Function Recognition Accelerator," in *Proc. Int. Conf. on Neural Networks*, vol. 2, pp. 1186–1190, 1994.

Simon-Zorita et al. (2001a). Simon-Zorita D., Ortega-Garcia J., Cruz-Llanas S., and Gonzalez-Rodriguez J., "Minutiae Extraction Scheme for Fingerprint Recognition Systems," in *Proc. Int. Conf. on Image Processing*, vol. 3, pp. 254–257, 2001.

Simon-Zorita et al. (2001b). Simon-Zorita D., Ortega-Garcia J., Cruz-Llanas S., Sanchez-Bote J.L., and Glez-Rodriguez J., "An Improved Image Enhancement Scheme for Fingerprint Minutiae Extraction in Biometric Identification," in *Proc. Int. Conf. on Audio- and Video-Based Biometric Person Authentication (3rd)*, pp. 218–223, 2001.

Singh, Gyergyek, and Pavesic (1977). Singh V.K., Gyergyek L., and Pavesic N., "Feature Recognition and Classification in Fingerprint Patterns," in *Proc. Int. Carnahan Conf. on Electronic Crime Countermeasures*, pp. 241–248, 1977.

Sjogaard (1992). Sjogaard S., "Discrete Neural Networks and Fingerprint Identification," in *Proc. Workshop on Signal Processing*, pp. 316–322, 1992.

Soifer et al. (1996). Soifer V., Kotlyar V., Khonina S., and Skidanov R., "Fingerprint Identification Using the Directions Fields," in *Proc. Int. Conf. on Pattern Recognition (13th)*, vol. 3, pp. 586–590, 1996.

Soutar (2002). Soutar C., "Biometric System Security," *Secure — the Silicon Trust Magazine*, no. 5, pp. 46–49, 2002.

Soutar and Tomko (1996). Soutar C. and Tomko G.J., "Secure Private key Generation Using a Fingerprint," in *Proc. CardTech/SecurTech Conf.*, vol. 1, pp. 245–252, 1996.

Soutar et al. (1998a). Soutar C., Roberge D., Stoianov A., Gilroy R., and Kumar B.V.K.V., "Biometric Encryption Using Image Processing," *Proc. of SPIE*, vol. 3314, pp. 178–188, 1998.

Soutar et al. (1998b). Soutar C., Roberge D., Stoianov A., Gilroy R., and Kumar B.V.K.V., "Biometric Encryption — Enrollment and Verification Precedures," *Proc. of SPIE*, vol. 3386, pp. 24–35, 1998.

Sparrow and Sparrow (1985a). Sparrow M. and Sparrow P., "A Topological Approach to the Matching of Single Fingerprints: Development of Algorithms for Use on Latent Fingermarks," U.S. Government Publication, Gaithersburg, MD: U.S. Dept. of Commerce, National Bureau of Standards; Washington, DC, 1985.

Sparrow and Sparrow (1985b). Sparrow M. and Sparrow P., "A Topological Approach to the Matching of Single Fingerprints: Development of Algorithms for use on Rolled Impressions," U.S. Government Publication, Gaithersburg, MD: U.S. Dept. of Commerce, National Bureau of Standards; Washington, DC, 1985.

Sprinzak and Werman (1994). Sprinzak J. and Werman M., "Affine Point Matching," *Pattern Recognition Letters*, vol. 15, pp. 337–339, 1994.

Srihari et al. (2001). Srihari S.N., Cha S.H., Arora H., and Lee S., "Individuality of Handwriting: A Validation Study," in *Proc. Int. Conf. on Document Analysis and Recognition (6th)*, pp. 106–109, 2001.

Srinivasan and Murthy (1992). Srinivasan V.S. and Murthy N.N., "Detection of Singular Points in Fingerprint Images," *Pattern Recognition*, vol. 25, no. 2, pp. 139–153, 1992.

Starink and Backer (1995). Starink J.P.P. and Backer E., "Finding Point Correspondence Using Simulated Annealing," *Pattern Recognition*, vol. 28, no. 2, pp. 231–240, 1995.

Stock (1977). Stock R.M., "Automatic Fingerprint Reading," in *Proc. Int. Carnahan Conf. on Electronic Crime Countermeasures*, pp. 16–28, 1977.

Stock and Swonger (1969). Stock R.M. and Swonger C.W., "Development and Evalutation of a Reader of Fingerprint Minutiae," Tech. Report: no. XM-2478-X-1:13–17, Cornell Aeronautical Labaratory, 1969.

Stockman, Kopstein, and Benett (1982). Stockman G., Kopstein S., and Benett S., "Matching Images to Models for Registration and Object Detection via Clustering," *IEEE Transactions on Pattern Analysis and Machine Intelligence*, vol. 4, no. 3, pp. 229–241, 1982.

Stoney (1985). Stoney D.A., "A Quantitative Assessment of Fingerprint Individuality," Ph.D. Thesis, University of California, Davis, 1985.

Stoney (1988). Stoney D.A., "Distribution of Epidermal Ridge Minutiae," *American Journal of Physical Anthropology*, vol. 77, 367–376, 1988.

Stoney and Thornton (1986). Stoney D.A. and Thornton J.I., "A Critical Analysis of Quantitative Fingerprints Individuality Models," *Journal of Forensic Sciences*, vol. 31, no. 4, pp. 1187–1216, 1986.

Stoney and Thornton (1987). Stoney D.A. and Thornton J.I., "A Systematic Study of Epidermal Ridge Minutiae," *Journal of Forensic Sciences*, vol. 32, no. 5, pp. 1182–1203, 1987.

Stosz and Alyea (1994). Stosz J.D. and Alyea L.A., "Automated System for Fingerprint Authentication Using Pores and Ridge Structure," *Proc. of SPIE (Automatic Systems for the Identification and Inspection of Humans)*, vol. 2277, pp. 210–223, 1994.

Sujan and Mulqueen (2002). Sujan V.A. and Mulqueen M.P., "Fingerprint Identification Using Space Invariant Transforms," *Pattern Recognition Letters*, vol. 23, no. 5, pp. 609–619, 2002.

Swonger (1973). Swonger C.W., "Application of Fingerprint Identification Technology to Criminal Identification and Security Systems," in *Proc. Int. Carnahan Conf. on Electronic Crime Countermeasures*, pp. 190–212, 1973.

Székely and Székely (1993). Székely E. and Székely V., "Image Recognition Problems of Fingerprint Identification," *Microprocessors and Microsystems*, vol. 17, no. 4, pp. 215–218, 1993.

Szu et al. (1995). Szu H., Hsu C., Garcia J., and Telfer B., "Fingerprint Data Acquisition, De-Smearing, Wavelet Feature Extraction and Identification," *Proc. of SPIE*, vol. 2491, pp. 96–118, 1995.

Takeda et al. (1990). Takeda M., Uchida S., Hiramatsu K., and Matsunami T., "Finger Image Identification Method for Personal Verification," in *Proc. Int. Conf. on Pattern Recognition (10th)*, vol. 1, pp. 761–766, 1990.

Tamura (1978). Tamura H., "A Comparison of Line Thinning Algorithms from Digital Topology Viewpoint," in *Proc. Int. Conf. on Pattern Recognition (4th)*, pp. 715–719, 1978.

Tartagni and Guerieri (1998). Tartagni M. and Guerieri R., "A Fingerprint Sensor Based on the Feedback Capacitive Sensing Scheme," *IEEE Journal of Solid-State Circuits*, vol. 33, no. 1, pp. 133–142, 1998.

Thomas and Bryant (2000). Thomas D.A. and Bryant F.R., "Electrostatic Discharge Protection for Integrated Circuit Sensor Passivation," US Patent 6091082, 2000.

Tico and Kuosmanen (1999). Tico M. and Kuosmanen P., "A Topographic Method for Fingerprint Segmentation," in *Proc. Int. Conf. on Image Processing*, vol. 1, pp. 36–40, 1999.

Tico and Kuosmanen (1999b). Tico M. and Kuosmanen P., "A Multiresolution Method for Singular Point Detection in Fingerprint Images," in *Proc. Int. Symp. on Circuit Systems*, vol. IV, pp. 183–186, 1999.

Tico, Kuosmanen, and Saarinen (2001). Tico M., Kuosmanen P., and Saarinen J., "Wavelet Domain Features for Fingerprint Recognition," *Electronics Letters*, vol. 37, no. 1 , pp. 21 -22, 2001.

Toh et al. (2001). Toh K.A., Yau W.Y., Jiang X., Chen T.P., Lu J., and Lim E., "Minutiae Data Synthesis for Fingerprint Identification Applications," in *Proc. Int. Conf. on Image Processing*, vol. 3, pp. 262–265, 2001.

Ton and Jain (1989). Ton J. and Jain A.K., "Registering Landsat Images by Point Matching," *IEEE Transactions Geoscience Remote Sensing*, vol. 27, no. 5, pp. 642–651, 1989.

Tou and Hankley (1968). Tou J.T. and Hankley W.J., *Automatic Fingerprint Interpretation and Classification via Contextual Analysis and Topological Coding*, C. Cheng, S. Ledley, D. Pollock, and A. Rosenfeld (Eds.), Thompson, Washington, DC, 1968.

Toussaint (1971). Toussaint G.T., "Note on Optimal Selection of Independent Binary-Valued Features for Pattern Recognition," *IEEE Transactions on Information Theory*, vol. IT-17, pp. 618, 1971.

Trauring (1963). Trauring M., "Automatic Comparison of Finger-Ridge Patterns," *Nature*, pp. 938–940, 1963.

Tresp and Taniguchi (1995). Tresp V. and Taniguchi M., "Combining Estimators Using Non-Constant Weighting Functions," in *Advances in Neural Information Processing Systems*, G. Tesauro, D.S. Touretzky, and T.K. Leen (Eds.), vol. 7, MIT Press, Cambridge, MA, 1995.

Trier and Jain (1995). Trier O. and Jain A.K., "Goal-Directed Evaluation of Binarization Methods," *IEEE Transactions on Pattern Analysis and Machine Intelligence*, vol. 17, no. 12, pp. 1191–1201, 1995.

Tsikos (1982). Tsikos C., "Capacitive Fingerprint Sensor," US Patent 4353056, 1982.

Turk and Pentland (1991). Turk M. and Pentland A., "Eigenface for Recognition," *Journal of Cognitive Neuroscience*, vol. 3, no. 1, pp. 71–86, 1991.

Uchida (2000). Uchida K., "Fingerprint-Based User-Friendly Interface and Pocket-PID for Mobile Authentication," in *Proc. Int. Conf. on Pattern Recognition (15th)*, vol. 4, pp. 205–209, 2000.

Uchida et al. (1998). Uchida K., Kamei T., Mizoguchi M., and Temma T., "Fingerprint Card Classification with Statistical Feature Integration," in *Proc. Int. Conf. on Pattern Recognition (14th)*, vol. 2, pp. 1833–1839, 1998.

Udupa, Garg, and Sharma (2001). Udupa R., Garg G., and Sharma P., "Fast and Accurate Fingerprint Verification," in *Proc. Int. Conf. on Audio- and Video-Based Biometric Person Authentication (3rd)*, pp. 192–197, 2001.

UKBWG (2002). United Kingdom Biometric Working Group, "Best Practices in Testing and Reporting Biometric Device Performance," Tech. Report: Version 2.01, Aug. 2002, available at: http://www.cesg.gov.uk/technology/biometrics/ .

Umeyama (1991). Umeyama S., "Least-Square Estimation of Transformation Parameters Between Two Point Patterns," *IEEE Transactions on Pattern Analysis and Machine Intelligence*, vol. 13, no. 4, pp. 376–380, 1991.

Verlinde, Chollet, and Acheroy (2000). Verlinde P., Chollet G., and Acheroy M., "Multi-Modal Identity Verification Using Expert Fusion," *Information Fusion*, vol. 1, no. 1, pp. 17–33, July 2000.

Verma and Chatterjee (1989). Verma M.R. and Chatterjee B., "Partial Fingerprint Pattern Classification," *Journal Institute Electronic & Telecom. Engineers*, vol. 3, no. 1, pp. 28–33, 1989.

Verma, Majumdar, and Chatterjee (1987). Verma M.R., Majumdar A.K., and Chatterjee B., "Edge Detection in Fingerprints," *Pattern Recognition*, vol. 20, pp. 513–523, 1987.

Viveros, Balasubramanian, and Mitas (1984). Viveros R., Balasubramanian K., and Mitas J.A., "Binomial and Negative Bionomial Analogues Under Correlated Bernoulli Trials," *Journal of the American Statistician*, vol. 48, no. 3, pp. 243–247, 1984.

Vizcaya and Gerhardt (1996). Vizcaya P.R. and Gerhardt L.A., "A Nonlinear Orientation Model for Global Description of Fingerprints," *Pattern Recognition*, vol. 29, no. 7, pp. 1221–1231, 1996.

Wahab, Chin, and Tan (1998). Wahab A., Chin S.H., and Tan E.C., "Novel Approach to Automated Fingerprint Recognition," *IEE Proceedings Vision Image and Signal Processing*, vol. 145, no. 3, pp. 160–166, 1998.

Wang and Pavlidig (1993). Wang L. and Pavlidis T., "Direct Gray-Scale Extraction of Features for Character Recognition," *IEEE Transactions on Pattern Analysis and Machine Intelligence*, vol. 15, no. 10, pp. 1053–1067, 1993.

Watson (1993a). Watson C.I., "NIST Special Database 14, Fingerprint Database," U.S. National Institute of Standards and Technology, 1993.

Watson (1993b). Watson C.I., "NIST Special Database 10, Supplemental Fingerprint Card Data (SFCD) for NIST Special Database 9, Fingerprint Database," U.S. National Institute of Standards and Technology, 1993.

Watson (1998). Watson C.I., "NIST Special Database 24, Digital Video of Live-Scan Fingerprint Data," U.S. National Institute of Standards and Technology, 1998.

Watson and Wilson (1992a). Watson C.I. and Wilson C.L., "NIST Special Database 4, Fingerprint Database," U.S. National Institute of Standards and Technology, 1992.

Watson and Wilson (1992b). Watson C.I. and Wilson C.L., "NIST Special Database 9, Fingerprint Database," U.S. National Institute of Standards and Technology, 1992.

Watson, Candela, and Grother (1994). Watson C.I., Candela G.I., and Grother P.J., "Comparison of FFT Fingerprint Filtering Methods for Neural Network Classification," Tech. Report: NIST TR 5493, Sept. 1994.

Watson, Grother, and Casasent (2000). Watson C.I., Grother P.J., and Casasent D.P., "Distortion-Tolerant Filter for Elastic-Distorted Fingerprint Matching," Tech. Report: NIST IR 6489, National Institute of Standards and Technology, Gaithersburg, MD, 2000.

Wayman (1999a). Wayman J.L., "Technical Testing and Evaluation of Biometric Identification Devices," in *Biometrics: Personal Identification in a Networked Society*, A.K. Jain, R. Bolle, and S. Pankanti (Eds.), pp. 345–368, Kluwer, New York, 1999.

Wayman (1999b). Wayman J.L., "Multi-finger Penetration Rate and ROC Variability for Automatic Fingerprint Identification Systems," Tech. Report: San Jose State University, 1999, available at: http://www.engr.sjsu.edu/biometrics/ .

Wayman (2001). Wayman J.L., "Confidence Interval and Test Size Estimation for Biometric Data," Personal Communication, 2001.

Weber (1992). Weber D.M., "A Cost Effective Fingerprint Verification Algorithm for Commercial Applications," in *Proc. South African Symp. on Communication and Signal Processing*, 1992.

Wegstein (1972). Wegstein J.H., "The M40 Fingerprint Matcher," U.S. Government Publication, Washington, DC: National Bureau of Standards, Technical Note 878, U.S Government Printing Office, 1972.

Wegstein (1982). Wegstein J.H., "An Automated Fingerprint Identification System," U.S. Government Publication, Washington, DC: U.S. Dept. of Commerce, National Bureau of Standards, 1982.

Wegstein and Rafferty (1978). Wegstein J.H. and Rafferty J.F., "The LX39 Latent Fingerprint Matcher," U.S. Government Publication, National Bureau of Standards, Institute for Computer Sciences and Technology, 1978.

Wei, Yuan, and Jie (1998). Wei D., Yuan Q., and Jie T., "Fingerprint Classification System with Feedback Mechanism Based on Genetic Algorithm," in *Proc. Int. Conf. on Pattern Recognition (14th)*, vol. 1, pp. 163–165, 1998.

Wentworth and Wilder (1918). Wentworth B. and Wilder H.H., *Personal Identification*, R.G. Badger, Boston, 1918.

Willis and Myers (2001). Willis A.J. and Myers L., "A Cost-Effective Fingerprint Recognition System for Use with Low-Quality Prints and Damaged Fingertips," *Pattern Recognition*, vol. 34, no. 2, pp. 255–270, 2001.

Wilson and Woodard (1987). Wilson T. and Woodard P., "Automated Fingerprint Identification Systems: Technology and Policy Issues," U.S. Government Publication, Washington, DC: U.S. Dept. of Justice, Bureau of Justice Statistics, 1987.

Wilson et al. (1992). Wilson C.L., Candela G.T., Grother P.J., Watson C.I., and Wilkinson, R.A., "Massively Parallel Network Fingerprint Classification System," Tech. Report: NIST TR 4880, Oct. 1992.

Wilson, Candela, and Watson (1994). Wilson C.L., Candela G.T., and Watson C.I., "Neural Network Fingerprint Classification," *Journal of Artificial Neural Networks*, vol. 1, no. 2, pp. 203–228, 1994.

Wilson, Watson, and Paek (1997). Wilson C.L., Watson C.I., and Paek E.G., "Combined Optical and Neural Network Fingerprint Matching," *Proc. of SPIE (Optical Pattern Recognition VIII)*, vol. 3073, pp. 373–382, 1997.

Wilson, Watson, and Paek (2000). Wilson C.L., Watson C.I., and Paek E.G., "Effect of Resolution and Image Quality on Combined Optical and Neural Network Fingerprint Matching," *Pattern Recognition*, vol. 33, no. 2, pp. 317–331, 2000.

Wolpert (1992). Wolper D., "Stacked Generalization," *Neural Networks*, vol. 5, pp. 241–259, 1992.

Woodward (1999). Woodward J., "Biometrics: Identifying Law and Policy Concerns," in *Biometrics: Personal Identification in a Networked Society*, A.K. Jain, R. Bolle, and S. Pankanti (Eds.), Kluwer, New York, 1999.

Xia and O'Gorman (2003). Xia X. and O'Gorman L., "Innovations in Fingerprint Capture Devices," *Pattern Recognition*, vol. 36, no. 2, pp 361–369, 2003.

Xiao and Bian (1986). Xiao Q. and Bian Z., "An Approach to Fingerprint Identification by Using the Attributes of Feature Lines of Fingerprint," in *Proc. Int. Conf. on Pattern Recognition (8th)*, pp. 663–665, 1986.

Xiao and Raafat (1991a). Xiao Q. and Raafat H., "Combining Statistical and Structural Information for Fingerprint Image Processing Classification and Identification," in *Pattern Recognition: Architectures, Algorithms and Applications*, R. Plamondon and H. Cheng (Eds.), pp. 335–354, World Scientific, River Edge, NJ, 1991.

Xiao and Raafat (1991b). Xiao Q. and Raafat H., "Fingerprint Image Post-Processing: A Combined Statistical and Structural Approach," *Pattern Recognition*, vol. 24, no. 10, pp. 985–992, 1991.

Xu, Krzyzac, and Suen (1992). Xu L., Krzyzak A., and Suen C.Y., "Methods for Combining Multiple Classifiers and Their Applications to Handwriting Recognition," *IEEE Transactions on Systems, Man, and Cybernetics*, vol. 22, no. 3, pp. 418–435, 1992.

Yahagi, Igaki, and Yamagishi (1990). Yahagi H., Igaki S., and Yamagishi F., "Moving-Window Algorithm For Fast Verification," in *Proc. Southeastcon Conf.*, pp. 343–348, 1990.

Yamazaki and Komatsu (2001). Yamazaki Y. and Komatsu N., "A Secure Communication System Using Biometric Identity Verification," *IEICE Transactions on Information and Systems*, vol. E84-D, no. 7, pp. 879–884, 2001.

Yao, Frasconi, and Pontil (2001). Yao Y., Frasconi P., and Pontil M., "Fingerprint Classification with Combination of Support Vector Machines," in *Proc. Int. Conf. on Audio- and Video-Based Biometric Person Authentication (3rd)*, pp. 253–258, 2001.

Yau et al. (2000). Yau W.Y., Toh K.A, Jiang X, Chen T.P, and Lu J., "On Fingerprint Template Synthesis," in *Proc. Int. Conf. on Control Automation Robotics and Vision (6th)*, 2000.

Yeung and Pankanti (2000). Yeung M. and Pankanti S., "Verification Watermarks on Fingerprint Recognition and Retrieval," *Journal of Electronic Imaging*, vol. 9, no. 4, pp. 468–476, 2000.

Young et al. (1997). Young N.D., Harkin G., Bunn R.M., McCulloch D.J., Wilks R.W., and Knapp A.G., "Novel Fingerprint Scanning Arrays Using Polysilicon Tft's on Glass and Polymer Substrates," *IEEE Electron Device Letters*, vol. 18, no. 1, pp. 19–20, 1997.

Zhang and Wang (2002). Zhang W. and Wang Y., "Core-Based Structure Matching Algorithm of Fingerprint Verification," in *Proc. Int. Conf. on Pattern Recognition (16th)*, vol. 1, pp. 70–74, 2002.

Zhou et al. (2001). Zhou J., He D., Rong G., and Qi Bian Z., "Effective Algorithm for Rolled Fingerprint Construction," *Electronics Letters*, vol. 37, no. 8 , pp. 492–94, 2001.

Zhou, Qiao, and Mok (1998). Zhou G., Qiao Y., and Mok F., "Fingerprint Sensing System Using a Sheet Prism," US Patent 5796858, 1998.

Index